AWAKENING CHILDREN'S MINDS

AWAKENING CHILDREN'S MINDS

How Parents and Teachers
Can Make a Difference

Laura E. Berk

OXFORD
UNIVERSITY PRESS

OXFORD
UNIVERSITY PRESS

Oxford New York
Auckland Bangkok Buenos Aires Cape Town Chennai
Dar es Salaam Delhi Hong Kong Istanbul
Karachi Kuala Lumpur Madrid Melbourne
Mexico City Mumbai Nairobi São Paulo Shanghai
Taipei Tokyo Toronto

Copyright © 2001 by Oxford University Press, Inc.

First published by Oxford University Press, Inc., 2001
First issued as an Oxford University Press paperback, 2004
198 Madison Avenue, New York, New York 10016

www.oup.com

Oxford is a registered trademark of Oxford University Press

Library of Congress Cataloging-in-Publication Data
Berk, Laura E.
Awakening children's minds : how parents and teachers can make a difference /
Laura E. Berk.
p. cm.
Includes bibliographical references and index.
ISBN-13 978-0-19-517155-6 (pbk.)
1. Child development.
2. Socialization.
3. Early childhood education—Parent participation.
4. Parenting.
I. Title.
HQ767.9 .B465 20001
649'.1—dc21   00-140080

3 5 7 9 8 6 4

Printed in the United States of America
on acid-free paper

To my brother, Martin,
an exemplary parent,
with admiration and affection

CONTENTS

I decided to write this book for parents and teachers of young children for several reasons. First, I was dissatisfied with the American parenting-advice literature. As I examined it, I found it to be contradictory, riddled with oversimplified messages, and often unrelated to or at odds with current scientific knowledge. Second, I felt certain after many years as a professor, researcher, and author of textbooks on child development, that contemporary scientific theory and research contain many vital, practical messages—ones crucial for parents and teachers to understand if they are to help children develop at their best. Finally, on countless occasions, parents have tapped me on the shoulder or written to me with questions and concerns. They appeared uncertain, uneasy, and sometimes highly frustrated in the face of a wide array of child rearing issues, from how to choose a child-care center to whether to make their children clean up their rooms. I became convinced that parents need a consistent way of thinking about their role in children's lives—one that can guide them in making effective child-rearing decisions.

It's little wonder that American parents are perplexed and conflicted about what course to steer in child rearing. They live in a world that makes parenting exceedingly challenging. The majority of mothers of preschool children are in the labor force, yet the United States stands out among industrialized nations in providing few supports to help employed parents in their child-rearing roles. At the same time, American parents complain that they are busier than ever, that the growing demands of their work lives leave them little time for their children. A nation of pressured, preoccupied parents has emerged in an era of grave public concern about the well-being of American youth, who are achieving less well than they should and often displaying a worrisome lack of direction and purpose, manifested at its worst in high rates of self-destructiveness and violence. These afflictions have permeated even the most economically privileged sectors of our population—young people who, on the face of things, have been granted the best of life's chances.

Many parents of young children have reacted to this youth disaffection with adaptive fear for their own children's futures. But unanimity on what parents can and should do to shield children from underachievement, indifference, and demoralization will elude those who seek it on the shelves of their local libraries and bookstores. Parenting advice has vacillated, and today it vacillates more than ever. Some authors, convinced that parents are in control of what their children become, advise a get-tough, directive approach. The educational parallel to this parent-power stance is to train and instruct as early as possible, variously justified by claims of maximizing brain growth or securing high achievement by starting sooner. Other authors locate today's youth problems in excessive adult pushing of children. According to these child-power advocates, children have their own, built-in timetables for maturing and learning. Waiting for children's readiness cues, these experts say, will relieve the stress that fuels youth discontent, estrangement, and rebellion.

These vicissitudes in child-rearing advice and educational practice mirror historical shifts in theories of child development and education. Until recently, major theories have not helped resolve these polarities. The most disturbing trend in this literature of contradiction has been a move to deny that parents make *any* notable contribution to their children's development. Children's genes and (secondarily) their peer groups, not parents, a highly publicized book claimed (Harris, *The Nurture Assumption),* are the supreme forces in how children turn out.

This public pronouncement of parental impotence comes at a time when many busy parents are poised to retreat from family responsibilities, and it grants them license to do so. Moreover, America's national unwillingness to invest heavily in humane family supports, such as high-quality child care and paid parental employment leave for childbirth and child emergencies, receives endorsement from the notion that parenting counts for little. If only genes and the peer group matter, then there is no need for generous government commitment to the family.

The heredity/peer supremacy thesis is partly aimed at discrediting, once and for all, the formerly widespread practice of blaming parents for any problem that surfaces in children's lives. But evidence pointing to parents as the sole cause of children's ills is old and outdated, harking back to the early 1980s and before. That was a time when researchers often ignored the role of children's genetic endowment and overstated findings on parenting effects. The field of child development has since taken steps to remedy the shortcomings of those early investigations. These efforts have yielded a research-based consensus that parents' influence on children, while far from exclusive, is nevertheless substantial.

Redirecting blame by heaping it on children—by asserting, on the basis of highly selective evidence, that anything good or bad in children's behavior is largely inborn and inevitable—is an even more dangerous excess. It risks leading us down a morally reprehensible path because it grants tacit permission for parental indifference, coldness, inconsistency, harshness, and even brutality—behaviors widely documented to damage children's development. After all, how parents treat children is irrelevant if parenting is inconsequential.

America's uncritical reception to the recent assertion of parents' insignificance is emblematic of widespread confusion about the role of parents—and other adults, such as teachers—in children's lives. Acknowledging that children need nurturance, protection, stimulation, and direction demands action—by individuals, communities, and the nation as a whole—to do everything possible to guarantee children the experiences they need to reach their potential. According to burgeoning evidence, those experiences include mothers and fathers involved in family life, a reasonable work–family balance, adequate parental leave provisions, excellent child care, and well-staffed and equipped schools that use the best teaching methods. This vision—and the commitment, effort, and sacrifice required to realize it—differ radically from the one emerging out of the view that children's genes and peers are supreme.

Despite the public attention granted to it, the genetic supremacy thesis is as passé in the field of child development as is the parent-blaming notion it aims to refute. Today's researchers have moved away from one-sided perspectives advocating that nature or nurture determines outcomes for children. Rather, a balanced, inclusive view has coalesced in the field, which asserts that *both* heredity and environment—children and important people in their lives—are powerful, interrelated influences. The new view also grants vital roles to children's extended environments. Neighborhoods, child-care centers, schools, workplace and government policies, and cultural values and priorities affect children's relationships and opportunities and, in turn, their development. According to this theoretical consensus, parents, teachers, and peers can modify children's genetic propensities, shifting, altering, and channeling them for better or for worse. Throughout development, children continue to bear the mark of their biological uniqueness, although not in raw, unchanged form. Instead, heredity combines with children's history of experiences to yield both similarities and wide individual differences in capacities and skills.

From the aggregate of theories representing this dynamic, synergistic view of nature and nurture, I have chosen one to serve as the framework for this book. It is *sociocultural theory*, which originated with the work of Russian psychologist Lev Vygotsky. Early in the twentieth century, he explained how children's social experiences transform their genetic endowment, leading their development forward and ensuring that they become competent, contributing members of their society.

Vygotsky proposed that as children engage in dialogues with more expert members of their culture, they integrate the language of those interactions into their inner mental lives and use it to think, overcome challenges, and guide their own behavior. The values, modes of reasoning, strategies, and skills that children acquire as adults converse with, assist, and encourage them are crucial for success in their families and communities. At the same time, children contribute significantly to those interactions; consequently, their dispositions, interests, talents, and limitations influence what they learn. But by tailoring communication to children's needs while promoting desirable competencies, adults can profoundly affect the formation of children's minds.

The fields of child development and education have welcomed Vygotsky's theory with enthusiasm. Many contemporary scholars have built on his ideas, which have inspired a growing research literature on the role of parents, of language and communication, and of everyday activities in children's psychological development. And because Vygotsky emphasized teaching as the major impetus for developmental change, his theory has energized new approaches to education and spawned investigations into classroom practices and school cultures that foster enthusiasm for learning, high achievement, and positive peer relationships. Moreover, Vygotsky spent much of his career thinking about how to educate children with physical and mental disabilities. Inspired by his theorizing, many researchers have addressed child-rearing and teaching strategies that promote social inclusion and optimum learning of special-needs children.

In this book, I convey to parents and teachers the essential principles and body of knowledge about child development emanating from sociocultural theory. I focus on early childhood, especially the years from 2 to 8, when language flourishes; the capacity to join in dialogues with others expands greatly; and children acquire a wealth of knowledge, become literate, and bring their behavior under the control of thought. To clarify the significance of adults' relationships with children, I also touch on infancy and on long-term consequences in adolescence and young adulthood.

My goal is to show that adult–child shared activities, mistakenly regarded as fleeting and inconsequential, affect children profoundly—often in lifelong ways. Throughout the book, I describe practices that can assist parents in their efforts to rear competent, caring, well-adjusted children. I also grant extensive attention to early childhood education—to learning activities, teaching techniques, and collaborative efforts between educators and parents. I hope to inform parents about excellent early childhood education and to inspire teachers and administrators to enhance the experiences they provide in child-care programs, preschools, and primary schools.

In Chapter 1, I discuss the challenges of contemporary parenthood; the vacillating, contradictory advice that has plagued the popular parenting literature; and the new wave of theories that offer a unified vision of the multiplicity of factors contributing to children's development. I show how Vygotsky's sociocultural theory, in highlighting the importance of adult–child dialogues during everyday, purposeful activities, clarifies the crucial role of parents and teachers in children's lives.

Chapter 2 describes the features of adult–child dialogues that enhance children's competencies. I introduce a major Vygotskian concept—the zone of proximal development, the region of challenging activities in which learning and development take place. Adults and children jointly create this "zone" through communication that stimulates children to think in new, more mature ways. Much of this chapter describes how parents and teachers can sustain the "zone," keeping children vitally connected to others and ever advancing to new heights.

Children's private (self-directed) speech is the focus of Chapter 3, in which I answer the question, "Why do children talk to themselves?" Drawing on a rich array of examples, I explain how children weave the voices of more expert cultural members into dialogues with themselves. When puzzling, difficult, or stressful circumstances arise, children call on this private speech to guide and control their thinking and behavior, in much the same way that dialogues with others previously helped them overcome obstacles and acquire new knowledge and skills. I highlight ways that parents and teachers can encourage children to use private speech adaptively, to aid their learning and self-control.

Chapter 4 addresses the significance of make-believe play, a compelling and absorbing activity of the preschool years. I show how pretending generates vital lessons in bringing action under the control of thought and fosters a wealth of cognitive and social capacities. From its beginnings, make-believe play is a social activity, and when parents and teachers play with young children, they promote skills that transfer to play with peers and that prepare children for the sophisticated game play of the school years. The chapter offers many recommendations for enhancing children's play.

In Chapter 5, I take up the development of children with deficits and disabilities, emphasizing the crucial importance of cultivating language and communication, of integrating these children into everyday social activities, and of making sure that their educational experiences are in their "zones"—optimal for promoting learning. I illustrate the power of these principles by describing the impact of social experiences on children with three distinct but serious childhood impairments: blindness, deafness, and attention-deficit hyperactivity disorder (ADHD).

Chapter 6 considers applications of sociocultural theory to early childhood classrooms. Three interrelated themes—teaching in the "zone," classrooms rich in dialogues, and abundant literacy activities—provide the framework for Vygotsky-inspired educational practices. Among the topics I discuss are classroom activities that maximize children's progress; teacher–child and child–child discourse that yields active, self-confident learners and that stretches children to higher levels; methods for assessing children's progress that help identify effective teaching strategies; and the creation of school- and communitywide contexts for educational excellence. I conclude with a summary of indicators of high-quality early childhood education to guide parents in selecting programs and advocating for their children's educational needs.

Finally, in Chapter 7, I address child-rearing dilemmas today's parents face by answering a set of twenty questions about children's learning and development drawn from an extensive survey of parents of 2- to 8-year-olds. By anchoring the answers in contemporary theory and research, I reaffirm that parents can do much to protect, restore, and enhance children's experiences, leading their development forward.

The sociocultural vision of adults as leaders in children's development is a beacon in the midst of confusion, a guiding light that can strengthen American parents' involvement in children's lives. Sociocultural theory has also inspired many successful innovations in early childhood education, offering models for teachers and goals for our nation. If I accomplish what I set out to do—to provide parents and teachers with renewed purpose and direction for engaging with children—this book will rank as my most gratifying professional achievement.

ACKNOWLEDGMENTS

For over a decade, I have discussed the ideas in this book with parents, teachers, university colleagues, undergraduate and graduate students, friends, and family members. In a very real way, it has been a collaborative endeavor.

I am grateful to a multitude of parents, teachers, and children for sharing their experiences and reflections and contributing their voices to the book through its many real-life examples. My colleagues at Illinois State University also offered suggestions, insights, and inspiring models of child-rearing and teaching practices. I am especially indebted to Laurie and Ray Bergner, Fran and Herm Brandau, Freda Briggs, Stephen and Ruth Ann Friedberg, Elaine Graybill, Steven Landau, Carolyn Merrill, Christine Mikitka, Mary Evelyn and Benjamin Moore, Carol Owles, Richard Payne, Karen Stephens, Victoria Whitington, and Elaine and Paul Vogt. Special thanks to scores of parents in my community who responded to a survey asking for their questions about children's learning and development, which provided the framework for Chapter 7.

I thank Alvin Goldfarb, Vice President and Provost at Illinois State University; Paul Schollaert, Dean of the College of Arts and Sciences; and John Pryor and David Barone, chairpersons of the Department of Psychology, for supporting my work through a sabbatical leave. Graduate students JoDe Paladino and Amy Petersen provided invaluable assistance with literature searches and gathering of reference materials. Susan Messer's outstanding editing contributed greatly to the readability of each page.

I owe a great debt of gratitude to Joan Bossert, psychology editor at Oxford University Press, for asking me to write this book; for her many perceptive comments on chapter drafts; and for her continuous encouragement and wise counsel—all of which helped make this project a peak experience. The final product also benefited immeasurably from the insights and enthusiasm of several scholars of sociocultural theory, child development, early childhood education, who reviewed the prospectus and/or the manuscript. They are Julie H. Haupt, Brigham Young University; Janet R. Jamieson, University of British Columbia; and James V. Wertsch, Washington University.

A final word of appreciation goes to my family. My husband Ken's generous love buoyed my energies at crucial junctures. Our sons, David and Peter, are living reminders of the fulfillment that accrues from investing in parenthood. Their keen interest in this book made working on it all the more meaningful and enriching.

L. E. B.

AWAKENING CHILDREN'S MINDS

ONE

A New View of Child Development

In my three decades of teaching university courses in child development, I have come to know thousands of students, many of whom were parents or who became parents soon after completing my class. I also served on boards of directors and advisory committees for child-care centers, preschools, elementary schools, and parent organizations. And my research continually drew me into classrooms, where for countless hours I observed and recorded preschool and school-age children's activities, social interactions, and solitary behaviors, in hopes of answering central questions about how they learn.

As a byproduct of those experiences, parents repeatedly approached me with concerns about how to foster their child's development in the early years. Their fervent questions, at times riddled with doubt and anxiety, revealed that creating optimum learning environments for young children at home—and ensuring their access to development-enhancing experiences in child care, preschool, and school—have become mounting parental challenges.

Consider the following problematic situations that parents recently raised with me:

- *Bob and Sharon, parents of a 4-year-old:* Our daughter, Lydia, could recite her ABCs and count from 1 to 20 by age 2 1/2. When we looked for a preschool, many programs appeared to do little more than let children play, so we chose one with lots of emphasis on academics. To me, Lydia's preschool seems like great preparation for kindergarten and first grade, but each morning, Lydia hates to go. Why is Lydia, who's always been an upbeat, curious child, so unhappy?

- *Angela, mother of a 4-year-old and 6-year-old:* My husband and I have demanding careers and need to bring work home in the evenings. I've read that it's the quality of time we spend with our children that's important, not the quantity. We try hard to give Victor and Jeannine our undivided attention, but they're often whiny, demanding, and quarrelsome. Many times we end up sending them to their rooms or letting them watch TV, just to get some peace after a long day. What's the best way to create quality parent–child time?
- *Talia, mother of a 7-year-old:* My son Anselmo, a first grader, constantly asks us to help him with his homework. His father firmly insists that he do it by himself. Anselmo tries, but he gets so frustrated and upset that I move in and help, even in the face of opposition from his dad. By that time, Anselmo is on such a short string that I do most of the assignment for him. Should we be helping Anselmo with his homework and, if so, how?
- *Noah and Suzanne, parents of a 2-year-old:* When our parents were raising us, they seemed confident of their power and influence. Recently we read that how children turn out is mostly written in their genes; there's little we as parents can do about it. Does parenting really matter?

BAFFLED, BEWILDERED PARENTS

Despite being well educated, intent on doing what's best for their children, and enlightened by a vast literature of child-rearing advice, many American parents appear uneasy and unsure of their roles at best, baffled and bewildered at worst. As the above sampling of concerns reveals, today's parents are not just worried about major transitions and traumas, such as the impact of marital breakup or community violence. They agonize over commonplace, recurrent, everyday situations—whether intensive preschool academic tutoring is crucial for later success in school, the meaning of "quality time" with children, and whether and how to help their child with homework. At an even more fundamental level, contemporary parents have begun to doubt their own efficacy in their children's development. Why is this so?

The reasons, I believe, are twofold. First, rapid societal changes have complicated parents' task, making child rearing more challenging than in previous generations. Second, information about child development disseminated to parents is increasingly voluminous but at the same time contradictory. It fails to offer a clear, consistent vision of good child rearing to guide daily decision making and practice. Let's take a closer look at these sources of parental frustration and confusion.

Societal Changes

Over the past three decades, external forces impinging on the family have transformed parents' and, therefore, children's lives. Overall, parents complain that they have less free time to spend with their children.[1] Witness a 1995 survey of a large, representative sample of American workers, nearly 25 percent of whom expressed the feeling that the demands of their jobs left them with "no time for family."[2] Compounding their worries, employed parents must, out of necessity, turn over many hours of child rearing to other adults. Yet once their children are beyond their grasp, they are hardly off the hook! Conscientious parents face an added responsibility: monitoring their child's whereabouts and activities, verifying from a distance that their youngster is physically safe, emotionally contented, and constructively engaged.

Although many societal conditions heighten parents' struggle to rear psychologically healthy children, two are especially pernicious, affecting even parents who manage to escape the trials and tribulations of divorce, single parenthood, stepchildren, serious financial worries, and other family stresses. The first is the dire shortage of acceptable child-care options in the United States, the second is the parental dilemma of "never enough time." In view of these difficulties, it is little wonder that so many American parents express a sense of powerlessness and inadequacy when it comes to affecting their children's development.

THE PROBLEM OF CHILD CARE.   In 1970, 30 percent of mothers with preschool children were in the labor force, a figure that increased more than twofold, to 62 percent, by 2000.[3] An obvious solution to reconciling parents' employment needs with young children's rearing needs is to make high-quality, nonparental care, with characteristics known to promote healthy psychological development, widely available and affordable. In Australia and Western Europe, child care is nationally regulated and liberally funded to ensure that it conforms to standards verified by research to foster children's learning, social competence, and emotional security.[4]

Without a nationally regulated and generously subsidized child-care system, formal child care in the United States is in much shorter supply and considerably more costly for parents than it is in other industrialized nations. And as our discussion in Chapter 6 will reveal, on the whole, the quality of American child care—whether center-based or home-based—is mediocre to abysmal.[5] Indeed, so widespread is poor-quality child care in the United States that Americans have acclimated to it. In a recent survey of parents whose children were enrolled in several hundred randomly chosen child-care centers across four states, over 90 percent believed that their preschoolers' experiences were far better than experts in early childhood development judged those experiences to be.[6] Parents seemed unable to distinguish "good" from "substandard" care.

THE "TIME BIND."   Like many parents, Angela, who raised the question of quality time, complains of being "torn in many directions." Often she leaves work in a hurry in the late afternoon to pick up Victor and Jeannine from child care, dashes to Victor's tumbling class or Jeannine's piano lesson, then stops at the grocery store to pick up something for dinner. When Angela and her husband, Tom, walk through their front door, they typically head to the phone or fax machine to take care of unfinished work while trying to quell Victor and Jeannine's hunger and irritability with a frozen dinner popped into the microwave and unlimited access to the TV set. Caught in a ceaseless sprint to reconcile job, marriage, and parenting, Angela and Tom feel drained at the end of the day—too tired to grant their children more than 10 or 15 minutes of focused time. When Victor and Jeannine do get their parents' undivided attention, they are argumentative and unruly, compounding their parents' fatigue and impatience.

Angela and Tom represent a growing number of American parents who try to pencil children into busy schedules, much like a business appointment. They love their children, but they also love and need their work, for personal and financial reasons. Hence they find themselves in a juggling act between the two, with work usually winning out. Tomorrow will be another day for the kids, they rationalize, but a business deal or a professional achievement, if not capitalized on at the moment, may evaporate. Their logic dovetails with the concept of "quality time" for children. In its commonly accepted meaning, quality time refers to an intense but brief contact. The term is a ready salve for the consciences of conflicted parents, who squeeze in a few moments with their children, catch-as-catch-can, yet sense deep down that they are robbing their youngsters—and themselves—of something vital.

The expression "quality time" dates back to the 1970s, a decade that witnessed the largest rise in women's participation in the labor force during this century. The notion was bolstered by observational studies of parent–child interaction. In these investigations, some parents exchanged positive emotional signals with and verbally stimulated their infants, and read to and conversed with their preschoolers. Other parents spent time with their children but were not actively engaged with them. Time and time again, children of the first set of parents developed more favorably, cognitively and socially, than did children of the second set of parents.[7]

A close look at the research reveals that children who fared well experienced effective interaction over an extended period. In studies following children from infancy into childhood and adolescence, early brief episodes of parental stimulation and sensitivity did not result in more competent children.[8] Instead, positive, supportive parenting that *endured,* even when it marked a change from an early period of parental retreat or negative interaction, was linked to favorable child development, including persistence in problem solving, high self-esteem, socially skilled behavior, closer friendships, and better peer relationships.[9] In sum, high-quality involvement with children requires a certain quantity of time—actually, a great deal, as I'll argue in this book.

In Angela and Tom's case, sandwiching concentrated time with Victor and Jeannine between work and other obligations, which often took precedence over family rituals, meant that routines that signal parental caring and that are major sources of development went by the wayside. For example, family dinnertimes and storybook reading at bedtime became rare events. So did the sheer enjoyment that comes from relaxed parent–child play; a joint cooking, art, or construction project; and a conversation based on real listening and exchange of ideas. Because these experiences were so few and short-lived, Angela and Tom were deprived of valuable opportunities to observe their children closely and to become intimately familiar with their talents, shortcomings, preferences, styles of learning, and ways of coping with hardship—knowledge that is crucial for helping children develop into mature, competent individuals.

Furthermore, the "time bind" stifles an essential child-rearing responsibility that I mentioned earlier and will return to again: monitoring children's experiences while they are both within and beyond parents' immediate reach. This includes frequently touching base with nonparental caregivers and teachers to find out what's happening at child care or in the classroom; looking in on sibling and peer interaction to make sure that it is positive and respectful; and controlling time spent watching TV and playing video games.

In a recent provocative study, sociologist Arlie Hochschild spent months getting to know employees at a large Midwestern corporation she called America. Whether clerical workers or executives, the majority confirmed the parental state of mind just described: They complained of overly long workdays and frenetic home lives. A surprising finding, however, was that few America workers had taken steps to make work and family more compatible.

For example, even well-paid employees were not taking the annual twelve weeks of federally guaranteed, unpaid family leave time, although they could afford to do so. Nor were they asking for job share or flextime, prominent company policies aimed at increasing the compatibility of work and home. Hochschild concludes, "Many working families are both prisoners and architects of the time bind in which they find themselves."[10]

As homes become frenzied places in which work encroaches on family time and parents are too exhausted or preoccupied to be physically and psychologically available, children quickly become discipline problems. Their disagreeable behavior often causes parents to retreat further into the haven of work. On the job, such parents feel competent and gratified; home has turned into a place where they are harried, annoyed, and must deal with children who sulk, complain, plead for gifts, and are obstinate until they get their way—reactions that cry out, "Fifteen minutes, here or there, with an essentially distracted parent, is not enough."

Fortunately, not all reports are as disturbing as Hochschild's. Psychologist Rosalind Barnett and journalist Caryl Rivers conducted extensive interviews with 300 dual-earner couples in the Boston area and found that despite stress at work and at home, most were highly satisfied and found child rearing to be both manageable and pleasurable.[11] And in a survey of 6,000 employees at DuPont, nearly half—and only slightly more women than men—turned down upward career moves to remain in jobs that allowed for more family commitment.[12] Barnett believes that parents most prone to a time bind in which work robs family life are at higher socioeconomic levels—in more pressured jobs that have less clearly defined limits and in which advancement typically depends on superlative performance. Ironically, she notes, economically less well off parents find it easier to establish a viable dividing line between workplace and home.[13]

Although the precise extent of family–work conflict in American culture is not clear, its presence and detrimental impact on parent-child interaction and children's development are well founded. Consider a series of studies that examined length of maternity leave in relation to employed mothers' psychological well-being and parenting behaviors. Short leaves of 6 weeks or less (the norm in the United States) were linked to maternal anxiety and depression and negative interactions with babies. But longer leaves, of 12 weeks or more, predicted favorable maternal mental health and sensitive, responsive parenting.[14]

Furthermore, long hours in child care during infancy and the preschool years are linked to less favorable parent–child interaction. One study included repeated observations of more than 1,200 mothers, of diverse socioeconomic and ethnic backgrounds, playing with their children between 6 months and 3 years of age. The more time children spent in child care (which ranged from 0 to 50 hours per week), the less positive and responsive their mothers' behavior tended to be. Children experiencing less positive interaction were less engaged with their mothers—more negative in mood and less affectionate.[15] Yet another study—this time, of 3- to 5-year-old firstborn sons—suggested that long child-care hours can translate into behavior problems. Mothers and fathers of boys with many hours in child care interacted less favorably with their sons. And such parents reported more noncompliant, defiant child behavior.[16]

These findings are not an indictment of maternal employment or nonparental child care. Rather, they underscore the importance of considering the needs of children when making work and child-care decisions. Studies carried out during the 1970s and 1980s on the relationship of maternal employment to children's development revealed many positive outcomes—higher self-esteem, better grades in school, more positive family and peer relations, and less gender-stereotyped beliefs.[17] But repeatedly, effective parenting mediated these favorable developments.

Employed mothers of cognitively competent, well-adjusted children value their parenting role and succeed at coordinating it with job responsibilities. Such mothers schedule regular times to devote to their children and combine warmth with consistent expectations for mature behavior.[18] Consider a study of the relationship of maternal employment to first graders' academic and social competence. Children of working mothers were equally or more competent than children of homemakers *only* if the children frequently experienced mother–child shared activities, such as warm conversation and play. Shared activities were especially crucial for children of mothers who had increased their hours of employment during the preceding 3 years, often from part-time to full-time. When a change in employment status was associated with high mother–child engagement, children fared well. When it led to reduced mother–child engagement, children's competence suffered greatly.[19]

Fathers' involvement in child rearing is an additional route to positive outcomes for children. Although women devote more than three times as many hours to child care as men do, fathers' involvement has risen in recent years.[20] Children of highly involved fathers score better on measures of intelligence, school achievement, mature social behavior, and flexible beliefs about gender roles—in short, on all the positive outcomes associated with maternal employment.[21] When mothers and fathers support each other and share child-rearing responsibilities, both engage in more effective parenting.[22]

In sum, increasingly pressured adult lives have contributed to parental difficulties in granting children the attention they need. When employed parents spend generous amounts of time engaged with their child, they safeguard the child's development. Under these conditions, children often reap extra benefits from more equitable involvement of both parents. In contrast, a pressured work life that pulls parents away from child rearing undermines infants' and children's well-being—cognitively, emotionally, and socially.

Probably because it reduces work overload, part-time maternal employment is associated with better academic and social development than is full-time employment.[23] Unfortunately, most American employers do not provide this option, and many parents—especially, single parents—cannot afford it. Yet as noted earlier, financially well-off parents are especially prone to the "time bind" but do not necessarily take advantage of available workplace options aimed at lessening it.

Child-Rearing Advice

Almost all parents—especially first-time parents—feel a need for sound advice on how to rear their children. The demand for expert advice is particularly great today, perhaps because parents, teachers, and the general public perceive that children's problematic behavior has increased. Widespread parent and teacher opinion, gathered from nearly 700 respondents in 1976 and again in 1989, revealed that during this 13-year period, children were viewed as more likely to "do poorly on schoolwork," "hang around with peers who get into trouble," and "destroy things belonging to others." Fewer were seen as involved in worthwhile activities that truly engaged them.[24] A 1997 survey of 4,500 American adults, 2,500 of whom were parents, echoed this disheartening trend. Most viewed today's youngsters as too out-of-control and undirected.[25]

The call for parenting advice has led to a proliferation of volumes, filling shelf after shelf in virtually every general-purpose bookstore and public library. The "correct methods" advocated in these books vary widely, with many addressing discipline and communication, thereby catering to rising numbers of parents with undercontrolled, apathetic, non-goal-directed children. Precious few of these parenting manuals are grounded in the explosion of contemporary research on child development that is of significant applied value. Rather, a plethora of opinion is available, some of it playing on and exacerbating parents' self-doubts with such titles as *Parenting for Dummies* and *The Seven Worst Things Parents Do.*[26]

ONE-SIDED VIEWS.   Well-known theories of child development—Freud's, Skinner's, Gesell's, and Piaget's, for example—provide little comfort, since dramatic shifts in favored theories have occurred since the launching of systematic study of children about 100 years ago. Indeed, this waxing and waning of theories has contributed greatly to discrepancies in expert child-rearing advice, which (like the theories) has fluctuated between extremes—swinging, like a rhythmic pendulum, from an adult-imposed, directive approach to a child-centered, laissez-faire approach, and back again. As one recent analyst commented, theories and the popular literature for parents "have done their share to undermine the wavering self-confidence of American parents."[27] The roots of these polarized perspectives can be found in centuries-old, dramatically opposing philosophies about the nature of children and child development.

Adult Supremacy. Writing at the end of the seventeenth century, British philosopher John Locke characterized the child as a *tabula rasa*. Translated from Latin, this means "blank slate" or "empty container," a being who can be freely "written on," or "filled," with socially acceptable knowledge and skills— in essence, molded in any way adults might desire through careful instruction, effective example, and rewards for good behavior. Lockean ideas provided the footing for American behaviorism, launched by John Watson in the early 1900s and built by B. F. Skinner into a powerful mid-century theoretical force heralding the supremacy of environment in its belief that behavior is shaped by external stimuli.

By the 1920s and 1930s, millions of parents had adopted behaviorist procedures in one form or another. The most committed were well-educated mothers, who read about conditioning methods in magazine articles and government bulletins on child care. Heeding Watson's warnings about the dangers of overindulgence, parents mapped out schedules and routines for their young children and tutored them in all manner of skills and in self-controlled conduct. In preschools and kindergartens, behaviorist tenets were used to justify large-group drill on letters, numbers, and general knowledge as well as repetitive worksheet practice that required young children to sit at their desks for long periods, filling in blanks, coloring within the lines, and otherwise following teacher prescriptions.

Parents anxious for their children to display mature behavior were convinced that these experiences would prime them for academic success. But research eventually documented otherwise—that regimented tutoring not adjusted to the child's interests and capabilities undermines rather than enhances learning, motivation, and self-control. In preschools and kindergartens where much time is spent sitting, listening to teachers, and doing worksheets, children exhibit high levels of stress behaviors, such as wiggling, withdrawal, and talking out. They also show a decline in self-confidence and motivation, expressing doubts about their own ability and retreating from challenging problems. Furthermore, when followed up during the first few years of school, children who spent their kindergarten year in a highly teacher-directed classroom achieve more poorly than do agemates who come from kindergartens emphasizing play and hands-on, small-group projects.[28]

Recall 4-year-old Lydia's dislike of her academic preschool, described at the beginning of this chapter. Lydia's negative reaction is certainly consistent with research findings. The behaviorist presumption that development can be mechanically engineered by social input, guaranteeing brighter, socially more mature children, is not borne out by the evidence.

Child Supremacy. Countering Locke's image of an all-powerful adult tutor, eighteenth-century French philosopher Jean Jacques Rousseau conceived of the child as a "noble savage"—untamed but naturally good, with an innate plan for orderly, healthy growth. According to Rousseau, adult training served only to thwart the child's inherently perceptive intelligence and moral sense, which unfolded naturally as children moved through a sequence of developmental stages.

The Rousseauian view provided the substrate for the twentieth-century counterpoint to behaviorism: a belief in the powerful role of children's inborn characteristics. At mid-century, Freud's psychoanalytic theory vied with behaviorism's reinforcement principles for parents' and educators' attentions. In the tradition of Rousseau, the psychoanalysts argued that powerful biological forces channel development through four psychosexual stages. Although psychoanalytic theory embraced a far less benign view of the child's "instincts" than did Rousseau's philosophy, Freudian ideas were nevertheless strongly child-centered in declaring that not much could be done about the child's basic nature. According to this view, the child's sexual and aggressive urges must be harnessed in the interests of society, but socializing too early or insistently can cause serious inner conflict and psychological disorder. Therefore, psychoanalytic experts advised parents to avoid the trauma of heavy adult demands and accept children's intrinsic dispositions and tendencies.[29]

The Rousseauian child-centered theme surfaced, as well, in the realm of the child's intellect. Swiss biologist Jean Piaget, twentieth-century giant of cognitive development, proposed a theory in which an intrinsically motivated child acts on the world, noticing discrepancies between the environment and inner structures, or ways of thinking. Gradually, the child transforms those structures so they better reflect reality and permit more flexible, efficient thinking and problem solving.

According to Piaget, as the brain matures and children's experiences expand, they move through a sequence of four cognitive stages, or reorganizations of thought: (1) *sensorimotor,* the stage of infancy, in which babies use their senses and movements to explore the world; (2) *preoperational,* the stage of early childhood, in which preschoolers use symbols, especially language and make-believe play, to represent their earlier sensorimotor discoveries, but thinking lacks the logic of older children; (3) *concrete operational,* in which cognition is well organized and logical but limited to coordinating only two or three variables when solving problems; and (4) *formal operational,* the stage of adolescence, which opens up the capacity for abstraction, permitting young people to coordinate an increasing number of variables and to imagine all possible outcomes in a problem, not just the most obvious.[30]

In contrast to the behaviorist emphasis on adult tutoring, Piaget believed that since development follows a natural, internally controlled stage sequence, what comes from within the child is paramount in guiding cognitive change. The environment, including the social environment, is available for children to interact with as they make sense of their experiences, but it does not determine the evolution of the child's mind. Instead, Piaget argued that children are in charge of changes in their own thinking and that biological readiness enables them to capitalize on a wider array of environmental opportunities, both physical and social, in revising inadequate, incorrect mental structures and creating new ones.

Piaget's contribution to the field of child development is enormous. He inspired more research on children's thinking than any other single theorist. Especially important, Piaget convinced the academic community—as well as many parents and teachers—that children are active contributors to their own development, have their own ways of understanding the world, and must be developmentally ready if teaching is to be successful.

In the field of early childhood education, Piaget's theory sparked preschool classrooms emphasizing discovery learning through children's spontaneous interaction with the environment. Rather than teaching didactically, teachers in Piagetian-based settings provide a rich variety of hands-on activities and encourage children's exploration and experimentation. Educators inspired by Piaget's work hope that by repeatedly applying cognitive structures in stimulating environments, children will notice and amend deficiencies in their thinking.

In a similar vein, Piaget's ideas served as a major impetus for the open education movement in elementary education, which rapidly gained ground in the late 1960s and early 1970s. It arose in reaction to the child passivity exacted in traditional classrooms, where pupils sat at their desks, listening to teachers transmit ready-made knowledge, and used textbooks as the main medium of learning.[31] A glance inside the door of an open classroom reveals richly equipped learning centers, small groups of pupils working on tasks they choose themselves, and a teacher who moves from one area to another, guiding and supporting in response to children's individual needs.

Furthermore, children's progress is evaluated differently in open education than in traditional education. Rather than tracking how well pupils keep pace with norms, or the average performance of same-age peers, open-classroom teachers evaluate children on an individual basis—in relation to their own prior development. Following Piaget's lead, this approach accepts the premise that children develop at different rates, although it assumes that all follow the same stage sequence. Undoubtedly because open education minimizes the importance of meeting normative standards, open-classroom school-age pupils fall slightly behind their traditional-classroom agemates in achievement test scores. Yet children in open settings display other benefits, including gains in critical thinking, greater respect for individual differences in their classmates, and more positive attitudes toward school.[32]

As our discussion already suggests, a central Piagetian tenet is that it is foolhardy to try to speed up development. If children are masters of their own learning, then adult efforts to teach them new skills before they indicate they are interested or ready are doomed to failure. Because Piaget stressed the supremacy of children's engagement with their surroundings over adult teaching, parents' and teachers' contributions to development are severely reduced relative to the child's. In sum, compared to the behaviorist, adult-supremacy perspective, the Piagetian view stands at the opposite pole.

Despite Piaget's overwhelming legacy, his theory has been challenged. Recent evidence indicates that Piaget underestimated the capabilities of infants and preschoolers and the direct contribution of adults—both parents and teachers—to cognitive change. To illustrate, let's look at preschoolers' responses to Piaget's conservation problems—the best-known examples of the odd logic of his preoperational stage. Shown two rows of six pennies each, after which the pennies in one row are spread out in a longer line, a 4-year-old is likely to say that the longer row has more pennies. Similarly, after a large ball of play dough is divided into six smaller pieces, a preschooler usually insists that the six pieces have more play dough than the ball, even though none was added during the transformation. Yet a wealth of research reveals that when such tasks are scaled down in difficulty (for example, using rows of three or four pennies rather than six or seven) or made relevant to children's everyday experiences (pretending the play dough is cupcake batter and the six pieces are little cupcakes), preschoolers' understandings appear closer to those of older children and adults than Piaget assumed.[33]

Furthermore, in tribal and village cultures without formal schooling, children who are cognitively adept in many ways master Piagetian conservation tasks much later than do children in industrialized nations.[34] This suggests that to grasp Piagetian concepts, children must take part in everyday activities, such as transforming the appearance of substances and reasoning about the result, that promote this way of thinking. Older children in preliterate communities who fail Piagetian tasks display other impressive cognitive capacities—ones required by and promoted in their culture. For example, among the Zinacanteco Indians of southern Mexico, girls become expert weavers of complex garments through the informal guidance of adults.[35] In Brazil, child street vendors with little or no schooling display sophisticated concepts of classification and equivalence as the result of buying candy from wholesalers, pricing it with the help of adults and experienced peers, and bargaining with customers on city streets. Yet when tested for similar understandings on Piagetian problems, these children do poorly.[36]

Finally, many studies show that children's performance on tasks such as conservation can be improved with training.[37] This, along with the cross-cultural findings just described, raises doubts about Piaget's assumption that discovery learning rather than adult teaching is the most effective way to foster development.

ABSENCE OF A UNIFIED VISION.   Parents trying to make their way through these opposing theories, and their attendant advice about child-rearing and educational practice, are likely to find themselves in a dim forest, without a discernible trail blazed before them. Those who respond with sympathy and patience to their child's inclinations and demands are as taken to task as those who set clear expectations and relentlessly insist that their child "shape up" and comply with them.

Parents who throw up their hands in desperation and search through their own parents' or grandparents' shelves for a more "tried and true" vision will find themselves mired in the same conundrum. They might, for example, run across Arnold Gesell's books of the 1940s and 1950s—*The Infant and Child in the Culture of Today, The First Five Years of Life,* and *The Child from Five to Ten*[38]—still prominent in many bookstores. Offering a lock-step description of physical, intellectual, and emotional milestones at each age, Gesell aimed to reassure uneasy parents that children's problematic behaviors were merely a phase—part of a biologically based sequence requiring understanding, not correction. A search of the previous generation's parenting handbooks might uncover other volumes of this child-centered wave, including *In Defense of Children, Children Have Their Reasons,* and even *Stop Annoying Your Children* and *Parents, Behave!*

Experts of Gesell's time complained that he went too far in downplaying the role of parents. His advice was soon overshadowed by Benjamin Spock's standby, *Baby and Child Care,* published in 1946 and selling millions of copies over seven editions, the most recent appearing in 1998.[39] Providing answers to virtually any question about child rearing that might occur to a parent, from physical care to emotional, disciplinary, and educational issues, Spock seemed, on many fronts, to lean toward parental firmness and away from children's rule-of-the-roost. A closer look, however, indicates that even Spock felt torn between the embattled forces of adult and child control. He tried to grant legitimacy to both poles, commenting that perhaps it's not what you do but how you do it:

> A strictness that comes from harsh feelings or a permissiveness that is timid or vacillating can each lead to poor results. The real issue is what spirit the parent puts into managing the child and what attitude is engendered in the child as a result.[40]

Above all, Spock admonished parents to trust themselves, to have the courage of their convictions. Yet many parents "at sea"—in search of a sound child-rearing ideology within the morass of clashing dictates—undoubtedly found Spock's directive hard to follow.

The past three decades have seen a continuation of this dichotomy of extremes in parenting advice and educational practice. In the 1970s, titles appeared that blew the whistle on permissiveness and child-centeredness, such as *Don't Be Afraid of Your Child* and *Power to the Parents.* As part of this rebound, Thomas Gordon's *Parent Effectiveness Training* [41] offered to rescue parents who had allowed their child to ride roughshod over them. In the realm of children's learning, books in the behaviorist tradition, advocating intensive, early academic training, resurfaced. A prominent example, Siegfried and Therese Engelmann's blueprint for raising a brighter preschooler, *Give Your Child a Superior Mind,* appealed to parents bent on boosting their child's IQ or—even better—producing a genius. In spelling out the theory, the Engelmanns dismissed the legitimacy of biological readiness and proclaimed,

> Every single genius at the top end of the IQ scale received early training. Every single one was subjected to an extremely active environment, not one that folded its hands and waited for the child to "mature." . . . The environment has to be empowered with the capacity to transform the "universal baby." . . . A child is the product of what he learns. His intelligence, capacity and range of skills reflect his environment—his teachers.[42]

Educational practice followed suit, moving back toward traditionalism. As Scholastic Aptitude Test (SAT) scores of American high school graduates plummeted and concern over the academic preparation of American children and youths became widespread, a "back to basics" movement arose that, by 1980, was in full swing. Academic preschools flourished, and kindergarten and primary classrooms returned to whole-class, teacher-directed instruction relying heavily on workbooks and frequent grading, a style still prevalent today.[43]

Bipolar tensions in parenting advice and in educational methods continue to the present day. David Elkind's book *The Hurried Child*[44] is among the best-known of parenting volumes in the child-centered, Piagetian tradition. Elkind appealed to parents prone to live for and through their child's accomplishments to give up their vain desire for a superkid, refrain from exaggerating the child's competence, and stop rushing and pushing the child into adulthood. In keeping with Rousseauian ideals, *The Hurried Child* advises parents to protect children from the harsh realities of the grown-up world and not to "stress them out" by expecting achievements beyond their biologically based limits.

As Elkind illustrates, a 10-year-old with many adult responsibilities—such as preparing breakfast, doing housecleaning after school, checking that a younger sibling is all right, assisting with meal preparation, and washing dishes—barely has time for her own personal, homework responsibilities and is in danger of excessive stress from "responsibility overload."[45] Schools, too, Elkind maintains, hurry and stress children by assigning too much tedious work and rushing them from one subject to another, depriving them of time to think and a sense of completion.

Harshly critical of the child-centered tenor of Elkind's message and pulling in the reverse direction is William Damon's *Greater Expectations*,[46] an impassioned plea to parents and teachers to eradicate what the author characterizes as a rising, insidious "culture of indulgence" in America's homes and schools: "Too many children—the affluent and the poor alike—are drifting through their childhood years without finding the skills, virtues or sense of purpose that they will need to sustain a fruitful life."[47]

As Damon explains, the child-centered philosophy was a major breakthrough when first introduced, in that it made parents and teachers aware that children have unique needs and benefit from warmth and encouragement. But, Damon contends, modern child-centeredness has been stretched to the point of unrestrained child gratification, resulting in a youth culture in which children and adolescents are less engaged, less purposeful, less accomplished academically, and more egoistic and antisocial than in previous generations.

Damon acknowledges that economic constraints and other family pressures play a part in this youth disaffection. But he places most blame on how contemporary children are reared. Child-centeredness, Damon explains, has become an excuse for a rudderless parenting and educational culture that makes few demands while fostering in children a stress-free, "feel-good" attitude in which children are told, "You're lovable," "You're great," "You're terrific," regardless of what they do. But because these messages have no basis in meaningful attainment, they are counterproductive. Sooner or later, children see through them, come to mistrust the adults who repeat them, and begin to doubt themselves.

Damon neither endorses the insensitivity of adult dominance nor the tumultuous reign of the child. Instead, he underscores that children are avid, active learners, but adults must cultivate their drive toward mastery. They must induce children to develop talents, skills, good values, and a sense of accomplishment through engagement not just in activities that are easy and fun, but in ones that are meaningful and challenging—that help them sustain effort in the face of difficulty, overcome obstacles, and advance to greater heights.

As Damon's message suggests, in building an effective vision of child development and child rearing, neither the child's inner thoughts and feelings nor the role of adult guidance can be singularly extolled or wholeheartedly ignored. To do either leads parents and educators to become trapped in a false opposition, to vacillate, and to think in oversimplified ways about how best to help children realize their potential to learn and become personally and socially responsible.

TOWARD A BALANCED PERSPECTIVE.   The popular parenting literature is notable for lagging substantially behind advances in child-development theory and research. Today, sound theories and educational strategies exist that are neither adult- nor child-centered but, instead, portray both as participating actively, jointly, and inseparably in the process of development.

On only one point is the popular parenting literature unanimous: the vital importance of getting development off to a good start during the preschool years. The earlier adults begin and the more continuously they engage in effective practices, the more likely children are to sustain effort, achieve in school, develop productive interests, and become responsible, caring individuals. The longer adults postpone and the more unpredictably and inconsistently they behave, the greater the chances that children will develop maladaptive habits and unfruitful interests, doubt their capacities, become dissatisfied with themselves, and despair about their prospects for the future.

After decades of theoretical division and debate, a new, more complex view of child development is coalescing in the field, supported by rapidly accumulating research evidence. The fragmented, polarized theories of the past are giving way to more equitable theories emphasizing that the child and the social environment interact and that the contributions of each to development cannot be separated and weighted in a simplistic, one-sided manner.[48]

Understanding this new view can be immeasurably helpful to parents, care-givers,[49] and teachers in providing children with development-enhancing experiences, since it offers a way of thinking about child rearing and education that they can call on to guide decision making in daily life. But a vital prerequisite for enacting this perspective is that parents, especially, must arrange their lives in such a way as to invest time and energy in young children. Indeed, as we will soon see, some children—because of genetic background, biological risk, or previous inept caregiving—require more intensive investment of parental energies than do others. Before we take up this emerging theoretical consensus, let's address the question of whether greater parental commitment, in the context of today's demanding and stressful work lives, is possible.

REEVALUATING THE TIME BIND

Parents, as I noted earlier, often complain that they have too little time for children—indeed, too little time to sleep, read, cook, exercise, and socialize as well! Their sense of being overworked and overcommitted, with few moments to spare, must be taken seriously. Feeling constantly frazzled can, in and of itself, interfere with relaxed, patient investment in children.

Yet how pernicious and unique to our lives is this time bind? To gain perspective on this question, I contacted a noted historian of family life,[50] who suggested that I consult John Ise's book, *Sod and Stubble,* in which Ide chronicles his mother Rosie's life on a homestead in rural Kansas in the late nineteenth century as she farmed, kept house, and reared eleven children.[51]

Settling with her husband, Henry, on the land in a one-room cabin, Rosie cooked on a stove so small that she could bake only two loaves of bread at a time, so she had to bake almost every day. She sewed to make the family's entire wardrobe—her own, her husband's, and each of her eleven children's. Keeping up the cabin posed constant difficulties. Cracks in the floor planks and in the log walls permitted various pests to enter, so Rosie battled bedbugs, grasshoppers, and ants, which required frequent searches of the house with a kettle of hot water in one hand and a can of kerosene and a feather in the other. Always, preparations had to be made for the next season—in the fall, for example, cooking enough molasses to last the winter, a task requiring weeks of work.

Outside, Rosie assisted Henry with myriad chores—herding and feeding livestock; making lye from wood ashes to be used in hulling corn for hominy; browning rye for coffee; harvesting wheat; and planting and caring for trees, flowers, grapevines, and a vegetable garden. When she was not helping with the crops and the garden, she could be seen washing and hanging out huge baskets of clothes. On rainy days, Rosie grabbed pans from the shelves to catch the water that dripped through the cabin's sod roof, remaining poised to shift the pans from place to place as new leaks sprang.

Still, Rosie and her husband Henry had time for their children, as well as time to participate in family gatherings, community events, and learning and literacy societies. While the children were small, they accompanied their parents on outings and during outdoor chores—for example, riding in the rear of the corn-husking wagon, where Rosie and Henry could easily see and talk to them. As they grew older, the children played at adult tasks and soon joined in and helped with many of them.

Despite grim work lives, Rosie and Henry, who had little schooling themselves, sent nine of their children to college and some to graduate school. They managed to be involved and caring parents, without all the comforts and time-saving conveniences that we now take for granted—a water-tight roof; central heating; fast foods; microwaves; vacuum cleaners; washing machines and dryers; automobiles; telephones; and much, much more.

Though Rosie's and Henry's way of life was hard, and we shouldn't go too far in romanticizing it, their story helps us put the contemporary time bind in perspective. It suggests that many parents who feel overwhelmed by life's demands ought to be able to free up more time for their children—the first step toward high-quality child rearing. Recent research by time-allocation experts John Robinson and Geoffrey Godbey substantiates this conclusion. Although Americans perceive their work hours as excessive, squeezing out other aspects of their lives, a different picture emerges when they keep detailed diaries of how they spend their time. Every 10 years since 1965, Robinson and Godbey have gathered daily time diaries from thousands of respondents, representing a cross-section of the American population. They discovered that not only are people's gross estimates of time per week devoted to work 6 to 8 hours higher than those recorded in their diaries, but free time—time unencumbered by any obligations—has actually increased!

Americans are working less than they did in 1965—about 6 fewer hours per week for men, 5 fewer for women.[52] Diary-obtained estimates of free time average 36 hours per week for employed men, 34 for employed women. Robinson and Godbey note that compared to a generation ago, the free time of Americans is more plentiful but also more disjointed—a half hour here, an hour there. How do they spend it? Americans report that TV viewing consumes nearly 40 percent—about 15 hours—of their unallocated moments. It seems easier to watch the news or an episode of a favorite TV show than to go to a concert, enjoy a leisurely family dinner, or take the children to a museum or the zoo.

Time-diary findings also verify that time constraints are greater for higher-income Americans. Yet the income gap in free time is not large; financially well-off individuals average only 2 to 4 hours a week less free time than do their less economically advantaged counterparts. Weekly free time for privileged Americans with demanding careers is still plentiful.

If free time is so abundant, why do so many parents say their lives are pressure cookers? The reason, Robinson and Godbey suggest, is that our pace of life is faster. People expect to do more, to live more intensely. Hence, they try to speed up the yield of time, often by doing several things at once—in the case of Angela and Tom, attending to work tasks while fixing dinner, watching TV, and fielding Victor and Jeannine's urgent pleas for attention. The very activity of squeezing more into the moment exacerbates the belief that time is scarce. This "time-famine" sensation is the wellspring of parental efforts to create quality time in the absence of quantity—a contradiction in terms.

How can parents beat the "time bind"? Rather than merely cultivating time-saving skills—a remedy that, by itself, may even further compress time spent with children—Robinson and Godbey recommend that parents find ways to meld time-saving with time-savoring. When parents have full-time jobs, some time pressure is bound to be present—in getting shopping, laundry, and cleaning done; meals on the table; and children to and from child care, school, and various activities. Yet to grant children adequate attention and involvement, there is no substitute for slowing down and reexamining the pace of everyday life. Parents must ask questions like these:

- Does my family have a sit-down meal together on most days of the week, free from the distractions of a blaring TV and a constantly ringing telephone?
- Do I have time on most days to interact one-on-one with each of my children?
- Do I involve my children positively and usefully in play and recreation and in accomplishing tasks of daily living—shopping, cleaning, gardening, cooking, decorating, and repairing?
- Do I provide my children with predictable routines; clear, consistently enforced rules; and sufficient oversight, while they are both within and beyond my immediate supervision—practices that help ensure that the time I share with them is plentiful, pleasurable, and constructively spent?

Clearly, true quality time for children is quantity time and more! Fashioning time for parents and children to be together is the first step toward implementing the ideas and practices I'll discuss in this book. A second step is an appreciation of the multiplicity of factors that contribute to development—an understanding that spells out parents' vital role yet clarifies how it joins with other forces to affect children's development and well-being.

CHILD DEVELOPMENT: A NEW CONSENSUS

At the dawn of a new millennium, a fresh set of theories of child development has blossomed. The new approaches are numerous—some more concerned with motor skills, others with cognitive competencies, and still others with emotional and social development. Yet they form a consensus, a set of variations on a unified theme.[53] Each borrows features from past perspectives that have withstood the test of time and integrates them with current evidence. The result is a new outlook on how children acquire more complex and effective skills.

Many Factors Contribute to Development

The new view assumes that many elements, internal and external to the child, work together as a dynamic, synergistic system to affect children's thinking, feeling, and acting. These elements include the child's heredity and biological constitution; the people and objects in the child's everyday settings of home, child-care center, school, and neighborhood; community resources for child rearing (such as family-friendly workplace policies and high-quality, affordable child care); and cultural values and customs related to child development and education.[54]

Look closely at these ideas—that children are affected by interwoven factors in biology, everyday contexts, and culture—and you will see that contemporary researchers are no longer one-sided in how they view the power of the child versus the adult, or heredity versus environment. Most have turned away from asking *which* influence is more important to uncovering *how* nature and nurture work together to affect the child's traits and capacities.

In addition, researchers now realize that quite normal children show both similarities and differences in pathways of change. A common human genetic heritage and basic regularities in children's physical and social environments yield certain universal, broad outlines of development. At the same time, biological makeup, everyday tasks, and the people who support children in mastery of those tasks vary greatly, resulting in wide individual differences in specific skills.[55] And because children build competencies by engaging in real activities in real contexts, different skills vary in maturity within the same child! Recall the Zinacanteco Indian child weavers and the Brazilian child street vendors, who are advanced in skills relevant to their own culture yet behind on tasks devised for children in Western industrialized nations. They offer a dramatic illustration of developmental variation—both between children and within the same child.

Heredity and Environment as Inseparable

Within this dynamic system in which inner and outer forces jointly engender development, each contributing factor influences—and is influenced by—the others. Therefore, the roles of heredity and environment, of the child and important people in his or her life, so closely interconnect that according to some experts, their influence is inseparable.[56] To illustrate, let's take two vibrant, contemporary research topics relevant to young children's learning: (1) the dramatic growth of the brain during the first 6 years, and (2) young children's temperaments, or genetically influenced styles of relating to their physical and social worlds.

BRAIN DEVELOPMENT. Many people think of infancy and early childhood as a time when the human brain is especially sensitive to experience. In line with this view, although genes provide the code for basic brain structures and functions, heredity goes only so far in affecting the organization of the child's brain and the rate at which it develops. The environment has a crucial, profound impact.

How does early experience join with biology to affect brain development? The cerebral cortex, seat of human intelligence, undergoes dramatic growth during the first few years. Almost all its neurons—cells that store and transmit information—are in place by the second trimester of pregnancy. Once established, neurons begin to take on unique functions by sending out branching fibers, which form elaborate connections with other neurons. Formation of this complex communication system contributes to an enormous increase in size of the brain—from nearly 30 percent of its adult weight at birth to 70 percent by age 2 and 90 percent by age 6.[57]

As neurons form connections, a new factor becomes vital in their survival: stimulation. Neurons stimulated by the surrounding environment continue to establish new connections, which support more complex functions. Neurons seldom stimulated soon lose their connections as their fibers atrophy. Notice how, for the biological side of brain development to go forward, appropriate stimulation is essential while formation of neural connections is at its peak.[58]

During early childhood, the brain is highly plastic, or adaptable, in that many brain regions are not yet committed to specific functions. This means that if a part of the brain is damaged, other parts can usually take over the tasks that would have been handled by the damaged region, provided they are granted the necessary stimulation. In a study of preschool children with a wide variety of brain injuries sustained in the first year of life, psychologist Joan Stiles found that cognitive deficits were milder than those observed in brain-injured adults. And by age 5, virtually all impairments had disappeared! As the children gained perceptual, cognitive, and motor experiences, stimulated intact areas of the cerebral cortex compensated for the early damage.[59] By age 8 to 10, most brain regions have taken on specific functions, so brain plasticity declines. Because of rapid brain growth and gradual decline in brain plasticity, the first 5 to 8 years of life are regarded as a sensitive phase of development in which appropriate stimulation is necessary for children to reach their full genetic potential.

In describing the close connection between brain growth and experience, I have used the expression "appropriate stimulation." By this, I mean neither impoverished conditions nor excessive bombardment with sights and sounds but input that the child can absorb, as indicated by his or her approach, interest, and concentration. In Burton White and Robert Held's classic study of the impact of early stimulation on development, young babies in a barren institution given a moderate amount of stimulation tailored to their ability to handle it—at first, a few simple designs on the side of their crib and later, a fancy mobile—reached for and explored objects six weeks earlier than did infants given nothing to look at. A third group of babies given massive stimulation—patterned crib bumpers and fancy mobiles beginning in the first few weeks of life—also reached for objects sooner than did unstimulated babies. But this heavy dose of enrichment took its toll. The massively enriched infants looked away and cried a great deal, and they were not as advanced in reaching and exploring as the moderately stimulated babies.[60]

Much research confirms that overloading children with input leads to disorganization of behavior. Excessive stimulation also causes them to withdraw as they try to shield themselves from a stimulus deluge, thereby creating conditions that, paradoxically, are much like stimulus deprivation![61] These findings help us understand, from a brain-development perspective, the detrimental impact of excessive adult tutoring on young children, described earlier in this chapter. They also raise grave concerns about the recent proliferation of expensive commercial early learning centers, in which infants are barraged with letter and number flashcards and slightly older toddlers are drenched in a full curriculum of reading, math, science, art, music, gym, and more.[62] Rather than optimizing early neurological growth (as proponents claim), these efforts to jump-start young children can inflict considerable harm, robbing them of a healthy start on the road to maturity.[63]

Our rapidly expanding knowledge base on brain development and children's learning reveals that a genetically influenced roadmap for brain growth and a developmentally appropriate environment go hand in hand; the impact of each depends on the other. Appropriate stimulation "wires" the brain, prompting it to form new connections and its regions to specialize. As this process goes forward, the brain gradually becomes receptive to increasingly complex and varied stimulation. This fosters further elaboration and specialization of brain structures and ever more advanced knowledge and skills.

TEMPERAMENT.   From the earliest ages, children vary greatly in preferences, interests, talents—and in temperament, or style of emotional responding, the most thoroughly studied of these sources of individual variation. Temperament encompasses activity level, ability to attend to stimuli, and capacity to adjust the intensity of emotions to a comfortable level so the child can remain adaptively engaged with his or her physical and social surroundings.[64]

Temperamental differences among infants and children are of great interest to researchers because temperament is believed to form the cornerstone of the adult personality. A wealth of research reveals that for children to develop at their best, the experiences adults provide must be adapted not just to children's general neurological progress, but also to their unique temperamental needs.

Temperamental traits most often studied include attention span, fear of novel experiences, irritability when desires are frustrated, and quality of mood (positive versus negative).[65] Parents can rate their children's temperamental qualities fairly accurately; their judgments show a reasonable correspondence with researchers' observations of children's behavior.[66] Teacher ratings are even more precise, since teachers are familiar with many children and therefore have a broader basis for judging whether a particular child is high, low, or intermediate on dimensions of temperament.

Let's see how temperament combines with brain development and experience, forming a complex, dynamic system that shapes the course of development. Take Larry, who when brought as an infant to a highly stimulating laboratory playroom, was agitated and upset by all the new sights, sounds, and people. Yet baby Mitch, when introduced to the very same playroom, watched with interest, laughed, and eagerly approached the exciting toys and strangers. Larry scores high on the temperamental dimension of fearful distress. On observing him, most of us would call him a very shy, inhibited child. Mitch, in contrast, scores low on fearful distress and high on positive mood. He is, in everyday language, an uninhibited, sociable child.

To chart the development of shy and sociable children, psychologist Jerome Kagan followed several hundred youngsters from infancy into the school years, repeatedly observing their behavior and measuring their physiological responses to highly stimulating, unfamiliar events. As babies, about 20 percent were easily upset (like Larry), whereas 40 percent were comfortable, even delighted, at new experiences (like Mitch).[67]

According to Kagan, individual differences in arousal of an inner brain structure called the amygdala, which controls avoidance reactions, underlie these contrasting temperamental styles. In shy, inhibited children, novel stimuli easily excite the amygdala and its connections to the cerebral cortex and sympathetic nervous system (which prepares the body to act in the face of threat). The same level of stimulation evokes minimal neural excitation in highly sociable, uninhibited children. Indeed, shy children's physiological responses to novelty—a rise in heart rate, pupil dilation, blood pressure, and blood concentration of cortisol (a hormone that combats stress)—resemble the reactions of very timid animals and are known to be mediated by the amygdala.[68] When neural messages from the amygdala reach the cortex, they lead a shy child to interpret new experiences negatively and a sociable child to interpret them positively. Indeed, brain waves in the cortex differ strikingly for these two types of children.[69]

Are these early, biologically based temperamental styles destined to last, restricting learning opportunities for shy children while opening new doors for their sociable counterparts? The answer, once again, depends on experience—especially, parenting practices. When parents shield infants and preschoolers who dislike novelty from minor stresses—such as eating and sleeping in a new setting or meeting new people—they make it harder for the child to overcome the urge to retreat from unfamiliar events. Under these conditions, heredity and environment act in concert to maintain the child's fear, increasing the likelihood that it will translate into long-term adjustment difficulties, such as excessive cautiousness, social withdrawal, loneliness, and (by school age) overwhelming anxiety in the face of academic challenges.

This does not mean that a shy child should be forced into new situations with coldness, harshness, and impatience—tactics that magnify their dread of new and unpredictable events. Instead, parents who warmly, but consistently and assertively, require their inhibited child to try new experiences and guide and support them in doing so actually reduce the child's physiological stress reactions, fostering a more adaptive style in the child. Indeed, adult efforts of this kind are believed to be largely responsible for the fact that about 70 percent of extremely inhibited babies cope with novelty more effectively as they get older (although practically none become highly sociable).

Shy and sociable children also require different adult interventions to promote exploration of their surroundings—an activity that (as Piaget pointed out) is essential for optimal cognitive development. Vivacious, stimulating parental behavior, including frequent questioning, instructing, and pointing out objects, is beneficial for reserved, inactive infants; it helps them become interested in and engaged with novel toys. Yet these same parental behaviors interfere with exploration in very active, outgoing children.[70] For these youngsters, too much adult intervention is intrusive; it dampens their natural curiosity. Consequently, "appropriate stimulation" varies for these two types of children.

Finally, culture affects the likelihood that parents and teachers will respond to shy children in ways that foster their development. In Western nations, shyness is regarded as a form of social maladjustment—a perspective that heightens the chances that adults and peers will react negatively to inhibited children's reticence and retreat. In China, adults evaluate shy children positively, as advanced in social maturity and understanding! The high value placed on self-restraint in Chinese culture leads shy children to receive very positive feedback from adults and peers. Consequently, inhibited Chinese youngsters appear particularly well adjusted during the school years—well liked by their classmates and rated by their teachers as academically and socially skilled.[71]

The Roles of Parents and Other Adults: Agents of Change, Buffers, Gatekeepers, and Conveyors of Culture

Environmental forces, from adult–child interaction to cultural values, join with heredity to affect the development of children with other temperamental dispositions as well. Throughout this book—and especially in Chapter 5, which addresses the development of children with physical and mental disabilities—we will see many more examples of these synergistic effects. In each, the role of parents and teachers as agents of change is vigorous and profound, although not sovereign and exclusive. Parents cannot erase their child's genetic propensities, but they can alter many of them in a favorable direction, especially if they have access to knowledge about effective child rearing and they intervene in early childhood, the years of greatest neurological malleability.

Furthermore, when parents and other adults apply good rearing practices, they serve as buffers, or sources of protection, for children against threatening forces in the wider world. A common thread in research on the impact of stressful life events and conditions (including poverty, divorce, abuse, community violence, and wartime trauma) is that a close relationship with a parent, relative, or teacher who introduces affection, assistance, and order into the child's life, fosters *resiliency*—mastery of cognitive and social skills that enable the child to withstand and even overcome adversity. To be sure, children who are relaxed, socially responsive, and able to deal with change are more likely to elicit the support of parents and other adults. At the same time, children can develop more attractive dispositions and adaptive skills as the result of parental warmth, attention, and consistent guidance.[72]

Parents and teachers also act as gatekeepers for young children. Depending on the experiences they offer, they open up or close off a great many avenues for learning. These include toys, books, television, computers, special lessons, weekend outings, time with grandparents and other extended family members, as well as the quality of child care, schooling, and the neighborhood they choose to live in (depending, of course, on the extent to which communities offer viable choices).

In all the ways just mentioned, parents and other adults are vital conveyers of culture, through direct teaching of attitudes and values and through the pervasive imprint of culture on the settings and activities they provide for children. In the hands of parents and teachers lies the awesome responsibility of conveying to the next generation the intellectual, scientific, aesthetic, and moral achievements that differentiate our species from others. From the simplest preliterate society to the most technologically advanced nation, adults are charged with ensuring that children acquire competencies that enable them to assume a responsible place in their society and, ultimately, participate in transmitting its values and practices to future generations.

Of course, children have an important say in the socialization process. For example, they usually become more expert at those skills that complement their native talents. And depending on their dispositions, the road to maturity may be rockier, requiring greater investment of parental energies and distinct child-rearing strategies. Moreover, without a doubt, peers contribute greatly to socialization—especially by helping children learn to resolve conflict, cooperate, share, form deep attachments beyond the family, and otherwise behave in ways that foster social harmony. But the recent, widely publicized claim of Judith Rich Harris, in her book entitled *The Nurture Assumption*[73]—that parents are minor players who are overshadowed by children's genetic makeup and peer culture—is not correct.

Indeed, many eminent child development researchers have countered Harris's thesis.[74] Genes and peers do not supplant adult agents, including parents, grandparents, aunts, uncles, family friends, and teachers. Harris draws on evidence suggesting that children's inherited intellectual and personality attributes lead them to evoke particular responses from adults, which further strengthen the child's inherited traits. For example, a friendly baby receives more social stimulation than a quiet, passive infant; a cooperative, attentive preschooler receives more patient and sensitive interaction than does an inattentive, distractible child; and a bright, advanced child is praised and stimulated more than a child developing more slowly. Hence, Harris concludes, most children follow a genetically preordained developmental course, regardless of parental influence.

Although Harris is correct that children often evoke behaviors from parents and others that strengthen their genetic tendencies, research clearly shows that parents can, and often do, uncouple these child-to-parent effects. Indeed, the substantial malleability of temperament in infancy and early childhood is explained, in large measure, by the fact that many parents and other adults are successful in guiding children with maladaptive tendencies toward more effective functioning. Moreover, decades of research on intelligence show that IQ, although not infinitely pliant, varies greatly with the stimulating quality of children's experiences.[75]

Furthermore, no conclusive evidence exists for the assertion that the most consequential environment for children's development is the peer group rather than the family. It is based on an array of selective and equivocal findings, mustered to convince readers that parenting effects are confined to how children behave in parents' presence and do not extend beyond the home. I will show repeatedly in this book that just the opposite is so — that parenting practices have much to do with children's competence at language and communication; sensitivity to others' feelings and needs; capacity to get along with others within and beyond the family; achievement in school; and guiding values, beliefs, and attitudes.

In fact, this overriding emphasis on peers as a source of positive development is itself a product of our culture. Compared to other nations, the United States is more peer-oriented; it places greater value on gregariousness and being liked by agemates.[76] As more American parents with busy, stressed lives retreat from their children, peers take over. Without a constructive link between the values taught at home and the values of the peer group, the consequences of high peer orientation are decidedly negative — a rise in school failure, aimlessness, drug use, teen pregnancy, antisocial behavior, and other youth problems of current concern in the United States.

Downplaying the role of parents—suggesting that they are relatively unimportant in socialization—does both families and society a disservice. It leads parents, like Noah and Suzanne, who are on the cusp of a dramatic period of development in their 2-year-old son's life, to express grave doubts about their own importance. Harvard University psychologist Howard Gardner notes:

> Children would not—could not—grow up to be members of a civilized culture if they were simply left to the examples of their peers. . . . A social science—or a layman's guide—that largely left out parents after birth would be absurd. So would a society.
>
> Whether on the scene, or behind the scenes, parents have jointly created the institutions that train and inspire children: apprenticeships, schools, works of art and literature, religious classes, playing fields, and even forms of resistance and rebellion. These institutions, and the adults who run them, sustain civilization and provide the disciplines—however fragile they may seem—that keep our societies from reverting to barbarism.[77]

SOCIOCULTURAL THEORY: DIALOGUES WITH CHILDREN

This book takes its inspiration from sociocultural theory, one of the dynamic, synergistic perspectives that has recently captivated the field. The central idea of sociocultural theory is that the child and his or her social surroundings join to provide direction to development; participation in social life guides and energizes the child's mastery of new, culturally adaptive skills. Because sociocultural theory focuses on children's access to and interaction with cultural experts, it has much to say to parents and teachers about how they can help children develop into responsible, contributing members of society.

Sociocultural theory originated with Russian psychologist Lev Vygotsky, who carried out his highly innovative research during the 1920s and early 1930s, writing prolifically on the contribution of social experience to children's learning. After the Soviet Union's twenty-year ban on Vygotsky's writings was lifted in the mid-1950s, his major works reached the West. They began to be translated into English in the 1960s and 1970s.[78] By the 1980s, many American psychologists and educators—doubting the Piagetian view of development and desiring to account for wide variation in children's competencies—embraced Vygotsky's ideas with enthusiasm.[79]

According to sociocultural theory, cooperative dialogues between children and more knowledgeable members of their society are necessary for children to acquire the ways of thinking and behaving that make up a community's culture. These dialogues occur frequently and spontaneously as adults and children spend time together—in everyday situations such as household chores, mealtimes, play, storybook reading, outings in the community, and children's efforts to acquire all sorts of skills. Although interactions that arise between adults and children may seem mundane and inconsequential at first glance, sociocultural theory emphasizes that they are powerful sources of children's learning.

Consider the following conversation between Mel and his 4-year-old son, Ben, as the pair took a summer-evening walk on a California beach near their home. Mel had brought along a plastic bag, as the beach was often littered with trash after a busy day.

Ben: (running ahead and calling out) Some bottles and cans. I'll get them.

Mel: If the bottles are broken, you could cut yourself, so let me get them. *(Catches up and holds out the bag as Ben drops items in)*

Ben: Dad, look at this shell. It's a whole one, really big. Colors all inside!

Mel: Hmmm, might be an abalone shell.

Ben: What's abalone?

Mel: Do you remember what I had in my sandwich on the wharf yesterday? That's abalone.

Ben: You eat it?

Mel: Well, you can. You eat a meaty part that the abalone uses to stick to rocks.

Ben: Ewww. I don't want to eat it. Can I keep the shell?

Mel: I think so. Maybe you can find some things in your room to put in it. *(Points to the shell's colors)* Sometimes people make jewelry out of these shells.

Ben: Like mom's necklace?

Mel: That's right. Mom's necklace is made out of a kind of abalone with a very colorful shell—pinks, purples, blues. It's called Paua. When you turn it, the colors change.

Ben: Wow! Let's look for Paua shells!

Mel: You can't find them here, only in New Zealand.

Ben: Where's that? Have you been there?

Mel: No, someone brought Mom the necklace as a gift. But I'll show you New Zealand on the globe. It's far away, halfway around the world.

In this dialogue, which lasted only a few minutes, Mel conveyed important social values and a wealth of information to Ben—about responsibility for preserving the environment, about safety precautions, about the wonders of an unusual sea creature, about the beauty and utility of natural objects, and even about world geography.

According to sociocultural theory, as adults—and more expert peers as well—help children participate in culturally meaningful activities, the communication between them becomes part of children's thinking. Once children internalize essential features of these dialogues, they use the language within them to accomplish new skills and to gain control over their own thought and behavior.[80] The young child speaking to herself when tempted by a forbidden object ("Don't touch!"), solving a difficult puzzle ("Where does this piece go?"), finding an interesting shell on the beach ("Looks like Mom's shiny necklace."), or acting out a scene in make-believe play ("What would you like for lunch? An abalone sandwich?") has started to produce the same kind of guiding comments that an adult previously used to help the child think about the world and engage in important tasks.

A Socially Formed Mind

Sociocultural theory is unique in viewing inner mental activity as profoundly social. The thoughts and imaginings that make us distinctly human are not regarded as independently constructed by the child. Rather, the child derives them from his or her history of relations with other people.

According to Vygotsky, infants are biologically endowed with basic perceptual, attentional, and memory capacities that they share with other animals. These undergo a natural course of development through direct contact with the environment during the first two years of life, similar to the process of exploration and discovery described by Piaget. For example, all babies gradually distinguish objects and people in their surroundings and realize that these entities continue to exist when out of sight. They also merge objects that are alike into categories (such as vehicles, animals, birds, and eating utensils), laying the foundation for mentally representing their experiences and thinking efficiently. And they become adept at imitating others, a powerful means for acquiring new skills. These and other infant capabilities set the stage for language, which develops with extraordinary speed after 1 year of age. By ages 2 to 3, most children are skilled conversationalists; by age 6, they have mastered most of the grammatical rules of their language and have vocabularies as large as ten thousand words.[81]

The milestones just cited are broad universals of development. They characterize children everywhere, as long as they are biologically prepared to learn and live in stimulating physical and social surroundings. But once children become capable of representing objects and events with symbols, especially language, their ability to participate in dialogues is greatly enhanced. This leads to a crucial change in development. The natural line of development makes closer contact with its surrounding social context, merges with it, and is transformed by it.[82] Children's social exchanges begin to influence their ways of thinking more profoundly than before, permitting them to acquire competencies in keeping with the requirements of their families and communities.

A basic premise of sociocultural theory is that all uniquely human, higher forms of thinking—including controlled attention to tasks, memory strategies, reflections on experiences and ideas, techniques for solving problems, and imagination—are deeply affected by children's social experiences. For example, when a parent suggests to a young ball player, "Watch me, keep your eyes on the ball!" the adult helps the child control attention, essential for mastering any complex task. When a teacher says, "Let's write the names of our snack helpers on the board," or "Put all the animals together and all the vehicles together," she teaches vital strategies for remembering. And a parent or teacher who asks, "Is Brenda crying because you took her colored pencils? What can you do to become friends again?" encourages children to reflect on their experiences and to think of effective techniques for solving social problems.

Vygotsky emphasized that to understand children's development, it is necessary to understand the social situations adults devise for them. Any higher form of thinking, he pointed out, first appears in social communication, *between* the child and representatives of his or her culture as they engage in a joint activity. Only later does it appear *within* the child, as an individual capacity or skill.[83] The child's mind, then, is a profoundly social organ. Through social life, it makes contact with and is influenced by other, more expert minds, permitting transfer of the values, knowledge, and skills essential for success in a particular culture.

The Importance of Language

Because Vygotsky regarded language as the major bridge between our social and mental worlds, he viewed language acquisition as the most significant milestone in children's cognitive development. Language is our primary avenue of communication with others and means through which we represent our experiences. Once children start to think with words, language becomes an indispensable "tool of the mind." Just as a hammer is a tool used to gain control over and transform physical objects, so we call on language to influence the thought and behavior of other people and ourselves.[84]

Language not only conveys culturally meaningful ideas but is itself deeply imbued with culture. It—along with other symbolic tools, such as gestures, aids to memory, systems for counting, works of art, diagrams, and maps—is the product of the social history of a cultural group, the result of members' efforts to create a communal way of life. Indeed, the central purpose of language, from its moment of emergence, is "communication, social contact, influencing surrounding individuals."[85] Then it becomes an individually applied tool for governing our own thoughts and actions.

To illustrate how Vygotsky envisioned this close connection between social interaction and children's thinking and behaving, let's look in on another verbal exchange between a parent and a young child. Deb is pulling weeds in the garden while 2 1/2-year-old Maggy follows along, alternately digging with her small spade and holding a toy telephone to her ear. Soon gray clouds appear along the horizon, and thunder can be heard. Maggy, frightened by the booming sounds, whimpers to Deb, "Scary, Mommy. Go inside!"

"That thunder is way up in the sky, far away," Deb explains, pointing off in the distance. "It can't hurt you. We need to get these weeds out before the rain comes. Just a little longer, and then we'll go inside."

Maggy listens and responds, "Not scary, far far away," and Deb nods in agreement. As Maggy waits, she paces back and forth near Deb, speaking into her toy phone, "Not scary thunder. Far away. Get the weeds. Not scary, boom boom! Like a big drum."

Maggy has taken the communication jointly generated with her mother and turned it toward herself. She uses speech derived from that conversation to reflect on the thunder, allay her fear, and help her wait until Deb's task is finished and they can go inside. As Maggy "thinks aloud" with words, she converses with herself, in much the same way that she interacted with her mother. Over time, Maggy will start to interact with herself silently, "inside her head." And as Maggie's social experiences expand and become more complex, she will continue to weave aspects of them into her inner dialogues, acquiring new, more advanced ways of thinking.

A final point about thinking as internalized social interaction: Note that Maggy's telephone conversation with herself is not a simple copy of Deb's remarks to her. The sociocultural vision is very different from behaviorism, which views development as directly imposed, or shaped, by external forces. Instead, children are active agents, contributing to the creation of their own thought processes by collaborating with more experienced cultural members in meaningful activities. The *combination* of child and adult leads to the communication between them. Then children actively take over this interaction and gradually adapt it for efficient and effective self-communication, shortening and personalizing it.

To capture this idea of children selecting from social interaction in ways that fit their goals, some experts like to say that the child "appropriates"—or adopts—tools of the mind.[86] Others continue to describe the child as "internalizing" social experience but emphasize the child's unique contribution to both adult–child interaction and its internalization. Whatever label is applied, active engagement on the part of both adult and child, resulting in a "meeting of minds," is central to this process.

Purposeful Activities and Culturally Adaptive Competencies

Children learn and practice thinking by participating in purposeful activities, organized by their cultural community. This ensures that they will acquire competencies that are adaptive in their culture.

At very young ages, when children are just beginning to acquire culturally valued skills, they depend almost entirely on interactions with more expert cultural members to make sense of their experiences. For example, when researchers tested 3-year-olds to find out what they remembered about a visit to a museum, the children recalled only information they had talked about with their mothers; everything else had been forgotten.[87]

When young children do not understand a concept or how to solve a problem, most often they lack experience in relevant activities with more expert individuals. For example, some ethnic minority children, who grow up in more "people-oriented" than "object-oriented" homes, do less well than they otherwise would on academic tasks because they rarely participate in activities involving "educational" toys, games, and a question–answer style of adult–child interaction ("What color is that?" How many wheels on that truck?"), which prime children for academic success.[88] Yet these very same children who do poorly in the classroom can be seen telling complex stories, engaging in elaborate artistic activities, competently watching over younger children, and accomplishing athletic feats in daily life.

The importance of activity contexts reminds us that all children do not face identical tasks. Cultures, and adults within them responsible for socialization, select different tasks for children's learning. As a result, children's cognition is contextualized; it emerges and derives meaning from particular activities and social experiences. Parents who spend little time in joint pursuits and conversation with their children convey to them a very different set of cultural values, practices, and cognitive strategies than do parents who involve their children in constructive play and projects; encourage them to participate in family routines and duties, such as meal preparation and cleaning; and plan parent–child outings. Similarly, teachers who require mostly solitary desk work from children, isolating the skills taught from their everyday use, promote values and competencies strikingly different from those cultivated by teachers who embed teaching and learning in meaningful collaborative activities.

The core lesson to be learned from our discussion so far is that development is a matter of children's genetic/biological potential undergoing a cultural metamorphosis, a process that cannot take place without parents and teachers as thoughtful and committed participants in children's lives. From the sociocultural perspective, parents and teachers are leaders in awakening children's minds and fostering their development; children are apprenticed to these experts.

Hence, to Talia's concern, posed at the start of our discussion: Should she and her husband, Jim, respond to 7-year-old Anselmo's pleas for help with his homework? Given what we currently know about how children develop, the answer is a resounding yes. Rather than promoting dependency (as Talia and her husband fear), assisting Anselmo is the surest route to competent functioning, provided parental interaction builds on Anselmo's current capacities and remains sensitive to his unique characteristics. Now let's turn to just how parents and teachers can advance children's knowledge and skills.

The Social Origins of Mental Life

Talia and Jim's fear of helping 7-year-old Anselmo with his homework, lest they create a dependent, immature child, is a peculiarly Western—and profoundly American—preoccupation. American middle-class parents typically regard young children as dependent beings who must be urged toward independence. In response to researchers' queries, they frequently say that babies should be trained to be self-reliant from the first few months.[1] Consequently, they place a high value on children's learning and doing on their own. Repeatedly relying on others for assistance is construed as weakness, uncertainty, and lack of capacity. In keeping with this view, many American parents worry that if their children seek help, they may become dependent.

A similar view permeates traditional classrooms, where an individualistic value system prevails. Children must "do their own work." In the most intensely individualistic of these settings, conferring with your neighbor is worse than dependency; it is cheating, and teachers go so far as to set up barriers between pupils, such as upright books and cardboard screens, to prevent it.

This emphasis on independent accomplishment is not broadly accepted around the world. Indeed, adults in some non-Western cultures regard American parents as rather merciless in pushing their young children toward independence—for example, when they insist that infants sleep alone rather than with their parents, or when they take pleasure in the earliest possible mastery of motor skills, such as crawling and walking, long before the child has acquired the reasoning powers to avoid steep staircases and busy roadways.[2]

Diverse non-Western peoples and American ethnic minorities stress *interdependence*—that children must feel intimately linked to others to become competent and self-reliant. Chinese, Japanese, Vietnamese, Guatemalan-Mayan, eastern Kentucky Appalachian, and many other cultural groups regard newborn infants as psychologically separate beings whose most important task is to develop an interdependent relationship with their community—an emotional and social foundation that is crucial for survival and learning.[3] Witness the following conclusion by a researcher who compared American with Japanese infant rearing practices: "An American mother–infant relationship consists of two individuals . . . a Japanese mother–infant relationship consists of only one individual, i.e., mother and infant are not divided."[4] These contrasting parenting perspectives reflect underlying family and community values. Japanese parents and other ethnic minorities adhere to a collectivist worldview, in which people define themselves in terms of their relationships with others.

Collectivist values also alter the way teachers and children think about classroom learning. Were you to visit a school on an Israeli kibbutz (cooperative agricultural settlement), you would find an explicit emphasis on cooperation and avoidance of pupil comparisons, and a far more positive attitude toward children who seek help than is common in American schools. When asked why children look at each others' work, kibbutz pupils mention the importance of connecting with others to acquire new skills. They explain, "If your picture looks crooked, you would want to see your friend's paper to learn how to make it straight," or "If you aren't sure what you're supposed to do, then you should check." To the same question, American and Israeli urban children typically respond, "I would want to see whose picture was the best," or "I might be wondering whether she got more right than I did."[5]

FROM INTERDEPENDENCY TO AUTONOMY

Vygotsky, who studied and wrote about children's development in Russia in the early twentieth century, was deeply interested in how interdependency—children's close ties to their community—can pave the way to competence and autonomy. His sociocultural theory has thoroughly collectivist cultural roots. Vygotsky stressed that children need social interaction and meaningful activities to develop, and he regarded high intrinsic motivation and mature, independent functioning as arising from the support granted by cultural experts as children attempt ever more challenging tasks. The child's mind, Vygotsky pointed out, "extends beyond the skin" and is inseparably joined with other minds. Out of this interconnection springs mastery, proficiency, and self-confidence.[6]

Nevertheless, a deeply ingrained American belief is that satisfying a young child's desire for social contact and assistance will be habit forming, leading to a clingy, spoiled youngster. Much evidence verifies that this is not ordinarily so.

Consider the early attachment bond that builds between caregiver and baby during the first year of life. By age 6 to 8 months, infants single out their parents and other stable, loving caregivers for expressions of joy and turn to them for comfort when anxious and afraid. An overwhelming consensus of research shows that *sensitive caregiving*—responding to the baby's cries for physical care and stimulation promptly, consistently, and appropriately—supports the development of a secure attachment relationship.[7] Securely attached infants actively seek contact with and are easily consoled by their familiar, responsive caregiver. Yet such infants are not destined to become immaturely dependent! Rather, by the end of the first year, their exploration of the physical world is confident, persistent, and complex. And they are less likely to cry and more likely to use gestures and words to express their desires than are infants whose parents delayed or failed to respond to their calls for help.[8]

Sensitive care builds an *interdependent relationship* between parent and baby—one in which physical and emotional closeness becomes the context for encouraging more mature behavior. Attachment serves as the springboard for a great many capacities that make their first appearance in the second year—self-confidence, compliance and cooperation; awareness of others' needs and desires, and empathy and sympathy (emotions that enable us to feel for and help others in need).[9] But the parent who fails to respond promptly and predictably, intervening only after the baby has become extremely agitated, teaches the infant to rise rapidly to intense distress. The baby has learned that only when he is distraught will the parent reliably come to his aid. As a result, he is more difficult to soothe, to encourage to communicate in ways other than crying, and to guide in acquiring other vital competencies.[10]

An analogous circumstance exists at older ages, as Anselmo's interactions with his parents reveal. Jim's refusal to help Anselmo with his homework, in hopes of instilling independence, is counterproductive. Anselmo's crying and pleading accelerate, to the point that anxiety prevents him from focusing on the task. Denying Anselmo assistance yields precisely what it was intended to prevent—a dependent, doubting child. As Anselmo's parents refrain from helping, they fuel his anger and demandingness, and ultimately his sense of helplessness. When Talia finally responds, she does so out of desperation—to stop Anselmo's agitated appeals, which are about to escalate beyond control. Consequently, Talia assists inappropriately, by doing the task for him.

Anselmo's resulting disorganized behavior and dependency prompt additional parental vacillation—sometimes refusals to help, at other times maladaptive helping—along with exasperation and criticism. Talia and Jim can be heard saying impatiently, "You aren't any good at this!" "Can't you do anything?"[11] Soon a barrier forms between Anselmo and the task he had previously wanted to master, and his motivation wanes.

In classrooms, the same sequence of events prevails. Teachers' communication plays a vital role in children's effort and learning. Consider a recent study, in which 1,600 elementary- and middle-school pupils were followed over a 3-year period. Those who viewed their teachers as warm and as providing helpful learning conditions—by making expectations clear and checking that the child understood—worked harder on assignments and participated more in class. Effort and participation, in turn, predicted better academic performance, which sustained the child's willingness to try hard in the future. In contrast, children who regarded their teachers as unsupportive were more likely to disengage, stop trying, and show declines in achievement. These negative outcomes led children to doubt their own ability, which perpetuated their reduced effort.[12]

How can adults build interdependent relationships with children that foster the development of culturally meaningful skills and mature, autonomous behavior? To answer this question, Vygotsky proposed a special concept: the *zone of proximal development*. Keeping it in mind can help parents and teachers interact with children in ways that lead their development forward.

THE ZONE OF PROXIMAL DEVELOPMENT

Take a few moments to list five or six competencies of a child you know well. If you are a parent, do so for your own child; if you are a teacher, choose a child in your class. Perhaps your list looks much like this one, recorded by Jessica, mother of 3-year-old Tyrone:

Just learned to cut paper with scissors.
Counts to four.
Looks at picture books and names many pictures.
Remembered two of the animals we saw at the zoo last Sunday.
Puts together puzzles with eight pieces.
Can sort shapes into categories.

Now indicate whether the skills on your list are ones that the child can do by himself, or whether they are ones that the child displays only when assisted by another person. Jessica, like most parents and teachers completing this exercise, limited her list to Tyrone's already acquired abilities — ones he can do alone.

Vygotsky pointed out that we are used to thinking of the child's capacities in static or "fossilized" terms — as finished achievements. In doing so, we look toward the past. What we should do, he advised, is to move beyond what children can do by themselves to what they can do with expert assistance and, therefore, have the potential to learn. In this way, we focus on the future — on the cognitive processes of today or tomorrow rather than those of yesterday, which are already mastered.[13]

Vygotsky defined the zone of proximal development as the distance between the child's actual development (the tasks the child can do individually) and the child's potential development, "determined through problem solving under adult guidance or in collaboration with more capable peers."[14] The "zone," as I'll call it from now on, is the dynamic region in which new capacities form as children tackle culturally meaningful tasks with a mentor's assistance. Had Jessica been thinking about Tyrone's "zone," she might have framed the items on her list this way:

> Just learned to cut paper with scissors. If I hold the paper while he cuts and prompt him, he can cut along straight or curved lines. He cut out a square and a circle with help today. I asked him which animals we saw at the zoo, and he mentioned giraffe and zebra. When I reminded him of the bird and pachyderm houses, he remembered a lot more: the flamingos, parrots, swans, elephants, hippos, and rhinos.

For Vygotsky, a crucial aspect of parenting and the central aim of education is to provide children with experiences in their "zone" — activities that challenge them but that can be accomplished with sensitive adult guidance. Consequently, parents and teachers carry much responsibility for ensuring that children's learning is maximized — for actively leading them along the developmental pathway. Rather than transmitting ready-made knowledge to a passive child or giving a child tasks for which he or she already has the requisite skills, the adult's role is to engage in dialogue with the child — by observing, conversing, questioning, assisting, and encouraging. During that dialogue, the adult continually assesses the child's progress and creates the "zone" by keeping the task "proximal" — slightly above the child's level of independent functioning. In this way, the adult "rouses to life" those cognitive processes that are just emerging in the child,[15] sustaining them socially so they can be refined and internalized as part of the child's psychological world.

CREATING THE "ZONE"

What features of adult–child shared activity forge the "zone"? Research documents several communicative ingredients that consistently foster development, in children of diverse ages and across a wide range of tasks.

Shared Understanding

For information, ideas, and skills to move from the social-interactive plane to the internal-thinking plane, the adult and child must strive for a common approach to the situation. They must desire genuine communication and work toward attaining it.

In sociocultural theory, this joint, mutual focus is called *intersubjectivity,* or shared understanding.[16] As the word suggests, each participant in the dialogue strives to grasp the subjective perspective of the other, an effort that results in a "meeting of minds," in which the partners' thoughts make contact, connect, and coincide. Intersubjectivity reaches its pinnacle in a love affair, where shared understanding is readily achieved through a glance, a touch, or a comment. Lovers in close psychological contact grasp one another's meanings quickly because each is on the lookout for and tries to satisfy the other's needs.[17] The opposite of intersubjectivity is total misunderstanding. In a failed love affair, widely divergent views of the same experiences cause people to say, "You don't understand me. You've become a stranger. We can't find common ground. We've grown apart."

The image of lovers communicating helps us appreciate the circumstances in which intersubjectivity is most likely to occur: in close relationships. Children most often attain it with parents, other family members, teachers, and eventually in friendships with peers. Of course, partners in teaching and learning do not need to attain the intersubjective heights of lovers to accomplish their goals. But a certain degree of intersubjectivity is necessary for any dialogue to be successful, and the love affair analogy reminds us that joint understanding, whether established in face-to-face interaction or as individuals work on a common task, combines both verbal and nonverbal cues. Sensitive emotional messages conveyed through gestures, facial expressions, and tone of voice are basic to it.[18]

Intersubjectivity is itself a developmental process. Since infants and young children are still acquiring communication skills, the younger the child, the greater the adult's responsibility for making mental contact and sustaining the interaction. Nevertheless, children of all ages actively join in, striving for a shared view of the world. Their participation results in gains in thought, language, and social skills. Gradually, the child takes increasing responsibility for attaining intersubjectivity, until both parties make similar contributions to the shared mental state that fuels children's learning in the "zone."[19] Let's see how, with adult support, the child's intersubjective competence increases.

INFANCY AND TODDLERHOOD.   Some researchers believe that the infant's capacity to share meaning with others is innate. Others think it is learned — that parents respond to infants' facial expressions, vocalizations, cries, and body movements as if they have meaning, and out of those responses infants pick up the meanings and expressive rhythms of human signals.[20] But all experts agree that subtle, sensitive, and mutually rewarding exchanges between parent and baby serve as the earliest context for intersubjectivity.

From the start, infants are equipped with capacities that draw adults into social exchanges with them. Newborn babies, for example, can make eye contact, and they prefer to look at people and to listen to human voices — especially their mother's familiar voice, to which they became accustomed during the months before birth.[21] Newborns also have a rudimentary ability to imitate facial expressions, opening their mouths or pursing their lips after an adult does so.[22] Their responsiveness encourages parents to look at, talk to, and imitate in return. Between 4 and 6 weeks of age, babies begin to smile at people, an irresistible signal that evokes smiles, cuddles, pats, and friendly, gentle verbalizations from their social world.[23] As cooing and babbling appear in the first half-year, adults again respond in kind, vocalizing and waiting for the baby to vocalize back.

By age 3 months, a complex communication system is in place in which parent and baby each respond in an appropriate and carefully timed fashion to the other's cues. As a result, babies experience and practice the give-and-take of human conversation. Disrupt this exchange of signals, and young babies' striving for connection with others becomes crystal clear. In several studies, researchers had the parent assume either a still-faced, unreactive pose or a depressed emotional state. Infants tried all manner of signals — facial expressions, vocalizations, and body movements — to get their mother or father to respond again. When these efforts failed, they reacted to the parent's sad, vacant gaze by turning away, frowning, and crying.[24] American, Canadian, and Chinese 3- to 6-month-olds respond to a parent's still face identically, suggesting a common, built-in protest response to caregivers' lack of engagement.[25]

When parents are attentive, patient, and interested in the baby's activities, their social signals sustain the infant's attention, essential for a shared focus. Around 4 months, infants begin to gaze in the same direction adults are looking, although their initial efforts are imperfect. Parents follow the baby's line of vision as well, often commenting on what the infant sees. This joint attention to objects and events fosters early language development. Mothers who maintain high levels of it during play have infants who comprehend more language, produce meaningful gestures and words earlier, and show faster vocabulary development between 1 and 2 years of age.[26]

Between 9 and 15 months, the capacity for intersubjectivity takes a giant leap forward. Toddlers use gestures to share their experiences with others. They touch an object, hold it up, or point to it while looking at another person to make sure he or she notices. Or they try to get another person to do something—to hand them an object or help them perform a task—by reaching, pointing, and making sounds at the same time.[27]

Look closely at these behaviors, and notice how toddlers *intentionally* try to establish common ground with another person by combining their interest in objects and events with communication.[28] When adults respond to their reaching and pointing gestures and also label them ("That's a kitty, isn't it?" "Oh, you want a cracker!"), toddlers learn that using language can quickly lead to a joint focus and desired results—the pleasurable object or experience the child wanted.[29] Soon the child utters words along with gestures, the gestures recede, and language is under way.

EARLY CHILDHOOD.   Spoken language brings vastly expanded potential for attaining intersubjectivity because it allows much greater clarification of purpose between participants in a dialogue. When a toddler points and reaches but cannot say what he means, the adult may need to search for the child's meaning, as this exchange between a mother and her 14-month-old son, Jordan, illustrates:

> Jordan: *(Points to one of the objects on the counter)*
> Mother: "Do you want this?" *(Holds up milk container)*
> Jordan: *(Shakes his head "no"; continues to point; two more tries)*
> Mother: "This?" *(Picks up sponge)*
> Jordan: *(Leans back in highchair, puts arms down, tension leaves body)*
> Mother: *(Hands Jordan sponge)*[30]

As language competence increases, shared meaning is established quickly, as when the child says, "Get the sponge, Mom. I need to wipe this up!" Then a joint focus becomes the springboard for achieving greater understanding, with children playing a strong, contributing role. This is evident in the impressive conversational skills of even young preschoolers. By 2 to 3 years, children take turns, make eye contact, and respond in a timely and relevant fashion to their partner's remarks.[31]

These capacities improve with conversational experience. Children become better at taking the perspective of their partner, especially a partner who adjusts his or her communication to the child's level and observes the child closely to assess his or her comprehension. By stretching up to grasp the adult's viewpoint, children acquire new knowledge, the basis for further growth. And with age, children exert greater effort to understand another person, a capacity first cultivated in adult–child interaction and then extended to peers. For example, in the following conversation, notice how 4-year-old Sammy assists his friend, Leah, in attaining intersubjectivity:

(Leah tells the teacher that she caught a fish while on vacation, when Sammy enters the conversation.)
Teacher: Did you have to scale the fish as well?
Leah: No, we eated them. *(The child misunderstands the meaning of the word "scale.")*
Sammy: You need to peel them . . . peel them. *(Sammy tries to clarify.)*
Teacher: *(Confirming Sammy's meaning)* You need to take the scales off, don't you?
Sammy: You can't do it with your hands; you need a peeler.
Teacher: Or a knife . . . a really sharp fishing knife.
Leah: They peeled the fishes with a fork. *(Leah now shares meaning with the teacher and Sammy.)*[32]

Between 3 and 5 years of age, preschoolers increasingly strive for intersubjectivity in dialogues with peers. They more often affirm playmates' messages, add new information to playmates' ideas, and make contributions to ongoing play to sustain it further.[33] They can also be heard making such statements as, "I think [this way]. What do you think?"—clear evidence of a willingness to share viewpoints, which assists preschoolers greatly when conflicts arise that must be resolved for play to continue.[34]

As the excerpts we have considered illustrate, participants in a dialogue may not attain intersubjectivity on a first try, and interaction between most people, whether adults or children, is not perfectly "in sync."[35] But by the preschool years, children can take a more active role in helping a partner reach a state of shared thinking and in correcting "misses" when they do occur.[36]

The communicative competence inherent in intersubjectivity blossoms within a zone of proximal development in which parents and other significant adults are "stimulating, attentive, confirmatory, interpretive, and highly supportive."[37] Parent–child intersubjectivity makes a vital contribution to the development of attachment, attention, language, and understanding of others' perspectives. These capacities, in turn, ease the task of establishing an intersubjective connection, and that connection provides the platform for the creation of additional "zones," enabling children to master complex, culturally adaptive skills.

Building a Support System for Acquiring New Knowledge and Skills

Intersubjectivity makes possible a second essential ingredient for creating the "zone": a support system that offers new ways of thinking about a situation. The quality of adult support varies with the type of joint activity. As we will see, a helpful parent or teacher interacts differently when assisting the child with tasks having clear learning goals, such as working a puzzle or mastering a homework assignment; when engaging the child in an open-ended conversation; and when enlisting the child in duties and routines of everyday living. But regardless of the activity, the adult adapts his or her support so the child can make use of it. As the child gains competence, adult support changes accordingly, granting the child a larger role.

CREATING A SCAFFOLD. The metaphor of a *scaffold* has been used to describe effective adult support as children work on tasks that teach culturally valued concepts and skills.[38] The learning goal might be built into the task materials, as when a child turns a crank to make a jack-in-the-box pop out, puts together a puzzle, or builds a structure out of blocks. Alternatively, the parent or teacher might specify the goal, as in matching shapes and colors, solving an arithmetic problem, or batting a ball.

In scaffolding, the child is viewed as a building—actively under construction. The adult provides a dynamic, flexible scaffold—or framework—that assists the child in mastering new competencies. To promote development, the adult varies his or her assistance to fit the child's changing level of performance, with the goal of keeping the child in the "zone." This is usually done in two ways: (1) by adjusting the task so the demands on the child at any given moment are appropriately challenging, and (2) tailoring the degree of adult intervention to the child's current learning needs.[39]

When a task is very new, the child may not yet be aware of its goal and need to be shown what to do, through demonstration. Consider, for example, a 9-month-old infant who has never before seen a jack-in-the-box. At first, the adult tries to capture the child's attention by working the toy and, as the clown emerges, exclaiming, "Pop! What happened?" Gradually, the adult redirects interaction toward how to use the jack-in-the-box. When the infant reaches for the toy, the adult guides the child's hand in turning the crank and pushing the clown down in the box. As motor, cognitive, and language skills improve in the second year, the toddler intentionally tries to turn the crank, looking at the adult or otherwise beckoning for assistance. The child's greater knowledge and communicative competence permit the adult to reduce her physical directiveness. Now the adult can help from a distance by using verbal instructions ("Turn, just a little more!") and gestures, such as a rotating hand resembling a turning motion, while the toddler tries to make the toy work.[40]

As children move into the preschool years, scaffolding becomes increasingly verbal and takes on the advantages of language—more ready attainment of intersubjectivity; flexible, efficient representation of meanings; and a powerful tool through which minds meet and the child adopts meanings into mental life. To illustrate, let's listen in as a father assists his 5-year-old daughter, Sydney, in putting together a difficult puzzle:

Sydney: I can't get this one in. *(Tries to insert a piece in the wrong place)*
Father: Which piece might go down here? *(Points to the bottom of the puzzle)*
Sydney: His shoes. *(Looks for a piece resembling the clown's shoes but tries the wrong one)*
Father: Well, find a piece that looks like this shape and matches this color. *(Points again to the bottom of the puzzle)*
Sydney: The brown one. *(Tries it and it fits; then attempts another piece and looks at her father)*
Father: There you have it! Now try turning that piece just a little. *(Gestures to show her)*
Sydney: There! *(Puts in several more pieces while commenting to herself, "Now a green piece to match," "Turn it [meaning the puzzle piece]," as the adult watches)*
Father: Now, Sydney, watch. Suppose I put this piece here. Will that work? *(Places a blue piece next to a second blue piece, but the space is too small and the wrong shape)*

Sydney: You can't do it that way. The piece is too big.

Father: What should I do?

Sydney: *(Places the piece in the correct space, using both color and shape as a guide.)*

Sydney and her father's interaction contains all the components and goals of effective scaffolding:

1. *Joint Problem Solving, Aimed at Keeping the Child in the "Zone."* Sydney and her father collaborate in overcoming obstacles that Sydney encounters. In doing so, father and daughter jointly work toward successful puzzle solution.

Sydney's father keeps the task within Sydney's "zone" by temporarily reducing the difficulty of the puzzle. He does so by breaking the task into smaller units, focusing Sydney's attention on the lower section—the part with the largest and most easily matched pieces. Then he assists with a general prompt, "Which piece might go down here?"

When Sydney's father observes that this suggestion is not sufficient for her to succeed, he offers additional support, "Find a piece that *looks like this shape* and *matches this color*" and *"Turn it."* His statements contain strategies (attending to color and shape, patiently adjusting pieces so they fit) that Sydney can use in future attempts. When Sydney experiments with the color-matching strategy and succeeds in placing the brown piece, she internalizes the technique. She applies it in subsequent efforts, regulating her behavior with self-directed language resembling her father's communication during joint problem solving. Consequently, Sydney begins to move toward independent solving of the puzzle.

Notice how, in scaffolding Sydney's puzzle solving, her father adapts the instruction he offers to Sydney's momentary competence. When Sydney has difficulty, he fortifies the scaffold, providing increased direction. Once Sydney starts to take over strategies generated during joint problem solving, her father pulls back, reducing the assistance provided.

Scaffolding provides parents and teachers with a sensible solution to the often-raised dilemma: Is it better to be directive or nondirective when helping children learn? As the scaffolding concept shows, this question has no pat answer. Rather, the intensity of adult support depends on where the task falls within the child's "zone." When a task lies at the outer edge of the child's current capabilities, more direct guidance is necessary to bring it within range of mastery. As the child's understanding and performance improve, less intervention is required.

How much assistance a child needs depends not just on cognitive maturity but also on other child characteristics. A temperamentally distractible child, an emotionally reactive child, or a fearful, inhibited child requires an especially sturdy scaffold—extra support and, at times, considerable adult perseverance to sustain a joint focus and keep the child engaged. Children who are good listeners, persistent in the face of difficulty, socially skilled, and therefore adept at attaining intersubjectivity need less adult vigilance and direction. At the same time, effective scaffolding can improve a difficult child's behavior, since it offers the child knowledge and procedures for solving problems, the security of adult support as long as it is needed, and the satisfaction of overcoming obstacles and mastering culturally valued skills.

2. *Self-regulation.* An important goal of scaffolding is to promote self-regulation—the capacity to use thought to guide behavior. The self-regulated child follows social rules; makes deliberate, well-reasoned choices and decisions; and takes responsibility for his or her own learning and behavior. Although self-regulation improves gradually throughout childhood and adolescence, early childhood is a crucial period for its development—a time when children learn to overcome impulses by thinking before they act.[41] Indeed, self-regulation is so important for children's cognitive and social development that we will return to it repeatedly in later chapters when we consider how other experiences—children's self-directed language, make-believe play, and learning in school—contribute to it.

How does scaffolding nurture a self-regulated child? It does so in two interrelated ways: (1) by providing children with strategies for working toward goals, and (2) by relinquishing adult control and assistance as soon as the child can work independently.[42]

In scaffolding, the adult encourages the child to grapple with questions and problems and, thereby, to contribute significantly to the dialogue. In this way, the adult evokes from the child his or her current knowledge and, on that basis, can scaffold more effectively. The parent or teacher intervenes only when the child is truly stuck, granting the child as much opportunity to master his or her own behavior as possible. Unless it is clear that the task is so new and obscure to the child that a demonstration would be helpful, the adult refrains from giving immediate answers to momentary difficulties. As our consideration of Anselmo and his parents revealed, doing the task for the child severely reduces learning and self-regulation.[43]

When adults ask children questions and make suggestions that permit them to participate in the discovery of solutions, then transfer of useful strategies to the child is maximized. By introducing language as a mediator of the child's activity, the adult's questions and prompts prevent the child from responding impulsively. They encourage the child to step back from the immediate situation and consider alternatives—in essence, to think.

Look at Sydney and her father's dialogue once again. When he asks, "Which piece might go down here?" he evokes Sydney's present strategic thinking, finding that it is still tied to immediate objects in the situation. Sydney looks for the clown's shoes but fails to find them. Then her father introduces a special form of strategic thinking called *distancing*. This method helps children move beyond concrete objects by looking for higher-order relationships—in Sydney's case, categorizing puzzle pieces by color and shape. Once Sydney succeeds in using color, her father encourages further distancing from the most obvious features of the clown image.[44] He places a piece incorrectly (by matching only on color) and queries, "Will that work?" In doing so, he helps Sydney analyze an error, consider how to correct it (by matching on both color and shape), and try out her conjecture. Sydney gains practice in applying strategies flexibly—in generating ideas to overcome obstacles. As a result, she acquires reasoning skills and can take initiative when faced with future problems.

3. *Warmth, Responsiveness, and Encouragement.* To work well, the emotional tone of scaffolding must be warm, sympathetic, and responsive. Children who experience warm adult relationships want to preserve that spirit of affection and cooperation—by joining in dialogues with adult partners and acquiring culturally valued skills.[45]

The standards for maturity parents set for young children vary widely, in ways that reflect family and cultural values. For example, Chinese-American immigrant parents report spending nearly ten times as much time as do Caucasian-American parents scaffolding their school-age children's mastery of reading, math, music, and drawing skills[46]—teaching that is undoubtedly a strong contributor to Chinese children's high achievement in both academic and artistic endeavors. Influenced by the Confucian belief in strict discipline to nurture socially desirable behavior, many Chinese and other Asian parents expect a great deal of their children and structure their time extensively.[47] But research indicates that their demands are imbued with warmth and caring—with deep concern for and involvement in their children's lives.

In a study of parenting in 180 societies, anthropologists Ronald and Evelyn Rohner found that warmth combined with at least moderate expectations for mature behavior and accomplishment is the most common child-rearing style around the world.[48] Why do so many cultures mingle concern and affection with guidance and control—a blend known as *authoritative parenting* in the child-rearing literature? Certainly because they sense its effectiveness, borne out by decades of research.

Authoritative parenting, whether assessed through direct observation or older children's ratings of their parents' communication, is linked to many aspects of competence. In early childhood, it predicts positive mood, self-confidence and independence in mastery of new tasks, cooperativeness, and resistance to engaging in disruptive behavior.[49] And in middle childhood, adolescence, and young adulthood, it is related to high self-esteem, social and moral maturity, academic achievement, and educational attainment.[50]

A major contributor to these favorable outcomes is the fuel that warmth grants to adult expectations. Warm, caring adults offer explanations and justifications for their demands. In doing so, they invite children to judge the appropriateness of their requirements. When children view demands as fair and reasonable, they are far more likely to heed and internalize them. A warm, involved adult is also more likely to be an effective reinforcing agent, praising children for striving to meet high standards. And when children stray from goals that a parent or teacher regards as important and it is necessary to be firm and disapproving, a warm adult has a much greater chance of changing the child's behavior than does an adult who has been indifferent or negative. Children of involved, caring parents find the interruption in parental affection that accompanies a reprimand to be especially unpleasant. They want to regain their parents' warmth and approval as quickly as possible.

In sum, scaffolding is a warm, sympathetic collaboration between a teacher and a learner on a challenging, goal-directed task that the adult helps bring within the child's "zone." Observations of adult–child pairs reveal that the diverse ingredients of scaffolding—matching the adult's assistance to the child's changing needs, suggesting effective strategies, posing questions that encourage children to think about higher-order relationships, and interacting warmly and praising children for competent performance—consistently relate to children's task engagement and learning.[51]

THE POWER OF CONVERSATION.   The instructional mode of communication inherent in scaffolding is well suited for tasks with clearly defined goals. Conversations, in which adult and child reflect on everyday events, are more free-ranging. They can dwell on virtually any aspect of experience—of living and working together. This makes them an especially powerful tool for assisting children in building an internal mental life infused with a cultural worldview.

When people converse with one another, they engage in a form of dialogue called *narrative*—a storylike mode of communicating, composed of a sequence of events with people as main characters. In the narrative, which may be real or imaginary, characters' roles and mental states—feelings, intentions, beliefs, opinions, and knowledge—are revealed.[52]

To illustrate, suppose someone asked you to "tell the story of your life." In forming a spontaneous autobiography, people link together smaller stories about incidents and occasions, with the self at their center and other influential people in supporting roles. The narrator arranges the stories sequentially, to conform to a culturally accepted organization of time. And he or she not only recounts, but *justifies* the stories—that is, makes them comprehensible by explaining why they happened as they did.[53]

The mini-stories in our life narratives focus on exceptional experiences—events that stand out against the backdrop of ordinariness in our daily lives.[54] For example, a move to a new neighborhood, a first date, a high school graduation, an important job interview, a wedding day, the birth of a baby, and special achievements or failings are likely to be included. The various entries are derived from our social interactions, at the time the events occurred and thereafter. When others join with us in celebration, approve or disapprove of our actions, or convey information or opinion that changes our outlook, they bestow special meaning on the events. And so we include those events in our autobiographies, elevating them to lifelong significance.

In everyday conversation, the events discussed resemble the mini-stories of our spontaneous autobiographies. For example, in recent narrative exchanges, I talked with a friend about her daughter's sudden breakup with a fiancé; with my husband about a controversial play we had seen; and with one of my students about how she might handle a troublesome roommate. Each narrative focused on a relatively exceptional personal experience. And in each, my partners and I addressed the legitimacy of characters' intentions, weighing personal desire against socially acceptable behavior.

For example, referring to her daughter's breakup, my friend complained, "It wasn't *that* she did it but *how* she did it. She shouldn't have promised she'd join him in Chicago and then reneged. His mother called a few days later and said how betrayed the young man feels. You can't back out like that, with no warning, no explanation, after he had already rented the apartment."

"The whole family knew the relationship had problems," I countered. "She's paying him for the apartment. Doesn't that lighten her obligation?"

During the conversation, my friend and I exchanged a wealth of cultural meanings about how relationships should be and about the maturity and morality of the daughter's behavior. The telling of the narrative also invited re-construction of what might have occurred between the daughter and her fiancé, thereby placing the event in a wider context of possibilities. In the process, the dialogue highlighted characters' internal states—the daughter's motivations, her boyfriend's feelings, and my friend's struggle to make sense of the breakup.

Readiness for Narrative. Our narrative dialogues with young children have the same features as do our narratives with adults, only in simplified form. In these conversations, we arrange events in logical, sequential order, and we focus on explaining unusual, hard-to-interpret occurrences, often by dwelling on characters' intentions and perspectives.

Even before they begin to talk, children display a readiness to participate in narrative.[55] After an adult describes and demonstrates some activity (for example, putting a teddy bear to bed), 1-year-olds who as yet have little language can easily reproduce the main steps in correct sequence with toys.[56] When toddlers begin to speak, their main interest is in talking about what people do and the conse-quences of their behavior. Listen to the two-word utterances that appear between 15 and 24 months of age, and you will find many expressions like these: "Tommy hit"; "Get cookie"; "Mommy truck" (meaning "Mommy push the truck"); "Daddy outside"; and "My dolly."[57] At the end of the second year, children begin to label their own and others' internal states with words, such as "want," "happy," "mad," "think," and "pretend."[58] These assertions about human action, desire, emotion, and perspective are the stuff of which narratives are made.

Early on, children are sensitive to yet another feature of narrative. At birth, they are captivated by unusual events, perking up their eyes and ears when something new and different happens. In keeping with this innate bias, the first narratives children produce focus on making sense of the atypical. "Look, the sun is sleepy, going to bed," said 2 1/2-year-old David while watching the sun disappear below the horizon at the end of a day at the beach. At the sight of a woman with her leg in a cast, 3-year-old Rachel re-marked, "Mommy, that lady got a big cut. The doctor sewed up her leg." (Rachel's brother had cut his leg a few days earlier and returned from the doctor with stitches and a bandage.)

An early armament of narrative tools enables children to quickly and easily comprehend and contribute to the narratives of expert members of their culture.[59] In families in which parents and children spend much time together, the flow of stories recreating personal experiences is abundant.[60] Through them, adults help children construct increasingly elaborate images of themselves and teach them culturally accepted ways of organizing and interpreting their experiences. As a byproduct of participation, children gain a rich understanding of their own and others' mental lives—powerful tools in predicting and explaining human behavior and, therefore, in getting along with others. And in enabling children to practice and perfect narrative skills, adult–child conversation provides crucial preparation for literacy. Let's take a closer look at these diverse benefits of narrative conversation.

Forming an Autobiographical Self. Consider, once again, the narrative task posed earlier, to relate "the story of your life." Think back to the earliest event you can remember. At what age did it occur?

For the large majority of people, memory for autobiographical events begins around age 3.[61] Practically none of us can retrieve happenings at younger ages—a phenomenon called *infantile amnesia.* What causes this early memory blackout, and how is it that after age 3, certain events differentiate themselves from a multitude of everyday experiences so they stand out for a lifetime?

Some researchers conjecture that growth of the cerebral cortex and other brain structures is necessary before children can store experiences in ways that permit them to be retrieved many years later.[62] Similarly, several psychological explanations focus on changes in the nature of memory during the preschool years—from an unconscious, automatic, and nonverbal system to one that is conscious, deliberate, and verbal.[63] Perhaps the second system cannot access events stored by the first, making the earliest events of our lives forever irretrievable.

Yet the idea of vastly different approaches to remembering at young and older ages has been questioned. Children 1 1/2 to 3 years old can describe their memories verbally.[64] And sometimes they even recall events that happened to them as preverbal infants! For example, while walking past a distinctive house with a fenced-in front yard, 22-month-old Lisa said to her mother, "Scary doggy!" Nine months earlier (before the child could talk), the family had taken the same walk. On that occasion, Lisa had seen a ferocious dog barking behind the chain-linked fence. Over time, neither the family walk nor the scary dog will be part of Lisa's personally relevant memory. Yet the train trip across the country she will take at age 3 1/2 and her first day of kindergarten at age 5 may still be memorable when she is 80.

A growing number of researchers believe that rather than a radical change in the way experience is coded into memory, two other milestones lead infantile amnesia to give way to memory for personally significant experiences:

1. *A Psychological Self.* To build an autobiographical memory, children must have a well-formed sense of self—as a person who, despite changes in appearance (a new haircut, becoming taller and more mature

looking), remains the same on the inside over time. Once constructed, this persisting *psychological self* serves as an anchor for unique experiences, which are retained easily as long as they become personally meaningful.[65] A psychological self is not firmly in place until age 3 or 4.

2. *An Autobiographical Narrative.* Besides a firm sense of an inner self, autobiographical memory depends on organizing personal experiences in narrative form so they become part of a life story. How do children learn to structure memories as narratives during the preschool years? Much evidence indicates that they acquire this skill through conversations with adults.

As early as 1 1/2 to 2 years, children begin to talk about the past, guided by adults who prompt them and expand on their fragmented recollections. At first, parents provide most of the content and structure of the story. But very soon, children's contribution increases, as can be seen in this short excerpt of a mother talking with her nearly 3-year-old daughter about a recent Halloween celebration:

Child: Once on Halloween the kids was over and I had a princess dress on me.
Mother: You had a princess dress on? Did you get any candy? Did you go door to door? What happened?
Child: We went treating.
Mother: You went treating! And who took you?
Child: Andrea's mother took us. And my mom . . . and we brought a pumpkin too.
Mother: What did you do with the pumpkin?
Child: We lighted it.
Mother: What did it look like? Was it scary?
Child: Uh-huh. Dad made cuts in it with a razor. He made a face too. That was funny.[66]

Notice how the mother provides details and, by asking "who" and "what," encourages her young daughter to enrich the narrative. As children participate in these dialogues, they adopt the narrative thinking generated in them and retain many details about past events, made personally meaningful in the context of parent–child conversation.

Observations of parent–child interaction reveal that parents vary in how they engage children in narrative talk. Some, like the mother in the conversation just given, use an *elaborative style,* in which they pose many, varied questions; add information by building on children's statements; and volunteer their own evaluations of events, as in "Was it scary?" Other parents use a *repetitive style.* Appearing rushed, impatient, and inattentive to the child's comments, they contribute little information and ask the same short-answer questions over and over: "Do you remember Halloween?" "What costume did you wear?" "Do you remember what you wore?" The elaborative style is considerably better at fostering preschoolers' narrative skill, since 2- and 3-year-olds who experience it produce more coherent and detailed personal stories when followed up 1 to 2 years later.[67]

Children's conversations with elaborative-style parents increase in complexity as language development proceeds, creating a zone of proximal development in which narrative competence expands. Between 3 and 6 years, children's descriptions of special, one-time events—a family excursion, a grandparent's visit, a first trip to the dentist—become better organized and more elaborate. Spurred by adult prompting, older children also add more background information—"when" and "where" the event took place and "who" was present. By including these details, children place personally significant experiences in the larger context of their lives.

Finally, between 4 and 6 years of age, evaluative statements, which help to clarify "why" an event is personally meaningful, become common. Older children more often embellish their descriptions with modifiers, such as "My mask was *ugly*" or "The kite flew *high.*" At times, they even add drama by intensifying these expressions, as in "The kite flew *very, very* high" and "Grandma ate a *huge* bowl of oatmeal for breakfast!" And like the autobiographical and everyday narratives that adults generate, children's narratives increasingly focus on people's internal states—their desires, feelings, and beliefs: "She *wanted it so much*" or "I *felt bad.*"[68] Furthermore, the richness of 6-year-olds' evaluative remarks can be predicted from their mother's evaluative statements in an adult–child conversation 3 years earlier[69]—a finding that underscores, once again, parents' vital role in creating a "zone" for narrative development.

In sum, as children share memories, mark them as personally meaningful, and begin to create their life story, the people to whom they are close become vigorous contributors to their self-constructions. From the beginning, the child's sense of self is not isolated, encapsulated inside the head. Rather, it is shaped by and situated in children's everyday social experiences—in the dialogues with parents, teachers, and other cultural experts within families, preschools, schools, and communities.

Acquiring Cultural Beliefs and Values. Through dialogues with adults, the child derives not just a self, but a *self imbued with culture.* The stories, both real and fictional, that parents and teachers relate to or jointly construct with young children are laced with cultural beliefs and values. They have profound socializing implications.[70]

At times, adults tell children stories that carry important self-relevant lessons. For example, recently I listened in as a father and his 5-year-old son waited in the foyer of a synagogue for a Jewish New Year service to begin. The father wove an animated tale about a boy named Chaim, who had great difficulty remaining quiet during the holiday service. Little Chaim had a brand new whistle in his back pocket, and he badly wanted to play it. With great effort, he resisted, turning and twisting in his seat until, finally, when the Rabbi blew the shofar (ceremonial ram's horn), Chaim could bear it no longer! A moment later, the clear, high-pitched sound of the whistle could be heard over the Rabbi's final shofar blast. Everyone in the sanctuary turned toward Chaim, who cringed with embarrassment. But much to Chaim's surprise, all the congregants cheered and thanked him for making the shofar ritual more beautiful than ever. And Chaim's father praised him for sitting quietly, *almost* to the end of the service.

Five-year-old Mark listened to his father's story with rapt attention, asking questions and adding personal comments: "Where did Chaim sit?" "Did he (like Mark) bring a book to read?" "Was Chaim allowed to get up and go to the bathroom?" "Was the Rabbi angry at Chaim?" The story disclosed that adults realize a long service is hard for a small boy to sit through, but exercising self-restraint and participating in communal rituals bring praise and acceptance from the community. The analogies Mark drew between his own life and Chaim's suggest that he had (as his father intended) experienced the story from a personal vantage point, identifying with its events and applying them to himself.[71]

Systematic research reveals both cultural similarities and differences in adult–child narratives. In an intensive observational study of daily storytelling in two communities—six middle-class Chinese families in Taipei, Taiwan, and six middle-class American families in an Irish-Catholic neighborhood in Chicago—Peggy Miller and her colleagues[72] found that preschoolers and their family members routinely narrated past experiences. Most often, they created joint accounts of pleasurable holidays and family excursions—birthday parties, the fair, the zoo, and McDonald's for the American children; the night market, the zoo, and riding on trains and horses for the Chinese children. Both groups also talked about times the children were ill, sad, or frightened.

In a smaller set of narratives, the topic addressed—either directly to the child or to someone else while the child listened—was the child's misbehavior. These stories, more than any others, seemed deliberately aimed at teaching social and moral standards. Chinese parents, however, were far more likely to initiate these tales of misdeeds than were Americans. In fact, 35 percent of Chinese adults' narratives with or in the presence of 2 1/2-year-old children focused on past transgressions, whereas only 7 percent of American narratives did.[73]

Furthermore, interpretations of children's misbehavior differed between the two cultures. Consistent with the Confucian parental obligation, "The deeper the love, the greater the correction," Chinese mothers' "misdeed" stories were much longer than those of the American mothers—in fact, the most lengthy and elaborate of all Chinese narrations. Sometimes they occurred right after the child committed a transgression; at other times, they reminded the child of earlier improper behavior. Chinese mothers typically corrected the child repeatedly: "What did you say?" "So, what *would* you say?" "Then how would Mom have reacted?" And in line with the Confucian reliance on formal stories with moral lessons, these informal narratives often ended with direct teaching of how to act: "Saying dirty words is not good," and (after the child agreed) an expression of affection—a hug, a tender touch.

In instances in which American stories referred to young children's misbehavior, mothers frequently deemphasized these acts, attributing them to the child's spunk and assertiveness. This does not mean that American parents seldom instruct their children in social and moral rules. They often do so, largely through guiding remarks that accompany children's ongoing actions, as in "Don't grab. Share the toy." "Hold hands when crossing the street." "You hurt Johnny. Say you're sorry."

As Miller notes, the way social and moral lessons are integrated into narratives affects children's frameworks for judging themselves and interpreting their social experiences. Through everyday stories, the Chinese adults personalized moral lessons and stressed obligations to parents and other authority figures. They also reminded children of the impact of their transgressions on others—an element dramatically illustrated in one mother's recounting of her 2 1/2-year-old's disruption of his older sister's music lesson: "Ai, you made Mama lose face. . . . I wanted to dig my head into the ground. Right? [Child smiles, shakes head]"[74] American narratives rarely dwelt on misdeeds and, at times, even recast children's offenses as strengths—as indicative of quick thinking and an active, spirited disposition.

Miller describes the generally high self-control the Chinese children in these families displayed—listening attentively to elders and complying without reminders. For example, even at age 2, they waited patiently to open a small gift until a guest had departed—proper etiquette in Chinese culture. Of course, this does not mean that Americans ought to change their child-oriented narratives to be just like those of the Chinese. The socializing impact of a particular narrative style is strengthened by its consistency with a family's and community's way of life. Also, the narrative variations we have considered tap only a small slice of cultural diversity in adult–child storytelling. The most important lesson we can take from Miller's provocative findings is that when parents and teachers take time to construct narratives with and about the young child, they create a "zone" that spurs children to weave moral and social rules into their self-definitions and to behave accordingly.

Understanding People as Mental Beings. We have seen that talking about mental states is a major focus of narrative conversation. In narrative, we express the "folk psychology" of our culture—our deeply ingrained assumptions about human desires, emotions, and beliefs, and our judgments of certain ones as more acceptable than others. Indeed, violations of our folk psychology are a major impetus for engaging in narrative.[75] Through conversing with others, we try to make puzzling events and behaviors understandable.

Because people's desires, feelings, and beliefs often differ, conversations are full of social negotiations—attempts to reconcile different versions of reality. Recall how I suggested to my distraught friend that her daughter's breakup with her fiancé might have been defensible, given problems in the relationship and the daughter's willingness to compensate the young man for his monetary losses. Similarly, a 2-year-old who says that the sun disappearing below the horizon is "sleepy" is likely to receive an alternative explanation. And as parents recount the misdeeds of their children, the children gain access to others' evaluations of their egocentric, inconsiderate acts.

According to psychologist Jerome Bruner, learning to negotiate differing viewpoints through narrative is a crowning achievement of human development.[76] Conversations about personal experiences are prime sources of social stability. When out-of-the-ordinary events occur and we experience clashing views, we often look for a good listener—a friend or a loved one we can talk to. By collaborating with this partner in conversation, we talk out our perspective, seek our partner's view, search for meaning in seemingly chaotic events, and try to reconstruct a comprehensible world. In these conversations, we may not agree with our partner's point of view, but we usually acknowledge that we comprehend and appreciate it—and our partner generally does the same.

By joining in conversation and listening to the narrative dialogues of others, children develop an understanding of their own and others' rich mental lives. Children with a good grasp of mental life can detect the likely inner causes of another person's behavior and use that information to anticipate what that person might do next. Such children are also more adept at empathizing—reading others' emotions and vicariously experiencing them—a response that increases the chances that they will react with sympathetic concern and help others in need.[77] As early as 3 to 5 years of age, emotion knowledge—awareness of the circumstances that prompt different emotional reactions and the social consequences of expressing one's feelings—is related to friendly considerate behavior, willingness to make amends after harming another, and peer acceptance.[78]

Research verifies that the more families talk about inner states, the greater children's knowledge of them. For example, mothers who frequently label and explain emotions have preschoolers who use more emotion words in conversation. Maternal prompting of emotional thoughts ("What makes him afraid?") is a good predictor of 2-year-olds' emotion language. Later in the preschool years, explanations ("He's sad because his dog ran away") are more predictive.[79] Consistent with Vygotsky's concept of the "zone," sensitive parents adjust the way they talk about emotions to fit children's increasing competence. And in line with what we have said about narrative as a vital context for negotiating differing viewpoints, discussions in which family members disagree about feelings seem particularly helpful in prompting children to step back from the experience of emotion and reflect on its causes and consequences.[80]

Attaining a Subtle Grasp of Mental Life. Around age 3 to 4, children's understanding of mental life undergoes a profound transformation. Older preschoolers realize that people's beliefs, not just their desires, affect their behavior. This advance is apparent in children's awareness that people can hold *false beliefs.* [81] To test for a child's grasp of false belief, researchers present situations like this one: Show a child two small closed boxes, one a familiar Band-Aid box and the other a plain, unmarked box. Then say, "Pick the box that you think has the Band-Aids in it." Almost always, children pick the marked container. Next, ask the child to look inside both boxes; when she does, contrary to her own belief, she will find that the marked one is empty and the unmarked one contains the Band-Aids. Finally, introduce the child to a hand puppet and explain, "Here's Pam. She has a cut, see? Where do you think she'll look for Band-Aids? Why would she look in there?" Only a handful of 3-year-olds but many 4-year-olds can explain why Pam would look in the marked box: "Because she *thinks* there's Band-Aids in it, but there aren't any."[82]

Mastery of false belief shows that children regard beliefs as *interpretations,* not just reflections, of reality. It marks the transition toward a more complex, active view of the mind, which will flourish over the next few years—the realization that people can engage in a great many inner activities, from concentrating, remembering, and understanding to guessing, comparing, and inferring.[83] Before age 4, most children assume that physical experience determines mental experience—that if Band-Aids *are* in the unmarked box, everyone will *just know* where they are. But preschoolers who grasp false belief recognize that people can, on the basis of prior knowledge and experience, interpret the same event differently—an understanding that is invaluable for social life. Children who are good at detecting others' points of view are better at thinking of effective ways to handle difficult social situations.[84] Rather than just asserting their own desires, they try friendly persuasion. Or they suggest that a conflict be solved by creating new, mutual goals.

Like emotion knowledge, preschoolers' grasp of false belief grows out of conversations that touch on the mental lives of others. Without those conversations, this level of insight is slow to develop. The Junín Quechua language of the Peruvian highlands is unique in lacking words that describe mental states, such as "think" and "believe," so Quechua adults refer to mentality indirectly. For example, they use the phrase, "What would he say?" in place of, "What would he think?" Junín Quechua children have difficulty with false-belief tasks for years after children in industrialized nations have mastered them.[85] Furthermore, clear evidence exists that preschoolers who frequently interact with more competent cultural members—parents, extended family members, neighbors, older siblings, and older peers—are advanced in false-belief reasoning.[86] These social encounters offer children many opportunities to hear people refer to their own mental states and those of others and, therefore, to observe different points of view. When 3- and 4-year-olds use their newfound capacity to talk about mental states during play with friends, their understanding of false belief improves further.[87]

Finally, as children participate in narratives and listen to those of others, they acquire culturally accepted ways for negotiating clashing viewpoints. This equips them with skills for engaging in conversation without confrontation and persistent conflict—competencies that are crucial for sustaining warm, pleasurable social relationships. Gratifying social ties, in turn, serve as vital contexts for further cognitive and social development.

Preparing for Literacy. Most parents hope that during the preschool years, their children will develop the knowledge, skills, and attitudes that prepare them to read and write in elementary school. This interest in literacy is well founded. Reading and writing are not just crucial for success in academic endeavors and later life. They are thoroughfares to vast realms of knowledge, enjoyable leisure pursuits, and contact with others at a distance—even in different historical time periods. Once children can read and write, they can explore the insights of countless authors and partake in their rich array of experiences. With those authors, they can forge highly varied and vastly expanded "zones" for learning.

Children can become competent readers and writers without being trained, pushed, or goaded into literacy learning in early childhood. As we saw earlier, preschools and kindergartens that emphasize drill on academic skills are detrimental. This way of teaching induces inattentiveness, restlessness, disengagement from challenging activities, and poorer achievement during the first few years of elementary school. Young children who are enthusiastic and self-confident about learning and who achieve at their best in the early grades have acquired literacy-relevant knowledge informally—through exposure to books and other reading materials at home, in preschool, and in child-care environments; through observing adults reading and writing in everyday life; and especially, through narrative conversation.

Literacy-related behaviors *emerge* in these contexts; consequently, early childhood educators refer to preschool competencies that lay the foundation for reading and writing as *emergent literacy*. Indeed, no clear dividing line exists between prereading and reading. As literacy experts Grover Whitehurst and Christopher Lonigan put it, "Reading, writing, and oral language develop concurrently and interdependently from an early age from children's exposure to interactions in social contexts in which literacy is a component, and in the absence of formal instruction."[88]

Research consistently demonstrates that language development in early childhood is strongly related to later reading competence—and to academic achievement in general during elementary school.[89] Furthermore, both language progress and an array of emergent-literacy skills can be predicted by the sheer amount of verbal interaction in the home during the first few years of life—a relationship that holds for children of all socioeconomic levels. Conversations with adults are especially powerful contributors to early childhood language proficiency and, in turn, to literacy development.[90]

A strong language foundation is vital for becoming literate because people read to extract meaning. Children can more easily derive meaning from the printed page when their vocabularies are large and they have come to think in ways that resemble the narrative styles on which the large majority of written texts are based. By repeatedly listening to and participating in narrative conversation, children develop mental scripts for the way narratives are typically organized. Then, when they start to read, the organization of text material readily makes sense to them, and they extract meaning more easily.

One of the clearest indicators of young children's understanding of stories, and other prereading skills, is the extent to which they can give elaborate, detailed accounts of past events.[91] Children sharpen this competency through conversing with adults, who add information, ask questions, and prompt children to increase the sophistication of their descriptions and explanations—in essence, who use an elaborative style of narrative talk. Whitehurst and his colleagues have encouraged parents and teachers of young children to integrate the elaborative narrative style into shared adult–child storybook reading, an approach called *dialogic reading*.[92]

Typically, an adult reads while a child listens—a format that is beneficial to early literacy development[93] but that cannot guarantee the child's attention, involvement, and comprehension. In dialogic reading, the adult encourages the child to become a participant in the narrative, even a storyteller. Using books with pictures that convey a story line but that have limited text so the adult is less likely to revert to straight reading, the parent or teacher has the child relate much of the story. The adult assumes the role of an active listener—querying, encouraging, and expanding on what the child has to say. As in other narrative talk, the adult increases the complexity of his or her questioning to fit the child's language progress. For 2- and 3-year-olds, questions focus mostly on describing events, actions, and objects. For 4- and 5-year-olds, questions more often address narrative organization ("What happens next?" "How does the story end?"); analyses of characters ("Why did the little girl want a teddy bear?"); and connections between the book and the child's everyday life ("Have *you* ever seen a fire engine on its way to a fire?").

When parents and teachers use dialogic reading consistently over several weeks to several months, children show gains in language development, print knowledge, and writing progress that are still present six months to a year later.[94] Although children differ widely in intrinsic interest in reading activities, shared reading can spark the interest of children who seldom seek out literacy-related pursuits on their own. Aspects of adult behavior—warmth, dramatic quality, and attempts to get the child to participate actively—heighten children's interest and involvement in reading.[95] An interested child is more likely to request shared reading times, notice features of print that are important for reading, ask questions about them, and (later on) read on his or her own.

As older preschoolers begin to attend to features of print, adults can combine shared book reading with scaffolding of children's knowledge of letter names, letter–sound correspondences, and print conventions (for example, that books are read from left to right and top to bottom of the page, that spaces are used to separate words and periods to end sentences). Adults can also assist young children as they become interested in writing by responding positively to their writing-like creations and helping them attain their writing goals in daily activities and play—printing their name or a message, making a storybook, or adding items to a shopping list. Along with general language and narrative competencies, relaxed informal teaching of basic reading and writing skills—in limited doses and without excessive feedback about right and wrong—fosters emergent literacy and aids the process of learning to read and write after children begin school.[96]

In sum, adult–child conversation—in book-reading and other contexts—is the best way to prime young children for becoming interested, accomplished readers and writers. Shared reading with parents is particularly influential—more so than reading with teachers. In one study, Lonigan and Whitehurst compared shared reading with teachers at preschool, shared reading with parents at home, and a combined condition. All three groups gained in oral language skills compared to children receiving no intervention. But children experiencing home reading improved the most.[97] Parents seem to be in the best position to read to their child often and to tailor their dialogues to the child's interests and abilities.

Other Contexts for Joint Adult–Child Engagement

When parents and children spend time together, opportunities for scaffolding of new skills and for conversation are nearly limitless. Parents who capitalize on these moments ensure that their children internalize the history, values, knowledge, skills, habits, practices, and understandings of their families and communities. We have already seen how academically related tasks, family celebrations, family outings, and adult–child storybook reading are excellent focal points for adult–child engagement. Make-believe play is yet another. Indeed, joint participation in make-believe with more expert cultural members is so important for development during early childhood that I devote an entire chapter to it. Other vital contexts for adult–child engagement include everyday routines and duties, mealtimes, and television viewing. Each of these settings has distinct and highly significant developmental benefits, as long as adults take time to enter into them and mentally connect with children.

EVERYDAY ROUTINES AND DUTIES.   By participating in everyday routines and duties at home and in preschool, children develop a sense of responsible participation in family and community life. At the same time, they acquire practical skills and a wealth of knowledge about their physical and social surroundings. The parent always in a hurry—who says, when the child desires involvement, "There isn't time," or who fails to insist that the child join in household tasks in keeping with his or her capacity—severely limits the child's learning.

In preindustrial times, children spent most of their day alongside parents as they went about housekeeping and earning a livelihood. As a result, children became deeply familiar with adults' daily activities, picking up many skills through observation and direct participation. (Recall John Ise's account of family life on a rural Kansas homestead, described in Chapter 1.) Greater parent–child togetherness throughout the day is also common in tribal and village societies, where adults spend less time supporting children's learning through verbal scaffolding because children have so many opportunities to observe and participate directly in the work of adults.[98]

Because fine-tuned scaffolding is seldom required, adult–child participation in everyday routines and duties—preparing a meal, washing dishes, raking and bagging leaves in the garden, buying groceries—offers extra time for conversation, with all its attendant benefits. In addition, many informal learning opportunities arise that will serve children well when they get to school. An astute mother I observed in the grocery store had her 3-year-old son, Ricky, reach for items on the shelf and put them in the cart. When at the checkout counter Ricky became restless and whiny, his mother handed him her credit card and directed him to watch closely for the moment the clerk would need it. As the boy turned toward the register, the mother pointed out how the price of each item appeared on a screen. Ricky alternately named the numbers he recognized and counted items as they passed through the checkout. Awed by the responsibility of handing over the credit card, a task he had seen performed only by adults, Ricky complied eagerly—and also saw numerical concepts in action! Although grocery shopping with Ricky might take 10 or 15 minutes longer than otherwise, it has wide-ranging benefits for his development.

Children, as parents and teachers well know, are not always eager to perform chores that adults set for them. But they are more willing when they see adults engaged in those duties, when adults explain why it's fair that everyone help, and when their relationship with those adults is warm and gratifying.[99] These communicative ingredients motivate children to join in with a cooperative spirit, which demonstrates that they have moved beyond the adult's position to one of their own—that is, internalized social norms with conviction.[100] In doing so, young children demonstrate once again their strong desire to become part of cultural life.

MEALTIME CONVERSATIONS.   Mealtimes—usually dinner—are special social contexts for families in complex societies. They are among the few occasions in which parents and children regularly gather after spending most of the day apart and in which the main family activity is relating to one another. Hence, mealtime talk overflows with opportunities for socialization.

Mealtimes and similar occasions for family togetherness open special conversational doors. Because all family members are present, dinner talk can convey to children a sense of family coherence and identity.[101] Most of us can still recapture the stories our parents told us, in which social and moral lessons were powerful and abundant. Here is one my mother told me, recalled in vivid detail nearly a half century later: "Once, when your grandfather was 16 years old, he came home weeping, his hands all bloody from working in the factory. His mother, your great grandmother, wiped away his tears and said, 'Don't cry, one day you'll own that factory.' And by the time he was 30, he did."

Dinnertime recaps of daily events also permit today's children, isolated from the adult world of real work, to gain access to their parents' daily lives. I learned much about my father's experiences as a retail merchant through stories he related to my mother at dinnertime: "Sofie, you'll never believe the customer who came into the store today. She complained so vehemently about a perfectly correct bill that it took two of us to escort her to the door."

Family mealtime conversations, whether children participate directly or listen to the exchanges of others, also provide special instruction in discussion skills, since they are among the few routine occasions in which children are permitted to enter an adult conversational world.[102] When meals are shared with children, parents can model and teach cultural rules regulating conversation—appropriate topics and politeness ("We don't say food is disgusting at the table") and subtle conversational strategies that children become proficient at only after much practice, such as how to enter a conversation and link with other participants' statements.

Finally, and perhaps most important, mealtimes allow parents to enter into their children's world and hear about the many facets of their lives, ranging from what the child did at school that day to reflections on how to solve peer or sibling problems.[103] Consequently, they serve to reinforce not just socialization but parental caring and support. The numerous benefits of this rich communal context are lost when family mealtime rituals diminish or disintegrate into frequent eating on the run or split adult–child meals.

The importance of family mealtimes is underscored by the fact that the most widely used research instrument for assessing the quality of young children's home environments asks parents whether the child eats at least one meal a day with a parent.[104] Scores on that instrument consistently predict early childhood mental development, no matter what the child's socioeconomic or ethnic background.[105]

TELEVISION VIEWING.   In Chapter 1, I noted that according to current survey findings, American adults spend over one-third of their free time—about

15 hours per week—watching TV. Estimates for children are even more ominous. Regular TV viewing typically begins between 2 and 3 years of age, consuming about 10.5 hours per week, or nearly 13 percent of the child's waking hours. It rises steadily over early childhood until it reaches an average of 28 hours per week for school-age children, or about 30 percent of the child's waking hours.[106] When we consider how much the set is on during school holidays and summer vacations, children spend more time watching TV than they do in any other waking activity, including going to school and interacting with family members or peers.

These statistics are averages; children differ in their attraction to television. For example, parents who watch a lot of TV tend to have children who do the same. Excessive TV viewing is associated with family and peer difficulties, poor school achievement, and serious health concerns—specifically, overweight and obesity as a result of hours of being sedentary and eating high-fat snacks while viewing.[107] Parents with stressful, unhappy lives often escape into television, and their children may do so as well.

It is crucial that parents exercise their gatekeeper role with respect to TV, limiting how much and what young children watch—to about an hour to an hour-and-a-half a day and to programs that are child-appropriate and informative and that teach positive social attitudes and behaviors. In addition, as much as possible, parents should watch with children and engage in joint conversation about televised information, helping them understand what they see. Parental oversight and involvement in children's TV viewing are essential for two reasons.

First, preschoolers easily misunderstand televised material. For example, at ages 2 and 3, they do not discriminate TV images from real objects; they say a bowl of popcorn on TV would spill if the set were turned upside down![108] When a child believes that all people, objects, and events on TV are authentic, violence—so pervasive on American TV—becomes particularly terrifying. Although by age 4 children know that not all TV programming is real, they judge TV reality according to whether the images resemble people and objects in everyday life. Not until age 8 do children fully grasp the unreality of TV fiction—that characters do not retain their roles outside the TV show.[109]

Furthermore, prior to this age, children have difficulty inferring characters' motives and connecting contradictory TV scenes into a coherent story line. They cannot appreciate why a character who at first seemed like a "good guy" but later behaves aggressively is really a "bad guy." They evaluate such characters and their actions much too favorably.[110] For example, psychologist Sharon Purdie showed second graders a complex dramatic program in which an accused kidnapper, who had at first appeared friendly, tried to shoot a prosecution witness and got arrested during the attempt. Children who failed to grasp the kidnapper's motive and the reason for the arrest judged him to be "good," not "bad."[111]

Second, weak government regulation of American TV means that without parental controls, child viewers are exposed repeatedly to antisocial attitudes and behaviors. The average American child finishing elementary school has seen more than 100,000 televised violent acts that provide "an extensive how-to course in aggression."[112] Television also hardens children to violence, making them more willing to tolerate it in others.[113] Furthermore, although educational programming for children is highly sensitive to issues of equity and diversity, entertainment programming often conveys ethnic and gender stereotypes—minorities as villains and victims of violence and in subservient roles; men as dominant, powerful, and competent and women as attractive, emotional, and submissive. The more children view, the more likely they are to endorse such stereotypes. [114] Finally, as many parents are aware, television advertising manipulates children's beliefs and preferences. Although children can distinguish a TV program from a commercial as early as age 3, below age 8 they seldom grasp the selling purpose of the ads.[115] Rather, they think that commercials are well-intentioned efforts to be helpful to viewers.

These worrisome findings are not an inherent part of the TV medium. Instead, they result from the way it is used in American culture. In actuality, television has as much potential for good as it does for ill. For example, TV content depicting acts of cooperating, helping, and comforting encourages these behaviors in children.[116] But most of the time, programs mix benevolent and hostile intentions in the same character. Unfortunately, children are riveted by a character's aggression and miss the caring message. Television promotes positive social behavior in young children only when it is free of violent content.[117]

Despite widespread public concern about the impact of TV on children's development, many parents do little to regulate or guide their children's viewing. When parents do make an effort, preschoolers watch less TV, find educational programs more appealing, and more often view shows with their parents.[118] Parent–child co-viewing creates conditions in which adults can raise questions about the realism of televised information, assist children in making sense of the story line, and express disapproval of negative on-screen behavior and commercial messages, thereby teaching children to evaluate TV content rather than to accept it uncritically.

Interestingly, parents who are warm, communicative, and firm but appropriate in their expectations have children who are less drawn to TV, particularly violent TV.[119] Very likely, these parents set an example through their own TV viewing, watch with their children whenever they can, and use TV programs in constructive ways, helping children move away from the set into worthwhile activities. A program about animals, for example, might spark a weekend trip to the zoo, a visit to the library for books about animals, or new ways of observing and caring for the family pet. Parents who intervene in their child's TV viewing so it is in keeping with the "zone" transform the TV medium from a negative to a positive force in the child's mental life, and they promote favorable cognitive and social development in many other ways as well.

DIALOGUES WITH CHILDREN: LARGER IMPLICATIONS

Compared to two or three generations ago, contemporary parents and children less often engage in the development-enhancing, joint activities discussed throughout this chapter. In 1970, long before parents became preoccupied with the "time bind," psychologist Urie Bronfenbrenner reflected that children "used to be brought up by their parents."[120] Although the family, Bronfenbrenner noted, continues to have primary responsibility for children's character development, it lacks the strength needed to do the job because parents and children no longer spend enough time together. Ours is a split society—adults in one world, children in another. Too many families have separate adult–child living areas, each equipped with its own TV and other leisure pursuits so that parent–child dialogues seldom take place. When parents and children spend most of their time apart, the result is a profound dampening of parents' socializing power.

In the past, extended family members or adults in the neighborhood more readily stepped in when parents, for one reason or another, could not invest enough time in their children's lives. Today, neighborhood experiences are much more restricted. Housing enclaves where families know each other well and interested adults are available to "mind children's business" are rare. Children who live close to their grandparents benefit greatly, enjoying affectionate, playful relationships with them at early ages and looking to them for information, role models, family history, and values later on. But greater family mobility means that more children live a considerable distance from grandparents and other relatives. And parental divorce, which will affect 50 to 60 percent of American children born in the current decade,[121] lessens contact with the non-custodial parent's extended family. In childhood, physical distance makes for a psychologically distant relationship.

Remove parents and other adults from active participation in the lives of young children, and the vacuum may be filled by unsupervised and ill-behaved peers and the moral vagaries of American TV fare. Continued disengagement of adults from children's lives, Bronfenbrenner prophesied, will result in greater alienation, indifference, antagonism, and violence on the part of young people from all sectors of society—a prediction that came to pass in the form of rapidly escalating youth crime between the 1970s and 1990s, with an increasing number of offenders from privileged homes.[122]

As media analysts try to make sense of the most heinous of these acts, including the recent spate of family, school, and neighborhood murders and maimings, parental retreat from a troubled child's life almost invariably surfaces as a contributing factor. Parents of these youngsters often appear to be good people, having provided their children with material comforts and having responded with anguish, remorse, and attempts to do the right thing in the face of their child's previous and current grievous behavior. But the cases suggest that stepping in only in at times of crisis cannot compensate for providing the ongoing togetherness and haven of a family. Such togetherness affects a child's development in countless ways, even through what appear to be trifling pursuits—help with homework; outings to the grocery store, the park, and the local library; dinnertime conversations; discussions of exciting or scary TV shows; and bedtime stories. Yet these are the key experiences of childhood, through which children appropriate mental tools from more capable and discerning social partners, become enculturated and, thereby, human—intelligent, responsible, and caring.

Of course, most youngsters with preoccupied parents do not become antisocial and violent. Yet over and over, commentary in the media and in the psychological literature confirms that too many of our youth are disaffected in less intense ways—self-absorbed, disgruntled, and lacking a clear sense of direction and purpose. In the words of psychologist William Damon, they are demoralized,[123] a term that suggests a break with their social world, a deficiency in internalization of worthwhile values and goals.

A provocative question is whether a craving for connection with family and community is at the heart of the floundering of many of today's youth, manifested in academic problems, poor peer relationships, low self-esteem, depression, angry, acting-out behavior, and—with the arrival of young adulthood—inability to make vocational commitments, attain financial independence, and forge healthy intimate relationships. Research documents that these difficulties are magnified two to threefold in children and adolescents who have been exposed to marital discord and divorce,[124] circumstances in which parents—at odds with one another—all too often are diverted from investing in their children's day-to-day lives.

Yet a certain number of children and adolescents, despite exposure to severe family adversity, escape these difficulties and adjust well. A common element in the lives of such resilient youngsters, as I noted in Chapter 1, is an unusually warm, positive relationship with at least one parent or a close tie with an adult outside the immediate family.[125] What happens within these alternative relationships that shields the young person from problems or restores effective functioning? Although little systematic evidence exists on the precise ingredients of such ties, I recently became familiar with the bond forged between Hannah, a 21-year-old college student, and her Aunt Eva and Uncle Charlie, two of my university colleagues. Hannah's parents divorced when she was 9 and her older sister Sarah was 15. Hannah related the story of her childhood and the genesis of her relationship with Eva and Charlie, who offered insights as well. What they had to say is enlightening.

"I can't remember much family togetherness when I was a kid," Hannah remarked. "Our parents couldn't talk things out with each other, and they rarely talked things out with us. Mom took Sarah and me to Girl Scouts, swimming, piano, and other lessons. We enjoyed the activities and the friends we made, but they couldn't compensate for what was missing: warm, family time. We almost never sat down to a meal together or went places together; we each went our own way. Our dad started going off on vacations by himself when holidays rolled around, so family get-togethers were rare.

"When our parents split up, we moved with our mom from Arkansas to Seattle. Mom worked all week, weekends, and most evenings. She had to get a career going so there'd be money to live on and to send us to college. Sarah hung out with another family in the neighborhood. A couple of times a week, she had dinner and went to church with them. Looking back, I'd say they were her substitute family; she 'adopted' them, and they 'adopted' her. I was too young to go off on my own that way. When I didn't have after-school activities, Mom insisted that I come home and do chores and homework. Sometimes I got to go to a friend's house to play, but many nights I'd open a can of spaghetti and have dinner by myself. I spent hours daydreaming and looking at old pictures of Mom, Dad, Sarah, and me."

On finishing high school, Sarah chose a religiously affiliated college of the same denomination as that of her "alternative" family. The year after her college graduation, Sarah married a devout classmate, entering into a culture in which family life was pivotal. Six years later, Hannah started college, but for her the road to maturity was rough. She had difficulty concentrating, earned uneven grades, and accumulated so many incompletes in courses that the university prohibited her from reenrolling until she wrapped up her "unfinished business." Frustrated with Hannah's undirectedness, her mother withdrew financial support and insisted that she get a job. Hannah's full-time waitressing soon became both an obstacle and an excuse for lack of progress in her studies. "I was at sea," Hannah recalled. "I didn't have any confidence in myself, and I didn't think I could do anything. So I started visiting Aunt Eva and Uncle Charlie, who lived three hours away."

"We hadn't known Hannah well while she was growing up," Eva continued, "so we were surprised but delighted when she started coming on weekends. It didn't matter what we were doing—birthday celebrations, dinner with friends, outings to movies and plays, shopping excursions, or leisurely breakfasts; Hannah hungered to be part of our family. During those times, she asked lots of questions about our work and home lives, and also about her parents, especially their early history: 'Was my mom close to her mom?' 'Did you know my mom and dad when they were in college?' 'What was my parents' wedding like?' I described these and many other earlier events. We also did our best to convince Hannah that believing in herself grows out of trying hard, taking risks, and following through. We talked about how important it was for her to return to school, helped her think through a change of major, and advised on time management and study skills."

Hannah completed her degree the following year. In a letter she wrote to Eva and Charlie shortly after her graduation, she attributed her turnabout in motivation and self-confidence to the connection, forged through dialogue, with her aunt and uncle:

> Thank you for everything you have provided, the time and effort you shared with me and the confidence you showed in me. It definitely enabled me to re-locate all of that within myself this year and even be pleasantly surprised by how each accomplishment facilitates the next one. This, and you, are among the greatest gifts I have ever received. The change in my ability to focus on my courses and the personal rewards have been immense. THANKS.[126]

What factors contributed to Hannah's turnabout? Shared understanding (intersubjectivity) between adult and child, scaffolding of new competencies, narrative conversations prompting a redefinition of self, and joint engagement in culturally meaningful activities—the diverse experiences we have considered that create the zone of proximal development—appear to be at the heart of her success story. Indeed, Hannah's tale suggests that young children denied these supports can still profit from them later, if such supports are available and they have the fortitude to capitalize on them. But not all young people are as fortunate as Hannah. Some remain profoundly impaired by inadequate adult investment in their childhoods. And even those who fare reasonably well may carry with them inner wounds—a sense of emptiness and regret at having missed self-defining, confidence-inducing early experiences that cannot, in the final analysis, be recaptured.

Experts asked to reflect on the malaise and problematic behavior of children today repeatedly comment that they lack sufficient adult guidance and involvement.[127] We have seen that children come into the world marvelously prepared to enter into partnerships with parents and other caregivers. In the course of this chapter, I have had much to say about just how parents and teachers can capitalize on children's natural propensities. Vygotsky's concept of the "zone" clarifies for us the meaning of true "quality time." What must we do to keep young children in the "zone," motivated, involved, and ever advancing to new heights? Here is a brief recap of the communicative principles we have considered:

- Forge an adult–child relationship based on shared understanding, or *intersubjectivity*—one in which the adult strives to "connect" with the child by "stretching down" to his or her point of view, thereby helping the child "stretch up" to the adult's more mature perspective. Intersubjectivity is essential for all successful dialogue.
- Offer a *scaffold* for mastery of tasks that teach culturally valued concepts and skills. Adjust the task to an appropriately challenging level, and tailor teaching and assistance to the child's changing needs. While supporting the child's efforts, ask questions and suggest strategies that help the child generate ideas and *distance* his or her thinking from the immediate features of the task. Turn over responsibility for the task to the child as soon as he or she can master it without assistance. Adult–child collaboration through scaffolding promotes self-regulation and independent accomplishment.
- Communicate with *high warmth,* using a positive emotional tone and providing explanations and justifications for your expectations. When adult–child relationships are sympathetic and caring, children want to acquire skills and behave in ways that preserve those gratifying ties. They are also more willing to work toward goals that are rational and reasonable. *Authoritative parenting,* which combines the motivating power of warmth with the guidance inherent in scaffolding, predicts many aspects of children's competence.
- Engage children in *narrative conversation* about personal experiences, using an *elaborative conversational style* that poses many varied questions

and that expands on the child's statements. Through narrative, children build an autobiographical self permeated with cultural beliefs and values; come to understand that people have rich mental lives and may view the same events differently; and acquire negotiation strategies for resolving disputes and getting along with others. Narrative conversation also fosters language development and emergent literacy, which greatly ease the task of learning to read and write when children get to school.

Through dialogues with children, adults play a formative role in the development of children's self-conceptions, sensitivity to others, cognition, academic knowledge, morality, social skills, and capacity to use language to gain control over thought and behavior. Can parents and teachers actually witness young children undergoing these social-to-psychological transformations? Let's turn now to a consideration of children's inner mental lives, as manifested in the dialogues they carry on with themselves. In the next chapter, I address a question that has long intrigued child development theorists and puzzled many parents and teachers: Why do children talk to themselves?

THREE

Why Children Talk to Themselves

If you could become the shadow of a 2- to 8-year-old, furtively tagging along as the child goes about his or her daily activities, you would notice a curious form of language behavior—remarks in which the child seems to talk to himself or herself or to no one in particular. This speech-to-self occurs frequently. It can surface in virtually any of the child's pursuits—during fantasy play, drawing and painting, building with blocks, tackling academic tasks, idly passing the time of day, and quieting down before naptime or nightly sleep. Researchers call this spontaneous, self-directed talk *private speech*.

Unlike adults, who self-consciously talk to themselves only in solitary moments, young children freely use private speech in public. So at ease are preschool and primary-school children in speaking to themselves in front of others that on observing this behavior, many adults question its normalcy! "Confused," "touched," and "strange" are among the descriptors I have heard them apply to self-talking children, generalizing from "crazy people," who not only speak aloud to fantasized audiences but also act improperly in a great many ways because they are indifferent to their social surroundings.

To be sure, talking to oneself in the midst of a roomful of people is not acceptable in the adult social world. Yet all of us engage in private speech from time to time. And it is ubiquitous in early childhood. When children between the ages of 3 and 10 are observed in classrooms, private speech makes up as much as 20 percent to 60 percent of their language.[1] Why do young children engage in it so frequently?

To grasp the significance of private speech in the life of the child, let's begin by looking at it in ourselves. When are you most likely to talk out loud to yourself? In response to this question, most adults say they engage in audible self-talk when they face cognitive, emotional, or social challenges. Here are some self-reports:

- "At the end of a busy day, when I'm tired and distracted, I sometimes find myself looking for an important document, for my keys, or even for where I parked my car. I say things like, 'Where was it when I last saw it? Did I put them [the keys] down while I was hanging up my coat?'"
- "Recently, I was angry at the way a sales clerk treated me, so I whispered to myself, 'Calm down. You can't change him, so move on from here.'"
- "I decided to ask my boss for a transfer to another department. I was so concerned about her reaction that I wrote out what I intended to say, imagined her response, and rehearsed about ten times in front of the mirror."

Of course, in surmounting daily challenges, we don't always speak aloud. Most of the time, we talk to ourselves silently, in a manner that resembles an inner dialogue. With the self as both speaker and social partner, we converse, instruct, explain, pose questions, and attempt to answer them. When we encounter an especially difficult situation, we turn parts of this mental dialogue outward, making our self-communication considerably more explicit and detailed than it ordinarily would be were we to speak to ourselves silently. Externalizing and elaborating our thinking seems to help us gain control of unmanageable circumstances. And if we cannot master them, we often turn to others, who may offer clarifying observations that we can integrate into our thinking. As a result, we can better grasp a situation, surmount an obstacle, or make a decision. As one adult remarked, "In looking for my keys, I might say to myself, 'Where are they?' But simultaneously, I'm also commenting to my wife, who might be able to help me think through what I did with them."

As these reflections suggest, our self-talk resembles and is intimately linked to our dialogues with others. Indeed, private speech—in children and adults alike—seems to grow from our history of supportive social interaction in the zone of proximal development. As more expert partners scaffold children's mastery of challenging tasks and converse with them in ways that enhance their knowledge and understanding, children incorporate those dialogues into their private speech. Over time, they weave into their self-talk an increasingly rich tapestry of voices from their social world—a process that ensures the transmission of values, strategies, and skills from the minds of one generation to the minds of the next.[2] At the same time, each child's private speech is unique, in that it bears the stamp of the child's active contribution to social interaction and of others' verbal adjustments to suit that child's individual needs.

In Vygotsky's sociocultural theory, this "communication with the self" becomes an indispensable tool for *self-regulation*—the central means through which children take over the support provided by others, turn it toward the self, and use it to guide and control their own thinking and behavior. Notice how self-talk induces a delay in responding, during which the child can think about past and present events, speculate about their possible consequences, discuss those alternatives with the self, formulate plans, and use that information to guide impending action. Private speech, then, permits children to create self-directed instructions and, thereby, becomes the fundamental tool for managing the self's activities.

A close look at children's private speech lends credibility to Vygotsky's conclusion that its broad function is self-regulation. Although self-talk takes many forms, in most instances children appear to be working through ideas, surmounting obstacles, mastering cognitive or social skills, or managing intense emotion. Here are some examples from my own observations of children:

- Two-year-old Peter experiments with language sounds, structures, and meanings as he sings to himself, *"Put the mushroom on your head. Put the mushroom in your pocket. Put the mushroom on your nose."* Then, as he eyes his cat, Tony, he exclaims, *"Put the mushroom on the Tony,"* and laughs.
- While counting raisins at snack time, 5-year-old Carla says out loud rapidly, *"One-two-three-four-five!"* Then she continues more slowly, *"Six, seven, eight, nine. Nine raisins!"* she emphasizes, with satisfaction.
- Standing in front of an easel, 4-year-old Omar picks up a brush, then stops and surveys other nearby easels. *"Where's the green? I need some green,"* he remarks, apparently referring to the missing green paint, which had been at the easels the day before.
- In his second-grade class, Tommy reads the text before him aloud, sounding out a hard-to-decipher name. *"Sher-lock Holmlock, Sherlock Holme,"* he says, leaving off the final "s" in his second, more successful attempt.
- Three-year-old Rachel leans against the wall, looks down, and mumbles to herself, *"Mommy's sick, Mommy's sick,"* in an apparent effort to come to terms with this stressful event.[3]

Private speech has not always been accorded the vital, positive role in children's development that Vygotsky bestowed on it. Observing preschoolers and kindergartners in the early part of his career, Piaget noticed that 3- to 7-year-olds often engage in speech not addressed to others. He called this speech "egocentric," a term expressing his view that it was a symptom of the child's cognitive immaturity.[4] Young children, Piaget claimed, engage in egocentric speech because they cannot adapt their remarks to the perspectives of others. For this reason, much of their talk is "talk for self" that accompanies or is stimulated by their actions but is not understandable to a listener. According to Piaget, brain development and repeated confrontations with peers—who are far less likely to try to make sense of children's egocentric statements than are adults—cause children to give up their egocentric ways. Eventually, their conversation becomes comprehensible, taking into account their listeners' perspectives.

Yet children's early communicative competencies—their striving for shared understanding and their remarkable conversational capacities, evident by age 2—are at odds with Piaget's view of their language as egocentric and nonsocial! In fact, prominent early childhood educators of the 1920s and 1930s challenged Piaget's theory of egocentric speech, based on their own observations of children. In England, Susan Isaacs collected detailed records of children's language in a small experimental nursery school. She found that when preschoolers *intended* to communicate with others, only a handful of their utterances could be called egocentric, or not adapted to the needs of their listeners.[5] Similarly, American educator Dorothea McCarthy watched closely as 1 1/2- to 4-year-olds played in the presence of an attentive adult; less than 5 percent of children's verbalizations were egocentric.[6]

Vygotsky, as well, voiced a powerful objection to Piaget's theory of egocentric speech. The direction of development, he emphasized, is not one in which initially self-absorbed, egocentric utterances are replaced by social speech. Instead, private speech originates in early social communication.[7] At first, private and social remarks are hard to distinguish, but gradually they differentiate. Social speech remains directed at conversing with others, whereas private speech becomes "communication with the self" for self-guidance and self-direction. The high rates of private speech observed in young children, then, represent a phase of development in between social speech and inner verbal thought. As children make the transition from private to inner speech—the silent dialogues we carry on with ourselves that are the essence of conscious mental activity—they internalize social communication and, thereby, build a socially formed mind.

Why is children's self-talk often hard for others to interpret? Not because of egocentrism, Vygotsky noted, but because once private speech separates from social speech and takes on its self-regulating function, it need no longer be as elaborate and complete as it was before. After all, when we talk to ourselves, we converse with a highly sympathetic and understanding listener! As a result, we shorten our private speech, leaving out assumed information, just as we would in conversing with a particularly intimate social partner.[8]

As children condense their self-directed remarks during early and middle childhood, private speech becomes more effective in guiding behavior. At first, Vygotsky explained, self-talk is little more than running commentary on the child's activity—a means of expressing oneself and releasing tension. Two- and 3-year-olds are too preoccupied with acquiring language and becoming proficient communicators for their statements to be very potent in managing thought and action. But gradually, private speech takes on its crucial self-regulating function;[9] children use it to comprehend their experiences and to plan and control action on a moment-by-moment basis.

As children talk their way through challenges, first with the assistance of more expert partners and then on their own, they acquire new strategies for handling difficulties. Soon, Vygotsky pointed out, they "think words instead of pronouncing them,"[10] and their self-talk becomes less audible, apparent only in whispers and silent lip movements as they work a puzzle, build a block structure, solve a math problem, or perfect the motor actions needed to ride a bicycle. In the older preschooler and school-age child, private speech becomes inner speech. It fuses with thought and compresses into even more efficient forms—perhaps a single word to stand for a great many words, just as the title of a book is imbued with the more elaborate meanings of its extended prose.[11] When children become very adept at a task, they no longer need conscious verbal guidance, since the necessary mental steps are so well practiced that they have become automatic. Consequently, children can turn their increasingly effective self-talk toward new challenges that have moved into their zone of proximal development.

Thanks to Vygotsky's astute theorizing then, we now know that children's private speech is far more than useless chatter, akin to the self-absorbed rantings of the mentally deranged or an annoying tic to be stamped out by impatient social partners. Instead, private speech is richly influenced by children's social experiences, and it is crucial for overcoming impulsive action and achieving conscious control over thought and behavior. Let's take a closer look.

SOCIAL ORIGINS

One day, 2 1/2-year-old Ellie arrived at our laboratory playroom, holding her mother Sasha's hand. I invited them to sit down at a table and asked Sasha to show Ellie how to construct a tower out of a set of brightly colored plastic pieces. The tower was much too difficult for Ellie to build on her own. So Sasha broke down the task into smaller parts, bringing it within Ellie's "zone" by holding a piece while Ellie locked another into it and commenting, "Look, Ellie! Each new piece has to be a different color, so our tower will have all the colors of the rainbow."

Ellie participated enthusiastically, adding new pieces and offering guiding comments of her own: "Not a yellow. We have yellow. Let's do purple! Push it in. There, got it. Now, let's do blue." Whether Ellie's remarks were social or private was not clear, but they appeared to assist her in identifying colors and adding new pieces to the structure.

Once the tower was built, we asked Sasha to sit to the side and read a magazine while we gave Ellie a much smaller tower, consisting of only a few pieces, to construct on her own. Although the task was simpler, for Ellie it was by no means easy. But once again, she cooperated with gusto, affirming "OK!" when I told her that Mommy wanted to read for a while and she should build by herself.

Very soon, Ellie began to talk out loud as she built. We heard, "Try yellow." "Push it [the piece] on." "New color." Then, as she grabbed the next piece, she exclaimed "Red!" But when the red piece would not fit, even with the aid of such remarks as, "Push, push," Ellie's speech became louder, and she alternately glanced at the partly built tower and her mother. Finally, we heard, "Mommy, push piece on, push on!" as Ellie pressed two pieces together unsuccessfully and looked at her mother with a frustrated, pleading expression. Sasha put aside her magazine, reached over, and assisted. Ellie had drawn her mother back into the task.

Relationship of Social and Private Speech

Like the adult who misplaces his keys and asks, "Where are they?" not just to guide his search but to solicit help from his wife, the speech of the 2- to 3-year-old child who is tackling a challenge is simultaneously private and social. In the young child's mind, the two types of utterances are as yet incompletely separated. During this period, children's remarks are not just a response to a difficult task; they often are an appeal for assistance from a potentially helpful person.

In a series of creative studies, Vygotsky sought to demonstrate the social origins of private speech and its close link to communication with others. He created situations that discouraged or prevented social interaction and tracked what happened to preschoolers' private speech. In one instance, he introduced so much noise into a classroom that children could not talk to one another comfortably. In a second experiment, he replaced familiar classmates with deaf children who had no verbal language. And in a third, he surrounded children with peers who spoke a foreign tongue. In each situation, preschoolers were deprived of the "illusion" that others could understand their private speech. Consequently, for most, self-talk declined to zero. Similarly, when Vygotsky placed preschoolers with unfamiliar peers or isolated them at a table in a corner of the classroom, self-directed speech dropped instantly and sharply.[12]

Other observations of children's language concur that social and private speech have common roots. For example, the most socially interactive preschool and kindergarten children tend to use the most private speech.[13] And just as Ellie freely engaged in self-talk during and after her mother's helpful scaffolding, several studies show that the private speech of preschoolers increases in the presence of a receptive social partner—either a peer or an adult.[14] Alternatively, when an adult places barriers between young children, such as cardboard screens or upright books that prevent easy visual access (a practice that, as noted in Chapter 2, American teachers often use to keep children from seeing one another's work), both social speech and self-guiding utterances that might be helpful in mastering a task diminish drastically.[15]

Are social and private speech so closely linked because private speech emerges out of early social communication? It appears so. Psychologist David Furrow analyzed the precise functions of 2-year-olds' social and self-directed utterances during a play session (for example, whether the utterance seemed to focus attention, direct action, express feelings, name objects, convey or seek information, or involve make-believe). He found that all the functions identified in self-talk were also represented in young children's social communication.[16] Between 2 and 4 years of age, social and private speech differentiate, just as Vygotsky surmised. Social speech increasingly emphasizes conveying or seeking information ("Daddy's at work!"), whereas private speech becomes more heavily laden with self-guiding remarks ("Put it [puzzle piece] here") and incomprehensible mutterings, which suggest movement toward inner speech.[17]

Further evidence for the social roots of private speech comes from studies of children whose family lives are limited in adult–child conversation. Consistently, such children are delayed in private speech development when compared to children from conversationally rich homes. For example, with graduate student Ruth Garvin, I collected extensive records of the classroom talk of 5- to 9-year-olds from impoverished families in Appalachian Kentucky.[18] We found that Appalachian schoolchildren engaged in high rates of immature private speech, such as word play and repetitive phrases—forms typical of much younger children. Furthermore, the Appalachian children's self-guiding comments remained audible well into the school years, suggesting a much later transition to inner speech than typically occurs for economically advantaged children.[19]

Not only does the stress of poverty restrict parent–child verbal communication, but the culture of Appalachia places little emphasis on parent–child dialogue. The verbal silence of many Appalachian homes, repeatedly noted by anthropologists studying the culture,[20] seems to have profound, negative consequences for the maturity of children's self-regulating language. Immature verbal self-regulation, in turn, impedes children's cognitive and social development and academic progress, as we'll se shortly.

Adult Communication and Children's Private Speech

Does a certain quality of adult–child communication, reflecting supportive interaction within the child's "zone," foster the development of private speech? Observations of children working on various problem-solving tasks suggest that this is so.

In one study, psychologists Douglas Behrend, Karl Rosengren, and Marion Perlmutter gave 3- and 5-year-olds puzzles of varying degrees of difficulty in two sessions, one with and one without the assistance of their mothers.[21] In the first session, observers rated each mother for the effectiveness of her scaffolding, noting the degree of emotional support she provided and the extent to which she adjusted the task to suit the child's needs and refrained from being too controlling (doing the task for the child, which discourages independent mastery). Three-year-olds whose mothers were effective scaffolders used more private speech during the mother–child session. And 5-year-olds whose mothers provided appropriate (not excessively controlling) guidance used more private speech when working on their own. Private speech, in turn, predicted children's successful puzzle solution.

Similarly, graduate student Sarah Spuhl and I asked mothers to help their 4- and 5-year-old children reproduce a complex model of a pyramid by fitting blocks together and matching colors and shapes.[22] We rated each mother's assistance for authoritative parenting—the extent to which she was warm, sensitive, and patient; held reasonable expectations for task mastery; and offered helpful guidance. Next, we had the children transfer the skills acquired in the pyramid task to a related construction problem, assembling Lego blocks into reproductions of models. We tracked their improvement in Lego building over three short sessions, scheduled 3 to 4 days apart. Our findings revealed that children of authoritative mothers more often used self-guiding private speech, in which they instructed themselves and commented on the task at hand. Four-year-olds experiencing authoritative assistance showed greater improvement in Lego-building skill over the three sessions. And their extensive use of self-talk appeared to facilitate these performance gains.

In sum, the very features of communication that create the "zone"—scaffolding with warmth, reasonable maturity demands, and helpful assistance—foster children's private speech. That conversing with the self occurs often in the context of and shortly after effective adult teaching suggests that children are adopting problem-solving strategies from their social world and applying them to their independent efforts, which yields gains in learning.

How do we know for sure that private speech, as Vygotsky claimed, is the supreme mental tool for self-regulation, the means through which children overcome impulsive action in favor of deliberate thought and action? Tracing the development of self-talk from the earliest ages and observing how children use it in diverse situations can help us clarify its self-guiding function.

A VITAL TOOL FOR SELF-REGULATION

Earlier I noted that adults tend to talk to themselves when they come face to face with challenges. Vygotsky was the first to observe that children's private speech, as well, increases with task difficulty. To explore the self-regulating function of private speech, he introduced obstacles into children's ongoing activities—for example, removing pencil or paper just as the child was about to draw. When the smooth flow of behavior was interrupted, preschoolers talked to themselves at nearly twice the rate as did classmates not exposed to obstacles. And the content of children's remarks suggested that they were using private speech to comprehend the situation and find a solution: "Where's the pencil? I need a blue pencil. Never mind, I'll draw with the red one and wet it with water; it will become dark and look like blue."[23]

Unlike preschoolers, Vygotsky noted, older children are less likely to speak aloud. Instead, confronted with an obstacle such as a missing pencil, they usually pause (as if to think) and quickly redirect their behavior. When Vygotsky asked school-age children for their thoughts, they described mental activities much like those reflected in preschoolers' private speech. He concluded that by the mid-elementary school years, self-communication has largely been transformed into highly efficient, soundless inner speech and that the steps needed to overcome disruptions in ongoing action had become fairly automatic, requiring less verbal intervention.[24]

Since Vygotsky's groundbreaking findings, researchers have confirmed and reconfirmed the rise in private speech as children work on more difficult tasks.[25] Children seem to rely on private speech to keep tasks within their "zone," just as adults aim to do when scaffolding children's learning. As soon as children can use language for social communication, they also turn it toward themselves, in an apparent effort to acquire new understandings and skills.

Dialogues from the Crib

Listen closely after 1 1/2- to 3-year-old children are left to fall asleep at naptime or at night. Many can be heard talking aloud to themselves. Several researchers have carefully recorded and analyzed these extended solitary monologues, known as "crib speech." Their findings reveal that bedtime narratives serve a rich array of self-regulating functions, including practicing diverse cognitive and language skills, reviewing and making sense of past or upcoming events, managing emotion, and engaging in imaginative expression. To illustrate, let's look in on the bedtime speech of Emily, a 2-year-old who regularly produced elaborate crib dialogues. Here she speaks about a recent trip to a department store in anticipation of Christmas:

1. We bought a baby
2. . . .'cause,
3. . . . the, well because,
4. when she, well,
5. we thought it was for Christmas,
6. but when we went to the s-s-store we didn't have our jacket on,
7. but I saw some dolly,
8. and I yelled at my mother and said
9. I want one of those dolly
10. So after we were finished with the store,
11. we went over to the dolly and she bought me one,
12. so I have one.[26]

For a 2-year-old child, Emily's story is impressively elaborate. It contains all the components of narrative considered in Chapter 2—a well-organized sequence of events based on an unusual happening; a set of main characters; and references to mental states, such as "thought" and "want." Recordings of Emily's bedtime musings reveal that they were often more complex in content and language than her everyday conversations—an observation that suggests crib speech is distinct from social speech and takes on its own special forms and functions considerably earlier than does private speech in other situations.[27] As Emily talked to herself at bedtime, she experimented with and practiced a variety of cognitive and communication skills, including memory for past events, rich vocabulary and complex grammatical forms, and logical organization of thoughts into coherent narratives.

Sometimes crib speech focuses directly on language play and mastery of verbal labels for concepts. So intense is this exploration of specific meanings that the narrative structure of the crib dialogue may temporarily recede in favor of it. In the following excerpt, 2 1/2-year-old Anthony explores the words "big" and "little" as he talks about an average-sized adult, Bob, whom he knows, and several additional invented characters (Bobby and Nancy). Along the way, Anthony practices his counting skills:

1. hi big Bob
2. that's Bob
3. that's Bob
4. big Bob
5. little Bob
6. big and little
7. little Bobby
8. little Nancy
9. big Nancy
10. big Bob and Nancy and Bobby
11. and Bob
12. and two, three Bobbys . . .
14. four Bobbys
15. six
16. tell the night, Bobby
17. big Bob
18. big Bobby not home[28]

Furthermore, children frequently focus on social routines and rules in their crib talk. Anthony, for example, often became preoccupied with activities he was forbidden to engage in during the day. A strict household rule was that he was not to play with anything on his parents' desks. One evening, he vocalized while rocking back and forth, just before he dropped off to sleep:

1. Don't touch Mommy Daddy's desk . . .

5. Don't go on the desk
6. Don't take Daddy's glasses
7. Don't take the glasses off . . .
12. Leave it
13. Daddy's glasses[29]

Once in a while, we can see all these functions in a single crib-speech episode. In the excerpt that follows, Emily created an intricate narrative about an anticipated trip to the ocean. Within it, she explored concepts of distance and location ("a little far away," "a couple blocks away," "downtown") and bodies of water (ocean, river, beach, bridge); addressed social routines and rules (where you get and eat hotdogs; going in the car with "the car seats"); and added imaginary events consistent with the theme of the story ("sharks go in the river and bite me"):

1. We are gonna . . .
2. at the ocean.
3. Ocean is a little far away
4. baw, baw, buh
5. far away . . .
6. I think it's . . .
7. couple blocks . . . away
8. Maybe it's down, downtown
9. and across the ocean,
10. and down the river,
11. and maybe it's in,
12. the hot dogs will be in a fridge
13. and the fridge (would) be in the water over by a shore
14. and then we could go in,
15. and get a hot dog and bring it out to the river,
16. and then sharks go in the river and bite me,
17. in the ocean,
18. we go into the ocean
19. and ocean by over by . . .
20. I think a couple of blocks away.
21. But we could be,
22. and we could find any hot dogs,
23. um the hot dogs gonna be for the for the beach.
24. Then the bridge is gonna,

25. we'll have to go in the green car.
26. 'cause that's where the car seats are.[30]

Why were Emily's crib soliloquies more complex and detailed than her so-cial conversations? One speculation is that this early self-talk is the most fully externalized form of private speech. In many instances, crib speech may reen-act dialogues children had with parents and other significant adults during the day and then extend them with the child's original contributions.[31] In this way, crib dialogues both capture and strengthen virtually all the benefits of chil-dren's conversations with more expert partners.

The conversational structure, tone, and content of private speech, in which a speaking self and a responding self interact, are especially evident in crib speech because of its completeness. Just as dialogues with others help children make sense of their experiences; acquire cultural beliefs, values, and problem-solving strategies; and marshal these tools to guide thought and behavior, dia-logues from the crib may assist very young children with self-regulation as soon as they are capable of conversational participation.

In fact, the conversational nature of crib speech and of later-emerging forms of self-talk, which blossom after age 3, may contribute in a special way to the success of children's private speech in regulating their thought and action.[32] Recall that through dialogue with adults and, especially, an elaborative narra-tive style, preschoolers' narrative capacities expand, and they become capable of imagining, reflecting on, and reconciling different perspectives. Conversa-tional self-talk, involving questions, answers, assertions, responses, and com-ments between a speaking self and a self talked to, makes private speech a remarkably flexible instrument of self-regulation——one able to adapt to the re-quirements of diverse situations, to negotiate unexpected difficulties, and to strengthen a wide array of new competencies.

Not all toddlers and young preschoolers engage in private dialogues at bed-time. Many generate similar self-directed conversations during the day at idle moments, perhaps while resting from vigorous play or riding from place to place in the backseat of the car. However, among children's earliest soliloquies, those occurring at bedtime have been the most convenient to study—and they have revealed an amazingly rich context of self-directed learning. By listening to these musings, we can discover much about the very young child's fascina-tions, preoccupations, imaginings, concerns, understandings, and internaliza-tion of cultural values and beliefs. Because crib speech is so elaborate, it provides us with a marvelous window into the young child's mind-in-the-mak-ing. Through it, we witness early learning and development as they take place.

Private Speech and Early Morality

One day, Judy—mother of 4-year-old Trevor—approached me, troubled by her son's private comments the previous day. Trevor's self-talk had seemed repetitive and peculiar, so much so that Judy admitted that she had wondered about Trevor's mental balance. After all, she blurted out apprehensively, disturbed people talk a lot to themselves!

Trevor's self-directed remarks had been sparked by an incident in which he had careened carelessly through the family living room, bumping into an end table on which an antique vase stood. Crash! went the vase, splitting into pieces. An anxious, sensitive child, Trevor was mortified. He knew he was not supposed to run in the house—certainly not in the living room, where his parents' fragile, most prized possessions were on display. His mother had stepped outside to water the plants on the patio. How would she react when she returned and saw the damage he had caused?

When Judy entered the room, she heard Trevor saying over and over, "Trevor did it. Trevor broke it. Trevor crashed it. Trevor broke it . . . ," as he stood forlornly before the fallen vase. After admonishing him to be more careful, Judy asked Trevor to fetch the plastic waste basket from the kitchen, into which she placed the broken pieces. She thought the unfortunate incident was over, but not for Trevor, who repeated every once in a while throughout the day, "Trevor broke it, Trevor's sorry . . . ."

As we saw in Chapter 2, preschoolers acquire standards for good conduct through adult conversation, guidance, and example. Anthony's crib soliloquy about not touching things on his parents' desk suggests that a strong desire to internalize and heed social and moral norms is evident as early as age 2. Soon this desire pervades preschoolers' make-believe play, which (as Chapter 4 will reveal) focuses heavily on rules and rule-following. Children's active desire to follow standards grows out of a commitment to parents who have been warm and sensitive and clear, consistent, and reasonable in their expectations.[33]

But the young child who wants so much to be good must assimilate a great many rules—rules for taking care of property; rules for respecting other people; rules for safety; rules for self-care, eating, and dressing; rules for doing chores; rules for good manners; and more.[34] Remembering all these standards, let alone following them, is a great challenge for a preschooler! As children's private speech develops, it assists them not only in recalling how to behave but in overcoming impulses and acting in accord with standards. In other words, talking to oneself is a highly effective tool for resisting temptation. Adults use private speech this way when they admonish themselves: "Don't take that second piece of cake!" or "Bite your tongue, don't say anything nasty!" Around age 1 1/2 to 2, children engage in similar self-talk. "Don't touch!" the toddler commands as he moves his hand toward a light socket, then quickly pulls it back. "Supposed to share!" the 2-year-old exclaims as she gives up a toy she had grabbed from a classmate.

Mustering the willpower to follow standards is at times difficult for adults, so it is not surprising that young children find it challenging. Inhibiting impulses and redirecting behavior depends in part on brain development—specifically, growth of neural connections in the frontal lobes of the cerebral cortex. Children show dramatic improvement in impulse control from the preschool to the school years, a period in which the frontal lobes are developing especially rapidly.[35] But frontal-lobe development alone cannot guarantee a well-behaved child. A major contributor is language development—in particular, private speech.[36] Self-directed language makes it possible for children to actualize their marvelous brain-based potential for suppressing impulses and following social rules.

How do young children react when placed in a tantalizing environment and asked to resist temptation? To find out, psychologists Brian Vaughn, Claire Kopp, and Joanne Krakow brought 1 1/2- to 2 1/2-year-olds into a laboratory and presented them with three delay-of-gratification tasks.[37] In the first, an adult told the child not to touch a fascinating toy telephone placed within arm's reach. Second, raisins were hidden under cups, and the child was told to wait until the adult said it was all right to pick up a cup and eat a raisin. In the third task, the child was asked not to open an attractive gift until the adult had finished her work. The youngest children, who had little language, could wait no more than 10 to 30 seconds before reaching for the desirable objects. Capacity to delay increased steadily with age, a time of rapid language gains. To help themselves wait, many 2-year-olds talked aloud to themselves. And the best predictor of individual differences in self-control was language development.

Once children show some capacity to inhibit undesirable acts and engage in socially approved behavior, caregivers expect more of them. When Heidi Gralinski and Claire Kopp asked mothers what they require their young children to do and what they insist they not do, they reported a gradual increase in rule expectations between ages 1 and 2 1/2—the period in which, as we have seen, the capacity to resist temptation rises dramatically.[38] Caregivers' expectations act as a scaffold for children's self-control, steadily introducing them to a wider array of standards, which preschoolers integrate into their private speech and then use to instruct themselves. When 2-year-olds experience warm, patient parent–child communication, they more often follow their mother's directives to clean up toys and not touch attractive objects. And they continue to obey after the mother steps out of a laboratory room and another adult tries to get them to violate standards by, for example, coaxing them to tear a page out of a book or throw a Nerf ball at someone's face.[39] Furthermore, getting moral internalization off to an early, good start appears to have lasting benefits. Two-year-olds who are advanced in the capacity to resist temptation remain ahead of their peers in this respect when observed again a year later.[40]

In everyday life, preschoolers find it difficult to keep their minds off tempting activities and objects for long. They profit greatly from adult suggestions for how to wait patiently ("Try thinking about other things") and how to resist engaging in unacceptable acts ("Imagine how sad Mary will feel if you take her toy. If you share, maybe she'll want to share, too"). When parents and teachers offer strategies that match children's capacity to understand, children can easily transfer those strategies to their self-talk, and their capacity to delay gratification increases greatly. By the school years, children become better at thinking up their own techniques for resisting temptation.[41] Brain development, cognitive development, and a history of adult-provided strategies integrated into private speech jointly foster a flexible capacity for moral self-regulation. Older children can monitor their own conduct, adjusting it as occasions arise that tempt them to violate inner standards.

Let's return now to Trevor, whose dash through the living room left his parents' treasured vase in ruins. When first under way, preschoolers' morally relevant self-talk is not very effective; it becomes so only over time, with much practice and continued adult oversight and prompting. Thus, Trevor's lapse in self-control is understandable and expected. As adults help children acquire the capacity to resist temptation and follow rules, they also encourage them to feel self-conscious emotions—such as pride, guilt, shame, and embarrassment.[42] These emotions energize moral action. They first appear between 1 1/2 and 2 years of age, and by age 3, they are clearly related to children's evaluations of their own behavior. For example, 3-year-olds express pride when they succeed at challenging tasks, and guilt and shame when they violate parents' standards.[43]

Initially, children experience self-conscious emotions only in the presence of others.[44] They depend on adults to tell them when to feel proud, guilty, or ashamed. As children form guidelines for good conduct and become better at following them, their morally relevant feelings, thoughts, and behavior come together. The child who succeeds in following rules feels proud, even in the absence of adult monitoring, and is likely to follow rules in the future. The child who transgresses feels guilty or ashamed and, faced with another temptation, is likely to resist.

From this vantage point, Trevor's reaction to the broken vase is remarkably mature—reason for Judy to be pleased rather than uneasy. Trevor's private speech shows that he steadfastly took personal responsibility for the damage, repeating again and again, "Trevor broke it. Trevor did it . . . " His unusual "out-of-body" references to himself—by proper name rather than "I" or "me"—puzzled and worried Judy. Yet notice how Trevor's remarks mirror the likely perspectives of outside observers. They reveal a concerted effort to weave others' voices into his self-directed dialogue.

Temperamentally sensitive, inhibited children like Trevor internalize standards relatively easily. On transgressing, they readily feel anxious and guilty. As long as parents refrain from harsh discipline so these emotions do not become overwhelming, inhibited preschoolers continue to show more mature conscience development, in the form of self-reported guilt and willingness to make amends after a transgression, during the school years.[45] Mild, patient discipline—polite requests, explanations, and suggestions for how to resist temptation—is generally all that is required for these children to acquire morally mature ways of thinking and behaving.

But what about relatively fearless, impulsive preschoolers, who respond to gentle interventions and reasoning with little or no emotional discomfort and remorse? Frequent use of harsh, power-assertive discipline does not work for them either. These tactics model impulsiveness and aggression. And they spark anger and resentment, which interfere with the child's ability to process adult teachings and, therefore, with internalization of standards. Furthermore, children who are repeatedly criticized, shouted at, or slapped soon learn to avoid the punishing adult. When the unpleasant parent or teacher comes their way, they quickly head in the other direction. As a result, the adult has little opportunity to engage in dialogue with the child and to encourage self-regulation through private speech.

How can adults promote conscience development in impulsive, hard-to-control preschoolers? An early warm, sensitive parent–child bond is a good predictor of conscience at age 5 in these children, as indicated by their not cheating in games and completing stories with moral themes by referring to standards (saying "I'm sorry," not taking someone else's toys, helping a child who is hurt).[46] Why is parental warmth vital? When children are so low in anxiety that typically effective parental discipline does not work well, a close parent–child bond seems to provide an alternative foundation for morality. It motivates children to listen to and internalize parental rules and to follow those rules as a means of preserving a spirit of affection and cooperation with the parent.

Impulsive preschoolers still need especially frequent, firm adult correction. But taking extra steps to build a warm, caring relationship when the child behaves well encourages the child to take over responsibility for moral behavior. As a result, the child's impulsive, rule-violating acts decline.

Private Speech and Mastering Emotions

Another important aspect of self-regulation during the preschool years involves learning to control socially unacceptable or overly intense emotion. Think back to the examples of private speech cited earlier in this chapter. The adult who whispered to herself, "Calm down . . . ," when faced with a rude sales clerk muted her own anger and impulse to lash out. When 3-year-old Rachel mumbled to herself, "Mommy's sick, Mommy's sick," she appeared to be trying to cope with rising fear and anxiety over her mother's illness.

Emotional self-regulation is crucial for two reasons. First, without it, we cannot get along well in our social world. Recognizing that favorable relationships depend on managing negative emotion, most cultures teach children to communicate positive feelings and inhibit unpleasant ones. Second, adjusting our emotions to a comfortable level is essential for accomplishing our goals.[47] If you are overly aroused, you engage in all manner of activities less effectively—driving a car, taking a test, conversing with others, or giving a speech. Too much emotion distracts us and disorganizes our behavior.

In Chapter 2, I noted that around age 2, language for talking about emotion increases. From conversing with others about inner states, preschoolers acquire a vocabulary of emotional terms and gain more knowledge about the causes and consequences of emotions. Infants and preschoolers can be seen blunting emotional arousal by covering their eyes and ears or turning away to block out unpleasant sights and sounds. As soon as children can talk about feelings, they try to use language to regulate emotion.[48] One 2 1/2-year-old reduced his discomfort at having been left with a baby-sitter by reassuring himself, "Mommy'll be back soon." On being excluded from a game by several classmates at preschool, a disappointed 3-year-old wandered off to another activity while saying, "I don't wanna play, anyway!" He eased his hurt feelings by changing his goal. As preschoolers become more aware of strategies for regulating emotion and better at applying them, emotional outbursts become less frequent.

The very factors that help children resist temptation help them manage their emotions—namely, a growing capacity to inhibit and redirect thoughts and actions, and adult guidance and examples in how to do so. Consider 4-year-old Tia, who had just gotten a face painting at an outdoor art fair. Holding her mother Sandi's hand, Tia explored the artists' booths and exuberantly showed off her elaborately decorated face until the heat of the afternoon caused her balloon to pop. As Tia's eyes welled up, Sandi bent down, dabbed away Tia's tears, and explained, "Oh, Tia, balloons aren't such a good idea when it's hot outside. We'll get another one on a cooler day. If you cry, you'll mess up your beautiful face painting."

As Tia listened to her mother point out the consequences of getting upset, her tears diminished to a trickle. Then she asked, "Can I see in your mirror? Is my face painting OK?" Tia made use of language to shift her attention away from the deflated balloon, back toward the art-fair festivities.

Through conversing with adults and watching them handle their own feelings, preschoolers pick up strategies for regulating emotion. When parents take time to prepare children for difficult experiences by describing and demonstrating ways to handle anxiety, they offer coping strategies that children can use on their own. One father, whose 5-year-old son was intensely afraid of dental treatment, read the boy an engrossing story while the dentist filled a cavity and cleaned his teeth. Afterward, the father explained, "See, Andy, if you think about other things, you won't feel so afraid!" At his next appointment, Andy tried the technique, concentrating on his birthday party. "It worked!" Andy happily reported to his father.

After children begin school, they receive much more feedback about the worth of their accomplishments and care more about peer approval. Consequently, they learn to manage negative emotion in a wider range of situations. By ages 8 to 10, children whose parents have provided effective instruction in emotion regulation typically have an adaptive set of techniques and can verbalize them.[49] In situations in which they have some control over an outcome (a difficult test or a friend who is angry), school-age children say they try to think of ways to solve the problem and, if none work, turn to others for help. When circumstances are beyond their control (having received a bad grade or awaiting a painful shot at the doctor's office), children report using private speech to distract themselves or redefine the situation.[50] To a low test score, one 9-year-old said, "I say to myself, 'Thing's could be worse. There'll be another test.'"

When children regulate emotion effectively, they feel in charge of their emotional experiences. This fosters a favorable self-image and an optimistic outlook, which assists them further in the face of emotional challenges.[51] But in addition to parenting, children's temperament is again influential. Children who experience negative emotion very intensely find it harder to use language to inhibit their feelings and to shift their attention from disturbing events. These emotionally reactive youngsters are more likely to respond to others with irritation and to get along poorly with peers.[52] Because they are difficult to rear, such children are often targets of parental anger and impatience—tactics that compound their poor emotional self-regulation.[53] They benefit from warm, patient parenting that places extra emphasis on management of emotion.

Private Speech and Social Competence

A socially competent child communicates clearly and pleasantly, is cooperative and a good listener, and considers the wants and needs of other children. Internalizing standards for good conduct and being able to delay gratification and regulate emotion contribute greatly to social competence. But other capacities enter into it as well. The communication skills and grasp of others' viewpoints that grow out of a rich history of adult–child dialogue are particularly important. They enable children to adapt to even highly challenging social circumstances, such as entering a community of people who speak another language.

COMMUNICATING IN A SECOND LANGUAGE.   Most children have a common linguistic basis for interacting with peers. But what happens when children of foreign-born parents arrive at school unable to speak the language of most of their classmates? Teachers report that such children, even after they have begun to comprehend the second language, can be strikingly quiet, rarely conversing with others. So characteristic of second-language learners is this initial speechless phase that it has come to be known as the "silent period."

What explains this curious period of silence? To find out, linguist Muriel Saville-Troike attached microphones to the collars of nine 3- to 8-year-old native speakers of Chinese, Japanese, or Korean.[54] Then she videotaped them as they first encountered English in their American classrooms, and she gathered follow-up observations at weekly intervals over the next six months. For as long as 4 to 12 weeks, two-thirds of the children were socially silent but privately talkative! They surreptitiously engaged in English conversation, using themselves as social partners. How did private speech help them use English adeptly once they felt ready to test their skills with their peers? Let's listen in and see.

Rehearsing social performance—saying to oneself what one wants to say before saying it aloud—was a common feature of the children's self-talk. Consider a Chinese 4-year-old who responded privately to the teacher's daily weather question for over a week before he raised his hand and, in a loud, self-assured voice, broadcast the weather report: "Sunny!" Several children—mostly the younger ones—spent much time repeating verbatim the phrases and sentences of others. They seemed to do so deliberately, to practice second-language communication, as illustrated by one child who, after saying "stop sign" to himself several times, turned to the teacher and declared, "Wo gang-gang shuo 'stop sign!'" ("I just now said 'stop sign!'").[55] At times, the children produced utterances they had heard but clearly did not understand, such as "Are you awesome?" Repetitions of others' speech often evolved into rhythmic sound play, as in these examples:

> S1: Jelly bean, jelly bean.
>   Jelly, jelly, jelly, jelly.
> S2: Yucky. Yucky scoop
>   Scoop scoop yucky scoop.
>   Yucky yucky yuck-yucky.[56]

Two- and 3-year-olds acquiring their first language also engage in much repetitive sound play (refer back to Peter's experimentation with the word "mushroom" on page 77 and Anthony's play with "big" and "little" on page 85). Besides offering pronunciation practice, soundplay probably helps young children attend to words and phrases so they recognize them when they next hear them socially. This assists them in deciphering meanings—a first step toward using the language for social communication.

The private speech of older second-language learners emphasized language structure, often through language pattern drills. Witness the systematic grammatical variations in the self-talk of this Japanese 5 1/2-year-old:

> S7: I finished.
>   I have finished.
>   I am finished.
>   I'm finished.
> S7: I want.
>   I paper. Paper. Paper.
>   I want paper.[57]

Notice how the child engaged in intentional transformations of sentence structures, using private speech to guide and control his language learning. At the same time, he used words and phrases meaningfully, in that his self-talk referred to the objects and activities with which he was involved.

In sum, the "silent period" is really not silent at all! During this time, private speech supports virtually all aspects of verbal communication, serving as a tool through which children create a "zone" for mastering the second language and extending their social competence.

SOCIAL PROBLEM SOLVING.   As parents and teachers well know, peer inter-action is not perfectly harmonious. Children, even when they are best friends, sometimes come into conflict. In these instances, private speech becomes an invaluable tool for solving social problems.

As we will see shortly, private speech has been observed extensively during cognitive problem solving, as children work on puzzles, picture-matching tasks, block constructions, and academic assignments. But there are few records of what children say to themselves as they grapple with challenges in peer relations—and understandably so. Smoothly crossing social hurdles—for example, gaining entry to ongoing play groups, working out disputes over toys, or resolving disagreements over facts, ideas, and beliefs—is incompatible with stopping to talk to yourself prior to deciding on a course of action. Part of getting along well with others is keeping up with rapid-paced social activity. Playmates might well be puzzled by a child who stops midstream to engage in self-talk!

As suggested by the "silent period" of second-language learning, most private speech aimed at solving social problems must take place apart from "online" social situations, which usually call for split-second decision making. When do children engage in this self-directed practice of social skills? For very young preschoolers, crib and idle-time soliloquies in part serve this purpose. Yet another important context for working out the nuances of socially skilled behavior is solitary make-believe play.

Both reserved and gregarious children draw on solitary make-believe to conjure up and experiment with social situations. When observed playing on their own in a laboratory playroom, preschoolers who seldom interact with peers in the classroom engage in more fantasized role play than do their more sociable agemates.[58] Their dialogues with make-believe partners may serve a special coping function, offering a safe context in which to practice social skills with nonthreatening "playmates" before transferring them to the real world of peer play. Consistent with this view, many preschoolers who interact little with peers and whom adults and peers judge to be shy are not socially anxious at all. When they want to, they can break away from their usual pattern of solitary play and interact skillfully with peers.[59] Make-believe may be an important means through which socially reserved children experiment with social skills and become more comfortable enacting them.

Nevertheless, solitary play—especially make-believe—is often a source of worry to parents and teachers, in much the same way that frequent self-talk sparks concern about whether a child is psychologically intact. "My daughter spends most of her time by herself drawing pictures and playing with dolls, even at preschool when children are all around her. Is she normal?" a mother of a 3-year-old once asked me. Only certain types of nonsocial activity—aimless wandering, repetitive motor action, and apprehensively hovering near peers without joining in their play—are signs of immaturity and cause for concern during the preschool years.

A close look at the private, imaginary worlds of highly sociable children reveals that many of them also use solitary make-believe for creating and playing out social scenarios. Several studies indicate that imaginary companions—fantasized friends endowed with humanlike qualities, such as a unique personality and voice, that persist for several weeks to months—are particularly common among gregarious children, although reserved and socially average children create them as well. According to recent estimates, between 25 and 45 percent of 3- to 7-year-olds have at least one imaginary friend, and many have more than one.[60]

Psychologist Marjorie Taylor, who has interviewed children extensively about their imaginary companions, reports that the characteristics of these fantasized buddies are highly diverse. Consider one 4-year-old, who created Nutsy and Nutsy, a pair of birds living outside her bedroom window. The two creatures were "talkative, raucous, and fun," quickly becoming part of the child's family and often going along on outings.[61] In another instance, Leanne, a 7-year-old I know, transformed her bike into a confidante named Betsy, who listened patiently as Leanne rode to and from school while mulling over daily concerns—the best strategy for securing a seat next to a favored lunch partner in the school cafeteria, what present to bring to the holiday gift exchange, and what Betsy and Leanne might talk about on the way home from school. Some children transform their stuffed animals into special friends. Still others create an imaginary personality and act it out themselves.

Regardless of the imaginary character's traits, the pretend play is generally vivid and elaborate. And it often reflects remarkable social competence. Taylor, for example, described the childhood memories of one of her graduate students, who invented a complex network of relations among her stuffed animals, which she mediated by encouraging considerate, sympathetic behavior. In one instance, she worried that the animals would be jealous of a particularly attractive member of this fantasized peer society, so she told them that she loved each equally. Larger animals, who might bully smaller ones, were instructed to be kind and gentle. And when one animal was chosen to go on a trip away from home, the others were assured that they, too, would have a turn.[62] Yet another inventor of an imaginary friend relied on his companion—an invisible little girl named Margarine who had long yellow braids that dragged on the floor behind her—to help him adjust to a new play group and, later, to a new set of preschool peers after a move across the country. Margarine came along during these anxiety-arousing transitions, invariably serving as a friendly, comforting companion until the small boy had established gratifying peer ties.[63]

Although imaginary companions and their creators are good friends, children can at times be critical of and impatient with them. Parents who know about their children's imaginary friends (many parents are totally unaware) often say they have witnessed the child arguing with the companion, trying to put the brakes on the friend's annoying and disruptive behaviors.[64] Imaginary friends have been known to make fun of others, refuse to share, stage temper tantrums, and even throw another child's favorite toy down the toilet—all very counterproductive ways of solving social problems! Their creators, much like their own parents, are faced with the task of discouraging these wayward acts.

Why might sociable children be particularly disposed to invent imaginary companions? According to Taylor, these invented creatures are fun, particularly for children who enjoy being with others. As a result, when alone, a friendly child is likely to make up a play partner to pass time in a pleasurable way. As children do so, their imaginary relationships become contexts for working out social problems. This makes it possible for the child and his or her fanciful playmate to continue their friendship—in much the same way that real friendships survive disagreements when partners resolve conflicts constructively.[65] When imaginary companions misbehave, harnessing their unruliness may help young children better manage their own social behavior in similar circumstances.

Although parents often say they do not want to encourage their children's imaginary friends, research suggests that these make-believe creations contribute to the development of self-regulation. Children with imaginary companions can better delay gratification than their less imaginative agemates can. When asked to sit quietly in a game, they do so for a longer time.[66] Perhaps the sustained attention required to devise and play with imaginary friends equips preschoolers with the capacity to inhibit impulses and wait. Children with imaginary companions are also advanced in their understanding of mental life, including appreciation of others' perspectives and of false belief.[67] This knowledge, so fundamental for getting along with others, is probably fostered by the elaborate negotiations that take place with imaginary friends, just as it is promoted by dialogues with real social partners (see Chapter 2).

In view of these benefits, it is not surprising that preschoolers who in solitary moments turn to fantasized friends for amusement engage in higher rates of peer interaction and more complex pretend play.[68] Undoubtedly they bring their social skills to bear on the imaginary companions they create, and this enhances their social skills further. In a recent study, my graduate students and I found that 4-year-olds with imaginary friends were better than their peers without these make-believe playmates at thinking up effective strategies for solving social problems. This social problem-solving advantage was particularly great for preschoolers who interacted infrequently with peers and who had one of these special friends[69]—an outcome consistent with the positive contribution of private make-believe to early social development.

In addition to social problem solving, imaginary companions foster other competencies that are supported by pretend play in general; I will take those up in Chapter 4. Indeed, observations during preschool free-choice periods reveal that fantasy play evokes the most private speech of all activities.[70] As I'll show in Chapter 4, Vygotsky regarded make-believe play as a vital context for the development of self-regulation—a conjecture supported by the rich, self-directed language that emerges as children spin fantasized characters, situations, and story lines.

Private Speech and Problem Solving

Private speech is an extraordinarily flexible mental tool. Think back to the Asian children who were learning a second language (English) and who spent weeks preparing for social engagement with their American peers by talking quietly to themselves in English. When focused on language and social concerns, such as how to enter a peer conversation or a game, bilingual children speak privately in their second language. But when immersed in solving cognitive problems, they generally talk to themselves in their native tongue[71]—the most facile instrument available to them for regulating thought and action.

Problem solving has been the most popular context for observing children's private speech. Researchers have watched carefully as children solve puzzles, sort and match pictures and shapes, make drawings, build models out of small blocks, and work on academic assignments—especially math problems, which present them with constant hurdles to overcome.

To evoke private speech, a task must be neither too easy nor too hard. Rather, it must be within the "zone"—appropriately demanding so that initially, the child benefits from an expert partner's scaffolding and gradually takes over that scaffolding role through self-guiding private speech.

When researchers carefully choose tasks so they are within each child's "zone," private speech is abundant.[72] Recall the study mentioned earlier in this chapter, in which my graduate student and I asked 4- and 5-year-olds to assemble Lego blocks into reproductions of models. While planning the study, I read a news report about a 5-year-old who had built miniature scenes out of thousands of Legos, producing elaborate boat harbors, factories, and cities. Had this young Lego expert participated in our study, he certainly would not have engaged in private speech! He was so familiar with Lego-building that the cognitive operations required to construct our 50-piece models would have been well practiced and automatic; he would no longer have needed verbal guidance to complete the task. Alternatively, most 2- and 3-year-olds would have found our Lego tasks much too difficult; they could not possibly complete them without a great deal of assistance from an adult. Here, too, private speech would not be expected.

When we pretested children and selected only those who were "Lego novices"—who could assemble no more than the beginnings of a Lego model (10 to 12 blocks) in a 10-minute period—all the 4- and 5-year-olds talked to themselves during our Lego-building tasks.[73] Other researchers have confirmed that private speech is especially prevalent when tasks are in the child's "zone"— cognitively demanding but within range of mastery. For example, preschoolers talk to themselves most when working on puzzles of intermediate difficulty. They rarely use self-talk when puzzles are very easy or very hard.[74]

Vygotsky's original investigations, and those of recent researchers, suggest that during the preschool years, when private and social speech are not yet completely differentiated, the presence of another person encourages private speech during problem solving.[75] Think back to 2 1/2-year-old Ellie's tower-building, scaffolded by her mother, described on page 80. Ellie engaged in extensive self-talk while her mother sat nearby. Had her mother or another partner not been available, Ellie's private speech would probably have evaporated. As children progress through the school years, circumstances conducive to self-talk may change dramatically. Once social and private speech are clearly distinct, children (much like adults) may be reluctant to talk aloud to themselves within earshot of others.

Still, self-talk is omnipresent in preschool and primary-school classrooms. If you stop and listen, even during quiet "work periods," you will hear a persistent, verbal undercurrent as children build, draw, read, and solve math problems. Teachers who try to subdue this rumble for fear that self-talkers might disturb their neighbors generally find that the vocal din is irrepressible. When told to "work quietly," children reduce the volume of their utterances to whispers, but the talking persists.[76] The relentlessness of private speech is yet another sign of its significance in children's development.

What do children actually say to themselves while working on challenging problems? Usually, they describe their actions, instruct themselves, ask questions, and answer them in words or behavior. "Put the green one here," "Wait, where's this piece go? Oh, I see," "Ready for the next one!" are typical private comments during problem solving. If reading is part of the task, children just beginning to decipher the printed page may read aloud.[77] These forms of private speech certainly seem to be directed at regulating thought and action. In addition, expressions that involve emotional release—"Oh, phooey, why can't I get that?"—can be heard after children make errors or when they have trouble deciding what to do.[78] Even these comments may be beneficial if they help children manage feelings of frustration and remain productively engaged in the task.

Nevertheless, we might reasonably question the value of any self-talk—regardless of how self-regulating it appears to be—that does not lead to positive changes in behavior and task performance. Yet researchers repeatedly find that the more children speak to themselves in a task-relevant fashion, the more competent their problem solving is when they are followed up from several days to as much as a year later. This positive relationship between private speech and gains in performance applies to preschool and school-age children working on a wide variety of tasks, including building Lego models, solving puzzles, classifying pictures and shapes, and completing daily math assignments.[79]

In one series of studies, my team of observers carefully recorded the private speech and behavior of first to third graders as they worked on math problems in their classrooms. Then graduate student Jennifer Bivens and I followed the first graders as they became second and third graders. The classrooms teemed with private speech as the children tackled their math assignments. Every child talked to him or herself—on average, 60 percent of the time.[80]

Our results indicated that first graders who made many self-guiding comments, either aloud or quietly, did better at second-grade math. By second grade, internalization of private speech was well under way; children often muttered and whispered as they worked. Second graders who often engaged in such mumbling grasped third-grade math more easily. Overall, children whose self-talk progressed most rapidly from audible remarks about the task to inner speech were more advanced in their ability to sustain attention and to inhibit distracting body movements (such as squirming in their seats and tapping or chewing their pencils). The development of private speech and self-regulation of behavior thus went hand in hand.

DEVELOPMENT OF PRIVATE SPEECH

Between the ages of 3 and 10, private speech gradually becomes softer and briefer, changing into whispers and lip movements—consistent with the internalization process Vygotsky described. By mid- to late-elementary school, the precise content of children's self-directed comments during academic work is hard to make out. Follow a child's mastery of a single task, and you will see that private speech undergoes similar changes. When the task is new and difficult, children speak aloud a great deal. As their performance improves, audible private speech declines in favor of the mutterings of inner speech.[81]

What encourages children's frequent use and eventual internalization of these self-directed dialogues? Warm, supportive teaching, challenging tasks within the child's "zone," the child's confidence that he or she can succeed, and the freedom to talk to oneself in learning environments are all involved. As I emphasized in Chapter 1, important developments in children's lives result from systems of influences, both internal and external to the child, with no single contributing factor being supreme. Private speech is no exception.

Nevertheless, the long-term path of private speech development is not a smooth, unfettered journey toward highly condensed and efficient internalized dialogues. Instead, the extent to which children talk to themselves varies widely in different activities, and it shows some curious peaks and troughs across the ages at which it has been studied. In no preschool activity is private speech more prevalent than in make-believe play, where it remains high at least through age 6, perhaps because of the opportunities fantasy play affords for children to create challenges for themselves[82]—a feature we'll take up in the next chapter. In contrast, self-talk during cognitive problem solving decreases between the ages of 3 and 6 as preschoolers become more skillful model builders, puzzle solvers, and picture matchers.[83]

Entry into first grade sparks another high water mark for private speech. In classrooms, it doubles in frequency from preschool and kindergarten to primary school.[84] Reading, writing, and mathematics are rich contexts for verbal self-regulation as children become immersed in manipulating and controlling the symbolic systems of their culture. School-age children's reliance on private speech for learning may be an important reason that flexibly organized classrooms, in which teachers provide supportive guidance while children work on challenging projects in small groups or independently, are particularly conducive to motivation, achievement, and positive school attitudes.[85] These conditions permit children to apply the self-directed dialogues essential for handling new academic demands at the start of formal schooling. As children master basic academic skills and use them to ease other school tasks, private speech trails off.

Still, great variation exists in children's penchant for engaging in private speech—individual differences that as yet have not been fully explained. We do know that preschoolers who are intellectually advanced (as indicated by higher IQ scores) display more task-relevant private speech during problem solving. Then, in elementary school, these children talk to themselves less often while working on academic tasks. In other words, high-IQ children are ahead in private speech development.[86] When faced with a new task, they deploy self-guiding speech adroitly and arrive at effective strategies quickly. This reduces their need to use private speech in the future.

In contrast, children whose intellectual development is slower rely on self-talk over an especially long age span.[87] And school-age children who are temperamentally impulsive or who suffer from disabilities that impede their learning also continue to engage in highly audible private speech after their classmates' self-talk has softened and abbreviated.[88] Why is the development of private speech delayed for these children? If we keep in mind that cognitive challenge stimulates private speech, then the high rates of self-talk among children with learning difficulties are understandable. These children find sustaining attention and completing academic work harder than do their peers, so they more often call on private speech to aid their efforts. In fact, many of these children appear academically engaged *only* while talking to themselves! I'll take up the special qualities of their private speech in Chapter 5.

In view of wide individual differences in private-speech development, to the oft-asked question, Is something wrong with my child because he frequently talks to himself?, we must answer: There is no special age at which using private speech to surmount challenges is immature or inappropriate. By the end of elementary school, as many as 20 to 30 percent of children remain frequent self-talkers during problem solving.[89]

Indeed, private speech is a central tool of self-regulation throughout development. Both children and adults engage in rich, inner dialogues as they go about their everyday lives. When seemingly intractable problems arise, they externalize their private ruminations—especially those that accentuate new, not yet understood aspects of their experiences.[90] Their remarks draw on their history of interaction with more expert cultural members, helping them focus their attention, mentally represent important aspects of a situation, become more conscious of their actions, recall and apply previously successful strategies, and inhibit impulses in favor of weighing alternatives and planning for the future. In sum, throughout life, private speech aids us in sustaining the intimate link between our sociocultural surroundings and our inner mental worlds and in attaining ever-higher levels of mastery over our thought and behavior.

NURTURING CHILDREN'S PRIVATE SPEECH

How can our current knowledge of private speech guide us in supporting children's learning and development? The evidence as a whole indicates that private speech is a problem-solving tool universally available to children who grow up in stimulating, socially interactive environments. Several factors—the communicative support available to the child, the demands of the task, its social context, and individual characteristics of the child—govern the extent and ease with which any one child uses self-directed speech to guide thought and action.

A first step to helping children use private speech to aid learning is for parents and teachers to be aware of its significance and how it develops. Private speech is healthy, adaptive, and essential behavior, and some children need to use it more than others. Still, many adults continue to regard children's self-talk as meaningless, socially unacceptable conduct—even a sign of mental illness! As a result, they often discourage children from talking to themselves. Alternatively, adults who know that private speech aids self-regulation at times err in trying to train it, especially in children who have trouble managing their behavior. These self-talk training programs have not been successful.[91] Adaptive private speech grows out of dialogues with more expert partners—namely, the sensitive scaffolding and the elaborative narrative style described in Chapter 2. It cannot be artificially glued into children's psyches by urging them to talk aloud and then silently.

Instead, the following experiences, which promote children's engagement with others and active, goal directed learning, encourage adaptive use of private speech:

• *Social play involving rich, verbal give-and-take.* The earliest forms of private speech—crib speech, make-believe dialogues, and experimentation with language—emerge out of playful social opportunities and conversation. In particular, fantasy play, in which children apply their communication skills while experimenting with different roles and situations, lays the foundation for diverse forms of self-communication.

• *Adult modeling and teaching of strategies for emotional self-regulation, resistance to temptation, and problem solving.* As adults describe, demonstrate, and justify ways to inhibit impulses and effectively manage behavior, children can integrate those strategies into their private speech. Joint adult–child activities and adult monitoring of children during play and problem solving abound with opportunities for teaching self-regulation. To capitalize on these moments, parents—as I have underscored before—must generously spend time with children.

Joint storybook reading is a particularly fruitful context for encouraging self-regulation, not just because it fosters language and literacy development but because children's stories are filled with characters who rely on private speech to overcome difficulties. A classic example is Watty Piper's *The Little Engine that Could,* in which a train carrying toys and food breaks down and needs help completing its journey over a steep mountain. In attempting to reach her goal, the little engine speaks to herself:

> Puff, puff, chug, chug, went the little blue engine. "I think I can—I think I can—I think I can—I think I can—I think I can—I think I can—I think I can—I think I can—I think I can." Up, up, up. Faster and faster and faster and faster the little engine climbed until at last they reached the top of the mountain.[92]

In another story, Elaine McMann Willoughby's *Boris and the Monsters,* the hero uses private speech to conquer his fear of the dark. Alone in his bedroom with the lights out and imagining monsters all around, Boris tries to shout, "There are no monsters!" But his fear is so intense that his words are reduced to a whisper. When his sympathetic father buys him a puppy to protect him from the monsters, Boris's private speech becomes more effective. Referring to his puppy, he speaks first to others and then to himself:

> "I will name him Ivan—Ivan the Terrible [statement to others]," said Boris. "Now I'll feel safe since Ivan the Terrible will keep away the monsters [message to self]. He even looks fierce now!"[93]

At the end of the story, Boris announces to his parents:

> "I do not need a light with Ivan the Terrible. Besides . . . THERE ARE NO MONSTERS IN THIS HOUSE!"[94]

In these storybook passages and many others, children can see explicitly how private speech helps characters grapple with difficulties, regulate their behavior, and attain their goals.

• *Careful listening by parents and teachers to children's private speech.* Parents and teachers who listen carefully to children's self-talk, evaluating its content for relevant new meanings and noticing whether it diminishes as children gain in competence, acquire information that enables them to scaffold more effectively. When children use guiding phrases derived from their interactions with adults, they signal that the task is within their "zone" and that they are ready to take over more responsibility for it. At the same time, children who rely on private speech to a greater extent than is typical for their age or who use high rates of immature forms irrelevant to their current activity could benefit from extra adult support and guidance.

• *Learning environments that permit children to be verbally active during problem solving.* When formal learning experiences begin in primary school, children are expected to sustain attention for longer periods, and more of the school day is devoted to academic pursuits of gradually increasing difficulty. As we have seen, one way children cope with this change is through greater use of self-guiding private speech. Teachers who try to suppress this speech by insisting that children work silently discourage an indispensable tool for learning.

In the first few grades, when a great many children speak aloud while working on assignments, a self-talking child does not bother nearby classmates, who are also engaging in much private speech. In fact, younger children seem to benefit from the private comments of their peers. Self-talk in one child often stimulates it in another, and children may pick up new ideas from their neighbors' remarks that they incorporate into their own self-guiding comments.[95]

With age, children transform their private speech into inner verbal thought and work more quietly. Nevertheless, under conditions of increased stress or task difficulty, they again talk aloud to organize their behavior and acquire new skills. School-age children who are less cognitively mature speak aloud to themselves long beyond the period in which their classmates internalize most of their private speech. For these children, teachers can arrange special areas in the classroom where task-related verbal activity can take place freely.

Once viewed as inconsequential—even disturbed—behavior, today private speech is recognized as a central force in development. In talking to themselves, children build a bridge between their social and mental worlds as they strive to become competent, self-regulated members of their cultural communities.

Learning Through Make-Believe Play

Two days a week, Kevin leaves his office 45 minutes early to take charge of his 2-year-old daughter, Sophie, while her mother, a university professor, teaches a late class. One balmy spring afternoon, Kevin retrieved Sophie at her child-care center and drove the 15-minute route home. Invited to look in on Sophie's play, I met the pair at the front door and nestled into a rocking chair from which to observe unobtrusively.

After downing the last bite of her snack, Sophie grabbed Kevin's hand and led him across the family room to a rug lined on two sides by shelves filled with books, stuffed animals, and other play props. Sophie moved a toy horse and cow inside a small, enclosed fence that she and Kevin had put together the day before. Then she turned the animals on their sides and moved them toward each other.

"Why are horse and cow lying down?" Kevin asked.

"'Cause they're tired," Sophie answered, pushing the two animals closer together.

"Oh, yes," Kevin affirmed. Then, building on Sophie's theme, he placed a teddy bear on another part of the rug and offered, "I think Ted's tired, too. I'm going to start a bed over here for some other animals."

Sophie turned toward the teddy bear, lifted his paw, and exclaimed, "She wants a lollipop to hold in her hand!"

"A lollipop in her hand? We haven't got any lollipops, have we?" answered Kevin.

"Laura has!" declared Sophie, glancing at me.

"Has Laura got a lollipop?" Kevin queried.

"Yes! She's got all of those, and a swing and a table, too!" Sophie remarked, referring to my chair, which rocked back and forth next to an end table.

"Maybe this could be a make-believe lollipop," suggested Kevin, placing a round piece on the end of a long TinkerToy stick and handing the structure to Sophie

"That's a lollipop," agreed Sophie, placing it in the paw of the teddy bear.

"Can she suck that while she's going off to sleep?" asked Kevin. "Do you think that's what she wants?"

"It's a pacifier," explained Sophie, renaming the object.

"A pacifier, do you think? The pacifier might help her get to sleep," Kevin confirmed.

"This long, long pacifier," Sophie answered, picking up the TinkerToy structure, looking at its long stick, and pausing as if to decide what to do next.

"Leprechaun is looking pretty tired," suggested Kevin, laying Sophie's stuffed leprechaun next to the teddy bear. "What do you think?"

"He wants a lollipop, too!"

"Oh, he wants a lollipop as well. What are we going to use for a lollipop for the leprechaun?" asked Kevin.

Pressing the teddy bear's and the leprechaun's arms together and the lollipop-turned-pacifier between them, Sophie readily came up with a solution. "He's sharing," she affirmed.

"Oh, they'll share! All right," Kevin agreed.

This scene is but a small excerpt from Sophie and Kevin's joint play session, which persisted for more than an hour—a remarkably long time for a 2-year-old to sustain any activity. Yet when the TV set is switched off and children are free to do as they choose, most preschoolers readily become absorbed in pretending. At times, their involvement is so intense that on being interrupted they react with shock and dismay, rejecting an adult who otherwise would be welcomed with joy and affection. One mother reported to me that her daughter Mattie reserved the period after she awoke in the morning for conversing with dolls and other imaginary characters. If a parent entered too soon to help her wash and dress, she dismissed the intruder, proclaiming sharply, "Busy! Don't stop my dollies!" Only smooth and clever entry into the make-believe activity—for example, inviting the dolls and stuffed animals to get up for breakfast—could lure Mattie into starting the "real" part of her day without protest.

The years of early childhood are often called the high season of imaginative play, and aptly so, since make-believe blossoms during this time, evolving from simple, imitative acts into highly elaborate, imaginative plots involving complex coordination of roles. Eminent child development theorists of the past attached great importance to the role of make-believe play in early development. All were convinced that anything so compelling and engrossing in the life of the young child must be profoundly significant.

THE ROLE OF MAKE-BELIEVE PLAY IN CHILDREN'S LIVES

Among influential explanations of why preschoolers are so drawn to pretending, Freud's psychoanalytic theory and Piaget's cognitive theory held sway for much of the twentieth century. Although each has made valuable contributions to our understanding, a new, more powerful view of the meaning of young children's play has arrived on the scene, thanks to Vygotsky's sociocultural theory.

The Psychoanalytic View: Wish Fulfillment and Insight into Social Roles

Freud regarded make-believe play as a form of pleasurable wish fulfillment that allows children to act out uncertainties, anxieties, and hoped for outcomes and, therefore, to master frightening and frustrating events. Young children, Freud noted, often revisit anxiety-provoking experiences, such as a trip to the doctor's office or discipline by a parent, but with roles reversed so the child is in command and compensates for unpleasant happenings. Sophie's parents, aware of the previous day's events, might have judged her pretend focus on bedtime, lollipops, and pacifiers to contain at least an element of wish fulfillment. The evening before, they had told her, "Only *one* lolly from the candy dish," and she had complained at having to go to bed while her parents continued to talk and laugh with their guests.

Psychoanalyst Erik Erikson built on Freud's vision, expanding his picture of make-believe. According to Erikson, children draw on fantasy play to find out about themselves and their social world.[1] In all cultures, children act out family roles and highly visible occupations — police officer, doctor, and nurse in our society; rabbit hunter and potter among the Hopi Indians; and hut builder and spear maker among the Baka of West Africa.[2] As they do so, they enter a small social organization whose members must cooperate to achieve common goals. And through observing and emulating admired adult figures, preschoolers internalize social norms and gain a sense of their future, of what they can become and how they can contribute to society.

Piaget's View: Exercising a New Symbolic Capacity

Piaget acknowledged the emotional function of play, and he agreed that through pretending, children become familiar with social-role possibilities. But he is best known for stressing the symbolic nature of make-believe. Pretending, Piaget pointed out, is a vital means of mentally representing the world that, along with gestures, language, and drawings, develops rapidly in early childhood. Through it, children practice and strengthen their capacity to represent their experiences.[3] For example, when Sophie pretended to put the animals to bed and used a TinkerToy to stand for a lollipop, she represented in her mind what formerly she could experience only directly—by going to bed or sucking a lollipop. Practicing and solidifying modes of representation, Piaget emphasized, make it possible for the child to free thought from the here and now; create larger images of reality that take into account past, present, and future; and transform those images mentally in the service of logical thinking.

Nevertheless, Piaget was convinced that by itself, make-believe play does little to advance children's development. Rather, children merely exercise playfully the symbols they have acquired in other contexts.[4] Much like his view of private speech as egocentric and nonsocial, Piaget believed that at first pretend play is a solitary activity in which the child uses highly personal symbols that cannot easily be interpreted by others. Sociodramatic play, involving joint make-believe with a partner, Piaget claimed, is not under way until age 3. As with other aspects of Piaget's theory, the direction of development for make-believe is from purely individual, egocentric symbols to social play and shared understanding.

Yet think back to 2-year-old Sophie's pretending. Sophie is socially engaged throughout! From the start, she draws Kevin into the activity, explains her pretend actions so he can build on them, and responds cooperatively and appropriately to Kevin's suggestions, as he does to hers. Vygotsky's theory has been the wellspring of our recent appreciation of the profoundly social nature of even very young children's imaginative play—and its wide-ranging influence on cognitive and social development.

Vygotsky's View: A Zone of Proximal Development

Vygotsky viewed make-believe play as crucial in children's learning.[5] He regarded it as a unique, broadly influential "zone" in which children try out a wide variety of challenging skills and acquire many culturally valued competencies. Consider the following frequently quoted remarks, taken from a brief lecture in which Vygotsky eloquently summed up his conviction that pretend play is a central force in children's development:

> [Make-believe] play creates a zone of proximal development in the child. In play, the child always behaves beyond his average age, above his daily behavior; in play it is as though he were a head taller than himself. As in the focus of a magnifying glass, play contains all developmental tendencies in condensed form and is itself a major source of development.[6]

Why did Vygotsky say that make-believe play creates a "zone" in which the child is "a head taller than himself"? If we stop every now and then to watch children at play, we can see what Vygotsky meant. Recall how Sophie satisfied both teddy bear's and leprechaun's desire for a lollipop, when just one Tinker-Toy lollipop was available. She had them share, a very mature response for a 2-year-old. In everyday life, Sophie, like many Western children her age, finds sharing to be difficult.

As another illustration, consider 5-year-old David, who has trouble sitting still during group storytime in kindergarten. He leans over and talks to the other children. In spite of the teacher's frequent prompting, he can't stay seated for more than a couple of minutes. But when David plays school with several of his friends, he can sit and pay attention for much longer—perhaps as long as 10 minutes. Play provides the roles, rules, and scenarios that enable David to concentrate at a much higher level than he typically does in nonpretend contexts.

UNIQUE FEATURES OF MAKE-BELIEVE PLAY

How do the make-believe scenes just described, and others like them, serve as major sources of development? To answer this question, Vygotsky pointed out, we must identify the distinctive features of make-believe play—those that make it unique among young children's experiences.

The widespread belief, originating with Freud, that play is pleasurable wish fulfillment characterizes certain playful pursuits—for example, acting out high-status roles, such as doctor, parent, or teacher, and thereby exercising authority over others instead of being directed and controlled. But not all fantasy qualifies as wish fulfillment. In the sociodramatic scenarios that young children create, a doctor must have patients to inoculate, a parent must have children to discipline, and a teacher must have pupils to do assignments. Make-believe roles are not equally pleasurable—a feature of cooperation that is as true in everyday life as it is in fantasy play.

Even when make-believe does fulfill a child's wishes, such pleasure is not unique to play. Many other activities, such as eating a favorite treat, being granted the undivided attention and affection of a parent, and listening to an exciting story, are at least as gratifying and sometimes more so than pretending. Indeed, imaginative wish fulfillment can, at times, be counterproductive. In well-known research on children's ability to delay gratification, psychologist Walter Mischel and his collaborators showed preschoolers some delicious marshmallows and told them that they could have one now or several if they waited until later. Children who spent the waiting period in a wish-fulfillment mode, thinking about what it would be like to eat those tasty marshmallows, were far less likely to wait patiently and successfully than children who turned their attention away from the treats and thought about other things.[7] In this situation and others, being caught up in fantasized wish fulfillment interferes with attaining larger, more rewarding outcomes in real life—ones that would have been realized had the child been able to exercise imaginative self-restraint.

What about Piaget's belief that through make-believe, young children solidify their new symbolic capacity? A burgeoning ability to use symbols certainly contributes to the emergence of make-believe, and (as we'll soon see) make-believe does much to extend young children's symbolic skills. Nevertheless, mental representation is yet another feature that is not exclusive to play. As we have already noted, it also characterizes gestures, language, and artistic pursuits as well as beginning literacy—preschoolers' first efforts to make sense of written symbols.

Vygotsky concluded that make-believe play has two crucial features that distinguish it from other childhood activities. First, the creation of imaginary situations in play helps children separate internal ideas from the objects and events for which they stand. Once young children realize that words, gestures, and other symbols are distinct from external reality, they are well on the way to using those representations as effective mental tools, calling on them to overcome impulses. Second, a careful look at children's pretend scenarios reveals that make-believe play is, above all, rule-based play. Inspired by experiences in their families and communities, children continually devise and follow social rules in imaginary situations. In doing so, they strive to bring their behavior in line with social expectations and acquire the rules of social life.

Consider these unique, complementary ingredients of make-believe. The first strengthens children's *internal capacity* to become civilized and socially responsible. The second provides children with powerful *external pressures* to act in socially desirable ways. Together, these features make fantasy play a supreme contributor to the development of self-regulation—one that extends the impact of adult teaching and example more than any other early childhood activity. To understand make-believe play's role in development, let's take a closer look at each of its unique features.

Overcoming Impulsive Action

Fantasy play makes its appearance in the second year of life, a time when children must start to suppress impulses and accept that certain desires will remain unsatisfied. In infancy, most of the child's wants—for food, stimulation, affection, and comfort—are gratified quickly. Such prompt satisfaction grants babies the security that their basic needs will be met. As a result, they do not have to be preoccupied with those needs and, instead, can turn their attention outward, toward acquiring physical, cognitive, and social skills. Warm, responsive caregiving also promotes a view of parents as kind and compassionate—an outlook essential for motivating children to emulate and take direction from parents.

Between 1 and 2 years of age, children begin to acquire language, greater understanding of the consequences of their actions, and the ability to comply with others' requests and directives. Consequently, caregivers' expectations change. They increasingly insist that children engage in socially appropriate conduct. During the very period in which children must learn to subordinate their desires to social life, imaginative play flourishes. For Vygotsky, this synchrony between socialization and make-believe is no coincidence. Pretend play fortifies children's capacity to use ideas to guide behavior. The young, immature child runs after a ball that rolls into the street, without considering consequences; drops toys on the spot when another activity engages her; and grabs an attractive object from a playmate, without regard for the playmate's rights and feelings. Make-believe play, Vygotsky asserted, helps preschoolers conquer these impulses by granting the child repeated practice "in acting independently of what he sees."[8]

Just how does imaginative play help children distinguish ideas from the enticing stimuli around them and use thought to guide behavior? According to Vygotsky, the *object substitutions* that permeate children's make-believe are crucial in this process. While pretending, children continually use one object to represent another. By making a TinkerToy stand for a lollypop or a folded blanket stand for a sleeping baby, children step back from reality. The TinkerToy becomes a means for separating the idea "lollipop" from a real lollipop; the blanket becomes a means for separating the idea "baby" from a real baby. This severing of thought from objects and actions occurs because, in play, children change an object's usual meaning. In calling the TinkerToy a lollipop, Sophie conjured up the idea of a lollipop and used it to alter the TinkerToy's identity. As a result, rather than reacting impulsively to the sight of a lollipop, Sophie relied on ideas to regulate the lollipop's very existence—and the teddy bear's, the leprechaun's, and her own actions toward it!

At first, children find it difficult to distinguish words and other mental symbols from the objects and actions to which they refer. Parents seem to realize this when, in the presence of their 1- or 2-year-old, they phrase things this way to an adult companion: "After we finish running errands, let's stop off for some i-c-e c-r-e-a-m." Ask parents why they spell rather than say the words, and they remark, "If you say 'ice cream,' he'll want it now. He won't be able to wait!"

Children's earliest efforts at make-believe also reveal how challenging they find the task of detaching thought from reality. Initially, object substitutions are closely tied to the real things they represent. Toddlers between ages 1 1/2 and 2 generally use only realistic-looking objects while pretending—a toy telephone to talk into or a cup to drink from.[9] Once, I handed a 21-month-old a small wooden block, put another to my ear, and called her on the phone: "Ring! Ring! Hello, Lynnay!" She responded by throwing down the block and turning to another activity. Yet when given a plastic replica of a push-button phone, Lynnay readily put the receiver to her ear and pretended to converse.

Around age 2, children begin to pretend with less realistic toys, such as a block for a telephone. And sometime during the third year, they can imagine objects and events with little or no support from the real world, as when they say to a play partner, "I'm calling Susie on the phone!" while dialing with their hands or without acting out the event at all. Between ages 3 and 4, this detachment of make-believe symbols from the real-life conditions they stand for is well developed. Let's look in on 4-year-old Alison as she draws her father into a make-believe scenario. Notice how Alison's imagination ranges far beyond the immediate play props before her—a tea set, a toy truck, and an ambulance. In the span of a few moments, she conjures up a fantastic, multicolored house and room and travels to a distant land where she witnesses a cataclysmic event!

Alison: *(while stacking multicolored plastic spoons)* I don't need my house
     painted. It just got painted today!
Father: Just got painted today?
Alison: Yep.
Father: What color was it painted?
Alison: It's kind of, it's got brown and red in it.
Father: Brown and red?

Alison: And a little peach color.

Father: A little peach color? What color is your bedroom?

Alison: Well, it's yellow and orange and red.

Father: That sounds pretty.

Alison: All mixed together!

Father: Oh, all mixed together.

Alison: Well, I have a dump truck. Or—what else would you like? An ambulance? *(Picks up toy ambulance and hands it to her father)*

Father: Did someone get in an accident?

Alison: Well, yes. *(Then, referring to a newspaper report her father had mentioned earlier in the day)* This morning, it said *(changes to a low-pitched, somber tone of voice)*, "Two trains crashing—in India."

Vygotsky maintained that in detaching symbols from objects and actions, make-believe play helps children use thought to choose deliberately among alternative courses of behavior. In play, Alison *thinks about* paint colors, which need not be the color of her real room. She learns that you can consider possibilities and choose among them, thereby controlling eventual outcomes.

Imaginative play, Vygotsky noted, also functions as a bridge from the concrete thought of the preschool and early school years to mature "adult thought, which can be totally free of real situations."[10] In helping children disengage thought from reality, pretend play is vital preparation for the much later development of abstract thinking, in which symbols are manipulated and hypothetical ideas are evaluated without referring to currently existing, real world conditions.[11]

When imagination eventually combines with the logical, abstract reasoning powers of adolescence, the stage is set for creativity. A truly creative work is both original and sensible; its novelty is culturally meaningful and useful. Almost always, creativity demands a high degree of self-regulation—pulling together previously unrelated ideas, critically evaluating those ideas, and persevering in the face of obstacles.[12] In make-believe, Alison experimented with the first step of this multistep process when she melded news of the train crash in India with the toy ambulance before her. As we will see shortly, people renowned for their creative accomplishments often report that make-believe play was a frequent, highly influential aspect of their early development.

Acquiring and Enacting the Rules of Social Life

Had Vygotsky lived long enough to become familiar with Erik Erikson's psychoanalytic theory, he would have agreed that make-believe play teaches children about social roles and provides them with insights into what they can become in their society. But Vygotsky was far more explicit about just how pretending helps children acquire dispositions that foster eager, willing participation in social life.

Children's imaginative play, Vygotsky pointed out, contains an interesting paradox. In play, preschoolers seem to do what they most feel like doing, and to an outside observer, their play appears free and spontaneous. Nevertheless, pretend play demands that children act against their immediate impulses because they must subject themselves to the rules of the make-believe scene.[13] A child pretending to go to sleep follows the rules of bedtime behavior. Another child imagining herself to be a mother and a doll to be a baby conforms to the rules of parental behavior. And a child playing astronaut obeys the rules of shuttle launch and space walk.

In this sense, make-believe is not really "free play," as we often assume it to be. Instead, its very essence is self-restraint—voluntarily following social rules. While pretending, Vygotsky explained, children repeatedly face conflicts between the rules of the make-believe situation and what they would do if they could act impulsively, and they usually decide in favor of the rules. When tired, Sophie's teddy bear and leprechaun don't stay up late doing just as they please. Instead, they obey their caregivers and go to bed. With only one lollipop, or pacifier, to go around, teddy bear and leprechaun share. They don't quarrel and grab, and if they had done so, Sophie or another make-believe character probably would have intervened and insisted on kind, considerate behavior.

According to Vygotsky, children's greatest self-control occurs during make-believe play. They achieve their maximum display of willpower when at their own initiative they renounce a momentary attraction in favor of rule-governed behavior.[14] The paradox of make-believe is that in everyday life, when children subordinate actions to rules, they usually give up something they want—instead of keeping a treasured toy all to themselves, they share it; instead of continuing to play, they clean up; instead of watching more TV, they go to bed. During fantasy play, however, renouncing impulse and following social rules are central to the fun of playing. Rather than frustrating or disappointing the child, self-restraint is the route to maximum pleasure.

In sum, subordinating immediate desires to the rules of make-believe scenes becomes a new form of desire[15]—one that responds to the child's need to become an accepted member of his or her culture. Indeed, if you watch preschoolers at play, you will see that they rarely violate the rules of their social world. And as they jointly create play scripts and follow social rules with peers, they come to appreciate society's norms and strive to uphold them. A child playing storekeeper experiences firsthand the reasons for having customers line up to pay, for making change accurately, and for being polite. A child playing parent in a household scene becomes aware of parental responsibilities and why it's important for children to follow their parents' directives.

In fact, an adult who breaks a rule in make-believe usually brings preschoolers' profound respect for social order into bold relief! Cara, a demanding but spirited 5-year-old, likes to initiate make-believe with the following transparent role reversal: "Mom, I'll be the mother, and you be my child *5 years old.*" Cara's mother plays along for a while and then deliberately transgresses, refusing to eat her vegetables or pick up her toys. At the first sign of misbehavior, Cara lectures in a tone of voice well beyond her years: "Children *must* obey their parents because their parents know things they don't, so the parents *must* take care of them." As Cara's pronouncement makes clear, play creates a "zone" through which preschoolers internalize a basic sense of social responsibility and morality. At the same time, they acquire a wealth of practical knowledge and skills.

In extreme circumstances, when the organization and predictability of the real world fall apart, young children whose prior lives have been filled with parental warmth and involvement often call on rules and rituals in make-believe to restore their social world. Recently, I came across the recollections of Alice Cahana, an elderly Holocaust survivor, recounting her days as a child in the death camp at Auschwitz. Alice explained that she and her sister Edith managed despite all odds to stay together. Their secret strategy was never to display any emotion that would give away their relationship, since a major objective of the SS was to break up families. Only at night did they dare to hug, whisper, and play together.

On Friday nights, they marked the Sabbath in a special way, by imagining that they were at home. They talked about the evening's events in minute detail to make the image of family life firm and real. Alice had always had the responsibility of setting the table, and her mother would correct her if she left out even small, nonessential items. In play, Edith would murmur, "Alice, it's time to set the table. Find the nicest tablecloths, and don't forget the flowers. Where are the napkins for the guests? You forgot the fork for Father. You really shined the candelabra beautifully this week, better than before." [16] After their pretend meal, the two sisters would whisper songs.

The rules of make-believe kept alive the integrity of the girls' lost social world. They kindled hope, or as Alice put it, "an inner light," fortifying the children with the self-restraint and forbearance they needed to endure the next day.

FROM MAKE-BELIEVE PLAY TO ORGANIZED GAMES
WITH RULES

Vygotsky regarded the sociodramatic play of the preschool years as essential for further development of play—specifically, for movement toward game play in middle childhood. In make-believe, the rules of play are implicit; preschoolers are hardly aware of enacting them. Instead, they are caught up in creating imaginary situations—putting a stuffed animal to bed, driving an ambulance to a train crash, or ringing up a customer's purchase at the cash register. Winning and losing, team membership and competition, and purposefully laying down rules are not of great interest to preschoolers. Try playing a rule-based game with a 3- or 4-year-old, and you are likely to find that the child is easily sidetracked. If, with your prompting and guidance, the child does finish the game, he or she might say, "I won!" or "Everybody won!" regardless of the outcome.

With age, the imaginativeness of play recedes. In the games that captivate school-age children, rules come to the forefront.[17] Six- to 8-year-olds are often preoccupied with working out the rules of a game and making sure all players follow them. They often spend as much or more time on the details of how a game should proceed as they do playing the game itself! Nevertheless, every organized game with rules contains an imaginary situation in veiled form. In *Monopoly*, children are real estate moguls; in baseball, they emulate Hall-of-Fame idols. Children retain both aspects of play, in changing balances, throughout development.

Increasing emphasis on the rule-oriented side of play extends the "zone" forged by fantasy play during the preschool years. By making children more aware of the goals of their play activities, game play further strengthens children's capacity to overcome impulse. Consciously striving to reach a goal requires planning—postponing action in favor of thinking out what to do in advance, organizing one's behavior in accord with the plan, evaluating how well the plan is working along the way, and revising the plan if necessary.

In the simple games of the late preschool and early school years, the play goal is very clear—in hide-and-seek, to keep the person who is "it" from finding you; in *Chutes and Ladders,* to travel a road with as many shortcuts and as few setbacks as possible, getting to the finish line first. Gradually, the goals of children's games become more distant and complex. Attaining those goals requires more intermediate steps and greater knowledge, skill, and coordination of play actions with those of others—in T-ball and kickball, scoring more runs than the other team while adhering to fair procedures for batting, pitching, and fielding; in chess, moving each type of piece according to its special rule in an effort to checkmate the opposing king.

Through game play, children receive additional experience in setting goals, in regulating behavior in pursuit of those goals, and in subordinating behavior to rules. And in negotiating rules in peer-organized games, children deepen their understanding of why rules are necessary and which ones work well. In the process, they form more mature concepts of fairness and justice. Indeed, parents and teachers often remark that game play prepares children for the inevitability of real downfalls and teaches perseverance and good sportsmanship.

In sum, the development of play proceeds from make-believe, with an overt imaginary situation and covert rules, to organized games, with overt rules and a covert imaginary situation. The vast yet nearly effortless learning that takes place through pretending makes it, for Vygotsky, "the highest level of preschool development. The child moves forward essentially through play activity."[18] Make-believe play, in Vygotsky's theory, is the preeminent educational activity of early childhood.

CONTRIBUTIONS OF MAKE-BELIEVE PLAY TO DEVELOPMENT

Vygotsky emphasized the development-enhancing, forward-moving consequences of make-believe. Was he correct that pretending in early childhood has a far-reaching impact on development, supporting the emergence and refinement of a wide variety of competencies? Indeed, much evidence fits with Vygotsky's conclusion.

Sociodramatic play with peers has been studied most thoroughly. Comparisons of preschoolers' sociodramatic activities with their social nonpretend pursuits, such as drawing pictures or putting puzzles together in the company of agemates, supports Vygotsky's view of make-believe as a "zone" in which children enhance their own development. In social pretending, preschoolers engage in lengthier interactions, are more involved, draw more children into their activity, and are more cooperative. In view of these findings, it is not surprising that 4- and 5-year-olds who spend more time at sociodramatic play are advanced in intellectual development and are judged more socially competent by their teachers.[19] Furthermore, pretend play fosters a diverse array of specific cognitive and social skills, which contribute to these broad-baseed outcomes. Let's take some examples.

Attention

Attention is fundamental to all human thinking. It determines the information considered in any task and whether the task will be completed. As any parent or teacher knows, young children spend only short times involved in most activities and are easily distracted. Yet attention becomes more sustained over early childhood—a development that equips children for concentrated involvement, which will be essential for success once they enter school.

Under what conditions are preschoolers most likely to display sustained attention? Think back to the examples of Sophie's and Mattie's behavior at the beginning of this chapter, and the answer will be clear: during play, especially complex play. In two studies, psychologist Holly Ruff and her collaborators sat toddlers and preschoolers at a table of toys. Children's patterns of attention changed dramatically with age.[20] After playing for a short time with a toy, 1- to 2-year-olds dropped it and turned to another. Their attention was externally controlled by the physical properties of the objects. Hence, they flitted from one toy to another and lost interest as the play session progressed. But once children began to set goals in play, the nature of their attention changed. It became *effortful,* as indicated by eyes fixed on the toys and a determined facial expression.

For the youngest children, play goals were often as simple as getting a cap off a bottle. With age, the problems and challenges children set for themselves became more elaborate, such as building an intricate structure out of small blocks or acting out a fantasy scenario. The more complex children's play goals, the more they displayed focused, effortful attention and the more such attention increased over the play session. And in one of the studies, both construction and imaginative play were powerful predictors of sustained attention between ages 2 and 5.[21] With respect to make-believe, when preschoolers create very intricate scenarios, either on their own or with play partners, they generally stay absorbed for a very long time.

Recall the anecdote about David, who remained an attentive pupil considerably longer while playing school than he did in other kindergarten activities. Preschoolers' sustained attention is more advanced in make-believe than in many real-life pursuits. When permitted to select freely among diverse activities at child care or preschool, young children overwhelmingly prefer fantasy play. Observing in a child-care center richly equipped with play materials, Kathleen Kirby, one of my graduate students, found that 2- to 4-year-olds spent 45 to 50 percent of free-choice periods immersed in make-believe—nearly twice as much time as they devoted to any other activity.[22] The rapt attention engendered in pretend play may eventually carry over to nonpretend contexts.

Memory

Fantasy play also strengthens young children's memories. Preschoolers remember information better in a play context than in a context in which information is isolated from its everyday use and they are told to remember deliberately.

Psychologist Lawrence Newman permitted one group of 4- and 5-year-olds to play with a set of toys and told another group simply to remember the toys. Play produced far better recall.[23] During the "remember" condition, children repeatedly named and touched the objects—a rehearsal strategy that, much like repeating a phone number, helped them hold on to information, but only briefly. In contrast, the "play" condition led to many spontaneous organizations of the toys that enabled children to recall effortlessly. Often these grew out of make-believe—for example, putting the *toy shoes* on the *doll* and pretending to feed her the *toy banana*. Narrating imaginative activities also yielded excellent recall, as in "I'm squeezing this *lemon*" or "Fly away in this *helicopter, doggie!*" When children embedded an object in meaningful make-believe, they increased its memorableness.

Furthermore, children acting out stories during pretend play are assisted in mastering the storytelling script, or basic framework of story organization. Preschoolers' pretend scenarios are often quite storylike, consisting of characters, settings, and plot sequences that include adventure, suspense, surprise, conflict, and resolution. Witness the following trip to Sea World, during which Emily and her friends save Baby Shamu from danger:

S: *(to Emily)* Would you come with us? Let's go to Sea World.

E: Sea World! Let's watch Shamu! I'm the mom. *(All three children run to one end of the room and sit down next to one another. They gaze toward the other end of the room.)*

S: Oh! I see Shamu.

E: It's starting *(presumably the show).*

A. J.: Yeah!

E: There's a little fish. There's a big mom.

S: There's a daddy.

E: Look! He fell on the ice. Look at 'em. Mommy and Daddy are fell! Oh-h-h-h!

S: *(Patting a pretend Baby Shamu)* Oh-h-h-h! I know you're all right. *(All make stroking motions on a pretend Baby Shamu.)*

E: Look! All better now. *(She pretends to lift Baby Shamu back into the water.)* [24]

Children like Emily, who have formed a *sense of story* through make-believe, more readily grasp the organization and meaning of new stories and are therefore more likely to remember them.[25] Young pretenders also impose the standards of story organization on the way they recall and explain their experiences to others. Their verbal narratives are more cohesive than those of agemates who prefer other forms of play.[26]

In helping children grasp the storytelling script (and in other ways we will take up next), make-believe play is wonderful preparation for literacy. Being able to anticipate story organization eases the task of making sense of written prose. It also grants children a firm foundation for authoring their first written narratives.

Language and Literacy

As the findings just mentioned illustrate, make-believe greatly enriches children's facility with language. During sociodramatic activities, preschoolers hear speech that describes and comments on actions going on at the moment. This helps ensure that language is understandable because it is in tune with ongoing events. Consequently, when new words arise in the course of a fantasy scene, children can determine their meaning easily from cues in the situation. In this way, vocabulary extends during make-believe as children introduce words they have heard during recent experiences. For example, "I'm going out. I need my *cloak*," said 5-year-old Lizzy, mimicking an expression she had heard in a TV movie while grabbing a dress-up raincoat from a hook in the housekeeping area at child care.

"You mean your coat?" asked Lizzie's playmate.

"Right, a *cloak* is a *coat*," Lizzie explained. The amount of time preschoolers spent talking with peers while pretending is positively associated with the size of their vocabularies at age 5.[27]

As children engage in play talk, they not only build their vocabularies but correct one another's errors, either directly or by demonstrating the acceptable way to speak. In one instance, a kindergartner enacting a telephone conversation said, "Hello, come to my house, please." Her play partner quickly countered with appropriate telephone greeting behavior: "No, first you've got to say 'How are you? What are you doing?' "[28]

Furthermore, the language skills required to express different points of view, resolve disagreements, and persuade peers to collaborate so play can continue are complex and often subtle. Emily's success in convincing several classmates to join the make-believe trip to Sea World was partly due to the way she approached them—by asking if they'd like to go. By experimenting with language during play, children can see how others react to various styles of communication and use that information to refine their way of speaking. In this way, play is an ideal arena for mastering all aspects of conversational dialogue.

Opportunities to acquire literacy-relevant skills also abound in make-believe play. In one kindergarten, children transformed the block-building area into a make-believe recycling center with the help of their teacher. Signs were prepared that advertised the new center, its hours, and what it would pay for various goods. As in other friendly businesses, attendants wore nametags, such as "Hi, I'm Charles!" When customers arrived with goods, the attendants had to fill out receipts listing each item, its quantity, and its value. Since many children could not yet spell, they used first letters or drew pictures of items. While doing so, they often became curious about how to write the full word and asked the teacher to help them.

What does research say about the role of make-believe in children's literacy development? The amount of time children devote to pretending at age 4 is positively related to reading and writing skills after entering kindergarten and first grade—specifically, the extent to which children spontaneously read words on game cards and signs, understand print concepts, and write letters and simple words.[29] The more children engage in literacy-relevant play (activities like the recycling center), the more advanced their literacy skills are as well.

Preschoolers' commentary about language while pretending, using such verbs as *say, talk, tell, write,* and *explain,* is a particularly good predictor of reading progress at age 5. Using language to talk about language happens often as peers jointly create fantasy scenes. Such talk may help children treat both oral and written narratives as objects of analysis; hence its benefits for early reading.[30]

With respect to writing, object substitutions and role play seem to have special benefits.[31] Frequently using objects to symbolize other objects and transforming oneself into various characters may encourage children to try to make sense of other symbol systems, such as how to express themselves with print. In their first efforts to write, preschoolers commonly assume that letters (just like pictures and first substitute objects) look like their meanings. In one instance, a child stated with certainty that the word *deer* begins with the letter O because O is shaped like a deer; then he demonstrated by drawing an O and adding antlers to it![32] Flexibly using make-believe symbols seems to assist children in revising early, incorrect ideas about how print is used to communicate.

Hypothetical Reasoning

During the preschool and elementary school years, thought is largely tied to the here-and-now. Children think in an organized fashion about concrete information they can directly perceive but have great difficulty reasoning about hypothetical situations—ones that do not make sense in the real world. For example, try giving a child between 4 and 9 the following problem: Suppose dogs are bigger than elephants and elephants are bigger than mice. Which one is the biggest: dogs, elephants, or mice? Most will insist that dogs couldn't possibly be bigger than elephants. "That's never true!" they exclaim.[33]

Yet with the help of make-believe, even preschoolers can transcend these limits and reason about situations that defy real-world knowledge. Consider the following "impossible" premises and question: All cats bark. Rex is a cat. Does Rex bark? Psychologists Maria Dias and Paul Harris had one group of 4- to 6-year-olds act out problems like this one, using toys that represented the content of the premises. A second group was told that the events were taking place on a pretend planet rather than on Earth. And a third group merely listened and answered the questions. Children in the two "play" conditions gave more hypothetical responses and also justified their answers with hypothetical ideas—for example, by saying "In the story, cats bark, so we can pretend they bark."[34]

The capacity to adopt a "theoretical" mode of reasoning in make-believe is highly consistent with Vygotsky's belief that pretending assists children in separating mental symbols from the objects and actions for which they stand, thereby permitting them to manipulate meanings in innovative ways. Reasoning about the nonreal is essential for abstract thinking and for many creative endeavors—that is, for human cognition to reach its highest potential.

Distinguishing Appearance from Reality

After kissing their preschooler goodnight and turning out the lights, many parents are accustomed to hearing refrains like this: "Mommy, Daddy, monsters are in my room again!" To rid the bedroom of scary creatures, pictures and mobiles may have to be removed and a thorough search conducted to assure the child that no monsters are lurking in the shadows, waiting to reappear as soon as the parent leaves. Uncertainty about the relation between appearance and reality also surfaces in other situations. On Halloween, a 3-year-old who eagerly dons her costume may become frightened at the sight of her animal- or witch-like appearance in the mirror. And a father who shaves off his beard and mustache may find that his young preschooler reacts with puzzlement and distress to his changed appearance.

Consistent with these all-too-familiar experiences, research confirms that preschoolers are easily tricked by the outward appearance of things. They mistakenly conclude that the way things look or sound is the way they really are. In several studies, psychologists John Flavell, Francis Green, and Eleanor Flavell presented children with appearance–reality problems in which objects were disguised in various ways. The children were asked what the objects were, "really and truly." Before age 6 or 7, most children took things at face value.[35] When asked whether a white piece of paper placed behind a blue filter is "really and truly" blue or whether a can that sounds like a baby crying when turned over is "really and truly a baby," they responded, "Yes!"

Yet in make-believe, children use objects to symbolize things that are very different from the objects themselves—a ball to stand for an apple, a laundry basket for a cradle. They do not judge these imaginary symbols to be real, so clearly they can tell the difference between pretend and real experiences long before they can answer many appearance–reality problems correctly.[36] The more 3- to 5-year-olds spontaneously engage in joint make-believe with classmates at preschool, the better they can distinguish the apparent and real identities of disguised objects.[37] Pretending with peers may help children master appearance–reality distinctions because it offers repeated practice in transforming a wide variety of objects from their real state to a pretend state and back again.

Understanding the Mind and Its Many Activities

Make-believe play provides a rich foundation for children's comprehension of the mind's wide-ranging capabilities. In Chapter 3, I noted that children's elaborate interactions with imaginary companions foster understanding of false belief and other people's perspectives. In sociodramatic play as well, opportunities to act out and coordinate various roles probably help children grasp similarities and differences between people in desires, beliefs, and feelings. Recently, a mother recounted to me a make-believe episode initiated by her 2 1/2-year-old daughter, Traci, involving extended experimentation with and reversals of roles, which led to abundant dialogue about mental states.

One evening, Traci, her two older sisters, and her parents had gathered in the living room to watch a video of *The Sound of Music*. Although Traci showed little interest in the movie, her ears perked up at a statement in the sound track reporting the death of the mother of the Trapp-family children. Traci began to ask questions, to talk about how the mother must have gotten sick and gone to the hospital, and to repeat that the mother had died. For the next hour and a half, she assigned her own mother and herself at least fifteen different roles—mother, father, baby, sister, doctor, nurse, and more—as she explored the idea of a mother dying:

> Traci: "Here, you're the baby and I'm the mama. Honey, I'm going to the hospital."

Mother: "Go to the hospital and have the doctor help you feel better."

Traci: "No, I'm not going to feel better. I'm going to die!"

Mother: *(frantically)* "No, no, I don't want you to die! I'll be very, very sad."

Traci: "OK, don't worry, it'll be all right."

Some scenarios (like this one) ended happily; others were filled with depressing events and ended sadly. In acting them out, Traci imagined and simulated diverse wants, hopes, worries, and strivings of people in her life.

As this brief vignette illustrates, sociodramatic play is rich in mental-state language, especially references to emotion. As children learn about mental states from conversing and engaging in make-believe with adults, they transfer this knowledge to sociodramatic play with peers. The more 3- and 4-year-old friends talk about mental states during joint make-believe, the better they perform and the more they improve over the following year on tasks assessing their grasp of mental life.[38] These include understanding of false belief, identifying the feelings of a puppet acting out emotionally charged situations (such as seeing a parent off on a trip), and explaining real-life causes of happiness, sadness, anger, fear, and mixed emotions (for example, why one might feel both happy and sad about winning a race against a friend).

Talk between siblings that focuses on feelings seems to play a particularly strong role in the diversity of themes that siblings act out in their joint make-believe. Complexity of play with siblings, in turn, is a good indicator of preschoolers' understanding of other people's feelings—more so than is their play with mothers.[39] Why might conversing and pretending with siblings make a special contribution to children's capacity to read others' emotions? In interacting with their child, mothers spend much time acknowledging and clarifying the child's feelings. Siblings (as well as preschool friends) frequently articulate how they themselves feel. Therefore, siblings more often expose the child to the inner states of someone other than the child himself or herself. The more affectionate and cooperative siblings' relationships are, the more sophisticated their sociodramatic play.[40] Siblings who get along well are probably better at creating and sustaining elaborate make-believe scenarios—play that contributes to their emotional sensitivity.

As children build on each other's play themes, they often refer to their make-believe with mental terms by making statements like these: "Let's *pretend*," "Let's *imagine*," "You *act like* a pilot, and I'll *make-believe* I'm in the control tower." Some experts believe that this suspension of play to communicate about it marks a major change in understanding.[41] Now children do not just represent experiences in play; they display *awareness* that make-believe is an activity in which the mind creates events. As a result, children become capable of consciously reflecting on and deliberately manipulating their own and others' fanciful representations, and their play becomes even more complex and imaginative.

Researchers continue to debate whether preschoolers actually view pretending as a mental state rather than just a series of actions mirroring real life.[42] But there is clear evidence that their grasp of make-believe as a mental activity improves steadily between ages 4 and 8. Over time, they can answer more subtle questions about the nature of make-believe. For example, by age 6 most realize that pretending depends on having prior knowledge about a make-believe role. That is, a person hopping can be pretending to be a rabbit only if he or she knows that rabbits hop.[43] Children age 6 and older also recognize that make-believe is something you can do just inside your head, without using your body at all.[44]

Why is this understanding of make-believe as mental representation so important? When children master this and other related ideas—that people are constantly engaged in thought, even when they have nothing to do; that mental inferences, not just direct observations, can lead to new knowledge; and that prior experiences affect people's interpretations of new experiences[45]—they show that they have begun to pay more attention to the processes of thought.[46] "Thinking about thought" makes possible a major advance in self-regulation. It permits children to call on what they know about mental life to surmount cognitive and social challenges. The child well aware of the mind's active, transforming capabilities is more likely to attend to relevant information, to plan, to use memory and problem-solving strategies, and to evaluate and revise his or her thinking to make it more effective. In sum, make-believe in early childhood is among those factors that promote reflective thought, which improves throughout the school years.

Self-Regulation

As we have just seen, pretend play, through its impact on children's awareness of the mind, fosters advanced forms of self-regulation. But what about the self-regulatory capacities that emerge earlier, during the preschool years—self-guiding private speech, willingness to take on chores, and capacity to delay gratification for brief periods? Does make-believe foster these early indicators of a self-regulated child? Findings of several studies I carried out with my graduate students suggest that it does.

PRIVATE SPEECH. In the first of these studies, we reasoned that if Vygotsky is correct that children learn to overcome impulse and manage their behavior through pretend play, then private speech should be especially frequent within make-believe activities. To find out, graduate student Kerry Krafft and I observed 3- to 5-year-olds during free-choice periods in two contexts differing sharply in encouragement of imaginative play: the Y Preschool (called this because it is sponsored by the YWCA) and the Montessori Preschool.[47]

In the Y Preschool, play formed the basis of the daily program. Children had easy access to a wide variety of toys, games, and books, and each classroom contained two centers especially conducive to sociodramatic play: a block-building area with hundreds of blocks varying in size and shape and a child-sized playhouse brimming with all manner of housekeeping props. The Montessori Preschool, in contrast, actively discouraged make-believe (although not all Montessori schools do so). Spurred by philosophical principles advocating realistic activities, the Montessori teachers set up "work stations" from which children selected. Typical options were puzzles, picture-matching and picture-sequencing tasks, letter tracing, small construction blocks, containers with water for pouring, books, and crayons and other tools for drawing and writing. When Montessori children strayed into make-believe, teachers often interrupted, drawing them back to work-station pursuits.

Nevertheless, Montessori children did engage in pretending, but it was sharply restricted relative to children in the Y Preschool, who displayed three times as much imaginative play. What happened to private speech? It showed a parallel trend. Children in the Y Preschool engaged in twice as much self-talk as did children in the Montessori preschool. Furthermore, pretend play emerged as the strongest correlate of both fantasy-play private speech and self-guiding private speech. That is, the more children engaged in make-believe, the more they talked to themselves to work out pretend characters' actions and to guide their thought and behavior during realistic tasks. This latter finding suggests that private speech, so rich in the make-believe context, may carry over to children's self-talk when they face real-world challenges.

Recall from Chapter 3 that as children master puzzles and other problem-solving tasks, their self-guiding speech declines. Yet when graduate student Tina Gillingham and I observed preschoolers in a laboratory playroom liberally equipped with fantasy-play props, we found that private speech during make-believe remained uniformly high from ages 2 to 4 and actually increased at age 5.[48] Our interpretation of the prevalence of private speech during make-believe is that children continually set challenges for themselves in fantasy play. Consistent with Vygotsky's theory, they create their own "zones," frequently calling on self-directed language to work out their imaginings and bring behavior under the control of thought.

SOCIALLY RESPONSIBLE BEHAVIOR.   In yet another study, graduate student Cynthia Elias and I addressed the question of whether complex make-believe—specifically, sociodramatic play involving elaborate communication between agemates—promotes socially responsible behavior.[49] During the fall of the school year, we observed 3- and 4-year-olds as they played in the block and housekeeping centers of their preschools and rated the quantity and maturity of their fantasy endeavors. Then we assessed social responsibility by observing the children during clean-up periods, recording the extent to which they willingly picked up and put away toys without prompting and assistance. We made these clean-up observations in the fall and again in the spring so we could measure gain in responsible behavior.

Our findings revealed that preschoolers who more often engaged in complex sociodramatic play showed greater improvement in social responsibility over the next 5 to 6 months. And this relationship was particularly strong for children rated by their parents as highly impulsive—that is, who were poorly self-regulated to begin with! In other words, children most in need of enhancing their self-regulatory abilities appeared especially sensitive to the benefits of sociodramatic play.

Imagination and Creativity

In addition to its contribution to many nonplay skills, make-believe can be examined on its own terms: as an imaginative activity that expresses salient aspects of the child's inner cognitive and emotional life. In Vygotsky's theory, the drive to fantasize and engage in role play does not fade away with childhood. Instead, he maintained, the imagination of later years is an internalized, condensed form of early childhood make-believe that can be considered play without action. We typically experience it as an elaborate stream of consciousness made up of mental images and silent self-talk that meanders along, remarking on new experiences, reflecting on the past, and predicting the future.[50]

By introducing fantasy elements into consciousness, this inventive private commentary probably helps us cope with the mundane, repetitive aspects of our daily lives. We resort to such ruminations while waiting; during long car trips or meetings; and at other monotonous or idle times. In this way, early make-believe fortifies us with a mental tool that is vital for adapting to everyday life! And from time to time, we apply logical, adaptive thinking to this inner playfulness to harness it for culturally worthwhile purposes. The result may be a creative idea or product.

Was Vygotsky correct that the imaginative mental combinations that form the basis for creativity originate in the pretend scenarios of early childhood?

Unfortunately, we have no long-term studies that systematically observed children for the imaginativeness of their play and then tracked them to document their creative accomplishments in adulthood. And even if such studies were available, many intervening events could blur the connection between early play and adult creativity. At present, all we have available to explore this relationship are the recollections of highly creative individuals about their childhoods or the reports of their biographers.

On a recent visit to my local library, I browsed the shelves devoted to biography, selecting several dozen life stories of accomplished writers, artists, and scientists. The accounts were remarkably consistent: For most, pretend play was an influential aspect of their early years. Often a significant person—a parent, an older sibling, or a relative—promoted imaginative experimentation and a sense of wonder by telling fantastic stories, initiating joint pretend, or offering gifts (such as books and puppets) that inspired make-believe.[51]

For example, biographical accounts of physicist Marie Curie, co-discoverer of radium and twice winner of the Nobel Prize, invariably make reference to her father's untiring efforts to provide his children with ideas and games to fill their spare time.[52] A chest of colored blocks had special meaning. Marie and her older siblings used the blocks to represent cities, mountains, rivers, countries, and continents. Their father, a high school science teacher, often joined in, capitalizing on play as a way to teach geography. In the home in which Marie Curie grew up, one biographer summed up, "play was learning and learning was play."[53]

In poet Sylvia Plath's childhood, stories and storytelling were pervasive. As a 2 1/2-year-old, Sylvia was intensely jealous of her sickly younger brother for consuming so much of her mother's attention. While the baby nursed, Sylvia sat nearby on the floor, impatient and unhappy. Her mother discovered that she could defuse Sylvia's envy with a game in which Sylvia spread out the newspaper before her, picked out all the capital letters on the page, and pretended, in a very grown-up way, to read—an achievement that attracted much parental admiration. Sylvia's mother often made up bedtime tales, serialized from one evening to the next. Almost as soon as they could talk, Sylvia and her brother responded in kind with limericks, poems, and fantastic stories of their own. On walks to their grandparents' house and on long car trips, favorite books invariably came along, offering ready inspiration for the children's imaginative creations.[54]

Filmstar Charlie Chaplin's mother was herself a talented comedy actress and singer. As a young child, Charlie often accompanied her when she went to work at the theater. As a result, playacting and impersonating became an early focus of Charlie's pretending. One evening during a performance, his mother's voice failed. In a pinch, the stage manager, who had seen Charlie at play, led the little boy onstage in her place. Charlie continued his playacting unabated, which included songs, dances, and impersonations from his mother's repertoire. He was demonstrating the wares of his first and best teacher in the art of make-believe, and the performance evoked a roar of appreciation and a shower of coins from the crowd.[55]

In these and many other similar biographical anecdotes, childhood make-believe engendered imaginativeness that was clearly related to outstanding accomplishment in adulthood. Of course, the scientific and artistic talents of individuals like Curie, Plath, and Chaplin are rare among us. Nevertheless, as play theorists Dorothy and Jerome Singer point out, all children have "that same potential for playfulness, for trying out possible lives, that is the foundation for a humbler but personally meaningful creativity."[56]

ADULT INVOLVEMENT IN CHILDREN'S MAKE-BELIEVE

Piaget's view of make-believe play, dominant until recently, asserts that pretending emerges spontaneously when children become capable of symbolic thought. He assumed that very young children could not share play symbols with others. Yet in instance after instance, we have seen that adults are central in preschoolers' play lives, often encouraging and elaborating on their imaginative strivings. If adults are prominent in early make-believe, how did researchers manage to adhere to an image of young children as solitary fantasizers for so long? The reason is that until recently, make-believe was largely studied in the laboratory, in sessions in which children arrived one-at-a-time and had no alternative but to play by themselves.

Only during the past 10 years have researchers seriously addressed the social context of make-believe. Their findings confirm that pretending, like other higher forms of thinking, flows from social collaboration. More competent partners *scaffold* young children's imaginative play, guiding its emergence and gradual refinement. Once pretend capacities are in place, children forge playful understandings with peers that serve as microcosms of cooperative activity, mirroring social relations and goal-oriented pursuits within the larger society.

Scaffolding Children's Play

Traci, the 2 ½-year-old who responded so strongly to the mother's death in *The Sound of Music*, often pretends with her own mother, Julie. For some weeks,

Traci had been talking about a mysterious creature she called a "maserus." Traci's description of the creature convinced Julie that the maserus was an imaginative friendly monster. Congested due to spring allergies, Traci was particularly irritable one morning. Well aware that Traci loves make-believe activities, her mother tried to distract her with a favorite pastime.

As Traci sneezed and whimpered, Julie spied a half-full white garbage bag in a corner, situated in such a way that it looked like an animal with a snout. "I think I see a maserus!" Julie declared, pointing to the garbage bag. Immediately Traci cast off her irritability and jumped into action. Over the next hour, she and her mother fed the maserus more trash, read books and sang songs to it, and laughed at the monster's antics. "By the end of our delightful session," Julie remarked, "I almost felt the bag was alive." When the activity changed to the more practical concerns of the day, Traci's problematic irritability resumed.

Recent research reveals that make-believe is, from the outset, a social activity.[57] In Western societies, it usually first appears between parents and children, although older siblings may participate as well. From these interactions, children derive many play skills that enhance their make-believe in other contexts.

In one of the most extensive studies tracing the development of make-believe play, psychologists Wendy Haight and Peggy Miller followed nine children from 1 to 4 years of age, repeatedly visiting their homes to make intensive observations of their pretending.[58] The researchers found that most make-believe—from 68 to 75 percent—was social across the entire age span. Mothers were the children's principal play partners from ages 1 to 3. Over time, mother–child play declined and child–child play increased. By age 4, children played about equally with their mothers and with other children—both siblings and peers.

The dominance of mother–child pretend at the youngest ages, however, was not due to lack of child playmates. Up to age 3, even if siblings and peers were present, children preferred playing with their mothers. Furthermore, Haight and Miller, as well as other researchers, report clear evidence that mothers teach their toddlers to pretend. At age 1, mothers initiate almost all make-believe episodes. They also demonstrate many pretend actions toward objects, thereby showing children how to use one object to represent another.[59] Around age 2, mothers begin to talk about nonexistent fantasy objects. In one instance, a mother suggested that an empty bowl was full of juicy oranges, one for each of her son's miniature zoo animals. This change may help children increase the range and complexity of their play symbols.[60]

Social Functions and Consequences of Adult–Child Play

Joint adult–child make-believe serves a wide variety of social purposes. Here is a sampling:

- *Teaching.* At times, caregivers use pretending as a pleasurable way to teach children real-world skills. For example, Michael's mother capitalized on make-believe to encourage her 3-year-old to use the toilet. Reluctant at first, Michael became an eager learner after being put in charge of toilet training his teddy bear.[61]
- *Enlivening daily routines.* Often children and their caregivers call on pretend play to relieve the monotony of chores and other repetitive tasks. While 2-year-old Molly folded socks with her mother, she put a pair together, held it up, and exclaimed, "Mommy, I made us something to eat!"[62]
- *Defusing conflict.* Occasionally, make-believe can defuse persistent caregiver–child conflicts. Concerned about 3-year-old Nancy's use of a pacifier, her mother had been trying to get her to give it up. Nancy resisted. As they played with puppets, Nancy announced, "I want a pacifier!" Her mother's puppet responded, "Little girl. You have only a red dot for a mouth. I don't think you can fit a pacifier in there!"[63]
- *Expressing and regulating emotion.* Traci's exploration, with her mother's help, of what it might be like to have a mother who got sick and died exemplifies how parents and children use make-believe to express and manage intense feelings. In pretend scenarios, Traci acted out feeling ill, feeling better, sadness, happiness, worry, love, and caring.
- *Influencing another's social behavior.* Joint make-believe can be an effective strategy for attaining a social goal. When 2-year-old Molly stood at the top of a slide and asked for help, her mother tried to get her to slide down on her own. Molly refused and stepped into pretend: "A shark . . . There's a shark in the sand!" Molly's mother immediately helped her down.[64]
- *Having fun.* As illustrations of adult–child make-believe throughout this chapter affirm, most of the time parents and children engage in imaginative play just for fun. In fact, some theorists have argued that the earliest expressions of humor emerge out of fantasy play.[65] Consistent with this claim, participating in adult–child make-believe seems to precede children's first verbal jokes. One toddler named Ari, having

become an avid make-believer, soon showed a corresponding rise in joking. At 20 months, he touched a picture of a sheep in a book his mother was reading to him, exclaimed "Neigh!" and laughed hysterically. At 21 months, while watching his mother wash dishes, he remarked, "Nutmeg [the family cat] drinks water with spoon" and then interpreted, "Funny thing! Ari tell Mommy joke."[66] As Ari's humor makes plain, pretending is not just a pleasurable activity in itself but brings pleasure to life in general.

That joint make-believe with adults is such great fun is undoubtedly a major reason that 1- to 3-year-olds are so attracted to it. But why is play with adults, at least initially, more engaging than play with peers? While children's play skills are still limited, adult scaffolding makes play more interesting, surprising, and absorbing. In several studies, 1- to 3-year-olds engaged in more than twice as much make-believe when their mothers were involved than when they were not. In addition, caregiver support led early make-believe to move toward a more advanced level.[67] For example, when mothers actively took part, children produced more complex pretend sequences—not just putting the doll to sleep but brushing her teeth, tucking her into bed, singing a lullaby, and kissing her good night. Furthermore, during parent–child play, make-believe themes are more varied, and parents' verbal commentary is especially effective in raising both the duration and the complexity of play.

In line with the "zone," children for whom make-believe is just emerging act more competently when playing with an adult partner than they otherwise would. In Haight and Miller's investigation, 1-year-olds whose mothers engaged in a great deal of pretending ranked especially high in peer play at age 4. And children of the most imaginative and enthusiastic parents were among the most highly skilled preschool pretenders.

Vital Features of Adult–Child Play

How should parents, caregivers, and teachers go about engaging young children in make-believe? Effective scaffolding of play is somewhat different from scaffolding of nonplay tasks. In fostering play, adults might have explicit goals, such as teaching culturally valued knowledge and skills and promoting self-regulation and imagination. But directiveness and didactic teaching are seldom, if ever, necessary.

As play theorist Brian Sutton-Smith pointed out more than a quarter-century ago, make-believe enables children who are still acquiring language to represent their everyday lives and inner thoughts and feelings more completely than is possible through any other symbolic means. This confirms Vygotsky's statement that "in play, the child always behaves beyond his average age, above his daily behavior." Look back at the vignettes described in this chapter—of Sophie giving a sleepy teddy bear a pacifier, of Alison recalling the train crash in India, of Emily traveling to Sea World, and of Traci role-playing a mother getting sick and dying—and note how difficult it would be for 2- to 4-year-olds to construct such well-articulated ideas only in words or in their drawings. Consequently, adults do not need to "tutor" preschoolers in pretending, as they sometimes do when helping them master puzzles or other similar tasks.

Instead, adult participation in make-believe works best when it responds to, guides, and builds on the child's behaviors with demonstrations and suggestions. In support of this approach, psychologist Barbara Fiese's observations of mothers playing with their 15- to 24-month-olds revealed that maternal questions, directions, and intrusions (initiating a new activity unrelated to the child's current play) led to immature behavior in which toddlers merely mouthed, touched, and looked at toys. Relentlessly barraging children with information that communicates "at" rather than "with" them fails to involve them in dialogue and interferes with optimum development of play. In contrast, turn-taking and joint involvement, in which mothers sustained or expanded on their child's play themes, evoked high levels of pretending.[68]

Maternal interactions that suggest play options related to 1 1/2-year-olds' ongoing activity—for example, saying "Oh, is the doll trying to swim?" as the child puts a doll into a toy cup—continue to predict extended make-believe sequences and imaginative object substitutions at age 3. In contrast, toddlers whose mothers negate and correct—"No, dolls don't go in cups, they go in the doll house"—tend to become 3-year-olds who spend much time in simple, immature manipulation of toys.[69]

Finally, the shared understanding underlying any type of adult–child communication that creates the "zone" is also essential in make-believe. Sensitive and mutually rewarding interaction between mother and baby in the first year of life predicts complexity of mother–child pretending and children's use of mental-state words during play at age 2.[70] Parental behaviors that assist infants in "connecting" socially and becoming effective conversationalists seem to enhance their play competence and ability to talk about others' thoughts and feelings later on. In sum, quality of adult–child social engagement, both within and outside of make-believe play, has much to do with the potential of such play to lead children's development forward.

ENHANCING SOCIODRAMATIC PLAY WITH PEERS

At child care, 4-year-old Sammy joins a group of children in the block area for a space shuttle launch. "That can be our control tower," he suggests to Vance, pointing to a corner by a bookshelf.

"Wait, I gotta get it ready," calls out Lynette, who is still arranging the astronauts (two dolls and a bear) inside a circle of large blocks, which represents the rocket.

"OK, all aboard Discovery!" Sammy broadcasts into a small wooden block, his pretend loudspeaker. After Lynette sets up the astronauts, Sammy announces, "Countdown!"

"Five, six, two, four one, blastoff!" responds Vance, commander of the control tower.

Lynette makes one of the dolls push a pretend button and reports, "Brrrm, brrrm, they're going up!"

Among children who have regular contact with peers, sociodramatic play with agemates increases greatly between ages 3 and 5.[71] As this excerpt reveals, by age 4 children can create and coordinate several characters in an elaborate plot and weave together intricate role relationships and story lines—factors that, as we have seen, contribute greatly to their cognitive and social competence.

Pretending with peers draws on the diverse communication skills children develop with adults. A secure infant–parent attachment bond, which grows out of caregiver warmth, responsiveness, and sensitive communication, predicts socially mature peer play in early childhood, including cooperation, empathy, and popularity.[72] And as I indicated in Chapter 2, the blend of warmth and expectations for mature behavior that make up authoritative parenting is linked to skilled peer interaction as well. Social play with agemates must be responsive and harmonious to result in pleasurable, satisfying, long-lasting play.

If sociodramatic play with agemates is to serve as a "zone" for learning, shared understanding, or intersubjectivity, is essential, just as it is in adult–child dialogues. In the shuttle-launch episode, Sammy, Vance, and Lynette reached a high level of intersubjectivity as they worked out a division of labor and responded to one another in a smooth, complementary fashion. Of course, children do argue and disagree. Piaget underscored the role of these conflicts in getting children to give up their egocentrism and notice others' perspectives.[73] Yet conflict is far less effective in promoting sensitivity to others' beliefs, thoughts, and feelings than is returning to a state of intersubjectivity— by engaging in cooperative dialogues and resolving differences of opinion.[74]

Intersubjectivity among preschool play partners increases with age. When psychologist Artin Göncü observed 3- and 4-year-olds engaged in sociodramatic pursuits, the 4-year-olds more often considered their partners' preferences and built on their partners' play acts—by asking a partner what he or she would like to do, introducing relevant new elements into the play narrative, compromising in instances of conflict, and expressing agreement with the partner's ideas. [75] These features of play reflect children's developing sensitivity to diverse points of view and their appreciation of the value of a meeting of minds for pleasurable, rewarding play.

Research indicates that parents and teachers rarely mediate preschoolers' peer relations unless intense disagreements arise that threaten safety or (in the case of teachers) classroom order. [76] And when adults do step in, they seldom use interventions that help children regulate their own interaction. Instead, adults often resort to directive strategies, in which they tell children exactly what to say and do and therefore solve the problem for them, as in, "Don't grab. Ask for a turn!" or "Wait until Sandra is finished." [77]

These techniques are appropriate for children who lack social skills and therefore, at least initially, benefit from clear direction. But adults need to modify these strategies to suit children's play maturity, providing assistance tailored to the child's "zone." Sticking with directive interventions does not prompt children to come up with effective solutions to conflict as it arises—strategies that work because they take into account both the child's and the playmate's desires.

At times, the adult might model a social skill or give the child examples of strategies, as in, "You could ask Paul, 'Would you let me try it for a while?' or you could say, 'May we share it?'" At other times, the adult might encourage the child to generate possible strategies: "What could you do to get Mary and Andrea to let you play, too?" In each instance, parents and teachers select the level of support that best matches the child's current social capacities and then pull back as the child acquires new social problem-solving skills.

Many parents and teachers hesitate to mediate children's play, perhaps because they believe (incorrectly) that children pick up social skills just by spending time with agemates. Vygotsky's theory tells us that adults are active agents in children's social development. If they wait until a child's negative acts become extreme, then their first impulse is to assert high control, and sometimes force. The following three suggestions can help parents and teachers select strategies that foster more mature social behavior:

- Intervene soon enough to prevent peer difficulties from escalating, thereby avoiding highly intrusive intervention tactics.

- Focus on developing the skills of each child, not just on quelling disturbances. Ask yourself, "What have I seen this child do in situations similar to this one? How can I help the child communicate more effectively?"
- Think in terms of the support that is necessary without taking over social responsibilities that children can assume on their own. Ask yourself, "How much of my help does the child require to meet his or her goals in this situation? A general prompt? Some suggested strategies? Or a specific directive and a demonstration?"[78]

Compared to sociodramatic play, preschoolers find it harder to establish a cooperative, shared framework when working together on realistic projects, such as construction, puzzle, and art activities.[79] To collaborate on these tasks, they need much more adult instruction and monitoring than they do in make-believe activities. Here, again, children's social competence is more advanced in make-believe play than in other situations. The social skills mastered in sociodramatic activities gradually generalize, helping children work toward shared goals in nonplay pursuits.

PHYSICAL CONTEXTS FOR MAKE-BELIEVE PLAY

Adults promote children's make-believe not just through scaffolding their pretending and social behavior but also through arranging a stimulating, appropriate play environment. The physical context of children's play is important because it shapes play themes and opportunities to interact with agemates. Consequently, it can have a profound impact on what children learn.

Play Materials

Toys and other play props should capitalize on children's current make-believe capacities while gently spurring children forward, toward a wider range of themes, roles, and characters and increasingly intricate story lines. As children become conscious of the goals of play and more concerned with rules and rule-following, adults can provide opportunities for game play. Then they can extend these understandings by gradually introducing more complex games.

Martha Bronson's *The Right Stuff for Children Birth to Age 8*[80] is an excellent resource for selecting play materials that support development in early childhood. Although it is written for teachers, preschool and child-care center directors, and elementary school principals, it can also guide parents. Here is an overview of changing needs for make-believe and game materials from toddlerhood into the primary grades.

BEGINNINGS: 15 MONTHS TO 2 YEARS.   Toddlers need a small selection of realistic-looking toys to support their beginning capacity to pretend. These include stuffed animals; soft, cloth-bodied or rubber dolls with simple care accessories; a play telephone and housekeeping items to support role play; large hand puppets for an adult and small hand puppets for the child; and transportation toys, both the large riding type and the smaller, hand-manipulated variety. Already, picture books can inspire make-believe, especially when they depict familiar objects and experiences.

By the end of this period, as toddlers begin to develop the representational capacities and fine motor skills for setting up scenes themselves, they enjoy small peg people that fit in cars, boats, and other vehicles. Soon after, they are ready for more complex scenes—dollhouse, garage, or barn. And some start to dress up, an activity that can be supported by old clothing of family members.

EXPANDING MAKE-BELIEVE SKILLS: 2 TO 3 YEARS.   Between ages 2 and 3, fantasy-theme repertoires expand greatly. Children take increasing responsibility for initiating and elaborating make-believe scenarios, first with adults and older siblings, then with agemates. During this period, they can make use of a wider array of make-believe materials—diverse dolls, from babies to children their own age and with physical and cultural differences they see in their communities; more feeding and care accessories; vehicles of different types and sizes; play scenes with a larger number of peg people, animals, and inanimate props; large and small blocks for putting together pretend structures; and a more varied array of dress-up clothing.

Around this age, placing pretend materials in sand and water-play areas begins to inspire highly imaginative and extended play. Also, books, videos, and TV programs with simple narratives offer models that young preschoolers can act out and embellish in make-believe. With respect to TV's potential for inspiring play, programs with slow-paced, nonviolent action and easy-to-follow story lines, such as "Barney and Friends" and "Mr. Rogers' Neighborhood," lead to more elaborate make-believe play than do those presenting quick, disconnected bits of information.[81]

BLOSSOMING OF SOCIODRAMATIC PLAY: 3 TO 5 YEARS.   The mid- to late-preschool years are a time of burgeoning capacity for sociodramatic play, especially group pretend. Children incorporate more detail into their play themes and benefit from increasingly varied and flexible props—hand and finger puppets; dolls with articulated limbs that can be manipulated; doll clothing with buttons, zippers, and other fasteners; more housekeeping accessories, such as high chairs, bassinets, and cooking, serving, and washing equipment; and diverse play animals, including fish, reptiles, dinosaurs, and exotic species.

Older preschoolers can comprehend and recall more complex stories, and they like books and videos about children their own age, animals, and everyday life, such as a visit to a hospital, a fire station, or a factory. They also like ridiculous, funny and dramatic, fantastic tales. Often they memorize those they like best and act them out in make-believe.

The years from 3 to 5 are a time of peak interest in play scenes, such as house, school, airport, farm, and zoo.[82] In addition to prepackaged scene sets, children can be provided the raw materials—shoe boxes, pipe cleaners, cardboard cylinders, aluminum foil, and art supplies—to create their own scenes. Whereas realistic toys encourage preschoolers to act out everyday roles, nonspecific materials often encourage fantastic role play, such as pirates or creatures from outer space. Fantastic roles, in turn, prompt more complex peer interaction, especially statements that plan and comment on the make-believe scenario itself, as in "I'll be the pirate and you be the prisoner."[83] Since fantastic make-believe does not follow highly familiar scripts, children must devote more energy to working out each episode and explaining what they are doing to their companions.

Literacy objects offer another powerful illustration of how play materials mold make-believe content. Early childhood educators Susan Neuman and Kathy Roskos provided 3- to 5-year-olds in a child-care program with literacy-enriched housekeeping, office, and library areas. For example, the housekeeping area included cookbooks, coupons, recipe cards, grocery packages, and pencils and notepads for list-making. Compared to agemates in a control program without extra literacy props, the children engaged in far more complex and extended literacy-related pretending.[84] They more often talked about literacy objects, pretended to read and write as part of role play, and transformed literacy props imaginatively, such as calling a cookbook a "magic, genie book" and a piece of paper "directions for ballet lessons."

Children at the upper end of this age range start to become interested in games. At first, simple games that depend on chance rather than strategy or skill are best—lotto, dominoes, and card games based on matching and visual memory (such as Concentration).

ADVANCED SOCIODRAMATIC AND GAME PLAY: 6 TO 8 YEARS.   In the early school grades, children display an even greater capacity to create replicas of the world around them—skills that teachers may build on in extended projects, such as studying a Native American village or the wildlife of a rain forest. Six-to 8-year-olds continue to like role play, and teachers can use it to foster their academic development. One third-grade teacher invented a magic carpet on which her class "traveled" to different countries, integrating all academic areas into the experience—reading, writing, math, science, and social studies.

Around ages 7 and 8, as children become more conscious of the rules of play, they like to act out scripted puppet shows and plays. As informal make-believe declines, game play strengthens. By the end of this period, children formulate and implement strategies and cooperate more effectively in games. They have also become interested in competition. Hence, they are ready for basic strategy games—checkers, chess, fantasy and adventure games, word games, and team sports, such as T-ball and soccer.

Equipping and Arranging the Play Environment

In addition to the appropriateness of play materials, their quantity and arrangement affect the maturity and diversity of themes in children's make-believe. These features of the environment also influence the congeniality of peer interaction.

With respect to quantity, children's behavior can tell us whether they have too many or too few toys. An excess of toys overwhelms and overstimulates. The child whose bedroom is piled high with all the latest playthings is likely to cherish and play with few of them. Alternatively, poor-quality child-care centers, widespread in the United States, are often underequipped with play materials. In one such program that I visited, the block-building area had only twenty blocks for sixty 2- to 5-year-olds. Although a stove, table, refrigerator, and crib lined the perimeter of the housekeeping area, there were just three dolls, a handful of dishes, one pan, and six dress-up garments to inspire role play. Without adults and play props to engage them, many younger children wandered aimlessly. And rather than becoming immersed in sociodramatic pursuits, older children quarreled over the few toys available. Research confirms that when playthings are in short supply, preschoolers' conflicts increase.[85]

The power of play spaces to affect the variety of make-believe themes is dramatically evident in preschoolers' gender-stereotyped toy choices and pretend themes. By age 2, gender differences in play are evident, and they strengthen over early childhood.[86] Parents vary greatly in their gender-role attitudes; the more traditional their beliefs, the more gender-stereotyped their toy purchases and the more stereotyped their children's play.[87] In many classrooms, the arrangement of play areas reinforces these sharp gender distinctions. Separate housekeeping and block-building areas—hubs of preschool pretending—result in girls gathering in housekeeping, where they enact domestic roles, and boys congregating in blocks, where they build intricate structures, play energetically with vehicles, and create fantastic and adventurous scenarios.

When graduate student Cheryl Kinsman and I collaborated with a kindergarten teacher to rearrange these play spaces, striking changes in children's play occurred. We removed the wall of shelves dividing housekeeping from blocks, joining the two areas into one.[88] While the shelves were in place, play was highly gender stereotyped. Children largely interacted with peers of their own gender, especially when girls were in housekeeping and boys in blocks. Also, when boys did enter housekeeping, their play was generally irrelevant to the goals of the setting. In one instance, several boys scurried on all fours around the kitchen table, each pushing a large wooden truck while a traffic director stood on a chair, shouting, "Green light, go! Red light, stop!"

But once the play areas were joined, boys and girls frequently played together. And girls, especially, engaged in more complex play, integrating materials from both areas into their fantasy themes. Finally, negative interactions between children declined after we removed the divider, perhaps because the more open play space reduced crowding and competition for materials. As these outcomes illustrate, play spaces often promote attitudes and practices of the surrounding culture—in ways not evident to teachers and parents. Our intervention encouraged this teacher to think more carefully about the impact her classroom design had on the quality of children's play experiences.

THE TRANSFORMATION OF THE CHILD'S PLAY WORLD

The make-believe play and games of early childhood offer an influential route to acquiring cultural values and the self-regulation children need to act in accord with those values. In the heat of the child's relentless requests for new toys advertised on TV and in the possession of playmates, parents seldom stop to ask the question: What activities will this toy inspire? What values will the activities teach? What social rules will my child learn to follow? A comparison of the fantasy activities of American children with those of children in other cultures spotlights potent lessons of the play world not given sufficient conscious consideration.

Children's make-believe places greater emphasis on imaginativeness and autonomy in Western individualistic nations than in collectivist societies. While American preschoolers often conjure up fantastic roles and vie with peers for the most stimulating and influential of them, children in Asian cultures devote more hours to play in which they perform actions in unison. For example, in a game called Bhatto Bhatto, East Indian children act out a trip to market requiring intricate touching of one another's elbows and hands as they pretend to cut and share a tasty vegetable.[89] On Children's Day in the Peoples Republic of China, preschoolers gather on lawns outside their classrooms to perform large-group, highly scripted activities for their families. They sing stories conveying social and moral lessons while dramatizing them with complex hand motions and body postures, in which each child acts identically.

The personal expressiveness and role negotiation in Western children's play are well suited for developing innovativeness, self-reliance, and social problem-solving skills—traits important for success in Western school and work worlds. Nevertheless, Western children's play has been transformed into an ever-enlarging culture of conspicuous consumption encompassing a seemingly endless array of costly, fancy amusements. Parents are quick to feel guilty about depriving children of the latest "educational" playthings or jeopardizing their integration into a peer network in which toys and other possessions are a salient basis for belonging. Yet parents' gatekeeper role with respect to play is as crucial as it is in the realm of TV.

An important point to note is that many contemporary toys undermine imagination and self-regulation. Aggressive toys are the most worrisome. Preschoolers who transform a stick or block into a weapon are doing little more than exploring a pervasive aspect of their culture. But equipping children with realistic-looking guns, swords, shields, and other tools of warfare is tantamount to setting up a training ground in aggression. Such toys foster both pretend and real hostility among peers.[90] Boys' penchant for high activity, excitement, and risk taking and their view of weaponry as the ultimate in masculinity attract them to war toys. Furthermore, when boys play with action figures modeled on violent TV and movie characters, such as Power Rangers, Transformers, and X-Men, their play narrows to mimicking the characters' televised behavior and is generally aggressive and stereotyped. Video games with violent plots in which children advance by shooting and evading the enemy are yet another fantasy pursuit that largely appeals to boys. A growing number of studies confirm that heavy playing of such games duplicates the effects of violent TV by promoting aggression and desensitizing children to violence.[91] Furthermore, video games, even more than TV, are riddled with ethnic and gender stereotypes.[92]

In watching what happens once fast-action video games have entered their households, many parents express another concern—that their children will become addicted to these violent amusements. About 5 percent, usually boys, develop into "passionate," or excessive, players during the elementary school years and desperately need parental intervention.[93] Compared to infrequent users, children highly involved in video games spend less time productively, more often watching cartoons and less often reading.[94] One parent whose son, Joey, spent his early childhood focused on play with Transformers and his school years immersed in video games complained about the boy's mediocre grades and lamented, "Nothing seems to interest him." Joey spent so much time with highly stimulating video games that he came to regard slower-paced pursuits that require greater initiative to reach a goal as dull.

Of course, preschoolers—even those as young as age 3—benefit from experience with computers as long as activities are constructive, adults are available to support them, and children are not diverted from other worthwhile activities. But in homes in which family members are preoccupied with the computer, especially the Internet, time spent communicating and enjoying joint leisure activities declines.[95] Therefore, the computer's value for acquiring new skills and information must be weighed against its potential for detracting from adult–child dialogues and other family activities.

Children's opportunities to engage in development-enhancing make-believe and game play are at risk in yet another way. Their lives are often heavily organized and scheduled. Many leave preschool, child-care, and primary-school settings, which may not recognize the value of play, for late-afternoon lessons and adult-organized sports leagues. Contributing to the rise in these adult-directed activities is a decline in neighborhood safety, making parents unwilling to allow their children to gather outside without supervision. In many American communities, child-organized games, handed down from one generation to the next—for example, red rover, statues, blind man's buff, leapfrog, and endless variants on popular sports—are a thing of the past.

Some experts worry that adult-structured athletics are robbing children of crucial learning experiences that accrue from spontaneous game play. When adults control children's games, place heavy pressure on them to win, and assign them to specific roles so they lose the opportunity to experiment with rules and strategies, then the arguments of critics are valid. Furthermore, children who join teams so early—by ages 4 or 5—that the physical, cognitive, and social skills demanded are well beyond their current capabilities usually lose interest and want to drop out.[96] And parents and coaches who criticize rather than encourage and do not let players forget about defeat prompt intense anxiety in some youngsters. Eventually, those children may avoid athletics entirely.[97]

To safeguard children's learning and enthusiasm, make-believe play rather than organized sports is best for preschoolers. When children are ready for game play, permitting them to select sports they enjoy, to progress at their own pace, and to participate in decisions about team rules preserves the positive lessons discussed in this chapter—in cooperation, fair play, and willingly following social rules. Finally, practice times must be adjusted to children's attention spans and need for unstructured time with family and peers. Two practices a week, each no longer than thirty minutes, is sufficient for 6- to 8-year-olds.[98]

By observing children's play themes, we can discover much about the values and identities that our culture—by way of homes, child-care centers, schools, and community youth activities—transmits to the next generation. As leaders in children's development, parents and teachers are in a prime position to design and influence children's play worlds in ways that shield them from acquiring materialistic and violent attitudes and behaviors and that accentuate play's cognitive, emotional, and social benefits. Vygotsky's theory reminds us that as long as we think carefully about the play materials we offer, the style and content of adult–child play, and the social skills we encourage in children's peer relations, make-believe play can nurture a wide range of capacities essential for academic, social, and later-life success.

FIVE

Helping Children with Deficits and Disabilities

The movie *Mr. Holland's Opus,* in its main plot and its subplot, is a thoroughly Vygotskian story. It chronicles a high-school music teacher's metamorphosis from a detached instructor, cynical about his students' interests and motivations, into an inspiring mentor for hundreds of young music appreciators and instrumentalists. Unable to make a living at his first love, composing, Mr. Holland turned to the professional safety net he had earned in college: his teaching credential. Reluctantly in the classroom, he drilled his students on textbook facts and conducted the school orchestra in a flat, lifeless fashion. Without a meeting of minds and a jointly constructed "zone," teacher and students disengaged, growing further and further apart.

Painfully aware of failing to "reach" his classes, Mr. Holland set aside assigned texts and musical scores one day and tried to "connect" with his students. "What kind of music do you like?" he asked. Noticing their shocked and confused expressions, he added sympathetically, "Don't be afraid."

"Rock 'n' roll!" was the nearly uniform answer. Next, Mr. Holland began to build a tie between students' current understandings and where he wanted to lead them. "What's this?" he asked as he played a lively rock tune on the piano.

The classroom came alive. For the first time, students smiled and looked alert. "'Lovers Concerto'!" they chorused.

Then Mr. Holland asked whether anyone liked the music of Johann Sebastian Bach. In the face of blank stares, he countered, "Sure you do," as he demonstrated how "Lovers Concerto" is a variation on Bach's "Minuet in G." The "zone" under way, teacher and students began to extend it. "Hands were up in the air, they were answering questions. It was so much fun!" Mr. Holland reported enthusiastically to his wife that evening, in a reversal of his usual pessimistic recap of the school day.

Mr. Holland discovered that teaching requires both "heart" and learning goals tailored to children's interests, knowledge, and skills. Each is essential for building a relationship that engages the learner.

Yet Mr. Holland could not transfer these basic realizations to the rearing of his own child, Col, born with a profound hearing loss. Refraining from gesturing to Col in hopes that he would lip read and speak, the Hollands failed to forge a basis for communication with their son. Hence, they lacked tools for inducting him into culturally valued ways of thinking and behaving.

As Mr. Holland's disappointment at being unable to share his passion for music with Col deepened, the gulf between father and son widened. Although he could coach an unmusical high-school athlete to find the beat on a drum and a faltering clarinetist to play with feeling, Mr. Holland could not exchange meanings with Col and, therefore, teach him to regulate his own thought and behavior.

As a preschooler, Col was impatient, demanding, and explosive. Only when his mother cried, "I can't talk to my son! I don't know what he wants, feels, thinks. I want to talk to my son!" did Mr. Holland agree to enroll him in a special school where, together, mother and child learned sign language and Col interacted with deaf peers, who shared his reliance on gesture. The capacity to converse with others enabled Col to develop into a sensitive, caring young man with a talent for science and auto mechanics. And eventually, it permitted him to appreciate the meaning of music, even though he could not hear it, and to draw on that understanding to find common ground with his father.

Engaging in parent–child dialogues is a formidable task when children bring to the relationship, through no fault of their own, deficits and disabilities that hinder their ability to interact with others. And as *Mr. Holland's Opus* so poignantly reveals, parents' characteristics—in this instance, a father's shattered hopes and dreams on learning of his child's disability—can further jeopardize communication, children's gateway to membership in their culture.

In this chapter, I take up Vygotsky's insights into the development and education of children who, because of biologically based impairments, face formidable learning problems. Vygotsky focused largely on children with sensory deficits, especially deafness and blindness, and on children with major psychological disorders, including mental retardation and schizophrenia. But his ideas apply to any type of physical or psychological difficulty, offering guiding principles for how to help all such children reach their potential.

Vygotsky's recommendations for special-needs children are variations on sociocultural themes we have already considered. The development of such children permits us to see, more conspicuously than with nondisabled children, the joint and interwoven influence of biology and environment on development. It also spotlights the vigorous role of social experiences—especially relationships with parents and teachers—in inducing favorable outcomes.

After introducing Vygotsky's main ideas, I'll apply them—first to children with severe visual and hearing deficits. Then I'll turn to the most widespread disability of the late preschool and school years—children whose inattentive, impulsive, and hyperactive behavior has led to a diagnosis of attention-deficit hyperactivity disorder (ADHD).

We will see that children with sensory deficits, although not inherently prone to difficulties with self-regulation, quickly develop them when deafness or blindness limits interaction with caring adults. And children with ADHD, most of whom are genetically disposed toward poor self-regulation, become increasingly inattentive and impulsive without firm, consistent, and caring adult guidance. By the school years, children with these highly dissimilar problems—blind, deaf, and attention-deficit—bear tragic similarities in behavior if they have become estranged from their sociocultural worlds.

VYGOTSKY'S APPROACH TO CHILDREN WITH DEFICITS AND DISABILITIES

Vygotsky regarded the most debilitating consequence of a physical or mental disability as not the disability itself but rather its implications for the child's participation in culturally meaningful activities. When a disability disrupts communication with more expert cultural members, then the development of all higher forms of thinking will be compromised.

All too often, Vygotsky pointed out, children with disabilities are not integrated into social life to the fullest extent possible. Consequently, on top of the primary deficit they develop a more serious secondary problem—a "cultural deficit"—because their learning of culturally valued ways of thinking and behaving is impaired.[1] Interference in social interaction hinders all uniquely human understandings and skills—controlled attention, memory strategies, reflective thought, problem solving, imagination, and most important, language and, with it, conversational practices that enable transfer of new competencies from collaboration with others. Under these circumstances, the effect of the disability is greatly magnified. And additional impairments emerge that could have been avoided if the child's social experiences had remained intact.[2]

Although Vygotsky regarded disrupted social experiences and, in turn, deficits in higher forms of thinking, as far more serious than the original disability, he also pointed out that social experiences are far more open to intervention than is the child's original problem.[3] A deaf child cannot be granted the ability to hear, a blind child the ability to see, and the child with attention deficits the ability to focus and inhibit impulses as if brain functioning were fully intact. But ways can be found to integrate the child into family, classroom, and community life—the most important focus of intervention and the path to ensuring that the child reaches his or her potential.

Vygotsky believed that the same general principles that govern the development of nondisabled children apply to children with physical and mental impairments. In children with disabilities, the course of development is altered, in part because of the defect's impact on social experiences and in part because such children develop behaviors aimed at compensating for their deficits.

As I will show, deaf children rely heavily on gesture to get their meaning across to others, blind children on touch and speech to "reach" their caregivers, and children with ADHD on high rates of private speech to exert control over their impulsive behavior. These compensatory skills provide clear evidence of the child's active striving to engage with social partners. Because a deficit or disability often hampers social contact and collaboration, carefully reconstructed social experiences—ones that establish shared understanding, scaffold new knowledge and skills, and include time for relaxed conversation and play—are crucial for ensuring that special-needs children develop at their best.

CHILDREN WITH SENSORY DEFICITS

Our eyes and ears are our sensory lifelines to affiliation, the foundation on which we rely for exchanging meanings through gesture and word. As Col's story illustrates, the burning desire of children with sensory deficits to communicate must be met halfway, by helping them establish alternative avenues for social connection. Otherwise, development will be profoundly compromised, and the child will remain forever a cultural outsider.

Children with hearing or visual impairments readily lean on their intact senses to communicate as long as adults encourage and assist them. When at long last Col was granted a stimulating language-learning environment, he capitalized on his visual sense to master American Sign Language (ASL), a gestural communication system that is as elaborate as any spoken language. The vast, symbolic power of language grants the deaf or blind child access to realities and ideas that would otherwise be unreachable, as demonstrated by Col's grasp of what music must be like and its significance to his father.

So driven are human children to connect with others that they try to invent language when they cannot acquire it from their social world. Psychologist Susan Goldin-Meadow and her colleagues followed the progress of a group of deaf preschoolers whose parents—like Mr. Holland—discouraged gesturing and addressed them verbally, in hopes that the children would use speech to communicate. None of the children acquired spoken language or used even the most common ASL gestures. Yet they spontaneously produced a gestural communication system, termed *homesign,* strikingly similar to hearing children's verbal language. For example, the homesigners had distinct gestural forms for nouns and verbs and combined them into simple sentences.[4] And over time, their language became an increasingly flexible symbolic tool as they began to represent not just the here and now but nonpresent objects and past and future events. In one instance, a child pointed over his shoulder to signify the past, pointed to a picture of a poodle, and finally pointed to the floor in front of him, saying, "I used to have a poodle!"[5]

Hearing children and deaf children acquiring ASL attain language milestones earlier and reach far greater linguistic heights than do homesign speakers, verifying that a rich language environment fosters rapid mastery of complex communication skills. But even without access to conventional language, these deaf children generated their own basic language system. What happens when they have willing conversational partners? Recently, linguists Judy Kegl, Ann Senghas, and Marie Coppola described a group of Nicaraguan homesigners who had been brought together to form a community. Although their simple gestural systems differed, over the next decade a common gestural language emerged, similar in complexity to well-established sign languages, such as ASL.[6] The wide gap between deaf children's self-generated gesture systems and the newly formed Nicaraguan Sign Language underscores the importance of a community of speakers for children to develop a full-blown language.

The inspiring story of Helen Keller shows that even in the absence of both vision and hearing, the child's thirst to be understood and to understand others endures. Helen's craving to connect with her social world ensured that with the help of Anne Sullivan, her sensitive, persistent teacher, she would acquire language. Before Anne arrived, 6-year-old Helen—much like the homesigning children just described—had invented just over sixty gestures. For example, she used a pulling motion to mean "come" and a pushing motion to mean "go," and she pretended to shiver and to turn on the freezer when she wanted "ice cream."[7] But without the language skills to converse with others, Helen remained locked, as she later described, in "an inhuman silence which severs and estranges."[8] Recounting her early childhood, she emphasized the isolation, disorientation, and desperation that resulted from being deprived of the ability to communicate and therefore to think—qualities, she reflected, that make a person human.

Recognizing the importance of teaching Helen language, Anne exploited Helen's sense of touch. She spelled words into Helen's hand using the manual alphabet. The famous moment, when Helen stood by a water pump and realized that "w-a-t-e-r" meant the cool liquid flowing over her hand, she called her "soul dawn."[9] The rest of the day, Helen touched numerous objects, eager to learn their names. Gradually, she added adjectives and verbs to her vocabulary and mastered the rules for expressing thoughts in sentences. And eventually, she acquired terms for intangible experiences and processes, such as *love* and *think*, essential for grasping others' mental states and perspectives.[10]

Language enabled Helen to undergo a transformation from a mimicking animal to a thinking, conversing human being. She wrote:

> Before my teacher came to me, I did not know that I am. I lived in a world
> that was a no-world . . . , I did not know that I knew [nothing], or that I
> lived or acted or desired. . . . I never contracted my forehead in the act of
> thinking. . . . My inner life, then, was a blank without past, present, or fu-
> ture, without hope or anticipation, without wonder or joy or faith.[11]

To reach out to her hearing partners, Helen resolved to learn to speak, doing so by lightly touching another's face to feel the position of the lips and tongue and then imitating the sounds. The process was slow and tedious, but she succeeded. Although her articulation remained imperfect, Helen became an accomplished orator, author, and crusader for the oppressed. Her extraordinary intellectual and social achievements sprang from sensitive scaffolding of language and communication by a highly gifted teacher. Anne insisted that Helen contribute to her own progress, just as preschoolers first acquiring language do. Rather than sitting Helen down for formal instruction, Anne permitted her to move freely among objects that interested her. Because of Helen's fascination with living things, most lessons took place outside, largely in the context of play.[12]

Few people can look back, as Helen could, on the personal impact of mastering language. Its central role in the formation of mind and in the transmission of culture is conspicuously evident when it is so drastically curtailed that it is nearly absent. With language, a recent biographer summed up, Helen's "blind eyes saw, her deaf ears heard, and her muted voice spoke."[13]

In one of her speeches, Helen claimed that deafness could result in a far greater catastrophe for development than could blindness. She explained,

> Blindness robs the day of its light and makes us physically helpless. . . . [But] deafness stops up the fountainhead of knowledge and turns life into a desert. For without language, intellectual life is impossible.

Vygotsky agreed that from a physical standpoint, the blind child has lost more than the deaf child. From the perspective of human social life, however, deafness is a more serious deficit because it can exclude the child from social contact. Blind children have greater potential for complete communication with others and can compensate more readily for their sensory loss through verbal speech. Consequently, they are less in danger of being denied important knowledge and skills and full-fledged membership in their community.[14]

Nevertheless, despite powerful compensatory behaviors and a strong drive to acquire language, both blind and deaf children are at risk for limited and insensitive social experiences. To safeguard their development, children with either deficit require adult support that uses the child's sensory strengths to enhance social relationships and language skills. Yet not all parents are equipped to surmount the impact of a child's sensory deficit on the parent–child relationship. A mismatch in sensory abilities between parent and child requires great effort and adaptation by the parent to establish and sustain sensitive, stimulating interaction.

The Blind Child

In a recent study, psychologist Deborah Hatton and her collaborators followed a group of children who had a visual acuity of 20/800 or worse from infancy into the preschool years. Although the children were free of any other disability, their vision was so poor that, at best, they had only dim light perception.[15] Compared to agemates who had less severe visual impairments, the blind or near-blind group showed serious delays in all aspects of development: motor, social, language, cognitive, and self-care skills.

What explains such profoundly restricted early development? Minimal or absent vision alters the child's experiences in at least two crucial, interrelated ways.

EXPLORATION AND UNDERSTANDING OF SPACE.   Infants with severe visual impairments attain motor milestones many months later than do their sighted agemates. On average, blind infants do not reach for and manipulate objects until 12 months—skills mastered by sighted babies around 4 months. With respect to moving independently, blind babies crawl around 13 months and walk at about 19 months; the averages for sighted infants are 7 months and 11 months.[16] Why is the blind infant uninterested in crawling and walking—feats that the sighted baby diligently pursues?

Infants strive to move so they can explore the world of objects. To identify an object's location, infants with severe visual impairments must rely on sound. But sound does not serve as a precise clue to object location until much later than vision—around the middle of the first year.[17] And because infants who cannot see have trouble engaging their caregivers (a difficulty we'll take up next), adults may not provide them with rich, early exposure to sounding objects. As a result, the baby comes to understand relatively late that the environment is full of tantalizing objects to investigate.

Not surprisingly, until blind infants "reach on sound," they do not try to move on their own.[18] Even after they do crawl, their motor control is poor due to many months of inactivity and lack of access to visual cues that assist the sighted baby with balance. Because of their own uncertainty and their parents' protection and restriction to prevent injury, blind infants are typically tentative in their movements. And they engage in high rates of self-stimulating behaviors, including rocking, eye-poking, and self-manipulation, believed to result from understimulation due to delayed mobility. These self-absorbed actions divert the child from turning outward toward the environment, delaying motor development and exploration further.

Motor progress, social stimulation, and cognitive development are closely linked. Babies who move independently become more aware of space and the location of objects—basic knowledge that paves the way to more sophisticated understanding of their physical surroundings.[19] Toddlers with less physical knowledge are delayed in language development. They have fewer things to name and to talk about with others.

When infants start to move about, parents relate to them differently. They increase their expressions of affection and play as the child seeks them out for greetings, hugs, assistance with objects, and social games.[20] Furthermore, gestures related to exploration, such as pointing and showing things, permit toddlers to communicate more effectively and are stepping-stones to language. And finally, babies' expressions of delight—laughing, smiling, and babbling—as they work on new motor competencies trigger pleasurable reactions in others, which encourage infants' efforts further.[21]

All these experiences occur much later and less frequently for blind than sighted infants. Inability to imitate the actions of others presents additional challenges as blind children get older, contributing to their slow motor and cognitive progress relative to children with better vision.[22]

SOCIAL RELATIONSHIPS.   Besides delayed motor development, blind infants elicit less stimulating interaction for other reasons. They cannot make eye contact, imitate, or otherwise respond contingently to their parents' communications. Nor can they pick up nonverbal social cues and jointly attend with another to objects in their surroundings. Their emotional expressions are muted; for example, their smile is fleeting and unpredictable.[23] Sighted people depend on these ingredients for reaching shared understanding in social interaction. Their constriction or absence in the blind infant often reduces parental attention and communication further.

When a visually impaired child does not learn how to participate in dialogues in infancy, capacity to interact with adults and peers is compromised in early childhood. Slow language development—limited vocabulary, difficulties comprehending and producing narratives, and incorrect use of pronouns (calling the self "you" and the other person "me")—are well documented in blind preschoolers.[24]

Weak language skills, in turn, contribute to delayed development of make-believe play and all its attendant cognitive and social benefits.[25] When blind children receive less frequent and sensitive parental communication, they have less social knowledge to represent in their pretending. Also, they may be less motivated to act out what they do know. Compared to their sighted agemates, blind preschoolers display simpler and more repetitive make-believe. The more deficient their language skills, the more impoverished their pretending.[26] In one study that sought information about children's play from parents, even 6-year-old blind children were reported to devote most of their play time to solitary exploration of toys and very little to imaginative play.[27]

As language and play skills fall behind, blind children face increasing social isolation, which leads to further lags in cognitive and social skills. In an observational study of blind children enrolled in preschools with sighted agemates, the blind children seldom initiated contact with peers and teachers. When they did interact, they had trouble interpreting the meaning of others' reactions and responding appropriately. As a result, their social partners turned their attentions elsewhere.[28]

INTERVENTION.   Although many blind infants and preschoolers are substantially delayed in development, wide variation exists. Once language is under way and the child can rely on verbal communication for learning, some children with little or no vision show impressive rebounds, becoming adept at practical and social skills and acquiring a unique capacity for imaginative thinking, which grants access to visual phenomena through touch and verbal comprehension.

As Helen Keller explained, this appreciation of the visual—of light, color, form, pattern, and depth—is not exactly the same as the sighted person's. But by using the same sensory language as all people, the child with a sensory deficit is influenced by the absent sense and can construct a representational world sufficiently similar to that of others to understand their experiences and be understood by them. She clarified:

> Perhaps my sun shines not as yours. The colors that glorify my world . . . may not correspond exactly with those you delight in; but they are nonetheless color to me. The sun does not shine for my physical eyes, . . . nor do the trees turn green in the spring; but they have not therefore ceased to exist, any more than the landscape is annihilated when you turn your back on it.[29]

Vygotsky concurred that "the education of a blind child must be organized on the same terms as the education of any child capable of normal development. . . . The main source from which this development draws its contents is the same for both—language."[30] From this perspective, overcoming loss of sight lies in abundant parental scaffolding of the child's exploration of the environment and in dialogue about those explorations. The blind child enriched in these ways can rise to extraordinary intellectual heights. Vygotsky noted the case of eighteenth-century mathematician Nicholas Saunderson, blinded by smallpox when only a year old, who lectured at Cambridge University on principles of Newtonian physics and wrote a geometry textbook. He not only rose above his spatial limitations, but "grasp[ed] the concept of space in its higher forms."[31]

Techniques that help blind babies become aware of their physical and social surroundings include combining touch and sound to create heightened sensory input. For example, the parent can hold, touch, and bring the baby's hands to his or her face while talking or singing. Encouraging manipulation of objects that make sounds is also important. These experiences foster "reaching on sound," which motivates independent movement.[32] Furthermore, parents must take special care to talk about objects the child is attending to in appropriately descriptive ways. Often they use general terms, such as "that" or "thing" instead of specifics, such as "soft, round ball," which foster both physical awareness and language.[33] Using many repetitions and consistently responding to the child's efforts to make physical and social contact help blind children derive meaning from nonvisual sensations and take the initiative to explore, communicate, and learn more.

Blind children usually do not become proficient at investigating objects with their hands until 4 to 6 years of age. Hence, they continue to benefit from play materials with interesting sounds and textured surfaces—and conversations about their features—throughout early childhood. Furthermore, blind preschoolers' limited pretend play is an especially important focus of intervention. The child's difficulty manipulating objects suggests that initially, parents' scaffolding of make-believe should rely heavily on language, sounds, and actions. As dexterity improves, parents and teachers can help the child integrate objects into pretend play.

We have seen that blind children's make-believe play is hampered by delays in other areas, including motor skills, general knowledge, and language. Therefore, adult involvement in play must extend well beyond the age at which sighted children have turned toward play with peers. In fact, rich and varied opportunities for adult-supported play can help overcome blind children's restricted experiences. Participation in pretend scenarios grants the blind child firsthand contact with real-life situations that are easily observed by the sighted child but relatively inaccessible to a child without vision. With a supportive adult, blind children can also obtain the extra prompting, explanation, and repeated practice they need to comprehend, refine, and combine imaginative play elements into complex scenarios for maximum pleasure and learning.

Far more than the sighted child, the blind child requires the help of adults in joining in sociodramatic play with peers. Because blind children often lack the manipulative, language, and social skills to participate in such play, parents and teachers need to provide assistance so that sighted playmates do not become frustrated and stop playing. As blind children acquire play skills and sighted children include them and help them further, adult intervention can be withdrawn.

Finally, because of their physical passivity and delayed language, blind children are at risk for severe deficits in everyday physical and social experiences. In the midst of active family environments and socially stimulating classrooms, too often they remain idle and alone.[34] Parents and teachers must ensure that blind children collaborate with adults and peers in a diverse array of culturally valued activities, including self-care and simple chores; problem solving tasks; narrative conversation; storybook reading; physical, imaginative, and game play; and "hands-on," richly narrated excursions in the neighborhood and community. Although the principles of intervention are the same for the blind and the sighted child, parents and teachers must exert much greater effort to intervene purposefully and systematically in blind children's development.

The Deaf Child

Whereas blind children's difficulties originate in limitation of free movement and inability to detect nonverbal social cues, deaf children are often confronted with a chasm in parent–child language that, try as they might, they cannot cross. During the first 2 years, blind children lag behind deaf children in exploration, play, and social development. But extensive adult–child conversation and other collaborative activities permit blind children to forge ahead, eventually catching up with their sighted counterparts and even, as Vygotsky noted, "bringing to life new [mental] forces."[35] Through language, blind people can acquire a much more elaborate understanding of sighted people's worlds than sighted people will ever know of theirs.

The deaf child deprived of a rich, flexible language system and a fluid means of engaging in dialogues with others can still explore and imitate. As a preschooler, Col visited his father's classroom and copied his conducting motions, waving his arms gleefully as the school orchestra played. But without conversation, explanation, and narrated pretend, Col was shut out of the meaning of those motions. His lack of language isolated him from parents, playmates, and cultural activities and, in turn, from himself. He could not engage in self-directed speech, using it as a tool for regulating thought and action.

DEAF VERSUS HEARING PARENTS: CONSEQUENCES FOR DEVELOPMENT. Comparisons of deaf children of deaf parents with deaf children of hearing parents verify, once again, the crucial role of supportive parent–child communication for optimum development. A deaf child of deaf parents learns sign language as a native tongue in early childhood. But like Col, over 90 percent of deaf children are born to hearing parents, who do not know sign language and cannot master it quickly. As with any second language, it takes years to become fluent in sign—and most adult learners never reach a level of competence that matches that of individuals who acquired the language in childhood.[36]

Deaf children of deaf parents experience early language environments that are just as sensitive, stimulating, and varied as those of their hearing agemates. Consequently, their language (use of sign) and play maturity are on a par with hearing children's, and their self-directed signs resemble hearing children's private speech.[37] When they reach school age, deaf children of deaf parents learn easily and are socially skilled, getting along well with adults and peers.[38]

For deaf children of hearing parents, language acquisition, self-directed communication, and self-regulation are strikingly different. As early as the first year of life, their parents are less effective at reaching shared understanding in parent–child interaction than are deaf parents of deaf children and hearing parents of hearing children. A hearing parent of a deaf baby is less likely to express pleasure, establish joint attention, and coordinate play actions. Hearing parents are also more directive and intrusive, interrupting and redirecting the deaf child's behavior while the child is engrossed in play.[39] These insensitive practices increase in the second year of life, around the time parents expect their child to talk. Hearing parents' more directive behavior may stem from a well-intentioned attempt to stimulate a child behind in communication skills. But in response, deaf toddlers become less involved, less positive, and less compliant.[40]

Communication poorly adjusted to deaf children's needs can extend into the preschool years. In observations of mothers helping their 4- and 5-year-olds solve a challenging puzzle, psychologist Janet Jamieson found that hearing mothers of deaf children did not scaffold effectively; they had trouble adjusting their verbal and nonverbal assistance to the child's efforts. Poor scaffolding was in part due to the child's difficulty in evoking support from the hearing parent, who customarily relied on verbal responses to sustain interaction. Deaf preschoolers could sense very few of their hearing mothers' verbal comments and could not reply verbally. Not surprisingly, their progress on the task suffered; their puzzle-solution attempts did not increase from the beginning to the end of the session.[41] Deaf children of hearing mothers also used less private speech—especially less self-guiding comments—than did deaf children of deaf parents, who signed to themselves freely to regulate their problem-solving behavior.[42]

Already used to communicating with gesture, deaf children of deaf parents are actually advanced in early development of pretend play over their hearing agemates.[43] But deaf children of hearing parents, once again, show a lag in play maturity, largely due to their impoverished symbolic experiences. As with blind preschoolers, their play themes are less complex and more repetitive and their make-believe episodes less sustained. They also move more slowly toward pretending with objects that do not physically resemble make-believe symbols (a block for a telephone receiver) and to pretending solely through imagination, without objects. Furthermore, their social-play skills are weak. At child care or preschool, they spend more time playing by themselves or watching others.[44] Overall, the quality of deaf children's communication with their parents and their language skills are strong predictors of the elaborateness of their imaginative play.[45]

Children with less sensitive parent interaction and limited language skills are behind their agemates in achieving control over their behavior. Without intervention, deaf children of hearing parents frequently display impulse-control problems. They are more likely than hearing children to have tantrums and to be easily distracted and angered—behaviors that lead to poor school performance and difficulty forming gratifying peer relationships.[46]

INTERVENTION.   Hearing parents are not at fault for their deaf child's language and self-regulation problems. Instead, they lack experience with communication based entirely on vision and gesture. Deaf parents, in contrast, know they must wait for the child to turn toward them before interacting.[47] Hearing parents tend to speak or gesture while the child's attention is directed at the object of communication—a strategy that works for hearing but not deaf children. Deaf preschoolers, understandably, attend visually to very little of hearing parents' verbal messages.[48] When their child is confused or unresponsive, hearing parents often feel overwhelmed and become intrusive, engaging in overly directive physical prompts and verbal commands to obtain an appropriate response from a child who has become a passive, unrewarding social partner.

The dramatic contrast in development between deaf children of hearing parents and deaf children of deaf parents confirms Vygotsky's observation that more devastating than the original defect are its consequences for the child's integration into social life. Absence of hearing, per se, does not compromise cognitive and social development. When granted the opportunity, deaf children easily acquire an alternative language system. Much evidence indicates that sign-language exposure is the most efficient and effective route to enhancing the intellectual and social functioning of deaf children. This means, as it did for Col, special teachers, classrooms, and schools beginning in early childhood.

Many hearing parents worry that a child who acquires sign language as his or her native tongue will remain isolated from the larger world of hearing people, including the parents themselves and other family members. This deeply felt concern underlies the long-standing, virulent debate over whether lip reading and speaking rather than signing should be the deaf child's major language. The answer, based on our knowledge of deaf children's cognitive and social development, is not which system deaf children should acquire but which one should be given priority as the child's first language. For children with severe to profound hearing loss, relying only on speech leads to a barren early language environment. Therefore, sign language is crucial for safeguarding young children's cognitive potential and social integration.

Even under difficult circumstances, some deaf children manage to acquire sufficient spoken language to function in a hearing world. But without a sign-language foundation, many others, like Col, learn very little language, either gestural or verbal. Controversy persists over whether to teach both systems at once and, if so, which combined method to use. Simultaneous signing and speaking is taxing, even for highly trained teachers. Some research indicates that the clarity and completeness of each type of message deteriorates and the rate of communication is reduced by half when adults try to use both.[49] Also, acquiring ASL first provides deaf children with a strong language base for learning a second language, such as verbal English. They master spoken language more easily when they have had early, consistent exposure to a highly accessible sign-language system.[50] Nevertheless, more needs to be learned about joint sign and speech communication before educators can be sure of the best way to combine them in deaf preschoolers' language development.

What is clear is that hearing parents need extensive coaching and assistance in communicating with a deaf son or daughter from infancy on. Even when their signing fluency remains limited, parents who start to acquire sign language soon after they learn of their child's deafness can become skilled enough to help their child. The more extensive the signing input, the more rapid the child's language progress.[51] Hearing parents must also change some of their communication habits, making sure to sign or speak in the child's visual field and to focus and comment on objects sequentially rather than simultaneously.[52]

When parents make these adjustments, deaf children readily meet them half way, devising innovative strategies to capture their parents' attention, initiate conversation, sustain it, and repair it when it breaks down. One deaf 4-year-old fluent in ASL, on meeting a hearing adult with "beginner" signing skills, pointed to the housekeeping area in a playroom, turned to the adult, and made a sign. When the adult failed to comprehend, the child adjusted quickly. She pantomimed putting bread in the toy toaster, pushing in down, taking it out, and taking a bite. Then she repeated her sign, "Toast!"[53] She had not only kept the channel of communication open but enlarged her partner's signing vocabulary.

What about the implications of sign language for children's literacy development, given that the visual-gestural code is different from the auditory-oral code on which reading is based? Research shows that ASL proficiency enhances deaf children's reading and writing performance. In fact, deaf children of hearing mothers who reach a high level of ASL competence by school age read, write, and achieve just as well as do other children.[54] Recall from Chapter 2 that literacy skills grow out of adult–child narrative conversation and literacy-rich informal experiences. These forerunners of competent reading and writing are far more available to deaf preschoolers acquiring sign language than to their counterparts for whom the verbal mode has been emphasized. The gap between sign and literacy codes is not problematic for language-proficient signing children, since various creative systems have been devised to assist them in building a bridge to written language.[55]

Deaf children fluent in signing who later master the spoken code reap multiple benefits. Able to form ties with both deaf and hearing communities, they profit from an enlarged cultural world. At the same time, they become bilingual—competent at two languages. A wealth of evidence reveals that bilingual children are cognitively advantaged. Compared to their single-language agemates, they think more flexibly and critically and are better at comprehending abstract concepts.[56] They are also more aware of language structure. For example, they readily notice errors of meaning and grammar in spoken and written prose—capacities that enhance their reading and writing achievement.[57]

In sum, when all the social ingredients for nurturing language in the nondisabled child are granted to the deaf child, deafness has no negative implications for psychological development. To the contrary, some children show special cognitive strengths. Alternatively, when deafness results in impoverished language experiences, it endangers development by leaving the child weak in both gestural and spoken codes—thereby, as Vygotsky pointed out, "tearing him away from the normal milieu, isolating and placing him in a narrow, closed-off world, . . . where everything reminds him of [his defect]."[58] Deaf children who know only a little sign and a little spoken language are denied full access to social life and, consequently, to the mental tools essential for becoming self-regulated, literate participants in their culture.

THE CHILD WITH ATTENTION-DEFICIT HYPERACTIVITY DISORDER (ADHD)

While the other second graders worked in groups on math problems, Cory squirmed in his seat, dropped his pencil, looked out the window, fiddled with his shoelaces, and talked out. "Hey, Benjie," he yelled over the top of several absorbed groups of children, "'wanna come to my house after school?"

Benjie didn't answer. He and the other children weren't eager to play with Cory. After all, Cory was always in trouble, the recurrent target of the teacher's reprimands: "Cory, you're not listening!" "Cory, why aren't you contributing to your group?" "Cory, stop wadding up that paper and dropping it on the floor!" "Cory, get your lunch bag and come along. We're all waiting." "Cory, don't interrupt Benjie. Get back to work."

On days that Cory was absent, a rare calm pervaded the class. Even on the playground, Cory was a poor listener and failed to follow rules. During a soccer game, he fiddled with his hair and clothing and faced the wrong way when the ball rolled toward him. "Cory, wake up!" his teammates chastised.

Without warning, Cory could become explosive, hitting and shouting at a child who annoyed him. At home, his parents were in constant conflict with him over homework, chores, and fights with playmates in the neighborhood. His backpack and room were a chaotic mess, despite his mother Janet's pleas that he put things away and her tireless efforts to help him. He often lost crayons, pencils, books, and other materials necessary for completing school assignments.

"I can't even have a calm conversation with him!" Janet blurted out during a parent–teacher conference, tears welling up in her eyes. "I'm always correcting, shouting, on the verge of blowing up. The pleasure, the love seems wrung out of our relationship. I don't know what to do," she said as her voice trailed off and the tears flowed.

Cory is one of 3 to 5 percent of school-age children with attention-deficit hyperactivity disorder (ADHD)—the most prevalent developmental disorder of childhood.[59] In all, about two million American school-age children have ADHD. This means that on average, one or two are in every elementary school classroom.[60]

Children with ADHD look perfectly normal; they bear no outward sign of disability and typically score average or above in general intelligence. Yet their difficulties have profound implications for their future in that basic ingredients of self-regulation are impaired. Children with sensory deficits experience self-regulatory problems entirely as a consequence of disrupted social interaction. Their underlying capacity for control of thought and action is fully intact. For the ADHD child, poorly regulated behavior is biologically based, central to the disorder, and often lifelong, causing grave relationship difficulties and placing the child at risk for school failure, antisocial behavior, unintentional injuries, and vocational and marital problems in adulthood.[61]

Positive, constructive relationships with parents and teachers are essential for ADHD children to realize their potential for self-regulation, although this potential is more limited than that of other children. When they experience favorable social ties, children with ADHD are protected from the most damaging consequences of the disorder.

Symptoms

ADHD children have great difficulty sustaining attention; they can't stay focused on a task or a play activity that requires mental effort for more than a few minutes. Instead, they are constantly drawn to nearby stimulating, low-effort activities that seem like more fun. This explains their attraction to television and computer games[62] and the frequent complaint of parents, "Why can't he pay attention in school? He sits glued to the TV and the computer for hours!" In addition, children with ADHD often act impulsively, ignoring social rules, interrupting others, and lashing out with hostility when frustrated. Many, but not all, are hyperactive. They charge through their days with excessive motor activity, running and climbing in inappropriate situations; constantly talking and making sounds; and fidgeting by tapping their pencils, shaking their legs, and manipulating objects unrelated to the task at hand.[63]

For a diagnosis of ADHD, these symptoms of inattention, impulsivity, and hyperactivity must have appeared before age 7; that is, they must have emerged as an early and persistent problem. They must also be pervasive—evident in at least two settings, such as home and school—and contribute to academic and social difficulties. Also, the child's disorganized behavior must be inconsistent with his or her age.[64] Children with ADHD behave like other children, but they resemble children much younger than themselves.

ADHD is often thought of as a boy's disorder, as boys are diagnosed far more often than are girls. However, many girls with symptoms seem to be overlooked. Others who are diagnosed do not receive special services in psychological clinics and schools because their symptoms are less flagrant than boys'. When researchers look at the prevalence of ADHD in communities and the number of children receiving clinic-based treatment, the boy-to-girl ratio in communities is 3 to 1, in clinics as much as 9 to 1[65]—a difference that supports the notion that girls are less likely to receive expert intervention than are boys.

When ADHD is missed because the child's behavior is labeled as "a phase to be outgrown" or is blamed on "irresponsible" parents, the toll on both child and parents can be severe. Hayley, third daughter of Vanessa and Owen, showed typical symptoms of ADHD throughout childhood. By age 2, she had trouble staying focused on just about anything. Starting in kindergarten, her report cards noted widespread academic problems, irresponsible and uncooperative behavior, and frequent peer conflicts. Just getting her to bring school assignments home, let alone complete them, was a constant battle. Hayley's excitability; loud, bossy style; inability to share and take turns; and argumentativeness estranged her from other girls. Through most of her childhood, she had no friends.

Hayley's two older sisters were outstanding students, popular with peers, and involved in worthwhile after-school pursuits—scouting, piano, and dance. At age 8, Vanessa tried music lessons with Hayley, believing that she needed some activity in which to excel and to feel good about herself. The lessons lasted only a few weeks. "She's not ready for this," the piano teacher reported. "She squirms, looks away, can't remember what I've just asked her to do. Today, I had her march around the room just to let off steam. Let's try again in a year or two."

Consumed with worry, Vanessa and Owen sought the help of school officials and a private psychologist. "She's your third child. You're worn out from child rearing, so you're not spending enough time with her," the psychologist interpreted. Yet Vanessa felt that her unsuccessful efforts to help Hayley were devouring her days and bringing her to the edge of emotional exhaustion. Her sense of guilt and powerlessness deepened and Hayley's inattentiveness and impulsivity worsened, translating into low self-esteem, failing grades, and, by adolescence, alienation from her parents, reckless driving, alcohol and substance abuse, early sexual activity, and repeated firings from after-school and summer jobs.

Hayley's sisters were so well organized and competent; surely those same qualities must lie dormant in Hayley, Vanessa reasoned to herself. "I've failed as a parent, lost my ability to reach her," she lamented with excruciating parental pain. No one had recognized Hayley's disorder, understood its origins, and therefore been able to intervene effectively to help both Hayley and her parents.

Origins

Although popular opinion has attributed the constellation of behaviors that make up ADHD to permissive, careless parenting, Vanessa and Owen did not cause Hayley's condition. Instead, Hayley's disorder had made parenting a trying ordeal. Research indicates that heredity plays a major role in ADHD. The disorder runs in families, and identical twins share it far more often than do fraternal twins. Also, an adopted child who is inattentive and hyperactive is likely to have a biological parent, but not an adoptive parent, with similar symptoms. [66] When Hayley was finally diagnosed as an 18-year-old and a wiser, better informed psychologist told Vanessa and Owen about its genetic roots in most cases, Vanessa thought back to her own distractibility as a child and recalled the impulsive, overactive behavior of one of her brothers.

Exactly what might be inherited by individuals with ADHD? Recent genome, electrical brain-wave, and magnetic-imaging studies suggest that problems in brain functioning underlie the disorder. Several genes that affect neurotransmitters and hormone levels have been implicated in ADHD.[67] The disorder also is linked to reduced electrical activity and blood flow in the frontal lobes of the cerebral cortex,[68] which are responsible for consciousness, inhibition of impulses, and regulation of behavior through language. In addition, children with ADHD have a smaller corpus callosum,[69] a structure that transfers information from one side of the brain to the other. Smooth, efficient communication between the brain's hemispheres enhances our capacity to engage in complex activities requiring collaboration between many brain regions, including coherent and sustained narrative conversation, problem solving, and abstract thinking. Children with ADHD are generally deficient in these skills. Finally, motor coordination problems sometimes accompany ADHD. The cerebellum, a structure that aids in balance and coordination of body movements, is smaller in ADHD children than in non-ADHD controls.[70]

As I have pointed out in many parts of this book, genetic and environmental factors do not operate in isolation; they are joint and synergistic. Among environmental influences linked to ADHD are home backgrounds in which marriages are unhappy and family stress is high. But researchers agree that a stressful homelife rarely causes ADHD. Instead, the behaviors of these children can contribute greatly to family strife and discontent[71]—circumstances that, in turn, are likely to intensify the child's preexisting difficulties.

Furthermore, the genetic basis of ADHD means that often one parent has the disorder. In fact, the likelihood that a child who has ADHD will have a parent with it is as high as 40 percent.[72] When a difficult child and an impulsive parent come together, the chances for marital discord and parent–child conflict are magnified. Under these circumstances, children with ADHD become not only more disorganized and impulsive but also defiant and aggressive.

In fact, half of ADHD children also show symptoms of oppositional-defiant disorder (ODD) and conduct disorder (CD).[73] In children with one or both of these additional diagnoses, stubbornness, noncompliance, and hostility plus rule violations, stealing, lying, and aggressive acts are common. But the genetic underpinnings of ADHD do not necessarily extend to ODD and CD. Instead, often maladaptive parenting triggered by the combination of a difficult child, parental traits, and a disrupted home life are at the heart of these serious accompanying disorders.

In Cory's case, his father, Claude, also had ADHD, and angry, explosive confrontations in the family were almost daily events. Claude's symptoms led to a checkered work history; eventually he quit work altogether and became the children's primary caregiver while Janet, Cory's mother, kept the family afloat financially. Claude's persistent unemployment and his brash, cantankerous style led to marital strife and heightened rather than eased Cory's problems. His school performance and social relations worsened.

Finally, maternal use of illegal drugs, alcohol, or cigarettes during pregnancy is linked to inattention and hyperactivity in children.[74] Each of these harmful prenatal factors might, in some cases, contribute to or even be fully responsible for the disorder. But parents who expose their unborn child to these harmful substances may have impulse-control problems themselves. So with respect to the association between the prenatal environment and ADHD, once again both heredity and environment may be involved.

Social Relationships

As with children who have sensory deficits, the course of development for children with ADHD hinges on the quality of their communication with adults and peers. What kinds of interactions do these children experience?

Let's begin with the parent–child relationship. Recognizing that shared understanding and scaffolding are as important for the ADHD child's mastery of new competencies as they are for any child, researchers have observed parent–child pairs working together on tasks. Recall that children with ADHD are restless and distractible. Parents complain that the child doesn't listen, has trouble finishing tasks, constantly seeks help, won't try to work independently, and turns elsewhere when no longer supervised. These behaviors help explain why parents step up their interaction when assisting a child with ADHD, giving more verbal directions, commands, corrections, and physical prompts than do parents of non-ADHD children.[75] Clearly, parents try hard to exert control over their children's behavior when children with ADHD display limited ability to control that behavior themselves.

Think about sustaining this degree of child management over time. It is stressful and draining. As the child responds with high rates of noncompliant, negative, and off-task behavior, many parents become overly controlling, negative, and less responsive. Often parent–child conflict and angry, explosive reactions follow.[76]

In one instance, Janet tried to help Cory with a math assignment. She stood behind him, encircling him with her arms and directing his pencil back to the page each time his attention wandered. After Cory had worked several problems, Janet was quick to criticize a couple of wrong answers. "Cory, you didn't add that correctly. And this one's wrong, too. Do that one over. What's 3 + 4? No, not that problem, this one over here!"

"Stop! Gimme my pencil!" Cory shouted, diverting his attention from the problems and yanking the pencil away in a wide, sweeping motion. When his arm bumped his mother's, she grabbed his wrist and pushed it back in the direction of the math paper. The muscles beneath her eyes stiffened and her teeth clenched. Janet's anger was on the rise, and she was doing all she could to suppress it.

"Let go! Let go! Ouch, that hurts. Lemme out!" Cory cried as he struggled to free himself from his mother's enveloping arms. The homework session was over.

Having become used to commanding, directing, and physically restraining Cory, Janet had failed to praise him for the problems he did get right. And on problems he missed, she didn't notice that Cory's answers were close to correct. Although he had been too impatient to work the problems thoroughly, he had done a good job of estimating the answers. Janet's unfavorable perceptions of and experiences with Cory had prevented her from granting him warmth, praise, and encouragement to take more responsibility for the task.

As this episode illustrates, both ADHD children and parents contribute to spiraling hostile, critical, and confrontational exchanges, undermining the child's opportunity to internalize culturally adaptive skills. But children with ADHD play a far greater role in this mounting conflict than psychologists had previously realized, although they certainly do not deliberately try to disappoint and enrage their parents.

One reason researchers view the child-to-adult direction of influence as particularly strong is that teachers also react to ADHD children with increased commands, reprimands, and negative sanctions,[77] and understandably so. The desk and cubbyhole of the child with ADHD is easily recognized as the most disorderly in the room.[78] And as ADHD children don't finish their work, impulsively violate classroom rules, and have trouble adjusting to transitions (such as returning to the classroom after recess or lunch), teachers' negative, corrective messages escalate, until they resemble the barrage of "You're not!" "Stop!" and "Don't!" that Cory's teacher visited on him daily. This negativity often spreads, pervading the entire class. For example, teachers tend to be more reprimanding with all their students when just one child with ADHD is in their class.[79]

Frequent unfavorable teacher feedback is strongly associated with peer rejection.[80] Both Cory and Hayley encountered serious peer difficulties because of their objectionable behavior—behavior that was not just unpleasant but antithetical to school values. Their classmates did not want to work or play with them, so Cory and Hayley had trouble establishing and sustaining rewarding friendships—contexts in which children receive confirmation of their self-worth, learn much about sensitivity to others' needs, and profit from a companion's help and acceptance. Having friends also fosters positive attitudes toward school and academic achievement,[81] perhaps because friendships make children's school experiences more enjoyable. Also, when a child's friends do well in school, the child generally wants to do the same.

These benefits are greatly reduced or unavailable to children with ADHD. Their actions are so unpalatable to their classmates that they can establish a negative peer reputation in a very brief period—in some cases, in as little as 8 minutes.[82] Children with ADHD are well aware of how they should behave; they can easily distinguish appropriate from inappropriate behavior.[83] But they seem unable to apply this knowledge to their interactions with others. Although their boisterous, intrusive, argumentative style contributes to active dislike and avoidance by their classmates, aggression seems to account for the largest share of their peer difficulties.[84]

When ADHD children do make friends, they are likely to choose younger children and classmates who are also unpopular, and their friendships are less caring and more conflict-ridden than are those of their peers.[85] These friendship qualities further limit their chances of acquiring social skills. Children with severe childhood peer difficulties show profound adjustment problems when they reach adolescence and early adulthood, including substance abuse, school failure and dropout, and law-breaking.[86] Poor peer relations, however, are not independent of poor parent–child relations. Many studies show that warmth, explanations, and pleasurable, well-coordinated conversation characterize the parenting of children who are well liked by their peers. In contrast, power-assertive discipline and insensitive, conflict-ridden dialogue tend to characterize the home lives of peer-rejected children.[87]

In sum, children with ADHD are disruptive forces—at home, at school, and in the peer group. Their cumulative history of negative exchanges with parents, teachers, and peers can set them on a lifelong course of academic and social tragedy.

Self-Regulation

Exactly what deficits lie along the pathway between this largely hereditary disorder and maladaptive adult–child communication, both of which cause self-regulation to go awry in the ADHD child? Although many accounts have been offered over the years, psychologist Russell Barkley's recently proposed theory of ADHD has amassed the largest research support.

According to Barkley, altered brain functioning in ADHD children leads to a basic impairment in inhibition of behavior—the ability to resist an urge to do something.[88] A deficit in behavioral inhibition can account for ADHD children's impulsivity and hyperactivity. It also explains why these children are so emotionally reactive. If you cannot inhibit an urge to respond, then your first reaction gets expressed—tantrums and hostility when you don't get your way with adults and peers. Impaired behavioral inhibition also may underlie ADHD children's problems with sustained attention; they cannot restrain the desire to do something they would rather be doing than the effortful task at hand.

Inability to delay responding prevents the child from holding information in memory, comparing it with past experiences, and projecting into the future by evaluating alternatives before deciding on a course of action. Barkley believes that a primary deficit in behavioral inhibition leads ADHD children to have a narrower time sense—less awareness of past and future.[89] In line with this idea, parents and teachers often comment that children with ADHD fail to learn from their mistakes or to benefit from warnings about what might happen if they engage in risky or unacceptable behavior. They leap into action so quickly that they do not think about prior experiences or future consequences. As a result, they break promises, miss due dates and appointments, and live in a state of perpetual disorganization—actions that evoke strong disapproval from others.[90] "Hayley often seems out of touch, in a fog, " Vanessa remarked in summing up this aspect of her daughter's difficulties.

Yet another consequence of ADHD children's difficulty in inhibiting behavior is immature and less effective private speech. Although psychologists used to assume that impulsive, inattentive children failed to engage in self-talk, we now know that this is not so. Like other children, they do communicate with themselves to manage and control their own thought and behavior. Collaborating with psychologist Steven Landau and graduate student Michael Potts, in several studies I observed 6- to 11-year-olds diagnosed with ADHD and children rated by their teachers as having poor impulse control. We recorded the children's verbalizations and behavior during academic tasks and compared them to the responses of agemates average in academic achievement and free of psychological difficulties. Both the ADHD and the impulsive children talked aloud to themselves much more often than did their peers.[91] They certainly did not suffer from a deficiency in amount of private speech!

But when we looked at how private speech changed with age, we found that children with ADHD and children with teacher-rated poor impulse control were delayed in internalizing their self-talk. Compared to the remarks of agemates, those of ADHD and impulsive children could be heard quite easily by a listener at older ages. In effect, ADHD children did not show the typical quieting and shortening of private speech that comes with mastery of new skills. Rather, their private speech remained loud, persistent, and—on the basis of our informal impressions—highly repetitive and inflexible. Furthermore, children with ADHD appeared to focus on their work only when they were remarking on their activity—reading assignments aloud and verbalizing what they were writing.

Additional findings suggested that this immaturity in private speech was due to an impairment that prevents self-guiding speech from gaining efficient mastery over thought and behavior. First, when we stepped up the difficulty of academic work slightly but not unreasonably, to a level well within the child's "zone," ADHD and impulsive children's task-relevant private speech became disorganized. Rather than increasing with task difficulty, the self-talk of these children decreased! At the same time, children with ADHD emitted more remarks irrelevant to the task—self-stimulating noises and comments about other events in the room. Furthermore, the private speech of ADHD and impulsive children failed to predict improved attention and gains in academic performance. Yet a clear relationship between task-relevant private speech and these indicators of self-regulation occurred for average-achieving, problem-free children.[92]

Like private speech, play is immature in children with ADHD. When psychologist Steven Alessandri observed 4- and 5-year-olds with and without ADHD during classroom free-play periods, ADHD preschoolers spent less time involved in play, especially construction with art materials and blocks and sociodramatic play with peers.[93] Instead, more than half of ADHD children's playtime was devoted to simple, repetitive motor movements, such as running around the room, rolling a toy car back and forth, or kneading play dough with no obvious intent to make something. These play behaviors are typical of children several years younger. The more inattentive, distractible, and noncompliant the ADHD child, the less involved he or she was in purposeful play activities.

With their genetically based deficit in behavioral inhibition, ADHD children face a monumental challenge in delaying action long enough to engage in strategic private speech and sustained, goal-oriented play. My impression of ADHD children's self-talk is that it is so single-mindedly aimed at holding impulses at bay and keeping attention on the task that the child has few mental resources left over for applying higher-level strategies. As a result, although ADHD children's private speech is abundant, it is limited in its effectiveness for regulating emotion and solving cognitive and social problems.

ADHD children's strife-ridden social experiences also reduce the potency of their private speech. Because of negative interactions with adults and peers, they learn fewer effective techniques for coping with challenges than do their agemates. Instead, they acquire some impatient, forceful strategies that are doomed to failure. But at the heart of both their social-participation and private-speech inadequacies is a formidable impulse-control deficit that ADHD children are helpless to undo. Directly intervening in that deficit is important for restoring the quality of their social experiences.

Intervention

In helping children with ADHD, it is important to remember that their symptom pattern is nothing other than an extreme of normal child behavior. Younger children have shorter attention spans, are more likely to react impulsively, and often engage in motor activity that seems excessive from an adult's perspective—behaviors that lessen with age as children use language to guide behavior. Children with ADHD benefit from the same family and school experiences that foster higher forms of thinking and culturally valued attitudes and skills in all children.

ADHD children's persistent, strenuous private speech reveals how much they want to gain control of their unmanageable impulses. They call on the most potent tool available to them for overcoming their impulse-control difficulties. But when children who talk out inappropriately in class and run on with idle, unfocused chatter during play are observed talking loudly and incessantly to themselves during cognitive problem solving, parents and teachers may assume that all their verbalizations—to others and to themselves—are maladaptive. All too often, adults suppress ADHD children's private speech as just one more sign of their unruliness.

From a sociocultural perspective, the major goal of intervention with ADHD children should be to repair damaged bonds with adults, especially parents, thereby paving the way for successful, fulfilling adult–child dialogues, on which development crucially depends. Rearing an ADHD child requires high parent involvement—more expressions of caring and much more organizing, planning, structuring, guiding, and monitoring of the child's experiences and behavior at home and at school than is required of most parents. To engage in such high-energy parenting, parents themselves benefit from the scaffolding, social support, and collaboration of experts—teachers, school psychologists, clinical child psychologists, and physicians.

Research consistently shows that the most effective intervention approach is multifaceted. Pediatricians and psychologists can try to modify children's deficient impulse control directly, through medication therapy and through changing aspects of their environments to better suit their limited attention spans and high need for activity. At the same time, adults must work to transform their negative, intrusive reactions to the child's impulsive style—a goal far easier to attain once the child's extreme behaviors are reduced.

MEDICATION THERAPY.   Medical science has not advanced far enough to grant a blind child sight or a deaf child hearing, at least in the large majority of cases. But drug therapy has been developed to temper the ADHD child's impulsivity. The most common drug treatment stimulates the central nervous system. Methylphenidate, or Ritalin®, is the most frequently prescribed stimulant medication. About 70 to 75 percent of ADHD children respond positively to it.[94] For children who react to stimulants favorably, the effects are substantial.

Recall that reduced electrical activity in the frontal lobes of the cerebral cortex is linked to ADHD. Stimulant medication attacks this problem head-on by increasing electrical activity in the frontal lobes. The result is a nearly immediate reduction in inattentive, impulsive, restless behavior. Usually behavior change is evident within 30 to 60 minutes, peaks in 2 hours, and dissipates after 4 hours as the drug wears off, although sustained-release forms that have longer-lasting but possibly less powerful effects are available. [95] Still, stimulant medication fails to help one-fourth to one-third of children with ADHD, who depend entirely on changes in adult–child interaction and environmental contexts for improved functioning. Furthermore, even when children do well on stimulants, drug therapy alone is not sufficient.

Cory's physician placed him on Ritalin® at age 7; Hayley began a stimulant regimen at age 18. Both young people talked less, followed social rules more consistently, and became entangled in fewer negative, explosive exchanges with parents, teachers, and peers—improvements that are typical for stimulant-treated youngsters. In addition, ADHD children being treated with stimulant medication can concentrate on schoolwork better; they finish more assignments and do them more accurately.[96]

With less disruptiveness and greater cooperation and sustained attention, ADHD children's social relations improve. Hence, the need for constant adult vigilance and supervision declines. Perhaps because adults permit the medicated child to assume more responsibility for his or her behavior, such children tend to credit themselves (and not external factors, such as the medication) for their successes; they feel more in control of their actions. Many report informally that they "can try harder."[97] ADHD children also show more mature private speech while "on" rather than "off" medication. With stimulant therapy, their self-talk is quieter and more abbreviated during academic tasks, and it "works" more effectively for them, predicting reduced wriggling and fidgeting and increased attention.[98]

In sum, medication improves ADHD children's behavior and helps them feel more positively about themselves—changes that increase the chances of more favorable social experiences. But stimulant drug therapy is far from a panacea. It works best for school-age children with more severe ADHD symptoms, and 4- and 5-year-olds benefit less than do older children.[99] Furthermore, stimulants allay but almost never erase the symptoms of ADHD; the vast majority of children continue to display difficult behaviors.

Perhaps for this reason, even though stimulant therapy enhances day-to-day schoolwork performance, it does not lead to gains on end-of-the-year achievement tests. And although stimulants improve the quality of peer interaction, they do not alleviate peer rejection—the extent to which classmates say they don't want to play with an ADHD child.[100] Peers often re-experience the child's unruly style from time to time and more so after the drug's 4-hour impact wears off—a reminder that gains from treatment are short term and must be combined with other interventions.

STIMULANT MEDICATION USE AND ABUSE.   Stimulant therapy is highly controversial. Some people claim that the drug is a dangerous, addictive, mood-altering substance that is being given to far too many children. Yet there are no reported instances of addiction, and young people on stimulants for ADHD do not tend to abuse other substances. In the rare instances in which medication leads to elevated or depressed mood, adjusting the dosage can usually lessen the problem. Other side effects, including reduced appetite, difficulty falling asleep at bedtime, nervous tics, and physical growth delays, are generally mild and short-lived in the few children who experience them.[101] Occasionally, though, a child reacts adversely and does not improve as treatment continues. Stimulants must be prescribed very carefully, with health professionals and parents tracking their behavioral effects and weighing pros and cons in each case. When this happens, the benefits of stimulant therapy greatly outweigh its risks.

How about overmedication of children? Is this a real and significant problem? Stimulants are prescribed to children more often than any other type of drug. Between 1990 and 1995, the most recent period for which information is available, the number of American school-age children and adolescents given stimulant prescriptions multiplied two-and-a-half fold, reaching an estimated 4 million.[102] Two explanations have been offered for this dramatic increase: better identification of ADHD and overprescribing. New studies, however, suggest a more complex picture. In some communities, children who do not exhibit behaviors extreme enough to warrant an ADHD diagnosis are given stimulants.[103] In these cases, medication is, indeed, being overprescribed. In other communities, the large majority of children with ADHD do not receive medication therapy.[104] Here, stimulants—in view of their documented short-term effectiveness in reducing ADHD symptoms—are underprescribed.

When medication therapy is not made available to a severely affected child struggling to meet responsibilities and get along with others, this is a serious breach. It can contribute to a tormented childhood like Hayley's, riddled with parental battles, school failure, peer rebuke, and self-deprecation. Ritalin® was prescribed for Hayley following a dreadful high school experience in which she barely graduated. Almost instantaneously, relations with parents, sisters, and coworkers relaxed. And she enrolled in a community college and earned a diploma in practical nursing—an accomplishment that, according to Owen and Vanessa, could not have happened without the assistance of stimulant treatment. On days when Hayley decided not to take her prescribed dosage, her parents and sisters reported immediate backsliding, toward greater distractibility, argumentativeness, and hostility. All too often, Owen and Vanessa have wondered how much easier life could have been for Hayley had she been properly diagnosed and had medication been offered when she was a child.

Still, in view of the sharp rise in children on medication therapy, overprescription is undoubtedly a much greater problem than is underprescription. A particularly worrisome trend is the enormous increase—as much as threefold from 1991 to 1995—in the numbers of preschoolers as young as 2 to 4 years of age on stimulants.[105] ADHD is extremely hard to diagnose with certainty at these ages. Many preschoolers whose parents complain about their inattentiveness, impulsivity, and overactivity are simply displaying age-appropriate behavior that will not translate into an ADHD diagnosis by school entry.[106]

The current trend to give preschoolers stimulants to calm their behavior may, in large measure, be due to a reduced tolerance for child-rearing stress in parents who lead increasingly busy, demanding lives. We have seen in this and earlier chapters that impatient, inattentive, inconsistent parenting promotes demandingness, anger, and poor emotional control in both ADHD and symptom-free children. That many American preschoolers spend their days in poor-quality child care further aggravates these reactions and, in turn, heightens parental exasperation when parents are reunited with the child at the end of the working day.

To our question—Is overmedication of young children a real and significant problem?—the answer is a resounding yes. Self-regulation originates in adult–child dialogues within the "zone"; if nondisabled children are denied that support system for bringing behavior under the control of thought, they will exhibit disorganized, unruly tendencies that can—in a world in which ADHD has achieved great notoriety—be mistaken for the disorder. Yet such children differ from their agemates with true ADHD in that they respond much more readily to improved parent–child communication and discipline. Warm, sensitive, appropriately demanding parenting returns them to a favorable course of development without the need for medication.

Medicating preschoolers to reduce annoying, impulsive behavior is rarely, if ever, warranted. As noted earlier, the documented effectiveness of stimulant therapy applies to school-age children; what little research there is on preschoolers reveals a reduced impact. Furthermore, stimulants may induce solitary play and clinginess in preschoolers—effects strong enough to disrupt rather than foster their social development.[107] The carefully controlled clinical trials required to demonstrate the efficacy and safety of stimulant medication for treatment of preschool-diagnosed ADHD have yet to be conducted.

Finally, no drug is available that can relieve parents of the extra time and energy required to rear a child with a disability. The great value of stimulant therapy is that for children with extreme symptoms, it makes possible vital social interventions—the route to self-control and social integration for ADHD children, as it is for all children.

ADULT–CHILD COMMUNICATION.   Whether receiving stimulant therapy or not, children with ADHD will violate rules, neglect homework and chores, and create disturbances in what otherwise might be a peaceful home or classroom. To create favorable conditions for development, parents and teachers must pave the way to cooperative relationships. Shared understanding and a support system for acquiring new skills—features of adult–child interaction that create the "zone"—are useful guiding principles for how to interact successfully with the ADHD child.

Because of Cory's inattention and impulsivity, his parents and teacher found themselves issuing constant commands and corrections and welling up with anger and impatience at his noncompliance. These harsh tactics were counterproductive; increasingly, Cory ignored or defied them. Yet defiance is not one of the core symptoms of ADHD. It is learned in response to adult criticism and negativity and through the child's successful avoidance of unpleasant tasks. To establish intersubjectivity—the cooperative, mutual focus that is the basis for all relationships—with a child who is in revolt against adult expectations means that parents and teachers must be firm and consistent. And at least initially, they must take responsibility for making social contact and sustaining it.

Cory's parents and teacher had to learn to make sure that Cory was paying attention—looking at them or at the focus of their remarks—before issuing requests and directives. Because of his distractibility and poor memory, their statements had to be specific and brief so he could more easily process and recall them, as in "Cory, free play is over. Please pick up the blocks." Vague or indirect messages—"Let's get back to work" or "What should you do after free play is over?"—rarely work with ADHD children. Also, statements that string together several directions—"Cory, put away the blocks, get the felt pens from your cubby and some paper from the table, and join your group for project time"—are unlikely to be followed.[108] The child simply cannot retain all parts of such intricate instructions.

When adults use communication techniques that "reach" ADHD children, they increase the child's cooperation, thereby preventing their own messages from escalating into anger and coercion. In scaffolding the child's mastery of new skills, for example, tasks cannot be too long, repetitive, intricate, or tedious. They must be adapted to the ADHD child's "zone," requiring a level of sustained attention typical for children considerably younger. And the number of times the adult must demonstrate, prompt, explain, praise, and draw the child's attention back to the activity is far greater than is necessary for other children. But gradually, the child will become better at participating in cooperative dialogues and assuming responsibility for the task.

Although progress in self-regulation is slower for children with ADHD than for other children, it is real and gratifying once the quality of adult–child interaction changes. Children receiving stimulant therapy who profit from good adult–child communication and discipline typically need lower doses of medication than do children whose parents rely exclusively on drug treatment.[109]

DISCIPLINE.   Most children do not need an intensive schedule of rewards and compliments to motivate acceptable behavior; they want to cooperate so they will be liked and respected by adults and peers. Because ADHD children find it so hard to inhibit their impulses, they are constant targets of reprimands and criticism. Soon they give up hope of warm, positive ties with adults; their self-esteem plummets; and they stop trying to engage in desired acts. Parents and teachers often become so used to the ADHD child's transgressions that they fail to notice when the child does show self-control! Frequent, affectionate praise for improved behavior can contribute to continued gains, to a warmer adult–child relationship, and to a more favorable self-image, all of which motivate compliance and rule following.

Again, conveying a specific message—by stating exactly what the praise is for—helps ADHD children figure out how they should act in the future.[110] For example, rather than just saying, "Great!" or "That's the way!", the adult might explain, "Cory, you did a fine job putting those blocks away neatly," or "I really liked the way you listened quietly during group time today. You gave the other children a chance to speak."

Many children with ADHD also respond to salient, concrete reminders and rewards in their efforts to conquer their impulses.[111] One teacher tied a colorful ribbon bracelet around a child's arm at storytime, explaining, "This pretty bracelet is to help you remember not to interrupt. When you're wearing your bracelet, that means don't talk out. Raise your hand." The bracelet served as a conspicuous symbol of how to act; the child leaned on it until she could recall the rule and tell her-self to follow it. Stickers placed in a special notebook can offer a cumulative record of how well the ADHD child has followed rules and completed tasks, reminding both children and parents of progress and accomplishments.

Even when adults make these efforts, ADHD children remain less coopera-tive than their agemates. Parents experiencing great difficulty handling their child profit from coaching in how to discipline—pairing directives with rea-sons and replacing verbal insults and spankings with effective tactics for dealing with an out-of-control child. One such discipline strategy is *time out,* which in-volves removing children from the immediate setting—for example, by having them sit to one side or go to their rooms—until they are ready to behave ap-propriately. When implemented consistently, time out calms an emotionally reactive child relatively quickly and offers angry parents a "cooling off" period, permitting them to refocus on encouraging good conduct through a warm, co-operative relationship with the child.

PEER RELATIONS.   Children with ADHD need special assistance in improv-ing peer relations. Conversation and collaboration with adults go a long way toward helping them acquire social skills for relating to agemates. And super-vising and intervening in peer interactions is vital for helping ADHD children learn to inhibit impulses, behave considerately, and see the results of sensitivity to others' needs in the peer situation.

In addition, social problem-solving training programs exist that teachers or psychologists can implement with small groups of children. In these interven-tions, children learn to recognize social problems, such as finding the best way to gain entry into an ongoing peer play activity. Then they think up strategies for solving the problem, assess the likely consequences of each strategy ("If I push my way into Jason and Mike's game, they'll be mad and not want to play with me"), and choose the one with the best potential for meeting both their own and others' needs ("Asking if I can play is the best thing to do").

Research reveals that after several months of social problem-solving train-ing, preschool and primary-school children improve in both ability to think of ways to solve peer conflicts and in teacher-rated peer relations relative to un-trained agemates.[112] During these interventions, ADHD children benefit from extensive practice of considerate social behaviors. But because they have re-acted with hostility so often after not getting their way, these children need to repeat socially acceptable acts many times to overcome their habitual re-sponses. And although children with ADHD engage in a variety of immature behaviors that irritate their peers, aggression is the largest contributor to their peer difficulties.[113]

When adults establish rapport, engage in supportive dialogues, and promote satisfying peer relations, they are apt to find that children with ADHD—like individuals with other disabilities—develop special strengths. Young people with ADHD are passionate and emotional in their actions and convictions; rarely are they self-conscious in performing before others. Consequently, they may excel at dramatic arts. Their talkativeness and penchant for socializing means that they have the potential to become expert at persuasion; politics, debate, and sales may be areas of unusual ability. And people with ADHD are likely to take chances where others would be more conservative. If their childhood social experiences have helped them channel their energies constructively, they may lead particularly innovative, exciting, and interesting lives.[114]

LEARNING ENVIRONMENTS. As long as teachers receive assistance from expert consultants, ADHD children's educational needs usually can be met in regular classrooms. Children with ADHD learn best in classrooms with the very same features that benefit their problem-free agemates. Therefore, designing learning environments so they enhance development is a major step toward helping children with ADHD manage their own behavior.

Many people assume that a highly structured, regimented learning situation is required to cope with the ADHD child's disorganized, reactive behavior. Yet recall from Chapter 1 that preschoolers and kindergartners enrolled in such classrooms show intense stress reactions. Their attention declines, and they wiggle and talk out. They also achieve less well than do agemates in more loosely structured settings. In other words, most children show signs of impulse-control difficulties when classrooms are rigidly organized and insensitive to their "zones" and to their need for active involvement in their own learning! Children with ADHD are no exception; in fact, they react more extremely than do other children to a traditional, adult-centered classroom, displaying greater difficulty with impulse control and becoming more troublesome to their teachers.[115]

In contrast, in classrooms where children are allowed to move about, are offered choices in activities, and collaborate in small groups on projects, children with ADHD appear less distinctive.[116] When they get up from their seats, wander, and talk out, their actions are not as disturbing to others as they would be if all activities required the whole class to orient toward the teacher. And tasks that require active engagement allow ADHD children to channel their otherwise disruptive behavior into constructive alternatives. Furthermore, under flexible classroom arrangements, teachers have more opportunity to scaffold and converse with the ADHD child, providing the guidance necessary to foster social skills and self-regulation. Small classes, with no more than twenty children, also promote this individualized attention and result in better achievement.[117]

In Chapter 4, I indicated that the relation between complex sociodramatic play and gains in social responsibility is especially strong for highly impulsive preschoolers. The chances that ADHD children will participate in sociodramatic activities are much greater in classrooms where teachers value imaginative play and scaffold children's play skills—events unlikely to occur in teacher-directed classrooms emphasizing whole-class academic instruction. Make-believe play with adults and peers is replete with opportunities for ADHD children to practice following social rules.

Furthermore, children with ADHD rely on private speech to gain control of their behavior over a much longer age period than do other children. Instead of suppressing such speech as socially inappropriate and disturbing to others, adults can listen to it, gaining insight into the child's plans, goals, and difficulties and using it as a resource to scaffold more effectively. A flexibly organized classroom emphasizing small-group and individualized activities is likely to be one in which the ADHD child's persistent self-talk is welcomed rather than dampened. In the next chapter, I will have more to say about Vygotsky-inspired classrooms and educational innovations that promote learning in young children, including children with impulse-control difficulties and academic and social problems.

VIEWING DEFICIT AND DISABILITY AS A SOURCE OF STRENGTH

Children who are blind, deaf, diagnosed with ADHD, or disabled in other ways depend—as do all children—on shared activities with more expert partners for acquiring culturally valued ways of thinking and behaving. The children considered in this chapter, although diverse in their deficits, have in common a strong desire to participate in and contribute to their social worlds. Yet in each disability, a biologically based impairment disrupts access to collaboration with adults and peers. All too often, such children provide a heartbreaking window into how severely development can be stunted when maladaptive adult–child interaction is allowed to persist. The repair of social dialogues should be central to intervention, regardless of the type of deficit.

To attain this goal, adults must understand the nature of the child's disability, just how it interferes with communication, and the tactics the child uses to compensate for it. Then parents and teachers can capitalize on the child's preferred mode or style of communication to strengthen both quantity and quality of social interaction. Adults can change or modify the communicative system— enrich touch, sound, and verbal language for the blind child; converse in sign language with the deaf child; and provide brief, specific requests and directions and positive feedback to the ADHD child—while still conveying the same meanings. To help children with disabilities, the social world must accommodate to their most efficient and effective means for conversing with others and allow them to acquire the mental tools necessary for self-regulation.

Vygotsky's sociocultural approach to children with disabilities is a highly optimistic vision; it accentuates the child's strengths. He underscored the importance of viewing the child not as abnormal or as underdeveloped but rather as having developed differently. When we regard children with sensory or psychological deficits as lacking important capacities, we impose our own vantage point on the child's experiences. Blind and deaf children do not experience blindness and deafness in the way most of us imagine—as the subtraction of normal sensation, as darkness or silence. And ADHD children do not regard their exuberant attraction to stimulation as an absence of self-control. To the affected child, his or her condition is "normal." Only as a result of social experiences does the child come to sense being different and "abnormal"—incomplete and divided from others.[118] Yet social interaction is equally capable of creating connection and integration if the child is viewed as having altered capacities and positive potential. With the assistance of others, children with disabilities can realize a wealth of possibilities and unique competencies.

Is the inclusion of children with disabilities in regular classrooms the solution to their educational needs? The answer depends on how well characteristics of the learning environment can help the child in question develop. Vygotsky was highly critical of special education settings in which the activities and the learning pace are beneath children's "zones." At the same time, he realized that children with disabilities often do best in classrooms designed to support their unique communication and learning styles and that have specially trained teachers and other experts exclusively devoted to helping them learn. If these criteria cannot be met in a regular classroom, then the child needs a special classroom with all the activities and positive adult and peer experiences necessary to create "zones" for optimum development.[119]

Vygotsky's theory provides a convincing rationale for parents and teachers to form strong, supportive, trustful relationships with disabled children; to work with them in creative collaboration; to be generous with time and involvement; and to be open to new ways of surmounting difficulties. Under these conditions, rearing and teaching children with disabilities is still challenging, but it is also satisfying and rewarding.

Learning in Classrooms

A visitor entering Tamara's combined kindergarten/first-grade classroom is likely to be struck by its atmosphere of calm purposefulness, given that so much is happening at once.[1] On a typical day, twenty-two 5- to 7-year-olds are busy working on diverse activities throughout the room.

At ten o'clock one Tuesday, several children were in the writing center—one preparing a thank you note and four others collaborating on making a list of the names of everyone in the class. In the reading center, five children were browsing the shelves or reading books, in pairs and individually. At a table next to shelves filled with math materials, four children worked in pairs on a problem requiring them to choose items from a restaurant menu without exceeding their budget. Yet another pair was immersed in an interactive computer activity about plants as sources of foods. Tamara was seated at a table, reading and discussing a story with a cluster of six children.

The children in Tamara's class come from a variety of ethnic and socioeconomic backgrounds. About three-fourths live in the middle-income neighborhood surrounding the school, located in a midsize Midwestern city. The rest are bussed from a housing project for low-income families several miles away. Two children have reading disabilities, and one has a speech and language delay. Several times a week, a learning disabilities teacher and a speech therapist come to the classroom to assist these children. Tamara's students present great variations in experiences, knowledge, and academic skills. She uses this diversity to enrich their learning.

The classroom is organized into seven clearly defined activity centers. The largest is the reading center, which doubles as a class meeting area. Others are the writing center, the math center, the life science center, the physical science center, the art center, and the imaginative play/extended project center. Computers can be found in the life science and writing centers. All centers are brimming with materials—on shelves and in boxes and baskets, clearly labeled and within children's easy reach. And each center contains a table to serve as a comfortable workspace for collaborative and individual pursuits.

Tamara's extensive planning and organization result in a remarkably smooth flow of classroom events. In a single day, an amazing amount happens. Children spend the first half-hour of the morning writing and drawing in their journals. Then they gather in the class-meeting area, where several share their journal entries with classmates, who ask questions and volunteer comments. Next, Tamara asks the children to "schedule centers." Quickly, they move into action. Each selects a center, places his or her name on a board to record the choice, goes to a specified area of the room, and becomes immersed in a task, a project, or a play activity.

Children rotate through all seven centers within four or five days. But the system is flexible; often they return to centers of special interest or to ones in which Tamara decides they need to spend more time. Each center offers an appealing array of activity options from which to choose. And center periods are long lasting, from 45 minutes to an hour, granting children ample time to become involved in a meaningful activity and the satisfaction of making good progress or completing it.

Mid-morning, the children clean up materials, gather for a snack, and go outside for recess. Tamara is constantly on the lookout for opportune moments to scaffold children's learning. As several children prepare the snack by pouring trail mix into small cups, she remarks, "We have twenty-two children, three teachers, and one guest. How many cups do we need for our snack?" Together, she and the children count, transforming an ordinary routine into mathematical thinking and problem solving.

After a visit to the school library, where each child checks out a book to take home, the children return to the classroom. Tamara is waiting in the rocking chair; the children join her in the meeting area. She reads a chapter from a novel, stopping now and then to discuss events in the story and to ask the children to draw inferences from them. "Who did Twig [the main character] find living in the little house she made?" "How did he get there?" "How did Twig feel about Elf moving into her house?" Lunchtime follows, then a brief rest period on mats around the room.

In the early afternoon, once again Tamara and the children gather briefly in the meeting area. She calls their attention to a new set of books, explaining that each contains lots of information about amphibians. Opening one, she reads a poem about frogs. From another, she shows the children several pictures of salamanders and reads about each. Then she asks a child to place the books in the life science center. Afterward, the children disperse for afternoon center time, the concluding period of the day. In the life science center, two children eagerly explore the new amphibians books, each carrying one back to show Tamara.

"Look! The frog laid some eggs, and the eggs are hatching into tadpoles!" Chuck exclaims, pointing to a picture.

"You've found some information about the life cycle of frogs," Tamara confirms. She helps Chuck read the caption under the picture.

Tamara moves from center to center. With the help of two parents, who volunteer several times a week, she questions, explains, demonstrates, models, acknowledges, and assists children in other ways. In the imaginative play/ extended project center, several children arrange a display of seashells that will become part of the class's natural history museum. Tamara talks with the children about how they might sort, label, and keep a record of the artifacts in the display. Other activities in the classroom help children acquire the information and skills they need to set up the museum. In several weeks, when it is complete, they will open it to visitors—teachers and children from other classes, school administrators, and family members. Through sociodramatic play, the children, posing as ticket agents, curators, tour guides, and museum store clerks, will express their new knowledge.

In this chapter, I address applications of sociocultural theory to teaching and learning in early childhood classrooms. As this glimpse into Tamara's classroom reveals, learning environments that actualize Vygotsky's ideas encompass but go far beyond the transmission of teacher-selected information and basic skills. The classroom is alive with a multiplicity of activities that are meaningful to children because they are stimulated by their experiences, interests, and imaginings, and they relate to their everyday lives.

Permeating those activities are lessons in literacy and mathematics that emerge from children's efforts to acquire knowledge, solve problems, and create products. Tamara's students want to master reading, writing, and math skills not because an adult tells them to but because those skills are essential to pursuing real-world practical goals and compelling topics in literature, social studies, and science. In Vygotsky-inspired classrooms, children discover that becoming literate opens enormous new vistas. It leads to vastly expanded understandings and relationships with people—teachers, classmates with common interests, authors whose minds children meet by reading their works, and experts in the wider community whom children can contact through letters and e-mail. Each of these social resources further advances children's development.

Tamara's classroom also illustrates that learning activities based on sociocultural theory are *shared*. Teachers take seriously the idea that mastery of increasingly complex, culturally valued ways of thinking and behaving depends on scaffolding by and narrative conversation with more expert partners—both adults and peers. One teacher described this philosophy to her students by stating, "Talking is probably the most important thing we do here because you learn most when you can talk while you work."[2] Her comment stands in stark contrast to directives for children to remain silent, which have permeated traditional, teacher-led whole-class instruction for centuries. Classrooms energized by Vygotsky's ideas are not quiet places. They are alive with discussion, negotiation, and collaboration.

Sociocultural theory has served as a provocative springboard for educational innovations. Most focus on the primary grades, the period during which "formal" education begins. In accord with this emphasis, our discussion of teaching practices will center on kindergarten through third grade. But many examples I will describe and the principles that underlie them can be adapted for younger children because no sharp dichotomy exists between preschool and school-age children's learning.

Vygotsky's major educational message for preschool teachers is to provide many, varied activities responsive to children's interests and a wealth of opportunities for make-believe play—the ultimate preparation for collaboration with other learners and mastery of academic tasks. Overall, preschool and primary-grade classrooms should differ only in their relative balance of play versus academic experiences; by school age, children become ready to handle more of the latter. Later in this chapter, I'll describe a unique, contemporary approach to preschool education that is highly consistent with Vygotsky's ideas. Then I'll conclude by summarizing signs of high-quality early childhood education that can help parents evaluate the appropriateness of preschool, child-care, and primary school settings for their child.

THE SOCIOCULTURAL APPROACH TO TEACHING AND LEARNING IN EARLY CHILDHOOD

Three interrelated themes that pervade Tamara's classroom are ever-present in applications of sociocultural ideas to early childhood education: teaching in the "zone," classrooms rich in dialogue, and abundant literacy activities.

Teaching in the "Zone"

Vygotsky regarded teaching and learning as supreme forces in development. Teaching, Vygotsky claimed, "brings out specifically human qualities of the mind and leads the child to new developmental levels."[3] How is this so? The answer lies in Vygotsky's concept of the "zone"—the range of tasks that the child cannot yet master independently but can accomplish by collaborating with more expert partners.

According to Vygotsky, education must capitalize on children's "zones." When teachers continually offer (or permit children to choose) tasks they can handle on their own, they focus on the past—what the child has already acquired. Teaching that enhances development is future oriented, aimed not so much at "the ripe as at the ripening functions."[4] It must immerse children in activities they have not yet mastered but have the potential to master with assistance—first with the help of others and, later, with the aid of private speech, through which they guide themselves. When teachers design activities to fit children's potential development, then they awaken those capacities that are ready to burst forth, thereby advancing children's actual development.[5]

Vygotsky argued that as teaching in the "zone" leads to new knowledge and skills, it permits children to attain new heights in self-regulation. Conversationally rich, challenging activities make children much more conscious of their own thought processes. The more aware they are of the strategies they use to solve problems and complete tasks, the more likely they are to reflect on those strategies, refine them, and apply them deliberately in new situations. Teaching in the "zone," Vygotsky claimed, is particularly powerful in directing development because it makes children think much more intently about their own thinking, bringing self-reflection and systematic reasoning to the child. Let's see how this happens.

Classrooms Rich in Dialogues

Imagine a child working a puzzle, drawing a picture, or printing her name on her own, without the collaboration of a more expert partner. The child focuses largely on the goal of her activity—the finished puzzle, the drawing, or the printed name. She rarely, if ever, stops to think about the best way to go about attaining her goal. Now think about a classroom in which dialogues saturate stimulating, challenging activities—teachers with children, children with children, and children with themselves. The environment constantly encourages children to engage in deliberate reasoning to guide their behavior, to stretch to new levels of "thinking about thought."

Vygotsky explained that classroom discourse—especially as children become ready for more academic learning in primary school—differs from most everyday interactions. In settings where learning is the primary goal of everything that happens, language serves not just as a means of communication but also as an object of reflection.[6] To become proficient at reading, writing, and mathematics and to acquire deeper understandings in social studies, science, and other areas, teachers and children must not just talk; they must talk about many language-based concepts and strategies.

Anyone listening in on the dialogues in Tamara's classroom—and other conversationally rich classrooms like it—will hear constant reflections on words, ideas, and ways to solve problems. Here are just a few instances:

- *During journal-writing time:* Carl appears to have trouble deciding what to write about. Tamara notices and explains that listening to others' ideas may help him think of something he'd like to write down. On a nearby wall is a large sheet of paper listing several "writing-idea" categories: Things I'm interested in; Things I've done; Things I want to do; and Things I know a lot about. Space is available for each child to make notes.

    Tamara calls Carl's attention to one of his classmate's jottings. "Look, Sharon's written the word 'bike.' I wonder what that means. Let's ask her!" Sharon explains that she's writing about the things she saw on a ride she took with her uncle on a bike trail. Tamara turns to Carl and asks him if he can think of an idea. He nods, turning back to his journal.

- *In the life science center:* Four children gather around a tray of starfish and shells of different shapes and sizes. Tamara joins them and reads from a book about starfish, "The surface of each of the five prongs of the starfish has warty tubercles and short spines." Then Tamara passes around a starfish so each child can count its "prongs" and feel its "warty tubercles" and "spines." "See, a warty tubercle is a bump on its skin," she explains. "Let's read further to find out why starfish have tubercles."

- *At class meeting time:* Tamara announces, "To prepare for our museum trip, there's something very important I need to do: Write a check for our entrance fees." She tears a check from a checkbook and holds it up. "It's two dollars a person, and we have twenty-two children. How much would that be?"

When none of the children responds, Tamara modifies her question: "How much for ten people to get into the museum? Let's have ten people stand up so we can see." Tamara asks Kara to tap ten children on the shoulder. After they form a line, she continues, "Now, if each ticket costs two dollars and we have ten people, how much will it cost? How could we find out?"

Several children chorus, "We can count by twos!"

Tamara nods and says, "Let's count," as she taps each child in the line.

When the class reaches "twenty," she asks ten more people to stand. The children continue counting, reaching "forty."

"Now, our last two people. Randy and Michael, please stand up."

A child calls out, "Forty-four dollars in all. That's a lot!" Tamara writes the check, pointing out the dollar sign followed by numerals 4-4.[7]

Hundreds of instances like these, in which Tamara and the children talk about language and think about how to reach their goals, occur in a single day. The more of these experiences children have, the more conscious they become of word meanings and of their own thought processes. In fact, research by one of Vygotsky's colleagues revealed that children are much better at consciously reflecting on and explaining concepts acquired through teaching than they are at explaining concepts picked up on their own.[8]

Abundant Literacy Activities

Vygotsky-inspired classrooms are burgeoning with literacy activities. Besides vastly increasing children's access to new knowledge, literacy adds to children's awareness of and regulation of their own thinking. As they become more skilled at reading, writing, math, and other forms of notation and talk about them, children develop the capacity to consciously manipulate and control the symbol systems of their culture.[9] This makes them much better communicators—with others and with themselves.

Mastery of written language is especially important in this process. Writing must be more precise and expanded than verbal dialogue because it cannot rely on extra supports, such as tone of voice and gesture, to clarify meaning. To ensure that our writing expresses what we want to say, we must think carefully about how to record our thoughts so that others can understand them. Writing, Vygotsky believed, demands exceptionally intense and frequent reflection on one's own thought and behavior. As teachers help children use different types of written language—stories, letters, journal entries, lists, labels, signs, and mathematical expressions—they empower children in self-regulation, especially in thinking about how to symbolize ideas in socially useful ways.

In Vygotsky-inspired classrooms, teachers provide opportunities for many forms of symbolic communication. But reading, writing, and mathematical reasoning are not taught in isolation or in a rigid, step-by-step manner emphasizing drill on component skills. For literacy activities to be meaningful and to advance cognitive and social development, children must read, write, and use math in authentic situations. "Teaching should be organized in such a way that reading and writing are necessary for something . . ." Vygotsky maintained. "[They] must be something the child needs . . . 'relevant to life.' "[10]

The whole-language movement, a current approach to early childhood literacy education, is based on these ideas.[11] It promotes reading and writing in ways that parallel natural language learning. Teachers expose the child to texts of all kinds in their "whole" forms; they do not give children highly simplified materials and emphasize coaching on phonics, the basic rules for translating written symbols into sounds. Keeping reading and writing activities whole and meaningful permits children to appreciate the communicative functions of written language. According to whole-language advocates, when children are drawn into literacy pursuits to attain real personal and social goals, they will be strongly motivated to acquire the skills they need to become competent readers and writers.

The whole-language approach has sparked heated debate. Psychologists and educators who favor a traditional, phonics-oriented approach claim that whole language does not teach children enough about the rules for reading so they can decipher words they have never seen before. But a recent investigation showed that kindergartners just beginning to read were more involved in literacy activities and made greater reading progress when they were in whole-language than in phonics-oriented classrooms.[12] In the primary grades, balancing whole-language and phonics seems particularly effective. In a study of 7-year-old poor readers, psychologists Peter Hatcher, Charles Hulme, and Andrew Ellis found that those assigned to combined "meaningful-reading plus phonics" teaching showed greater gains in reading achievement than did those receiving either "meaningful-reading alone" or "phonics alone" teaching.[13]

Overall, these findings lend strong support to the view that children benefit from activities that demonstrate the role of reading and writing in everyday communication, in seeking new knowledge, and in pleasurable storytelling. As school-age children become familiar with written language, they are ready to acquire specific reading strategies.[14] Yet when practice in phonics is overemphasized, literacy experiences are splintered into senseless pieces, and children can easily lose sight of the goal of reading—understanding. Many primary-grade teachers report cases of children who can read aloud fluently but who register very little meaning. These children might have been spared serious reading problems had they been exposed to rich, whole-language experiences followed by a combination of meaning-based teaching and attention to basic skills in the primary grades.

Finally, recall from earlier chapters that formal instruction in reading and writing, unless initiated by children's questions and guided by their interest level, is not appropriate for preschoolers. Instead, before the primary grades, literacy emerges from everyday life. It grows out of narrative conversation; homes, preschools, and child-care settings with abundant literacy materials; and literacy-relevant make-believe play. The evidence I reviewed in Chapters 2 and 4 amply demonstrates that these emergent-literacy experiences are vital for optimum reading and writing development. And as we'll see next, the power of emergent learning does not stop with the beginning of formal schooling.

ACTIVITIES THAT CREATE "ZONES"

The design of classroom activities influences the quality of teacher–child and child–child interaction, which molds children's cognitive and social development.[15] Collaboration and dialogue are restricted in traditional classrooms because the main activities are whole-class lessons in which all children sit at desks facing the teacher and work on the same textbook assignments. When teachers rely on scripts from teaching manuals to guide classroom talk, not surprisingly, the main form of discourse is recitation; teachers ask questions of children, who try to give the expected responses.

This style of interaction permits whole-class lessons to flow smoothly. But it also leads teacher–child exchanges to emphasize rote, repetitive drill rather than higher-level processes, such as comparing, contrasting, analyzing, evaluating, and applying ideas and concepts. Recent national assessments of the quality of discourse in American schools reveal that teachers devote far more time to low-level memorization than to challenging thinking.[16] In fact, up to 20 percent of questions in classrooms that rely on recitation discourse can be answered with a simple "yes" or "no."[17]

Teaching limited to whole-class activities constrains interaction so that conversational give-and-take and scaffolding rarely, if ever, occur. Teachers trying to keep whole-class activities intact through most of the day cannot attend to individual children's needs. If the teacher stops to help one or two children, pockets of inattention and withdrawal already under way elsewhere quickly escalate into management difficulties.[18] Furthermore, to maintain order and a smooth flow of classroom events, whole-class teaching requires a large power difference between teachers and children. When children have no more than a reactive voice in classroom dialogues, they have little opportunity to experiment with ways of thinking under the watchful eye of an adult expert and to indicate—in words or in behavior—the kind of assistance they need to advance.

This does not mean that whole-class teaching should never occur, only that it should be a secondary type of classroom interaction supporting activities that create "zones" for learning. At times, Tamara gathered all her children in the meeting area to orient them to activity-center possibilities. At other times, she brought the class together to discuss a topic relevant to everyone—something related to an in-depth class project, an approaching holiday, a field trip, or a special school event. As needed, she conducted a class-wide lesson on academic content that many children appeared ready to master. Or she focused on social problem solving and values essential for a harmonious classroom community.

Furthermore, when Tamara did organize whole-class lessons, she retained the active involvement and relaxed conversational style of other activities in the room, as the check-writing activity in preparation for the museum field trip illustrates. The meeting area where the whole class gathers is warmly appointed, with a rocking chair for the teacher and several beanbag chairs and large pillows for the children. These informal furnishings enhance the climate of respectful listening and open exchange of thoughts and feelings that Tamara establishes during whole-class gatherings.

In classrooms sensitive to children's "zones," teachers cannot map out experiences months in advance according to a lock-step, textbook format. To provide assistance that respects children's diversity and active involvement in their own learning, teachers must make plans based on children's evolving interests and competencies. An *emergent curriculum*, meaning a curriculum that is open to revision and redirection based on children's changing learning needs,[19] is highly consistent with sociocultural theory, since it integrates child spontaneity with flexible but deliberate teacher planning and guidance. The presence of children with diverse, ever-evolving "zones" in every classroom means that a variety of activities is essential, including many that can be approached in different ways. Activity centers and extended projects allow for high-interest, emergent curricula that translate Vygotsky's concept of the "zone" into action.

Activity Centers: Small Groups, Pairs, and the Individual Child

Activity centers are special areas liberally equipped with materials that convey a particular theme. They are a common way of organizing learning experiences in preschool classrooms. But all too often, the activity-center approach is scaled back or abandoned in kindergarten and the primary grades rather than expanded and deepened.

The physical design of activity centers encourages intimate social gatherings—small groups and pairs of children who work together, assist one another, and comment on center happenings that interest them. These interactions ensure children an active voice in their learning and permit teachers to impart a voice to them through scaffolding and narrative conversation. Centers are best designed and equipped so limits are not placed on what children can learn from them. In this way, their possibilities are responsive to each child's dynamically changing "zone."

Tamara's writing center, for example, is bursting with enticing materials. On one shelf is a wide range of writing tools, sorted into baskets and jars, that suggest interesting, varied ways to create written messages—lead and colored pencils, crayons, felt-tip markers, glitter markers, word and graphic stamps, ink pads, rulers, scissors, glue, tape, and staplers. On another shelf is a wide assortment of writing paper—lined and unlined sheets of different sizes, note pads, small blank books, stickers, and stamps. A third shelf offers reference materials—picture dictionaries, regular dictionaries, "new-word" books compiled by the children, magnetic alphabet letters on trays, alphabet stencils, and alphabet puzzles. Also included is a basket, labeled "Your Classmates," containing large cards with each child's name and picture and a corresponding basket, labeled "Your Teachers," with similar cards for Tamara, the learning disabilities teacher, the speech therapist, the parent volunteers, the lunchroom helper, and the cook.

When they are richly stocked and address stimulating, challenging topics to which children can relate, activity centers are ideally suited for the joint pursuit of meaningful goals. They foster elaborate classroom talk that promotes high-level reasoning and literate modes of communicating. Activity-center structures enable teachers to assist children in raising questions, explaining ideas, overcoming fears of risk taking when challenges arise, and working together despite differences in capacities and backgrounds.

Although many activity-center tasks are collaborative, children in Tamara's classroom often can be seen working on their own, transferring understandings and skills gleaned from participating with others to their own projects so they can gain independent mastery. For Vygotsky, one of the most important autonomous learning activities involves children interacting with texts—written by adult authors or by children themselves. In these activities, children learn to converse not just with themselves but also with written narratives. Eventually, dialogues with others speaking through texts become the most common context for learning, offering a lifetime of occasions to acquire new knowledge.

Extended Projects

Extended projects, such as "The Natural History Museum" in Tamara's classroom, are in-depth studies of special topics. They may be undertaken by a small group of children who collaborate because of a common interest or by the whole class, with responsibilities distributed across individuals and groups. During a project, children investigate, deeply and fully, phenomena in their own community or the wider world, seeking answers to questions they raise on their own, with classmates, and with teachers. Projects stimulate children to find out: "How do things work? What do people do? What tools do they use? What goes on behind the scenes?"[20]

Other projects in Tamara's classroom included "What Happens at the Airport?" "An Imaginary Trip to Japan," and "All about Balls." Each lasted from 2 weeks to several months and was closely tied to other parts of the curriculum. Reading, writing, math, life science, physical science, art, and make-believe play supported each project, and project work, in turn, enriched learning in each subject.

In "The Natural History Museum," for example, Tamara modified the life science and physical science centers to impart project-relevant knowledge. In life science, books, pictures, posters, and charts about amphibians and echinoderms (prickly sea creatures, such as starfish) were available. The table and shelves were filled with real examples and tools of study—magnifying glasses and instruments with which to pick up delicate specimens. During the project, frogs, turtles, sea crabs, and snails lived in the center so children could observe their behavior, and children drew and wrote about what they saw in science logs. In physical science, Tamara and the children brought in many kinds of rocks and labeled and sorted them, referring to charts and maps to identify their type and geographic origins.

To help the children understand what museums are and what goes on in them, Tamara arranged a field trip. To prepare for the trip, the children read books and watched videos about museums. With Tamara's help, they made a list of jobs performed at the natural history museum, learned about the job of curator, and formulated questions they wanted to ask the curator of rocks and fossils, whom Tamara had arranged for the children to interview. They also discussed displays they wanted to include in their own museum, for which the field trip would provide inspiration. Small groups of children chose different parts of the museum in which to become expert, bringing back specialized knowledge to the class as a whole.

Sometimes, one project supports another, offering children an example of the interconnectedness of knowledge in the real world. In "What Happens at the Airport," Tamara's class took a field trip to the municipal airport and built an airport terminal in the classroom. They learned about airport jobs, airport operations, and different kinds of airplanes. Then they prepared for "An Imaginary Trip to Japan." Before "takeoff" for Tokyo, volunteer parents came to school and played the roles of ticket agents, security guards, baggage workers, and air traffic controllers. Several children went along as pilots and flight attendants, the remainder as passengers.

When the children "arrived," they "checked into" a *ryokan,* or traditional Japanese inn, and the imaginative play/extended project center became a traditional Japanese room. They set up a Japanese restaurant, designed menus, used Japanese phrases to order food, and ate with *hashi,* or chopsticks. In the math center, they learned about different foreign currencies, tracked daily exchange rates, and kept a record of their travel expenditures. As tour guide, Tamara took the children by *Shinkansen* (bullet train) to visit several Japanese cities. They went to famous tourist sites and to several museums, building on what they had learned in "The Natural History Museum" project. This sparked new museum displays in several activity centers—the Tokyo National Museum in the art center, the National Science Museum in the physical science center, and the Shinagawa Aquarium in the life science center.

Not all projects need have as many components and last as long as "The Natural History Museum" and "An Imaginary Trip to Japan." In a two-week project called "All about Balls,"[21] Tamara's children addressed the many possibilities of an everyday object. They gathered old balls from relatives, friends, and others and came up with many facets to investigate. The more than thirty types of balls they collected included a globe of the earth, a gumball, and a cotton ball. Small groups of children addressed different questions—about texture, size, material, and use. After each group recorded and reported its findings, the children tested predictions about the balls involving weight, height of bounce, flotation, and distance rolled on different surfaces. As the children experimented, Tamara scaffolded their introduction to diverse math and science concepts, including circumference, volume, friction, resistance, and speed.

Regardless of a project's scope, it always addresses a topic related to children's everyday experiences, allows integration of a range of subjects, and involves children in "fieldwork"—deciding what questions to ask and what work needs to be done; collecting information from diverse sources; making observations; constructing models; recording findings; and cataloguing, discussing, and dramatizing new knowledge. Project work requires sustained collaboration between teachers and children; literacy skills and many higher forms of thinking; and a level of planning, organization, and child responsibility well beyond that required in day-to-day activity-center tasks.[22]

In all these ways, the project approach helps children reach new heights of understanding, self-confidence as learners, and self-regulation. Especially when extended in the later grades, early project experiences may launch lifelong dispositions to seek in-depth understandings of meaningful topics.[23]

TEACHER–CHILD DIALOGUES

What kinds of teacher–child dialogues constantly stretch children to higher levels, developing active, self-confident learners with a firm foundation in literate modes of expression? To find out, educators have designed innovative teaching interventions based on Vygotsky's ideas that emphasize teacher–child interaction in reading and math. Each approach is highly successful in spurring children's academic development in the primary grades.

Reciprocal Teaching

Originally aimed at improving reading comprehension in children achieving poorly, *reciprocal teaching* is an interactive teaching method that its designers, Annemarie Palincsar and Ann Brown, have extended to other subjects and to all school-age children.[24] A teacher and two to four children form a collaborative learning group and take turns leading a discussion aimed at helping children understand text passages. As group members engage in dialogue, they flexibly apply four strategies: *questioning, summarizing, clarifying,* and *predicting.*

At first, the teacher scaffolds, explaining and modeling the strategies. As children become proficient at them, the teacher draws back, turning the discussion over to the children. The four strategies ensure that children will link new information to previously acquired knowledge, explain their ideas, use what they have learned to acquire new knowledge, and keep their interaction goal oriented.

Once the group has read a passage, the dialogue leader (at first the teacher, later a child) begins by *asking questions* about it. Children offer answers, raise additional questions, and in case of disagreement about content, reread the text. Next, the leader *summarizes* the passage, and children discuss the summary and *clarify* ideas that are unfamiliar to any group members. Finally, the leader encourages children to *predict* future content based on prior knowledge and clues in the text narrative. Over several sessions, children discuss passages with related themes, deepening their understanding of important concepts. In this way, children notice that they can use information from one text passage to better grasp the meaning of others.[25]

Let's look in on a reciprocal teaching session in which four first graders and their teacher have begun to read a series of stories on animal survival. Just before this dialogue, the group had read a passage about the birth and rearing of baby snowshoe rabbits:

Kam *(dialogue leader):* When [were] the babies born?
Teacher: That's a good question to ask. Call on someone to answer that question.
Kam: Robby? Milly?
Milly: Summer.
Teacher: What would happen if the babies were born in the winter? Let's think.
Several children make a number of responses including: "The baby would be very cold." "They would need food." "They don't have fur when they are just born."
Kam: I have another question. How does she get the babies safe?
Kris: She hides them.
Kam: That's right but something else . . .
Teacher: There is something very unusual about how she hides them that surprised me. I didn't know this.
Travis: They are all in a different place.
Teacher: Why do you think she does this?
Milly: Probably because I heard another story and when they're babies they usually eat each other or fight with each other.
Teacher: That could be! And what about when the lynx comes?
Several children comment that [the lynx] would be the end of all the babies.
Kris: If the babies are hidden and the mom wants to go and look at them, how can she remember where they are?
Teacher: Good question. Because she does have to find them again. Why? What does she bring them?

Milly: She needs to bring food. She probably leaves a twig or something.

Teacher: Do you think she puts out a twig like we mark a trail?

Several children disagree and suggest that she uses her sense of smell. One child, recalling that the snowshoe rabbit is not all white in the winter, suggests that the mother might be able to tell her babies apart by their coloring.

Teacher: So we agree that the mother rabbit uses her senses to find her babies after she hides them. Kam, can you summarize for us now?

Kam: The babies are born in the summer . . .

Teacher: The mother . . .

Kam: The mother hides the babies in different places.

Teacher: And she visits them . . .

Kam: To bring them food.

Travis: She keeps them safe.

Teacher: Any predictions?

Milly: What she teaches her babies like how to hop.

Kris: They know how to hop already.

Teacher: Well, let's read and see.[26]

Kam, Milly, Kris, and Travis are already experienced enough with reciprocal teaching to implement its four strategies with only occasional teacher support. The children's dialogue is saturated with high-level cognitive processes, including analysis of text content, synthesis with previous knowledge, question asking, and inference making. Each child strives to clarify and extend the story and search for new discoveries by combining it with information gleaned from previous texts. Palincsar and Brown report that as children make these connections, they often voice them with great excitement, expressed as "squeals of delight"![27]

Research verifies that children from the primary through middle-school grades who experience reciprocal teaching show impressive gains in reading comprehension.[28] In one study, Palincsar and Brown reported that first graders with as few as twenty sessions, one per day, displayed markedly improved story understanding when compared with agemates taught in other ways using the same reading materials. In addition, when given a sorting task in which they had to classify animals by themes emphasized in the stories, reciprocal-teaching children did far better.[29] They grouped animals that, for example, gave birth at the same time of the year, engaged in similar infant care practices, ate the same foods, and were predators. Although they had read the same text passages, comparison children largely grouped animals by physical characteristics.

Although reciprocal teaching is among the most structured of Vygotsky-inspired teaching interventions, its originators comment that they intended it to be this way. Its four strategies are precisely what successful text comprehenders do when conversing with themselves about text passages. Furthermore, reciprocal teaching provides children with the systematic social experiences they need to internalize those strategies. Then children can call on the strategies in their private speech when reading on their own.

The structure of reciprocal teaching makes it particularly helpful to teachers who are just beginning to integrate Vygotsky-inspired narrative dialogues into their classroom activities. All new learners—teachers and children alike—benefit from a clear road map when first acquiring a new skill. Also, the four strategies offer parents an excellent guide for how to read with their child. The approach may remind you of dialogic reading, the adult–child storybook-reading technique for preschoolers discussed in Chapter 2. Reciprocal teaching can be viewed as an upward extension of dialogic reading—one that increases the complexity of the dialogue and, thereby, responds to older children's "zones" for literacy learning. Both approaches have amassed track records of extraordinary success.

As reciprocal-teaching procedures become well practiced, teachers can adapt them to serve new learning goals. Observations of teachers and children engaged in reciprocal-teaching dialogues reveal that over time, they apply the strategies more flexibly. Children develop such an enthusiastic, inquisitive mind-set from participating in reciprocal teaching that they interject questions and clarifying remarks from the very outset, when embarking on reading a text passage.

Inquiry in Mathematics

Mathematics educators Paul Cobb, Terry Wood, and Erna Yackel observed mid-year in a second-grade classroom in which they had taught the teacher to use a unique approach to teaching called *inquiry math*. There, children given the addition problem, 39 + 53 = ?, to work in their heads offered the following richly varied solutions:

> Anna: 50 plus 30 is 80, then 9 plus 1 more would be 90, plus 2 more would be 92.
> Joel: You have 53, 10 more is 63, plus 10 more is 73, plus 10 more 83, plus 9 . . . 92.
> Jenny: See, 39 and 50 more is 89, then add 3 makes 92.
> Eric: 30 plus 50 is 80 and 9 plus 3 is 12. Put all those together and I came up with 92. [30]

Mathematics is often conveyed in such a way that children view knowledge as ready-made—as if there is only one way to solve problems, which teachers must transmit. Inquiry math combats this view through learning activities in which children jointly construct increasingly advanced math concepts and procedures. As a result, children see that people solve problems in different ways and that they themselves use different procedures from one occasion to the next—procedures that gradually become more effective as they revise them on the basis of shared information. The contrast between traditional math teaching and inquiry-math teaching is captured by the difference between the questions, "What was I told to do?" and "How can I figure this out?"[31]

Rather than memorizing standard procedures, students in inquiry-math classrooms meet in small groups to work problems and explain their personally invented procedures to one another. With the teacher's guidance, they engage in mathematical dialogues, in which they discuss, critique, and justify their solution processes and answers. After members of a small group reach consensus on a way of solving a problem, they bring their method and answer to the whole class for further discussion. In the process, they learn to engage in analytical reasoning.[32]

Inquiry math emphasizes inventing and revising problem-solving strategies as a means of nurturing mathematical practices valued by the wider society. Consequently, it does not neglect the development of powerful computational techniques. Rather, it assumes that the best way to foster high-quality math procedures is to encourage children's understanding of their current strategies by having them explain those strategies to others.[33] Through this focus on understanding rather than mechanical answer finding, children acquire better computational procedures because they find those procedures to be sensible. Then, in classrooms with many opportunities to practice improved computation, children solidify and perfect those skills.

Because inquiry math enhances math concepts and computation in an integrated manner, children rarely give wildly unreasonable answers of the sort that frequently occur in traditional classrooms—for example, $39 + 53 = 812$ (arrived at by treating the two columns as if they were separate problems—that is, $9 + 3 = 12$ And $3 + 5 = 8$). Anna, Joel, Jenny, and Eric know that the solution, 812, is way out of range because of their extensive experience in relying on mathematical reasoning.

As in other Vygotsky-based educational interventions, the teacher's role in inquiry math is complex and demanding. It includes helping students develop productive small-group dialogues, getting children to comprehend one another's procedures, pointing out multiple routes to solutions and important differences between them, emphasizing contributions to discussions that are fruitful for advancing classmates' thinking, and recasting children's explanations in more advanced ways.

Let's join a second-grade inquiry-math session in which a teacher guides children's attempts to engage in genuine mathematical communication. Craig and Karen are working on the problems $47 + 19 =$ ___ , $48 + 18 =$ ___ , and $49 + 17 =$ ___ . As yet, they have not had much experience in small-group collaboration:

Karen *[having worked the first problem and moved to the second, holds up her thumb and starts to count]:* Forty-eight, forty . . . That's just the same. *(Karen excitedly points to 47 + 19 = 66 on the activity sheet, but Craig ignores and continues to write his answer to the previous problem. The teacher then takes his turn in the dialogue and asks Karen, "What is just the same?")*

Karen: If you take 1 from the 19 and put it with the 7 *(She hesitates and looks at the teacher, while Craig leans forward to look closely at the problem)*, and [it] makes 48 and that makes just the same [as 48 plus 18].

Teacher: Do you see that, Craig? Do you see what she is trying to say? *(The teacher . . . reminds Craig of his obligation to listen and try to understand Karen's explanation. . . .)*

Teacher: Look at the next problem, 48 plus 18 equals. She said it is the same number.

Karen: Ya, because you take 1 from the 19 and add it to the 47 and that makes . . . *(Hesitates).*

Teacher: Forty-eight.

Karen: Forty-eight and 18 . . .

Craig *(Interrupts):* Oh! I know what she's trying to say. Take 1 from here and add it here.

Teacher: Right!

Craig: It's got to be the same answer, or you can add it here and add it to here *(Points from 47 to 48 and from 18 to 19).*

Karen: No, take one from . . . *(She points to 19)* and add it here *(Points to 47).*[34]

As this episode illustrates, in inquiry math, children construct understandings as they engage in stimulating problem solving and, with teacher assistance, make sense of others' methods and explanations. The teacher helps Karen and Craig grasp a mathematical pattern by encouraging them to reflect on one another's strategies, to agree or disagree, and to work toward a common perspective. Karen and Craig reach consensus readily, but sometimes problems remain unresolved for hours or days, during which children can be seen engaging in animated discussion about them at lunch or recess.[35]

What does research say about the impact of inquiry math on learning? Comparisons of children's performance in inquiry and non-inquiry second-grade classrooms revealed that inquiry children were substantially ahead in their grasp of math concepts at the end of the school year.[36] And they continued to show that advantage a full year later, after completing a traditional, textbook-based math curriculum in third grade.[37] Furthermore, at the end of both second and third grades, inquiry-math students did just as well as their non-inquiry peers in math computation. In other words, inquiry children showed no deficiencies in math technique due to teaching that emphasized math concepts.

Finally, inquiry children gained much more than a deeper grasp of mathematical knowledge; their beliefs about mathematics changed. They were far more likely than non-inquiry children to say that success in math depends on understanding and collaborating rather than on accepting an adult's solutions, turning in neat papers, and being quiet in the classroom. They also believed more strongly in the relevance of working hard, being interested in math, and coming up with personally meaningful solution methods for enjoying and being good at math. Inquiry children continued to hold these beliefs after spending a year in a traditional third grade.[38] They had formed an enduring appreciation of math activity—not as applying adults' rules but rather as an exciting adventure involving communicating, reasoning, and discovering new meanings.

CHILD–CHILD DIALOGUES

In Vygotsky-inspired classrooms, children spend much time engaged in joint activities with classmates, who assist them in mastering tasks within their "zones." We have seen in previous chapters that young preschoolers are already competent conversationalists. This sets the stage for collaboration with peers, first in pretend play and later in other activities. In defining the "zone," Vygotsky explicitly mentioned peer collaboration. He noted, further, that *collaboration with more capable peers* is an excellent means for leading children forward.

Cooperative Learning

In both reciprocal teaching and inquiry math, teachers engage in considerable scaffolding to get children to create "zones" for one another's learning. Clearly, adapting communication so it helps a peer partner is quite challenging, even for older children. Teachers must model effective dialogue, help children verbalize their thinking, and encourage them to comprehend, respect, and build on their classmates' ideas and opinions. Tamara and a student teacher or parent volunteer often demonstrated how to work together on a task. After describing the activity, the two adults began, engaging in patient listening, explaining, questioning, and turn-taking as the children looked on.

These efforts are vital because peer collaboration fosters academic progress only under certain conditions. A crucial factor is *cooperative learning*—structuring the peer group so students work toward common goals. Inevitably when they collaborate, children argue and disagree—events that remind them that people often hold different viewpoints. But by themselves, conflict and disagreement do not advance children's learning. Rather, striving for intersubjectivity—by resolving differences of opinion, sharing responsibility, and engaging in cooperative dialogues—leads to gains in academic knowledge.[39] For example, in a study of school-age children jointly solving math problems, psychologists Shari Ellis, David Klahr, and Robert Siegler found that partners were far more likely to move toward effective strategies if they clarified, explained, and tried to apply each others' ideas.[40] Notice how these features of peer dialogue are central to both reciprocal teaching and inquiry math.

Cultural values and practices influence the ease with which children engage in cooperative learning. Working productively in groups comes more naturally to children reared in collectivist rather than in individualistic cultures. For example, Navajo children cooperate more readily than do Caucasian-American children.[41] Japanese classroom practices, in which children begin learning in the preschool years how to work effectively in groups[42] and to solve problems by building on one another's ideas, are situated in a larger culture that values interdependence in family and work life.[43] The consistently superior math and science achievements of Japanese students over American students[44] from elementary school through high school is believed to be partly due to the many opportunities for harmonious small-group and whole-class problem solving, in which Japanese children explain, reflect on, and revise their math concepts and procedures.

Mixed-Age Classrooms

Tamara's classroom includes both kindergartners and first graders—an even balance of 5-, 6-, and 7-year-olds. Mixed-age grouping expands the heterogeneity of children in the same class, creating conditions that support Vygotsky's vision of more competent children spurring the development of their less advanced peers.[45] In laboratory studies, children's planning and problem solving improve most when they work cooperatively with a partner who is an "expert"—especially capable at the task.[46] Mixed-age grouping also enhances children's learning in classrooms, preschool and primary school alike.

Among preschoolers, the play of younger children is more cognitively and socially advanced in mixed-age settings spanning two to three years than in single-age settings.[47] Older preschoolers seem to stimulate their younger classmates to reach greater heights in play. As early as age 3 or 4, children can modify their behavior to fit the needs of a less advanced child, simplifying and reducing their rate of communication and taking more responsibility for a task.[48] Younger preschoolers are captivated by their older classmates' superior knowledge and exciting play ideas and are highly motivated to learn from them.

In the primary grades, when academic performance differs between mixed-age and single-age classrooms, it consistently favors the mixed-age arrangement. Also, self-esteem and attitudes toward school are more positive in mixed-age environments,[49] very likely because these settings decrease competition and increase harmony among children. When children of diverse ages learn together, they spend more time facilitating and emulating the efforts of other classmates rather than trying to outdo them. And in such classrooms, older children helping younger children often becomes a norm of classroom life, especially when cooperative learning is central to children's activities.

Mixed-age classrooms are not just beneficial for younger children. Older, more expert children gain as well. As they remind younger peers of classroom rules and assist them in their learning, older children practice nurturing and help-giving—important life skills that are challenging in their own right. In a study of kindergartners interacting with classmates, some of whom were one year older and some of whom were one year younger, psychologists Adam Winsler and Rafael Diaz found that the kindergartners used more private speech when collaborating with younger children.[50] The researchers informally noted that this extra self-talk seemed to be sparked by the challenges of mentoring. In carefully planned and supervised programs in which older or more rapidly developing children tutor those progressing more slowly, both tutors and tutees gain in self-esteem and academic achievement.[51] The oft-heard remark—that a good way to learn is to teach another—seems to be as true for children as it is for adults.

Mixed-age classrooms are far more likely to promote cognitive and social development when they exist in a supportive context. When principals create them not because they believe in them but merely for convenience (to deal with uneven enrollments in some grades), such classrooms have fewer benefits. In some schools with both mixed-age and single-age classes, principals tend to place higher-performing pupils in mixed-age settings to ease the demands on teachers.[52] This undermines the strengths of the mixed-age arrangement by replacing it with an alternative form of homogenous grouping.

Finally, recall that more expert children can foster learning in less expert children as long as both work cooperatively toward common goals. In many classrooms, groups of children who differ in skill level engage in poor-quality interaction, exchanging unclear and inaccurate explanations and answers[53] because teachers fail to guide them in how to communicate. When teachers provide this assistance, mixed-age classrooms not only support development throughout the preschool and elementary school years but better prepare children for everyday life. In communities and work settings, people are not age segregated. Instead, individuals of diverse ages, capabilities, and skill levels must find ways to interact in mutually beneficial ways.

EVALUATING PROGRESS: DYNAMIC ASSESSMENT

One day, 6-year-old Carrie eagerly showed her science log to Tamara. Carrie had filled several pages with pictures of starfish, writing a few words and letters beneath each. Tamara sensed that Carrie's writing symbolized much more than she had recorded on the page. She asked Carrie to read from her log, continuing, "Can I write the words you say so I will remember your ideas?" In response, Carrie rendered an elaborate narrative:

> Starfish sometimes have long legs. Starfish can be small and skinny. Starfish eat from their stomachs. This is a backside of the starfish. Starfish live in the sea. Starfish are big. Starfish are not bumpy on the back side.[54]

As Carrie read and Tamara wrote beneath Carrie's writing, Tamara learned much about Carrie's current capacities. More important, she picked up a great deal about what Carrie was ready to master with assistance. Carrie had learned easily from hands-on exploration and from reading about starfish. Her memory for detail was sharp, and her verbal narrative was clear and precise. Although she could not yet convey much of what she knew in conventional writing and spelling, she could read back most of what Tamara had recorded.

Tamara could see that Carrie was ready to learn to write many of the words in her narrative, so she included several in Carrie's spelling list for the week and suggested that Carrie create some labels using those words for the starfish display. She also asked Carrie to add more pictures and writing to her science log. As Carrie wrote, Tamara assisted, using a method called *scaffolded writing,* developed by early childhood educators Elena Bodrova and Deborah Leong.[55] It helps children make the transition between dictating to others and independent writing.

Instead of "taking dictation," this time Tamara drew horizontal lines, each standing for a word in Carrie's sentences. Then Carrie wrote as much of each word on each line as she could. Scaffolded writing provides beginning writers with enough structure for their writing that they write more elaborate messages and add more syllables to each word than they otherwise would.[56] In each scaffolded writing session, Tamara assessed Carrie's progress and used it as the basis for prompting her to expand her writing. Soon Carrie was able to write in complete words and sentences.

The concept of the "zone" serves not just as a guide for how to teach but how to evaluate children's progress. Vygotsky was critical of traditional intelligence and achievement tests. Their usefulness is limited, he argued, because they assess only children's current competencies. They tell us nothing about what children are ready to learn. Vygotsky pointed out that two children can obtain the same test score but differ greatly in the breadth of their "zones."[57] The child whose "zone" is narrow profits most from teaching just slightly ahead of his or her independent capacities. Carrie's "zone" for expressing her ideas in writing is broad; during scaffolded writing, she performed at a much higher level than when working independently.

Unlike static assessment procedures that emphasize already acquired knowledge and skills, *dynamic assessment* is a general, ongoing assessment approach that introduces purposeful teaching into testing situations.[58] Its goal is to find out what the child can attain with scaffolding. Dynamic assessment stresses the process of teaching and learning rather than how many correct answers children give. The adult tries to find the teaching style to which the child is most responsive and to suggest strategies that the child can apply in new situations, noting the extent to which the child performs more competently than before.

Various dynamic assessment procedures exist. Most use traditional intelligence-test items as the basis for scaffolding.[59] In each of these systems, a test–intervene–retest sequence is used in which children are first tested to see what they can do independently. Then an adult scaffolds their efforts on tasks they have not yet mastered. Finally the adult again assesses what the child can do without help. Consequently, teachers and other school staff can discern the extent to which traditional test scores underestimate a child's potential to learn.

Another approach to dynamic assessment embeds it in classroom learning. The teacher or another trained adult observes and tries to facilitate mastery of academic tasks children encounter in their classrooms, keeping a record of children's responses.[60] This technique is especially helpful to teachers because it identifies teaching interventions likely to foster a particular child's academic development. Bodrova and Leong have built a dynamic assessment procedure into scaffolded writing. The teacher continually notes each child's progress. Then, to make the best use of the information, the teacher enters it into a computerized "expert" system that suggests next steps for helping that child meet writing goals for the primary grades in most school districts.[61]

How effective is dynamic assessment? Research shows that children often do much better at mastering cognitive tasks with scaffolded assistance than their IQ scores predict they should.[62] As yet, dynamic assessment is not more effective at forecasting children's academic achievement at the end of the school year than is IQ. But better correspondence between dynamic assessment and academic achievement may emerge in classrooms where children receive individualized scaffolding as part of their daily learning experiences[63]—teaching that is integral to the dynamic assessment approach.

Dynamic assessment is challenging and time consuming. To implement it, the adult must determine the child's learning needs and respond to those needs during repeated testing situations. But it is just this aspect of dynamic assessment that offers promise for identifying effective teaching practices, especially for children who have difficulty learning. Dynamic assessment reduces the possibility that a child will be denied stimulating opportunities to learn because of a poor score on a traditional test. And for children with fairly narrow "zones," the scaffolding built into dynamic assessment yields information about interventions that are likely to improve their academic progress.

Keeping track of each child's dynamic assessment data so they can be used to decide on teaching strategies is a significant hurdle for teachers. But with new computer software like that Bodrova and Leong designed, which helps teachers conveniently record each child's most recent progress and consider what to do next, dynamic assessment may soon be more widespread.

Besides being a useful procedure, dynamic assessment conveys an optimistic attitude. School personnel who use it with special-needs children are convinced that the key to their academic progress lies in finding the means by which each child can profit from intervention.[64] The focus of dynamic assessment is not on children verifying their abilities to adults. Instead, it is on systematically promoting all children's learning, using their "zones" as guides.

COMMUNITIES OF LEARNERS

Sympathetic values and goals on the part of school administrators and the surrounding community are essential if learning environments with the features I have described are to become widespread. Recognizing this need for favorable larger contexts, a new educational approach inspired by sociocultural theory transforms the ingredients of educational excellence—abundant cooperative dialogues, literacy-rich activities and projects relevant to children's experiences, and diverse mixtures of children creating "zones" for one another—into school-wide values.

The *community-of-learners model* assumes that each person has a different area of expertise that can help other community members, depending on the task at hand. Both adults and children are regarded as learners; all collaborate and develop in their respective roles. In classrooms, teachers assist children and children assist one another; at home, parents help their children learn, supported by contact with teachers. Then other levels of the school champion and nurture the collaborative work of teachers, parents, and children.[65]

Teacher–Parent Partnerships

In communities of learners, parents and teachers communicate often, keeping one another abreast of children's reactions and progress at home and at school. Teachers suggest ways that parents can foster children's learning. They also invite parents to visit and participate in the classroom. As a result, parents learn firsthand about effective educational practices, and they enrich classroom life through assisting with activities or contributing special expertise. In addition, teachers and parents work to build bridges between children's home cultures and the culture of the classroom. And schools include parents in basic planning and governance to ensure their understanding of, investment in, and contribution to educational goals and practices.

When parents are involved in school activities, talk regularly with teachers, monitor their child's learning progress, and help their child with homework, children show better academic achievement.[66] Yet teacher–parent partnerships are harder to realize in urban areas than in small towns, where most residents know one another and schools serve as centers of community life.[67] Also, some ethnic minority parents feel uncomfortable about coming to school. And parents who face many daily stresses have reduced time and energy for classroom involvement. Under these conditions, teachers working within a community-of-learners model must take extra steps to reach out to parents—by integrating ethnic minority values and practices into classroom life[68] and regularly contacting parents who do not come to conferences and other school events.

Tamara built strong parental ties by conferring with parents often— through notes, letters, informational meetings, classroom visits, and workshops to plan and implement classroom projects. She also initiated projects that utilized parents' expertise. In one project, "African-American Hair Braiding," several parents came to class and shared their knowledge and experiences. One mother demonstrated different types of braiding. Another arranged a display of the various combs, clips, tools, hair gels, and lotions used. Each mother explained how she had learned the art of braiding from her own mother and would teach her daughter to braid.

Stressing themes of cooperation and connection, here is what one parent said about Tamara's success in including parents as crucial members of the learning community:

> She worked with parents from the beginning. She established a trust level and created a partnership with us. I think almost all parents felt this way, even if they couldn't be in the room to participate a lot. . . . We learned right along with our children. She talked with us when we needed that, kept us informed, reassured us, and included us as important contributors to our children's education.[69]

Teacher–School Partnerships

Classrooms that consistently create "zones" for children's learning rarely operate autonomously. As members of the learning community, teachers need support and scaffolding to carry out the complex tasks of effective teaching and to become more expert at their work. When other participants in the educational system—teacher-colleagues, supervisors, and principals—provide this assistance, children reap many benefits.

Tamara often engages in supportive exchanges with Rita, a teacher who shares her educational values. Tamara and Rita have collaborated for many years, designing classroom activities and projects and engaging in dialogue about effective teaching—exploring, questioning, and looking at teaching strategies in different ways. Tamara's principal has also created a climate in which teachers can experiment, rethink, and revise their teaching strategies. Nevertheless, no unified philosophy of teaching and learning exists in Tamara's school. Aside from Tamara and Rita, all teachers lean toward traditional education. As Tamara noted, "When you . . . have different views about curriculum and how your classroom should be run, you can feel isolated. . . . I miss conversations and interactions with other people about issues, about children, and about the things I am doing."[70]

Occasionally, schools can be found in which administrators, education specialists, and teachers join forces to create and implement an educational philosophy that pervades all levels of the school. Cooperative dialogues, joint problem solving, and scaffolding of teachers by expert educators are central to the school's day-to-day operation. Interactions between adult members of the learning community nurture and sustain improved teacher performance—in the form of experiences for children that are as encouraging, enriching, and educative as possible.

EXEMPLARY PROGRAMS

Two exemplary programs—one for preschoolers and one for children in the primary grades—have achieved international acclaim for their success in translating the community-of-learners model into action. Let's visit each of them.

Reggio Emilia

In Reggio Emilia, a small town in north-central Italy, an extraordinary preschool program has captured the attention of educators worldwide. Capitalizing on the enthusiasm and commitment of parents who built their own preschool using materials left over from the rubble of World War II, founder Loris Malaguzzi devised a city-sponsored educational system over 40 years ago that today includes thirteen centers for infants and toddlers and twenty-two preschools for 3- to 6-year-olds. Its educational vision has evolved over time, with Vygotsky's ideas serving as a major stimulus along with other philosophies and theories of child development and education.[71]

Reggio Emilia education views the child as a complex, capable being who is motivated by and learns from social interaction and relationships.[72] The approach is based on strong community ties—a major reason for its excellence. Together, parents, teachers, administrative staff, and government officials support the program's educational goals. Parents meet with teachers and other staff members for program planning, and they volunteer in classrooms. Teachers routinely collaborate with other teachers and with specially trained educational advisors, called *pedagogistas,* in devising new ways to assist children's learning.[73]

A strong spirit of collaboration permeates teacher–child communication. In each classroom, pairs of teachers work together as equals, modeling cooperation. Children stay with the same teachers and classmates for three years—a continuity that ensures that they will form the meaningful relationships essential for mastering high-level cognitive and social skills.[74] The design of physical space, with many inviting, intimate alcoves, promotes small-group activities for two, three, or four children—regarded as "the most favorable organization for an education based on relationships" because they increase the likelihood of complex interactions, constructive conflict resolution, and self-regulation.[75] Each building also has a common space, or *piazza*—a central area referred to with the same term used for city square. In the piazza, children and adults gather to reaffirm their membership in the community and to reassert school-wide values and goals. The piazza serves as a passageway to other areas of the building, physically linking the social whole with its diverse parts.[76]

The *atelierista*, a full-time specialist and artist, is responsible for implementing an essential component of Reggio Emilia education. In a special room, or set of rooms, called the *atelier,* the atelierista supports teachers and children as they work with a wide variety of artistic media. An important part of the children's day is symbolizing activities in diverse ways—through paintings, drawings, photographs, clay, audio- and videotapes, music, and transcriptions of conversations. Teachers encourage children to represent everything they think about, including such challenging concepts as shadows, feelings, growth, time, and motion. According to atelierista Vea Vecchi, the atelier "provides a place for children to become masters of all kinds of techniques . . . —all the symbolic languages."[77] Reggio Emilia preschoolers become skilled at using an impressive range of representational tools for communicating with others and with themselves.

Reggio Emilia also makes extensive use of long-term, multifaceted projects that offer a broad, integrative framework for exploration and interaction. Parents, teachers, pedagogistas, and atelieristas meet to select project themes, which must allow for both individual expression and collective contributions; provide general goals within which children decide on subgoals; promote lively, cooperative dialogues; and permit many modes of representation.

For example, in an 8-week project called "The Long Jump," children engaged in such interconnected activities as building a long-jump track; advertising and holding an Olympic sports event; experimenting with the relation between running speed and jumping distance; and communicating their knowledge through diverse symbol systems. These included drawing plans of the track layout, run-up, and landing areas; designing posters with contest rules, jumper registration information, and advertising to be displayed city-wide; writing letters of invitation; measuring the length of jumps with string, tape measure, and carpenter's rule; designing an insignia for each jumper to wear at the meet; writing rules for the referees; and posting contest results.[78]

Reggio Emilia education includes extensive documentation of children's experiences and work. These records focus on the processes of learning, not just the end results. They typically include transcriptions of children's discussions about intentions, photographs of work in progress, comments by adults working with children, and finished products. The atelierista organizes and stores these materials for future reference by all members of the learning community.

Documentation makes possible public exhibits of children's creations accompanied by written explanations—a means for informing the community about what happens in its preschools. By referring to archived materials, family members can track children's progress at any time. And children can see what they have accomplished. As they revisit their work, they usually feel a sense of pride and self-confidence that sparks further curiosity and effort.[79] Finally, documentation permits school staff to reflect on classroom events and children's development as a basis for coming up with new ideas for activities and projects and improving teaching practices.[80]

Children's enthusiasm and the complexity and originality of their artistic creations, shared worldwide through traveling exhibits, attest to the success of Reggio Emilia preschools. The Reggio Emilia approach explicitly recognizes that ongoing dialogue throughout the educational system and with the surrounding community—resulting in socially and symbolically rich classroom experiences—creates ideal conditions for teaching and learning.

The Kamehameha Early Education Program (KEEP)

The most well-known and extensive educational reform movement based on Vygotsky's theory is the Kamehameha Elementary Education Program (KEEP). It began in Honolulu as an innovative system of education for the primary grades serving ethnic minority children at risk for academic difficulties and soon spread to serve thousands of children on several Hawaiian islands, on a Navajo reservation in Arizona, and in Los Angeles. KEEP's theme is "assisted performance"[81]—scaffolding of all child and adult members of the learning community so each advances within his or her "zone."

Much like Tamara's classroom, KEEP classrooms are organized into activity centers designed to foster teacher–child and child–child cooperative dialogues. Each center—for example, the library center, the art center, and the game center—encourages a different set of cognitive and social skills. Small groups of five to six children rotate through the centers over a week's time, working cooperatively on a wide range of meaningful academic tasks.

All children enter a leading activity center, called "Center One," at least once each morning for scaffolding of challenging literacy skills. With the teacher's assistance, children read text materials that relate to their experiences. Then the teacher engages them in extensive discussion of what they have read by questioning, responding to, and building on the children's ideas. Other activity centers extend the literacy goals of Center One and are rich in peer collaboration. Each child's weekly selection of activity centers is tailored to his or her specific learning needs. And the design of centers is adjusted to fit the backgrounds and learning styles of the children in each KEEP classroom, creating culturally responsive environments.[82]

The KEEP approach insists that just as children require scaffolded support, teachers teach best when they receive assistance from other educators. Principals, consultants with specialized expertise, and teacher-colleagues design activity settings in which teachers enhance their skills for promoting children's learning. These settings take a wide variety of forms, including workshops, retreats, individual consultation, and enrollment in university courses.

The most important activity settings for teachers are observation-and-conference sessions and peer coaching. A consultant observes each teacher at least once a week. Then the consultant and teacher schedule a conference in which they work together to identify ways of better assisting children, often by reviewing audio- or videotapes of classroom interaction. As a result, new goals for improving teaching are set. Similar activities occur in peer coaching, in which teachers volunteer to assist their colleagues.

KEEP schools are cultures of learning for all involved, and the approach is highly effective. Ethnic minority children enrolled in first- through third-grade KEEP classrooms perform far better in reading achievement than do their counterparts in traditional classrooms. Furthermore, KEEP pupils more often participate in animated dialogues with teachers and other children, use more elaborate language structures, and more often support one another's learning than do their traditionally educated peers.[83] KEEP's two main themes—(1) developing children's literacy skills through collaborative activities relevant to their cultural backgrounds and experiences, and (2) involving everyone in assisted performance—make it an unusually comprehensive realization of Vygotsky's teaching and learning principles for the primary grades.

INDICATORS OF HIGH-QUALITY EARLY CHILDHOOD EDUCATION

The educational practices, programs, and related findings I have described demonstrate that children do not develop at their best by taking in ready-made information from external authorities. Such teaching is intellectually impoverished, greatly underestimates children's motivational and cognitive capacities, and dulls their appetite for learning. Nor do children develop effectively by being left to their own devices, until they indicate naturally and unambiguously that they want and are prepared to learn. This approach wastes valuable time and prevents children who do not announce in words or deeds, "I'm ready now," from receiving crucial adult support. A child can be ready to learn a great deal before he or she recognizes possibilities or knows how to request them.

Instead, children master language, literacy, and other symbolic tools; a wealth of knowledge and practical skills; and advanced means for regulating thinking and behavior through interacting with adults and peers in expertly designed activity settings that mirror the stimulating challenges of real life. Educative experiences consistent with sociocultural theory are not yet prevalent in American child-care, preschool, and primary school environments. Where they are present, they are more likely to be germinating and blossoming than to be in the full flower of classrooms like Tamara's.

Currently, there remain both ideological and economic obstacles to widespread, outstanding early childhood education in the United States. With respect to preschoolers, our nation has not yet recognized that one of the significant ways to support the American family while fostering children's academic preparedness and social development is through liberally subsidized, high-quality child care. And with regard to primary school, breaking down the regimented practices of traditional, whole-class instruction remains difficult, even in the face of evidence that the teaching and learning strategies I have described consistently yield better cognitive, emotional, and social outcomes.

But there is reason for optimism. Early childhood professional and advocacy organizations, such as the National Association for the Education of Young Children and the Children's Defense Fund, are working avidly for child-care and school reforms, and some state and local governments, child-care centers, and school districts have responded. These "top-down" efforts to improve children's educational experiences can be greatly aided by complementary, "bottom-up" support from parents, who have a crucial role to play—in becoming knowledgeable about what makes for first-rate early childhood education and pressing for it.

Once parents are aware of the learning experiences that lead children forward, they can select programs and classrooms with development-enhancing characteristics. When these are scarce or unavailable, parents can become advocates for children's educational needs, urging communities and school systems to upgrade quality. In virtually every locale, pockets of excellent early childhood education exist that offer models for what is possible.

What indicators of high-quality early childhood education should parents use as guides? Let's begin with preschool and child care and then turn to kindergarten and primary school.

Preschool and Child Care

Because the majority of American mothers of preschool children are in the labor force, child-care settings are the out-of-home contexts with the largest influence on preschool children's development. Child care is not a situation in which children should merely be watched, amused, and kept from danger. Rather, it should embody excellent early childhood education, no different from that found in the best preschools.

About 40 percent of American preschoolers whose mothers work are enrolled in child-care centers—the most prevalent type of care setting. Another 12 percent are in child-care homes. The remainder experience diverse arrangements, with most being cared for in their own home by a relative or a nonrelative baby-sitter. Furthermore, over one-fourth of preschoolers experience more than one type of care on a daily basis, a circumstance that is particularly hard on children who, due to their temperaments or to high life stress, do not adjust to change easily.

In Chapter 1, I noted that the overall quality of American child care is mediocre to abysmal—among the worst in the industrialized world. Its alarming inadequacy stems from a complete absence of any national standards for quality combined with weak government funding. Without federal leadership, child-care standards are set by the states and vary greatly across the nation. In some places, adults need no special preparation in child development or early childhood education, and as many as twelve or thirteen 2-year-olds and fifteen to twenty 3- and 4-year-olds may be looked after by just one caregiver. Under these conditions, individualized adult–child dialogues and scaffolding within well-planned learning activities are virtually impossible.[84]

In a study of several hundred randomly chosen child-care centers in California, Colorado, Connecticut, and North Carolina, researchers judged that only 1 in 7 centers provided a level of care sufficient to promote healthy psychological development.[85] Similar conclusions have been reached about American child-care homes.[86] Far too many are unlicensed and unmonitored and therefore not held to any standards of quality. Regardless of whether preschoolers come from economically advantaged or disadvantaged homes, those in poor-quality child care develop less favorably than their peers, cognitively and socially.[87]

Below is a list of indicators of high-quality education for 2- to 5-year-olds that parents can use as a checklist when looking for a preschool or child-care setting or when evaluating their child's current setting. These signs of good early education are based on *standards for developmentally appropriate practice* devised by the National Association for the Education of Young Children (NAEYC), an organization of more than 100,000 early childhood educators.[88]

They specify program characteristics that meet the developmental and individual needs of young children, based on current research and the consensus of experts. NAEYC has established a voluntary accreditation system for preschools and child-care centers. It grants special professional recognition to programs that meet rigorous standards of quality. The National Association for Family Child Care (NAFCC) has a similar accreditation system for child-care homes.

Parents should always ask if the preschool or child-care setting they are considering is NAEYC- or NAFCC-accredited. If it is, then it satisfies most or all of the quality indicators that follow. Signs of teacher–child involvement and teacher specialized knowledge in early childhood development and education are especially powerful predictors of children's daily experiences and development. When group size, teacher–child ratio, and teachers' educational preparation are favorable, teachers are more verbally stimulating and sensitive to preschoolers' needs. And children do especially well on measures of cognitive, language, and social competence.[89]

INDICATORS OF HIGH-QUALITY PRESCHOOL EDUCATION, AGES 2 TO 5 [90]

CLIMATE FOR LEARNING: Teachers help children begin to form a sense of the classroom as a community of learners. Some activities involve all children—for example, creating a mural for the classroom or planning a special event for parents. Teachers provide experiences indicating that each child is valued, such as sending a "We miss you!" card to a sick classmate. They bring children's home cultures and languages into the shared classroom culture, and they guide and assist children in relating to classmates with disabilities.

PHYSICAL SETTING AND DAILY SCHEDULE: Space is divided into richly equipped activity centers, such as make-believe play, block building, science, math, games and puzzles, books, art, and music. A fenced outdoor play space is equipped with swings, climbing equipment, tricycles, and sandbox and waterplay. The daily schedule allows for alternating periods of active and quiet time. Periods of at least one hour permit children to become immersed in play and projects.

GROUP SIZE (NUMBER OF CHILDREN IN A SINGLE SPACE) AND TEACHER–CHILD RATIO: In preschools and child-care centers, group size for 2-year-olds is no greater than 12 children with two teachers, one adult for no more than 6 children. Group size for 3- to 5-year-olds is no greater than 20 children with two teachers, one teacher for no more than 10 children. In child-care homes, the adult is responsible for no more than 6 children; no more than 3 of these are infants and toddlers.

DAILY ACTIVITIES: Most of the time, children play and work in small groups and individually. Subject matter content, such as literacy, math, social studies, and science, is integrated through thematic activities, extended projects, and play. Children select many of their own activities and learn through experiences relevant to their own lives. Teachers facilitate involvement in challenging pursuits adjusted to children's developing capacities. They accept individual differences in styles and rates of learning.

INTERACTIONS BETWEEN TEACHERS AND CHILDREN: Teachers move between groups and individuals, demonstrating, asking questions, offering suggestions, engaging in discussion, and adding more complex ideas. They use positive guidance techniques, such as modeling and encouraging expected behavior and redirecting children who are misbehaving to more acceptable activities.

RELATIONSHIPS WITH PARENTS: Parents are encouraged to visit any time, to observe, and to participate in the classroom. Teachers communicate often with parents about children's behavior and development.

TEACHER QUALIFICATIONS: Teachers have college-level specialized preparation in early childhood development, early childhood education, or a related field. Preferably, they have a two-year college degree or, even better, a four-year degree plus teacher certification in early childhood education.

LICENSING AND ACCREDITATION: The program is licensed by the state. If a preschool or child-care center, accreditation by NAEYC's National Academy of Early Childhood Programs is evidence of high quality. If a child-care home, accreditation by the NAFCC is evidence of high quality.

Kindergarten through Third Grade

The most recent international study of mathematics and science achievement, released in 1998, extends the disheartening picture of the academic accomplishments of American youth evident for several decades. Although average to above-average in elementary school, U.S. performance declined sharply with increasing grades; by high school, it was near the bottom.[91] In more focused comparisons of American students with Japanese and Taiwanese students, who are consistently among top performers, differences in math competence were present in kindergarten and widened over elementary and secondary school. Although less extreme gaps occurred in reading, by high school both Asian groups scored better in this area as well.[92]

The periodic National Assessment of Educational Progress (NAEP), which tracks American students' academic performance, confirms their mediocre to weak overall standing. Although performance in reading, math, and science is improving, the majority of fourth graders are not proficient in these subjects, and their writing competence is particularly weak.[93] Underachievement is especially great for children from low-income and certain ethnic minority families, but the current learning crisis is not limited to these groups. Many economically well-off children have also fallen behind academically.

These sobering statistics are among the most powerful driving forces for critical examination of our nation's educational system, including the quality of primary-school education. The Carnegie Task Force on Learning in the Primary Grades noted that stressful family experiences and poor-quality child care during the preschool years undercut many children's chances for high achievement after school entry. But once in school, "a great many lose their natural curiosity and enthusiasm for learning."[94] According to NAEYC's position statement on early childhood education,

> Too many schools narrow the curriculum or adopt instructional approaches that are incompatible with current knowledge about how children learn and develop. Specifically, schools often emphasize rote learning of academic skills rather than active, experiential learning in a meaningful context. As a result, many children are being taught basic academic skills, but they are not learning to apply those skills to problems and real situations. They are not developing complex thinking skills, such as conceptualizing and problem solving.[95]

Besides academic progress, children's emotional, social, and moral growth is of great concern. The teaching strategies and programs considered in this chapter demonstrate that children immersed in stimulating, relevant, collaborative tasks advance in many more ways than academics. Their learning is also evident in how they manage themselves and get along with others in daily life.

Through sensitive scaffolding, children acquire adaptive help-seeking techniques as the basis for a mature sense of independence. They take increasing initiative, assume more responsibility, and become better at planning and making reasoned decisions and choices. Teacher-guided cooperative learning enhances children's skill at reconciling personal desires with group goals, their capacity to help others, and their acceptance of individual differences in feelings, interests, intellectual perspectives, competencies, and cultural backgrounds. Furthermore, children become better communicators—more observant, thoughtful, and articulate in their exchanges with others. When conflicts arise, they draw on dialogue to negotiate rather than lashing out with impulsive hostility.

Below I list indicators of high-quality primary-school education, again based on NAEYC's standards for developmentally appropriate practice. Together, these indicators embrace a view of the classroom as a community of learners—respectful, constructive relationships between teachers and children as the basis for vigorously grappling with academic challenges and acquiring ethical values and behaviors.

The content of the curriculum and the strategies for imparting it are the result of complex decision making at many levels of school systems; teachers do not design classroom experiences in isolation. But even in schools embracing a traditional approach, most teachers can take steps toward better practices. And with the support of parents who are knowledgeable about first-rate classroom experiences, teachers are in a far better position to guide administrators toward a new vision of the classroom—as a context of collaborative inquiry that sparks exhilaration for learning and that awakens every child's mind.

INDICATORS OF HIGH-QUALITY EDUCATION IN THE
PRIMARY GRADES: AGES 5 TO 8 [96]

CLIMATE FOR LEARNING: Teachers ensure that the classroom functions as a community of learners in which all members—children and adults—feel accepted and respected. Class meetings occur regularly. Children participate in devising rules for fulfilling responsibilities and getting along with others. They also have a say in decisions about projects and other class activities. Teachers bring children's home cultures and languages into the shared culture of the classroom, and they guide children in including classmates with disabilities as full members of the community.

PHYSICAL SETTING AND DAILY SCHEDULE: Space is divided into richly equipped activity centers—special places for reading, writing, playing math or language games, exploring science, working on construction projects, using computers, and engaging in other academic pursuits. A variety of work spaces are used flexibly for individual and small-group activities and whole-class gatherings. The daily schedule allows for alternating periods of active and quiet time. Periods of at least one hour permit children to become immersed in investigating problems, creating products, and making progress on extended projects.

CLASS SIZE AND TEACHER–CHILD RATIO: Optimum class size is 15 to 18 children with one teacher or up to 25 children with a second adult.

CURRICULUM: The curriculum helps children achieve national, state, and local academic standards while satisfying their eagerness to make sense of their experiences in all content areas: language and literacy, mathematics, social studies, art, music, health, and physical education. The curriculum is well organized and integrated so children can apply knowledge gleaned in one area to other areas and begin to grasp connections across subjects. It is implemented through activities responsive to children's interests, ideas, and everyday experiences, including their cultural backgrounds.

DAILY ACTIVITIES: Teachers provide interesting, challenging learning activities that include opportunities for individual choice and both small-group and independent work. Groupings vary in size and makeup of children, depending on the activity and children's needs. Together, teachers and children develop extended projects with tasks to be carried out by small groups and individuals, who report back to the whole class. Teachers encourage cooperative learning.

INTERACTIONS BETWEEN TEACHERS AND CHILDREN: Diverse, flexible teaching strategies ensure each child's progress, including children with academic difficulties and children capable of advanced performance. Teachers move between groups and individuals using intellectually engaging strategies, including posing problems, asking thought-provoking questions, discussing ideas, and adding complexity to tasks. They also demonstrate, explain, coach, directly instruct, and use other assistance, depending on children's needs.

EVALUATING PROGRESS: Teachers evaluate children's progress through written observations and work samples obtained at regular intervals, which they use to improve and individualize teaching. In addition, they involve children and parents in the evaluation process. On a day-to-day basis, teachers guide children in reflecting on their work and in deciding how to improve it; errors are viewed as opportunities for new teaching and learning. Teachers seek information and perspectives from parents about children's progress and include it in ongoing evaluations.

TEACHER QUALIFICATIONS: Teachers have a four-year college degree in early childhood education or in elementary education with a concentrated course of study in early childhood education.

RELATIONSHIPS WITH PARENTS: Teachers collaborate with parents in decisions about children's education. They initiate periodic conferences and encourage parents to visit at any time, to observe, and to participate in the classroom.

SEVEN

The Child in Contemporary Culture

In this chapter, I take up dilemmas that today's parents face in rearing young children. Throughout this book, we have touched on myriad forces that make contemporary parenting highly challenging. These include one-sided, contradictory messages in the parenting-advice literature; career pressures that impinge on parent involvement in children's lives; abysmally weak American child-care services to assist employed parents in their child-rearing roles; cultural violence and excessive materialism permeating children's worlds; schools with less than optimal conditions for children's learning; and impediments to granting children with deficits and disabilities social experiences that maximize their development.

Contemporary parents do not just find child rearing more difficult; they feel more uncertainty than their predecessors about whether and how to intervene in their children's activities and behavior. In the pages that follow, I draw on major themes of this book—the power of adult warmth, appropriate expectations, narrative conversation, make-believe play, and teaching in the "zone"—to show how Vygotsky's sociocultural approach can serve as a guide for resolving a great many child-rearing concerns.

This chapter answers twenty questions drawn from a survey of over four hundred parents of 2- to 8-year-olds living in a Midwestern city with a population of one hundred thousand. In that survey, I asked parents to list any questions about young children's development and learning that interested or worried them. The questions I answer here address issues that appeared most often in parents' responses. Each represents a concern that surfaced in three or more parental replies.

I intend these answers to parents' questions to reflect a way of thinking about child rearing, not a set of recipes for dealing with specific events. When parents are familiar with principles that are grounded in contemporary theory and research on children's development, they can better deal with the quandaries generated by the changing home, school, and community contexts in which today's children grow up. Although adverse cultural trends have complicated and threatened good child rearing, parents—as agents of change, buffers against stressful life circumstances, and gatekeepers of learning opportunities—can do much to protect, restore, and reshape children's experiences.

My 7-year-old doesn't think very well of himself. Is poor self-esteem a major cause of learning problems? How can I increase my child's self-esteem? Should I be praising him more?

When we speak of self-esteem, we refer to the judgments we make of our own worth and the feelings associated with those judgments. People with high self-esteem, although recognizing their limitations, are fundamentally satisfied with their characteristics and competencies. Their self-confidence, self-respect, and realistic appraisal of their current skills fortify them in the face of failure, motivating them to try hard to surmount challenges.

By the school years, individual differences in self-esteem are clearly evident and strongly related to children's everyday behaviors. That is, most school-age children are quite good at judging their own strengths and limitations. For example, children who agree with such statements as, "I'm good at schoolwork," tend to achieve well academically; children who concur that "most kids like me" get along well with their classmates; and children who say that they're "usually the one chosen for games" are more advanced in physical skills.[1] Many parents sense this strong link between children's self-esteem and accomplishment. Consequently, they may try to build their child's self-esteem with praise and reassuring comments.

Although self-esteem and favorable development are related, high self-esteem does not necessarily cause effortful behavior and achievement. Rather, to help sustain good outcomes, self-esteem must be earned through commitment, responsibility, and mastery of meaningful skills.[2] Children whose parents combine warmth with reasonable expectations for mature behavior feel especially good about themselves.[3] Warm parenting lets children know that adults believe they can succeed. And firm but appropriate expectations prompt children to strive for attainable goals and to use those goals as reasonable standards against which to evaluate their behavior.

Parents who deliver praise not based on real attainment actually undermine their child's development. It does not take long for most children to see through these false compliments and to question their self-worth. For others, this unconditional parental acceptance may contribute to an unrealistic, overly inflated sense of self-esteem, which is also linked to adjustment problems. In one study, second and third graders identified by their teachers as frequently teasing, starting fights with, and excluding other children were far more likely than their classmates to rate themselves as perfect on a self-esteem questionnaire.[4] Their distorted view of their own competence appeared to undermine any motivation to improve their social behavior.

Just as parents can't solve a child's motivational and self-esteem difficulties through indiscriminate praise, they also can't do so through critical, impatient remarks or harsh, forceful tactics, as in "You're lazy!" "Why don't you try hard like your sister!" "Do that homework or you'll be punished!" These strategies spark anger and resentment in children and undermine a positive parent–child relationship, on which motivation and effort thrive. And they destroy self-esteem by conveying a sense of inadequacy to children—that their behavior needs to be controlled by adults because they are unable to manage it themselves.

Instead, parents can foster high but realistic self-esteem by asking themselves three crucial questions:

- Are the demands I make of my child within his or her "zone"—neither too high nor too low?
- Have I forged a warm parent–child relationship so my child is fueled with the desire to meet my expectations?
- Have I used firm but encouraging tactics—scaffolding of academic tasks to promote autonomous mastery; narrative conversation about the importance of trying hard to convey strong work-ethic values; and joint participation in routines and duties, such as meal preparation and household chores, to assist in developing responsibility?

Finally, children don't need to feel great about everything they try. None of us is adept in every area. Rather, during the school years, self-esteem differentiates into an array of self-evaluations. For example, children judge themselves to be good at some school subjects and physical skills but not so good at others. Eventually, they combine these separate self-evaluations into a general appraisal—an overall sense of self-esteem. It remains positive so long as the child feels that he or she is competent at *some* worthwhile skills.[5]

In sum, the route to favorable self-esteem lies in parents' encouragement of achievement and responsibility. Then children have something worth feeling good about. Praise should be tied to real progress and attainment. Encouraging words are particularly helpful when children are trying their best but gains in performance are hard won. And most children greatly appreciate a parent's congratulations for a job well done. Positive self-judgments formed in these ways foster continued effort and mastery, which in turn promote high self-esteem.

How much television and what kinds of programs should I permit my preschool child to watch?

The typical preschool child devotes nearly 13 percent of his or her waking hours to watching television, a figure that rises to 30 percent by school age. Clearly today's children spend far too many hours in front of the TV set, a circumstance that restricts time available for joint parent–child activities, play, reading, and other worthwhile pursuits. Television is so pervasive an influence in children's lives that I discussed it at length in Chapter 2.

Parents are wise to limit children's access to TV to about one to one-and-a-half hours a day—no more than 10 hours a week. Following that guideline would cut the exorbitant number of hours children spend watching TV by 50 to 75 percent. Parents also need to prohibit violent TV and orient children toward educational programs that inform them about their world and toward entertainment shows that teach positive values and social skills. In Chapter 2, I explained how readily children can pick up negative attitudes and behaviors from television. Fortunately, children can just as easily absorb worthwhile messages and information from TV, so parental guidance in this area can have great benefits for development.

In Chapter 2, I also noted that it is crucial for parents to model good viewing practices; to watch TV with children, helping them understand and evaluate what they see; and to use televised content as inspiration for make-believe play and other enriching activities. Another suggestion: Try not to use television to reward or punish children. This increases its attractiveness, making children want to watch all the more.

My 20-month-old daughter and husband enjoy going to the Public Broadcasting System website. I'm delighted that they spend time together, but the whole computer concept makes me nervous. Already, my daughter bangs on the keys and uses the mouse. How much is too much and how young is too young?

More than half of American families own a personal computer, and one-third of these have access to the Internet—rates that are growing rapidly.[6] It's not surprising that even very young children are attracted to the computer—often more so than to television. As one school-age child commented, "It's fun because you can control it. TV controls itself."[7] Your key-banging, mouse-clicking 20-month-old already seems to appreciate this sense of electronic control!

As I noted in Chapter 4, the computer, like TV, has just as much potential for good as for ill. Hence it's another alluring device that requires close parental monitoring and intervention—to prevent children from becoming addictive users; from immersing themselves in violent, gender-stereotyped video games; and from accessing websites and web pages with sexual, aggressive, or other inappropriate content.

Undoubtedly, father and daughter are benefiting greatly from their time together at the computer. The warmth, exploration, conversation, and fun involved in this and other joint parent–child activities strengthen emotional bonds and foster both cognitive and social development. But such an early introduction to the computer is not necessary. Young children orient to computers because they frequently see adults using these stimulating devices, so they want to do so, too.

Almost all American public-school classrooms have at least one computer,[8] and many preschools have them as well. But for the computer to enhance learning in early childhood, adults must guide children in its constructive use and help them acquire computer-literacy skills. Around 3 years of age, children can type in simple commands and play educational games. Although they like the computer, most preschoolers do not find it so captivating that it diverts them from other worthwhile activities.

A common parental worry is that computers will channel children into solitary pursuits and disrupt their social development. To the contrary, children generally prefer to use computers socially. At home, they often like to engage in computer activities with a parent or older sibling because they can do much more with the help of an expert partner. And at school, small groups often gather around the machine to solve problems collaboratively.

How can parents capitalize on the computer's potential for spurring their child's development? A variety of educational software is available that permits children to practice academic skills and acquire new knowledge through discovery learning, reasoning, and problem solving. As soon as children begin to read and write, they can use the computer for word processing. It permits them to write freely without having to struggle with handwriting, and they can plan and revise their work easily. As a result, young writers worry less about making mistakes, and their written products are longer and of higher quality.[9] However, computers by themselves do not help children master the mechanics of writing, such as spelling and grammar.[10] Consequently, they are best used to build on, not replace, other writing experiences.

Beginning in the late preschool years, children can learn to program. Specially designed computer languages, such as LOGO, are available for this purpose. As long as adults provide the necessary scaffold, children benefit greatly from programming experiences. They not only acquire a valuable new skill but master new concepts, become better problem solvers, and think more creatively.[11] Also, since children must detect errors in their programs to get them to work, programming helps them reflect on their thinking and regulate their own behavior.[12]

How much is too much and how young is too young? There's no evidence that computer experiences make toddlers more skilled computer users or thinkers. By kindergarten and primary school, children can gain much from computer activities. As far as how much computer time parents should permit, the answer depends on what children are doing. When they are involved in writing, problem solving, or other educational pursuits, there's no special reason to be very restrictive. But not all software called "educational" is the same quality, so parents are wise to evaluate what their children are learning. Moreover, parents must ensure that time at the computer does not interfere with the variety of experiences children need to learn at their best. And playing violent video games and freely accessing the Internet should be prohibited.

How many and what kinds of toys does a young child need? My 3-year-old son is attracted to guns and war toys. How should I handle this type of play?

Martha Bronson's *The Right Stuff for Children Birth to 8*[13] is as an excellent resource for selecting play materials that provide children of varying ages with both pleasure and an appropriate challenge. On pages 138 to 141 of Chapter 4, I provided an overview of play-material suggestions for stimulating make-believe and game play in children between 2 and 8 years of age. In Bronson's book, you'll find additional recommendations, organized into four broad play-activity categories: social and fantasy play; exploration and cognitive mastery; music, art, and movement; and gross motor play.

Children's rooms and play spaces need not be filled with every toy imaginable. A modest number of toys is sufficient. Children who have too much typically care little for what they have. When given a chance to acquire something new, they usually don't react with much excitement or selectivity. For materially indulged children, new toys are such a common event that a complacent attitude sets in. The child comes to think, if I don't like what I just got, I can always discard it for something else. A bedroom or playroom heaped high with a jumble of toys, many broken and mistreated, also teaches children that possessions need not be cared for and respected.

Parents often assume that the play materials children choose are the ones that are best for their development. To some degree, this assumption makes sense: If a toy isn't appealing to the child, the child isn't going to spend time with it. So it's important to provide children with a variety of play materials responsive to their interests.

Nevertheless, preference is not the same as appropriateness. Children sometimes choose toys with very limited play possibilities and soon ignore them. Other toys should not be given to children because they encourage undesirable play behaviors. Guns and other forms of weaponry fall into this category. In Chapter 4, I pointed to research demonstrating that these aggressive play materials promote both make-believe and real hostility in children's interactions with peers.

When thinking about purchasing a new toy for your child, ask yourself these questions:

- Does my child already have too many toys, and am I adding to this overabundance?
- Is the toy responsive to my child's interests, and is it likely to sustain his or her involvement over time?
- Do I want my child to acquire the values and skills the toy teaches?
- How will the toy help provide a foundation for my child's future learning and development?

I'm expecting a new baby. How much is too much information for a 4-year-old about pregnancy and childbirth?

It's easy to tell preschool and young school-age children too much about pregnancy and childbirth—more than they are capable of understanding. The best approach is to respond to their questions with simple, direct answers. The younger the preschooler, the less likely he or she is to notice the pregnant mother's growing tummy and to be interested in how the baby got in there. Such questions as, "Where do babies come from?" "Where did I come from?" and "How does a baby get born?" rarely occur before age 5.

When children do ask these questions, parents vary widely in how much information they are comfortable in providing. Up to age 8 or 9, most children are satisfied with such general explanations as it "starts as a little seed inside the mother, which grows into a baby," "grows in a special space in the mother's tummy called a uterus," and "when the baby's ready to be born, the mother's uterus squeezes and squeezes, and the baby comes out." Some parents show their child books with pictures of fetuses, identifying those that are about the same age as the forthcoming sibling and discussing the baby's development as it progresses. There's no evidence that this is in any way harmful or that it's necessary during early childhood; rather, it's a matter of parental choice.

Eight- to 9-year-olds are ready for more detailed knowledge about how babies are conceived and grow, as children of this age are getting closer to puberty. A variety of well-written and illustrated books are available to help parents discuss love between partners, conception, birth, and rearing of children. Parents need to select carefully, making sure they agree with the book's values. Two books that I like are *How Babies Are Made,* by Andrew Audrey and Steven Schep,[14] and *Where Did I Come From?* by Peter Mayle.[15] *How I Was Adopted,* by Joanna Cole,[16] is an excellent starting point for discussion with preschool and young school-age children who are adopted.

I don't believe in spanking. We do time outs, which seem to work for our 4-year-old. How long is time out effective, and what's the next step?

Although spanking has declined over the past 50 years, the majority of parents in the United States admit to slapping or hitting their child for misbehaving.[17] There is good reason not to believe in spanking. A great deal of research shows that it promotes only temporary compliance, not lasting changes in children's behavior. Children who are repeatedly criticized, shouted at, and slapped are likely to display the unacceptable response again as soon as adults are out of sight and they can get away with it. In fact, children of harshly punishing parents develop into especially disobedient and aggressive youngsters. In a study of a national sample of over twelve hundred mothers of 6- to 9-year-olds, psychologists Murray Straus, David Sugarman, and Jean Giles-Sims found that the more spanking the mothers reported, the more antisocial behavior their children displayed two years later—cheating, telling lies, being mean to classmates, and disobeying teachers.[18]

Why doesn't spanking work? First, when parents spank, they often do so in response to children's defiance and aggression.[19] Yet the punishment itself models aggression! Second, children who are frequently punished soon learn to avoid the punishing adult. When children evade their parents, they reduce parents' opportunity to teach desirable behaviors. Finally, as spanking "works" to stop children's misbehavior temporarily, it offers immediate relief to parents, which rewards them for spanking. For this reason, the parent is likely to spank with greater frequency and intensity over time, a course of action that can spiral into serious abuse.

This does not mean that parents should never express anger at or punish a child. An otherwise warm parent who is disappointed and disapproving lets the child know that the transgression is serious. When children realize that adults regard their misdeed as very important, they listen more closely.[20] And punishment is warranted after repeated infractions.

But parents have far better ways to punish than spanking. One of these is time out—requiring a child to sit aside or to go to his or her room. Another is withdrawal of privileges, such as a visit to the playground or a weekly allowance. These mild punishments derive their potency from warm parent–child bonds. Children of involved, caring parents find the interruption in parental affection that accompanies punishment to be very unpleasant. As a result, they want to regain the warmth and approval of the parent as quickly as possible.

An important preventive of misbehavior—and a vital element of effective punishment—is explanation. Pairing reasons with mild punishment (such as time out) leads to a far greater reduction in rule violations than using punishment alone.[21] The reason the adult gives the child must match the child's capacity to understand. At ages 2 to 3, referring to simple, direct outcomes works best, as in, "If you keep pushing Tommy, he'll fall down and cry." By age 4, parents can give more complex and subtle explanations. For example, they can refer to others' intentions ("Don't yell at Jessica. She was only trying to help"), to others' feelings ("He's proud of his tower, and you knocked it down; now he's very sad"), and to issues of rights and fairness ("That toy belongs to Rudy, so you must ask for a turn").[22]

Explaining to children what they did wrong, why it was wrong, and how they should have acted helps them recall the misdeed and relate it to expectations for future behavior. Furthermore, by pointing out the impact of the child's actions on others, parents prompt children to feel empathy and sympathy—emotions that motivate concern for others.[23] And giving children reasons for changing their behavior invites them to judge the appropriateness of parents' expectations—to see that parents are not being arbitrary or autocratic. Explanations lead children to strive to meet parental standards because those standards make sense.

In sum, when time out is combined with reasoning, it remains effective through the school years. You can tell that your approach to discipline is working when time out and other punishments become less necessary as your child shifts from externally controlled responses to behavior based on inner standards and compassion for others. Typically this shift is well under way between ages 4 and 7.[24]

If parents find themselves punishing frequently, then they need to reconsider the basis of their discipline. When sensitivity, cooperation, and exchanges of affection are evident in parent–child interaction, children as young as 2 years of age more often follow parental directives.[25] Children with an affectionate, mutually gratifying parental tie want to heed parents' demands because they feel a sense of commitment to the relationship. This reduces the need for punishment, freeing parents to focus on encouraging children's competent behavior.

Three additional ways to avoid excessive punishment are worth mentioning. First, changing aspects of the environment can reduce children's problematic behavior. One parent arranged for her younger child to play at a friend's house during his sister's birthday party, realizing that the boy wasn't yet ready to join in the party's activities and would likely disrupt them. Second, a close look at the reasonableness of the rules can be helpful. Another parent caught herself before yelling, "Don't roll down that hill!" at her daughter. She realized that the child was unlikely to hurt herself on the gentle, grassy slope and that any grass-stained clothing could easily be washed. With a moment of reflection, the parent backed off from an almost-delivered rebuke to allow a pleasurable play activity. Finally, sensitivity to children's physical and emotional resources helps prevent inappropriate punishment. When children are tired, ill, or bored, they are likely to engage in attention-getting, disorganized, or otherwise improper behavior as a reaction to discomfort rather than as an affront to authority. In these instances, meeting the child's needs makes more sense than punishing.

What's the best way to deal with repeated tantrums in a 3-year-old child who gets so enraged that he hits and throws things at you? How can you calm a preschooler when the situation requires him to listen and pay attention?

When a tantrum occurs, time out is useful—transferring the child to an unstimulating area where he can't throw things until the emotional storm is over. If he tries to throw anything or to hit you, you need to prevent him from doing so, gently but firmly. It's crucial to remain calm and to avoid harsh, coercive tactics, which will only fuel the child's rage and poor emotional control.

It's also important to figure out why these persistent tantrums are occurring. As the often-heard phrase "terrible twos" suggests, many people assume that tantrums are a fact of life for 2- and even 3-year-olds. Once toddlers acquire the ability to follow adult directives, one way they assert their autonomy is by resisting parents' requests and demands, using the familiar refrain, "No!" And from time to time, toddlers lose control. When frustrated, they haven't yet developed many techniques for regulating their emotions. But parents who take mental notes for a day on the number of compliant acts versus the number of tantrums are likely to gain a new appreciation for how infrequent their child"s tantrums really are. For most young children, eager, willing cooperation is much more common than opposition.[26]

If your child has been emotionally reactive and difficult to soothe since infancy, then temperament is probably a significant contributor to his behavior. You'll also want to consider whether any changes in your family or the child's daily life might be sparking intense anxiety—marital conflict, divorce or remarriage, a new baby brother or sister, starting preschool or child care, or a parent going to work when the child is used to having him or her at home. Parenting practices can modify children's temperaments and assist them in coping with stressful life events. Protection from family discord; extra parental warmth, affection, and pleasurable time together when the child is behaving well; and firm, calm, and consistent discipline will help.

Most children build up to a tantrum gradually. Parents can tell it's in the offing, and sometimes they can distract the child before it reaches a peak. For example, if the child is about to "blow" while you're out shopping, try involving the child in the shopping experience—pointing out things of interest to the child; asking the child to help you select and carry purchases; and reminding the child that after the shopping is finished, you are going to do something the child enjoys. When parents interrupt a tantrum on the rise by redirecting the child's attention, they provide strategies children can use on their own to regulate emotion. If parents always wait to intervene after the child has become intensely distressed, it's harder not only for the parent to calm the child but for the child to learn to calm down. And once the child regains emotional control, reassuring the child of parental love with hugs and comforting words restores the parent–child relationship and strengthens the child's sense of security.

Make-believe play is an effective context in which preschoolers can practice what to do when frustrated. Parent and child can take turns acting out the "parent" and "child" roles. While playing the "child," the parent can get upset. Then parent and child can come up with ways to help the "child" control intense feelings. Occasionally during make-believe, children send parents clear messages about disciplinary tactics they want and need to quell tantrums. In one instance, Sonja, a mother at wit's end over her 4-year-old daughter Meredith's frequent fits of kicking and screaming, consulted a child psychologist. The psychologist had Meredith play the "mother" and Sonja play the "child."

When the "child" asked for a cookie, the "mother" said, "No cookies before dinner. You can have a cookie after dinner."

Sonja the "child" began to mimic her daughter's tantrums. "I want a cookie. I want two cookies! Gimme my cookies!" she shouted.

"No!" Meredith the "mother" answered, "No cookies until after dinner."

"I want cookies now!" Sonja the "child" wailed while thrashing about in Meredith's usual fashion.

Meredith looked on, dismayed by her mother's unruly behavior. Then she stepped out of the play and instructed, "You're supposed to say, 'No cookies 'til later,' Mommy."

When Sonja the "child" continued her screaming and crying, Meredith stated more insistently, "Mommy, say, '*No* cookies! You *can't* have cookies before dinner!'"

With the psychologist's help, Sonja reflected on the play episode, realizing that she'd been inconsistent in handling Meredith's outbursts, sometimes resisting, at other times giving in. As a result, Meredith continued the tantrums to get her way, yet she desperately wanted to stop these explosions and to follow sensible, consistent rules. To do so, she needed her mother to send a clear, rational, and steadfast message that tantrums are inappropriate and ineffectual and that cookies are eaten after dinner.

What suggestions do you have for disciplining a strong-willed, stubborn child? Nothing seems to work, including time out and loss of privileges.

As this question makes clear, some children are far harder to discipline than others. A child's temperament affects the ease with which he or she will follow parental directives and listen to explanations. In Chapter 5, I indicated that the impulsivity and emotional reactivity of children with ADHD make them very hard to rear and often lead to strife-ridden adult–child relationships, which further reduce children's cooperation. Willful, stubborn children are also challenging to discipline. They tend to evoke harsh punishment, which heightens their resistance.

A seemingly stubborn child may feel so little anxiety that parental disapproval and mild punishment do not spark enough inner discomfort to motivate compliance. Consequently, parents of headstrong children must use firm, consistent discipline and repeatedly explain how to behave and why. At the same time, such parents must resist the temptation to engage in carping criticism, harshness, and force. A warm parent–child bond based on cooperation is especially vital for helping recalcitrant children internalize parents' standards. It provides the obstinate youngster, who feels little or no anxiety when reprimanded, with an alternative foundation for meeting parents' expectations: a desire to preserve a spirit of affection and harmony with the parent.[27]

Because parents' communication with noncompliant children is often riddled with negativity, it can take time to get the relationship on a better track. Arranging regular times for joint parent–child pleasurable activities is vital. Making sure to notice and praise the child's favorable behavior also reduces the negative cloud hanging over parent–child interaction.

Finally, looking for the "silver lining" in the child's difficult disposition can help parents muster the fortitude needed to rear a child with a difficult disposition. Consider Carl, one of the most obstinate participants in a study of the combined impact that temperament and child rearing have on long-term development.[28] Beginning in infancy, Carl rejected many routines and experiences, including baths, bedtime, and new foods. He shrieked, cried, and struggled to get away. Yet his parents regarded his emotional intensity as a sign of inner strength and vigor. They believed that if they were patient and firmly insistent, Carl would, in the end, adapt positively.

By the time Carl reached school age, he was doing remarkably well. The energies he had previously invested in stubborn rebellion were channeled constructively. He did well in school and became enthusiastically involved in several activities. One of these was playing the piano—lessons that he had asked for but (in his typical fashion) at first disliked intensely. Carl's mother had granted his request for piano instruction under one condition: that he stick to the lessons for six months. She held him to this agreement despite his protests, which gradually subsided. Carl came to love his introduction to music. His parents' warmth, determination, and consistency had helped him gain control of his behavior and benefit from new learning opportunities.

How can you get an inactive child who loves quiet play to be more active and sociable?

Parents of quiet children often wonder whether their youngster is developing normally. Preschoolers whose play and behavior are typically mature for their age but who prefer solitary, tranquil activities are probably doing just fine, both cognitively and socially. As I indicated in Chapter 3, only *certain kinds* of nonsocial activity—aimless wandering; immature, repetitive motor action; and anxious hovering around peers without joining in their play—are cause for concern.[29] Most play of quiet preschoolers is not of this kind. Instead, it is positive and constructive, consisting of such activities as art, make-believe play, puzzles, and block-building.

Our society places such a high value on sociability that adults often regard quiet reserve as a sign of maladjustment. Yet not all cultures see things this way. Chinese adults, for example, view quiet children very positively—as advanced in social maturity.[30] Thai primary-school teachers also value restrained, persistent child behavior, and they regard children who would be average in activity level in the United States as poorly behaved and unmotivated.[31] Equating an energetic pace and gregariousness with normality is a Western cultural phenomenon—one that does not match what we know about quiet, nonanxious children. Most are bright youngsters with intense interests who, when they do play with peers, show socially skilled behavior.[32]

Nevertheless, you might want to encourage a quiet, inactive child to engage in active play from time to time—to ensure healthy exercise and to broaden the child's experiences. The best way to do this is to join the child in active games, such as tag, relay races, hide-and-seek, and throwing and catching. Creating a "zone" for learning—by ensuring that active play is fun, provides plenty of opportunity to practice physical skills, and is not overstimulating for the quiet child—will increase the success of these efforts. You won't be able to transform a quiet child into a physical dynamo, but you can help the child learn to enjoy moderate physical activity. Finally, parents of quiet children may be gratified to learn that a calm, less active nature typically makes a child easier to rear.

How does a parent gain respect from a child who sees the other parent acting disrespectfully toward his or her spouse?

Children learn much about how to relate to others by observing their parents' day-to-day communication. Marital conflict is linked to hostile behavior and poor emotional adjustment in children, including feeling sad and engaging in aggressive acts.[33] Hearing one or both parents berate the other leads children to act similarly—toward parents, siblings, teachers, and peers. If disrespect between parents includes physical harm, then children's difficulties can escalate further.[34]

Besides modeling destructive forms of interaction, parents who behave hurtfully toward each other generally interact hostilely with their children.[35] They also tend to use inconsistent discipline—alternately strict and lax.[36] When parents scold children on some occasions but permit them to act inappropriately on others, children are confused about how to behave and engage in especially high rates of disobedience.

In sum, parents behaving insolently to each other are up against a brick wall in getting a child to behave respectfully. They need to repair their relationship. Seeking the help of a marriage and family counselor without delay is the best way to prevent the child's emotionally despondent and angry reactions from spiraling into lasting adjustment problems.

Any tips on raising an only child?

The best way for parents to ensure that only children fare well is to engage them in development-enhancing dialogues, to impose reasonable expectations for mature behavior, and to discipline effectively. Overall, parents of only children are quite successful in attaining these child-rearing goals. Contrary to popular belief, only children are not destined to become spoiled and selfish. Instead, research consistently shows that they are as well adjusted and as socially competent as other children. And they form just as close and as rewarding friendships as do children with siblings, suggesting that they can and do learn to share and to be considerate of others' needs. Furthermore, only children have a more positive sense of self-esteem and do better in school than do children growing up in families with two or more children.[37]

A major reason for these positive outcomes is that having just one child generally means a closer parent–child relationship; more time for high-quality parent–child interaction; and greater encouragement for mastery and accomplishment.[38] But because only children lose the lifelong benefits of positive sibling ties, parents might take steps to enrich the child's life with sibling-like relationships—for example, by cultivating warm bonds with cousins or the children of close family friends. In sum, with good parenting, only children fare extremely well.

How can you keep a child's self-esteem high while still praising a sibling's achievements and good behavior? When a child "acts out" because of sibling jealousy, what's the best way to handle it?

Children display wide individual differences in the quality of their sibling ties. Once again, temperament makes a difference. For example, arguments between siblings increase when one child is emotionally intense and highly active.[39] But parents can do much to foster favorable sibling interaction. During the preschool years, mothers tend to be more positive and playful with second-borns than first-borns, and they discipline the older child more.[40] This differential treatment is understandable, in that older children are more competent and capable, so parents expect more. But being older also means more privileges—for example, being able to stay overnight at a friend's house or enroll in certain after-school activities and lessons. These advantages may help compensate for an older child's perception that a younger sibling is receiving better treatment.

If parents experience intensifying sibling conflict, they may want to reevaluate their communication with each child. Warmth and frequent expressions of affection are associated with positive sibling interaction, whereas harshness and coldness are associated with sibling antagonism.[41] Once established, this link between parent–child and sibling relationships is self-perpetuating. Warm parenting fosters considerate sibling interaction, which prompts positive parental communication in the future. When parents are hostile and coercive, children act similarly toward their siblings, and parental anger escalates.

The elementary school years are a time when sibling conflict can increase. As children get feedback about how well they are doing in school and in other activities (such as sports and music lessons), parents may compare their accomplishments, especially when siblings are close in age and the same gender. The child who feels less valued is likely to resent a sibling whom parents seem to prefer. Therefore, when praising one child, parents should try not to diminish the merits of another. If a sibling expresses jealousy, parents can remind the envious child of an admirable personal trait or a recent commendable performance. But be careful not to give empty praise (not based on real accomplishment), which children quickly come to mistrust. It may fuel jealousy of a sibling, whom the child concludes parents *really* appreciate.

In sum, parents can foster positive sibling ties through expressing warmth and affection, stressing each child's positive qualities and achievements, and refraining from making comparisons. When sibling relationships are friendly and sympathetic, they bring many benefits, including gratifying companionship, emotional support, and assistance with everyday tasks.

Should you try to curb bossy behavior when siblings or peers are playing together? If so, at what age?

Yes, you should step in and teach alternative, cooperative modes of interaction—at as early an age as you observe bossiness. A child who has trouble engaging in give and take during play with siblings or peers will quickly become embroiled in conflict.

As I noted in Chapter 4, pleasurable, rewarding play depends on attaining intersubjectivity, or shared understanding. Children must resolve differences of opinion and find ways to meet both their own needs and those of their playmates. When domineering, uncooperative behavior is extreme, the bossy child is likely to be rejected by agemates. Long-term peer rejection, as I indicated in Chapter 5, not only leads to an unhappy social life but to serious adjustment problems in adolescence and early adulthood.

When a child uses bossy tactics, interrupt the play and ask the child to think of a better way to get others to cooperate, such as making requests and taking into account the playmate's preferences. If the child can't think of alternatives, suggest and model several. If bossiness continues unabated, insist that the child leave the play area, explaining why he or she must do so. During times when you're alone with the child, talk about problems that have arisen in peer and sibling play and help the child think of good social problem-solving strategies. Then act out these situations in make-believe, granting the child plenty of practice in applying effective social skills and showing the child how others are likely to react if bossy behavior returns.

How can a parent identify the difference between a language disorder and normal language development? What resources are available?

If your child's language development is delayed by several months when compared to norms for early language milestones, then your child might have a language disorder. But keep in mind that children vary greatly in their pace of language learning. For example, girls are slightly ahead of boys in early vocabulary growth, and reserved, cautious children often wait until they understand a great deal before trying to speak.[42] When they finally do speak, their vocabularies grow rapidly.

Here is a summary of major language milestones for the first 2 years:

Approximate Age	*Milestone*
2 months	Coos, or makes pleasurable vowel sounds, such as "aaaaa" or "oooo."
6 months	Babbles, or repeats consonant–vowel sounds in long strings, as in "babababababa."
6–14 months	Babbled sounds expand greatly; around 1 year, they reflect the sounds and rhythms of the infant's language community.
8–12 months	Understands some words.
12 months	Says first recognizable word.

18–24 months	Vocabulary expands from about 50 to 200 words.
20–26 months	Combines two words.
27 months and on	Speaks in longer sentences; participates easily in a conversation with an adult.

Because of wide individual differences, it's sometimes hard to tell a language disorder from normal variation in language development. If you're concerned about your child's language progress, consult a trained speech–language pathologist. The American Speech–Language–Hearing Association (ASHA) maintains a list of certified speech–language pathologists for referrals. You can contact the association at (800) 638-8255.

The most common cause of early language problems is a hearing loss. Typically, children with hearing impairments are not identified until 12 to 25 months of age, when speech and language development is already delayed. Therefore, ASHA recommends that all newborn babies be screened for hearing disorders before they leave the hospital. Newborn testing takes only a few minutes and permits problems to be addressed early, preventing negative consequences for all aspects of psychological development.

Hearing loss can also emerge later. The most common cause during toddlerhood and the preschool years is repeated otitis media, or middle ear infection. Some episodes are painful, so parents detect them, but many are accompanied by few or no symptoms. Children with recurrent otitis media bouts have trouble making out what others are saying. Hence they are distractible, behind in language progress, and socially isolated; and they also achieve poorly in school.[43]

When children begin preschool or child care, they are more susceptible to otitis media because of close contact with other children. Therefore, frequent screening for the disease, followed by prompt medical intervention, is vital. Interestingly, verbally stimulating adult–child interaction and high-quality child care help reduce developmental problems associated with otitis media.[44] When adults converse often with children and keep environmental noise to a minimum, children with persistent ear infections have more opportunities to hear and respond to spoken language.

I'm trying to decide whether to enroll my 5-year-old son in kindergarten or wait until next year. How can I tell if he's ready for kindergarten? If he doesn't do well in kindergarten, should he repeat it or go into a "transition" class?

Many parents struggle with the decision of whether to enroll their child in kindergarten once the child meets the age requirements. Most often, they consider delaying the start of school for boys, who as a group tend to lag behind girls in cognitive and social development. At the heart of parents' concern is whether their child will be able to meet the academic and social demands of the kindergarten classroom.

Although many teachers believe that a 5-year-old who's on the young side can benefit from waiting another year before enrolling in kindergarten and advise parents to hold the child out, research has not revealed any advantages for delayed entry. A host of studies indicate that younger children make just as much progress, academically and socially, as do older children enrolled in the same grade. No difference exists between younger and older classmates in achievement test scores.[45]

A related dilemma involves whether to retain a kindergartner for a second kindergarten year if he or she is not progressing well. More than a half-century of research has failed to show any learning benefits for children retained in grade, and mounting evidence indicates that retention can be harmful, prompting negative attitudes toward school and a drop in self-esteem and in academic motivation, even as early as kindergarten.[46] In one study, retained kindergarten children, despite the extra year of school, scored lower than their classmates in academic achievement after entering the primary grades. In contrast, children recommended for retention but who nevertheless went on to first grade were doing just as well as classmates who had been promoted in the standard fashion.[47]

Yet another alternative is to place a poorly performing kindergarten child in a "transition" class—a waystation between kindergarten and first grade. Transition classes, however, are a form of homogeneous grouping that gathers children judged by the school system as less likely to succeed. As with other "low-ability" groups, teachers often have lower expectations for transition-class students and teach them in a less stimulating fashion than they do other children.[48]

Notice that each of the options just mentioned assumes that readiness is inherent in the child—that a 5-year-old must have reached a certain level of development to profit from classroom experiences. Consider, once again, the concept of the "zone," in which teaching leads development. It tells us that children don't just grow into school readiness. Rather, they acquire the knowledge, skills, and attitudes necessary for successfully participating in classroom life through the assistance of others. This means that readiness is not something we must wait for. Instead, we can cultivate it. Parents, teachers, and school systems can work together to ensure that each child takes the next appropriate steps toward mastering the range of capabilities needed for school success.

The National Association for the Education of Young Children (NAEYC) recommends that every child of legal age start kindergarten. It also recommends against school readiness testing as a means for deciding whether a child should be admitted to kindergarten, be retained in kindergarten, or enroll in a "transition" class rather than a first-grade class after completing kindergarten.[49] School readiness tests are poor predictors of children's future school performance and identify many children as unready who are quite ready to handle school experiences.[50]

As long as teachers are sensitive to children's diversity and work with small groups and individual children within their "zones," there is no reason to hold a child out of kindergarten. Deciding not to enroll a child and opting for an alternative experience is justifiable only when the kindergarten environment is so rigid and unaccommodating to individual differences that the child would be frustrated and unhappy and would have an unproductive year.

My first grader has homework to do several times a week. Should I help her with her homework, and if so, how should I do so?

American parents often express uncertainty about helping their child with homework. They worry that by providing help, they will discourage self-reliance in thinking and problem solving. Vygotsky's concept of the "zone" underscores that children acquire the many capacities they need to learn autonomously from the assistance of parents, teachers, and other more expert adults. By collaborating with the child on a challenging task, the adult assesses what the child can already do and what the child is ready to learn, providing a support system for mastery.

The metaphor of a *scaffold,* discussed in Chapter 2, is an excellent guide for how to help your child with homework. Scaffolding involves varying your assistance to fit the child's changing competence. When the child says, "I don't understand," you can adjust the task, breaking it into smaller parts. You can also provide prompts, hints, and explanations, increasing the amount and directiveness of your guidance until the child makes progress. As you do so, you can assist the child in analyzing why certain problem-solving approaches work and others do not, encouraging her to come up with ideas for surmounting difficulties. As she starts to apply the strategies derived from your dialogue, you can reduce the intensity of your intervention, letting her take over responsibility for the task.

Too often, parents imagine that their child's classmates *can* do the homework assignment independently. After all, they say to themselves, why would the teacher have assigned it if this weren't so? This pattern of reasoning leads parents down a counterproductive path. "What's wrong with my child?" they say to themselves. "She *should* be able to do the assignment, just like everyone else!" But recall that children of the same age differ widely in their "zones." And rooted in the very idea of the "zone" is that learning requires teaching! Children in our culture frequently are rebuked for seeking help, a response that promotes dependency, helplessness, and retreat from challenge, not competence and autonomy.

Chinese and Japanese parents spend a great deal of time helping their children with homework—far more than American parents do. Asian parents also communicate often with teachers about how to help their child learn at his or her best. Rather than being dependent, Chinese and Japanese students develop into well adjusted, excellent students[51]—at the top in academic achievement in the world.

When does math become a greater problem for girls than for boys? What can be done to help girls do well in math?

Throughout elementary school, girls get better grades in math—and other academic subjects—than do boys. At times, school-age boys outperform girls on math achievement tests,[52] but boys' advantage in math isn't clearly evident until secondary school. A close look at children's performance on specific test items reveals that both genders do equally well in basic math knowledge, and girls do better in computational skills. Boys' advantage appears on tests of math reasoning, primarily on complex word problems and in geometry.[53]

The cause of boys' late-appearing math advantage is a matter of controversy. Some experts believe the difference is rooted in boys' superior ability to reason about spatial relations. Gender differences in spatial skills are present by elementary school and persist throughout life.[54] Young people who are good at spatial reasoning are, indeed, better at solving complex math problems.[55] One conjecture is that male (androgen) hormones may play some role in enhancing boys' spatial skills. But evidence favoring this idea is inconsistent.[56]

Although heredity may contribute to boys' spatial superiority, experience also makes a difference. Children who engage in manipulative activities involving spatial relations, such as block play, model building, and carpentry, do better on spatial reasoning tasks. Also, playing video games that require rapid mental rotation of visual images enhances the spatial test scores of boys and girls alike.[57] Yet boys spend far more time at all these pursuits than do girls.

Furthermore, children's and adolescents' attitudes toward math and their belief in their capacity to do well at it affect their math achievement. Boys feel more confident about their math ability, even when their grades are poorer than girls'.[58] Why might this be so?

Shortly after entering primary school, children regard math as a boys' subject—a stereotype that prompts girls to like math less than boys do. Girls also predict poorer math performances for themselves than boys predict for themselves.[59] Children derive these views from their social surroundings. They listen to what parents and teachers say about who is "good at math," and they see more men in math-related careers—from math teachers in the upper school grades to scientists in the wider community.

Also, subtle feedback from adults undermines girls' confidence in their ability to do well at math. If a parent or teacher believes that a child is not very capable at a school subject, the adult may act surprised when the child succeeds, ascribing good performance to luck by saying something like this: "Gee, you did a lot better than I expected!" And when the child fails, the adult may explain the failure by referring to mediocre ability: "You're not very good at that, are you?" Girls get much more of this type of feedback than do boys, especially in math.[60] In contrast, parents and teachers often attribute boys' poor performance to misbehavior and lack of motivation. "If only you'd listen and try," they say, "you'd do much better."

As a result of these messages, too many girls come to believe that when they succeed at math, their ability didn't help them. And after failure, they reason that weak ability, not insufficient effort, was at fault. Children who hold these discouraging explanations for their performance often come apart with anxiety when a task is difficult. They say to themselves, "I can't do this! It's too hard!" before they have really tried.[61] Although eventually young people figure out that effort can compensate for low ability, girls may conclude that mastering complex math is not worth the cost—extremely high effort.[62] So in high school, they retreat from advanced math courses and math-related careers.

Fortunately, parents can do much to foster girls' self-confidence and achievement in math. Beginning in the preschool years, they can provide girls with toys and activities that promote spatial reasoning and scaffold their mastery of those tasks. And they can assist children of both genders in interpreting their math successes as due to both effort and ability, in understanding that ability accrues from trying hard, and in taking failure as a sign that more effort and better problem-solving strategies are needed.

A positive sign is that the gap between boys' and girls' math achievement is declining. In addition, more girls are enrolling in advanced math and science courses in high school, and slowly but steadily, women are entering male-dominated math-related professions.[63] The more parents hold nonstereotyped values about what males and females can and should do, the more likely girls are to sustain their high elementary-school math and science achievement in secondary school.[64]

Why do boys lag behind girls in reading and writing in primary school? Do they catch up later?

Throughout the school years, girls attain higher scores on reading and writing achievement tests and account for a lower percentage of children referred for remedial reading instruction.[65] Part of the reason for girls' advantage in literacy development is that they undergo a faster rate of physical maturation, believed to promote slightly earlier development of the left hemisphere of the cerebral cortex, where language functions are housed for most people.[66] In addition, many types of developmental problems are more common among boys, including speech and language disorders, reading disabilities, and inattention and hyperactivity. Boys' and girls' differing genetic makeups probably underlie these gender differences, which affect reading and writing performance.[67]

By secondary school, girls' advantage on tests of general verbal ability is so slight that it is not really meaningful.[68] Consequently, boys who are free of reading disabilities have the potential to achieve just as well as girls in reading and writing. Still, girls continue to outperform boys in these subjects. Home and school experiences contribute, although less is known about them than those that underlie boys' advantage in mathematics.

Just as children think of math as a masculine subject, they regard reading and writing as feminine subjects. Parents rate daughters as more capable at reading than they rate sons—beliefs that children adopt. [69] Furthermore, traditional primary-school classrooms, in which teacher-directed, whole-class lessons are the major activity, require children to sit still and concentrate for long periods of time on academic tasks that often are irrelevant to their interests. In previous chapters, I indicated that such classrooms are poorly suited to the learning needs of both boys and girls. But boys adapt especially poorly to the regimentation of traditional classrooms because of their generally shorter attention spans, higher activity levels, and less compliant dispositions. Consequently, they often are targets of teacher disapproval, which sparks negative attitudes toward school and dampens their enthusiasm for learning.[70]

In a recent Australian study carried out by psychologist Freda Briggs, several hundred schoolchildren were asked for their views on school and classroom activities. Many boys between 5 and 9 years of age expressed dissatisfaction with school and said that their favorite activities were recess and lunchtime. But in four classrooms, distinguished by an activity-center curriculum offering opportunities for individual choice, small-group work, and literacy experiences responsive to children's interests, boys reported strong liking for school. And they named reading and writing as their favorite activities. They particularly enjoyed making their own books, based on themes of sports and hobbies.[71]

Although more evidence is needed to be sure, perhaps classrooms that create "zones" for learning, with many of the features I described in Chapter 6, spark sufficient enthusiasm for literacy pursuits among boys that they reduce the well-known gender gap in reading and writing achievement. Finally, the trend for boys to learn to read more slowly than girls is less pronounced in countries where reading is not stereotyped as feminine but regarded as well suited to the masculine gender role.[72]

Is learning and development affected if the father becomes less involved or absent after a divorce?

Divorce is invariably painful for children, and learning and development can be affected—temporarily and long term.[73] Preschool and young school-age children are often profoundly upset. Because they have great difficulty grasping the reasons for their parents' divorce, they may blame themselves and take the marital breakup as a sign that they could be abandoned by both parents. As a result, they may cry and cling, refuse to go to school, and show a drop in enthusiasm for play and learning. Young children need extra affection and reassurance along with gentle reminders that their parents' separation is permanent. Of all age groups, preschoolers are most likely to have trouble accepting the reality of divorce and to fantasize that their parents will get back together.[74]

Many school-age children and adolescents also react strongly to the end of their parents' marriage, particularly when family conflict is high and parent involvement with children is low. Around the time of divorce and for up to several years after, children tend to be emotionally volatile, displaying both depression and demandingness, noncompliance, and aggression.[75] Boys in mother-custody families seem to have the hardest time. Research reveals that before the marital breakup, many sons of divorcing couples were impulsive and defiant—traits that may have contributed to as well as been caused by their parents' marital problems. Thus, boys often enter the period of family turmoil surrounding divorce with behavior problems and a reduced capacity to cope with stress.[76] Custodial mothers tend to have difficulty handling sons on their own. Both boys and girls show declines in academic achievement during the aftermath of divorce, but school problems are greater for boys.[77]

Most children improve in adjustment by two years after divorce. Yet for some, emotional distress and poor school performance persist, contributing to lasting problems into adolescence and young adulthood. Adults whose parents divorced during their childhoods tend to do less well in terms of educational, vocational, and economic attainment than their counterparts from stable families.[78] Regardless of whether fathers remain salient figures in children's lives, the strongest predictor of good outcomes following divorce is effective parenting—combining warmth with reasonable maturity demands, limiting family conflict, and using consistent, nonpunitive discipline.[79] Fathers who remain involved and who use good child-rearing techniques contribute greatly to the psychological well-being of children of both genders, with boys showing special benefits.[80]

I have a child with physical disabilities (cerebral palsy) but who's very smart. Will his intellectual growth continue as long as it's promoted?

Your child's intellectual growth will definitely continue as long as you and other important adults in his life promote it. Chapter 5 of this book is devoted to the development of children with deficits and disabilities. Although I don't discuss children with cerebral palsy specifically, the same general principles for fostering continued learning in all children apply to your child. Children—with and without disabilities—acquire new competencies through dialogues with more expert partners, who are sensitive to what the child is ready to master and foster it in culturally meaningful activities.

All too often, children's disabilities are viewed as entirely biological, much like an incurable disease. Vygotsky's theory emphasizes that the most serious consequence of a physical or mental defect is not the biological impairment itself but the disruption it causes in the child's social relationships. You can help your child compensate for his physical limitations through social contact and communication aimed at strengthening the higher thought processes—voluntary attention, deliberate memory, concept formation, logical reasoning, problem solving, and imagination. "The mightiness of the mind," Vygotsky wrote, "has virtually no limits."[81]

When cerebral palsy results in speech, hearing, or visual impairments, promoting language proficiency through alternative means is crucial for enhancing development. Parents and teachers who maximize children's communicative capabilities, through sign language, finger spelling, special computer technology, and other symbolic innovations, grant them access to the minds of others and to tools for collaborating with more capable partners in their "zones"—sure routes to realizing their potential.

A Vision for Parenting
and Educational Practice

Vygotsky's sociocultural theory is an empowering perspective for parents and teachers. In underscoring the role of adult–child dialogues in children's development, it offers a balanced resolution to the dichotomy between adult directiveness and child-centeredness that has, for decades, permeated American parenting advice and educational practice.

Consistent with a wealth of current research, sociocultural theory stresses that children contribute actively to their own development, etching their unique imprint on everything they learn. To implement sociocultural concepts of child rearing and teaching, parents and teachers must have a firm grasp of children's temperaments, interests, knowledge, skills, and strengths and weaknesses. Yet each ingredient of effective dialogue—the shared understanding essential for genuine communication, the sensitive guidance inherent in scaffolding, the narrative conversation that builds the child's cultural worldview, and the meaningful activities that spark learning of all kinds—requires that adults and children join forces. To create the "zone"—the dynamic region in which children acquire cognitive and social competencies and the capacity to use thought to guide behavior—children and important adults in their lives must collaborate.

Adults are leaders in this collaborative process. Through dialogues, they fashion the child's lifeline with humanity. Weaken or sever that line, and no matter how well endowed children are genetically, they become less than they otherwise could be. Although not the sole influence, adult–child togetherness through the give-and-take of communication indelibly affects children's development. Dialogues with parents, teachers, and other significant adults transform the child's mind, connecting it with other minds and transferring to it a wealth of understandings and skills.

A VISION FOR PARENTING

From the sociocultural perspective, parents help children realize their potential by making a long-term commitment to sensitivity, consistency, and richness of interaction, not by offering brief bursts of attention interspersed with little involvement. This means that good parenting is possible only through great investments of time. Early in this book, I cited evidence indicating that contemporary parents—even those with demanding careers who claim the greatest time scarcity—have ample time for generous involvement in their children's lives. Nevertheless, today's parents spend far less time than they could conversing and playing with children, teaching them important skills, and participating with them in the routine responsibilities of everyday life. As a culture, we seem to have lost sight of why such joint parent–child engagement is so important.

A wealth of research inspired by Vygotsky's sociocultural ideas highlights the many essential capacities that emerge when parents and children engage in such seemingly mundane pursuits as a conversation, a pretend-play episode, a bedtime story, a homework assignment, or a shopping excursion. Through these activities, children acquire wide-ranging knowledge about their physical and social worlds, ways of relating to other people, strategies for surmounting challenges, a sense of family and community belonging, and a personal history imbued with cultural beliefs and values. They also become adept at using powerful symbolic tools for communicating and thinking, which open up virtually unlimited "zones" for learning.

Furthermore, through conversation, children and parents enter one another's daily worlds—worlds that are far more segregated today than they once were. Children learn about parents' work and other aspects of adult life—arenas they will one day join. And parents find out about children's experiences. This affords parents additional opportunities to support their child's development and to convey the message, "I care deeply about what your days are like."

The field of child development has reached a broad, research-based consensus that parents' influence on children, while far from exclusive, is nevertheless considerable.[1] I have reviewed many of those findings within the pages of this book. Collectively, they indicate that parental warmth combined with firm, consistent, rational, and appropriate expectations for mature behavior promotes favorable child development broadly—across different ages, temperaments, socioeconomic levels, and cultural backgrounds.[2] And an increasing number of studies also show that children with certain extreme traits, such as shyness, impulsivity, or emotional reactivity, benefit when parents make sensitive but persistent efforts to modify the child's maladaptive style rather than reacting in impatient, hostile, and ignoring ways.[3]

For today's parents to be effective at child rearing, they must move beyond the now obsolete doctrines that construe parents as all-powerful or dismiss them as ineffectual. Parents act in synergy with many influences, most notably, the child's biologically based characteristics but also other wide-ranging forces in the environment, including the family, preschool, child-care center, school, neighborhood, community, and larger culture. Some experts despair of American parents fully appreciating this complexity. They worry that parents have become too used to facile sound bites of information and to recipes offering short-term fixes for children's problems. In contrast, I believe that parents *can* grasp the intricate mix of factors that contribute to children's development, that they *can* apply a new, more refined understanding of their own indispensable role in helping children become productive, responsible adults.

The current consensus of research is unequivocal in declaring that parenting requires sustained emotional investment and reasoned judgment—all the more so in view of the many factors in American society that have complicated it. Among these are weak supports for families in the workplace, poor-quality child care, less than optimum schools, a media riddled with violence and stereotypes, and a culture of acquisitiveness and indiscriminate consumerism. Without policies that do a better job of helping parents with the awesome task of child rearing, parents must be even more vigilant in their roles as gatekeepers of children's experiences and as conveyors of values and attitudes.

The sociocultural metaphor of parents as leaders in their children's development offers direction and guidance as parents grapple with myriad dilemmas—whether to purchase a popular toy, to permit the child to watch another hour of TV, to insist that the child clean up his or her room, to have dinner with the child, or to spend a morning in the child's classroom. Those decisions are weighty and significant; to minimize or retreat from them downplays children's needs and endangers their development. Indeed, it can be argued that those decisions are the essence of parenting, and parenting today not only matters greatly, but matters more than ever.

A VISION FOR EDUCATIONAL PRACTICE

More than any other contemporary perspective, sociocultural theory has advanced our knowledge of educational practices that foster children's enthusiasm for learning and academic progress. Educational innovations and research stimulated by Vygotsky's ideas are helping to release teachers and school administrators from a quagmire of extreme approaches to teaching and learning, each of which is poorly suited to children's needs.

Early childhood marks the dawning of children's capacity to interact skillfully with others, to reflect on their own thinking, and to plan and guide their own behavior. These developments are crucial for academic success and gratifying peer relationships. A child-centered educational philosophy that imposes little or no structure and waits for children to discover knowledge or to announce their readiness to learn deprives them of the direction they need to acquire these vital capabilities. And an adult-centered philosophy that grants children little or no leeway for self-direction and drills them on ready-made academic facts makes children dependent on external control and stifles their motivation, involvement, understanding, critical thinking, and originality.

Sociocultural theory offers a balanced alternative to this seesaw between educational extremes. It grants vital roles to both child and adult by advocating that adults respond to children's current capacities with teaching strategies that lead development forward. Through teaching in the "zone," education simultaneously considers where children are and what they are capable of becoming, thereby strengthening readiness for academic learning in the preschool years and continued academic progress in elementary school.

Like its vision of parenting, the sociocultural vision of early childhood education depends on adult warmth, sensitivity, and expectations for maturity tailored to children's readiness to learn. But readiness is neither totally determined by children's preferences nor exacted by teachers who focus on a narrow head start in academic knowledge. Instead, all children are regarded as ready to learn—to progress through their "zones" with the help of more expert partners.

Below are key tenets of early childhood education stimulated by sociocultural theory, ones that I hope will inspire better child-care, preschool, and primary school experiences and also assist parents in their efforts to help children learn.

- *Teachers and children contribute jointly to development.* Teachers design rich, varied environments sensitive to individual differences in children's interests, competencies, and learning styles. The activities teachers provide foster children's active involvement in learning because they are meaningful—relevant to children's everyday lives.
- *Activities focus on language and literacy development.* Teachers give language and literacy the utmost attention because mastery of conversation, reading, and writing permits children to communicate with an

unlimited range of expert partners, thereby greatly enlarging their opportunities to learn. Becoming literate also enables children to attain new heights in self-regulation. Learning to read and write encourages children to think about how to communicate more effectively—with others and with themselves.

- *Educational goals spur children to new levels of competence.* Learning activities are challenging and offer ready access to the assistance of more expert partners to surmount those challenges. To ensure that children progress through their "zones," teachers help them select tasks that fit their learning needs; continually adjust the difficulty of those tasks, the degree of adult assistance, or both to suit children's changing capabilities; and set expectations for classroom behavior consistent with children's cognitive and social capacities. Teachers also promote cooperative learning, through which children assist one another.

- *Make-believe play is a vital activity of early childhood.* Teachers grant make-believe play an important place in the curriculum. Through pretending, preschoolers use ideas to guide thought and action and willingly follow social rules, bringing their behavior in line with social norms and expectations. In make-believe, children also create "zones" for a wide variety of cognitive and social competencies and informally acquire many literacy-relevant skills. And they prepare for game play, which strengthens their ability to devise and follow social rules and their understanding of fairness and justice.

  Teachers scaffold young preschoolers' make-believe play, preparing them for sociodramatic play with peers. When children jointly create imaginative scenarios, they receive vital lessons in resolving conflicts and cooperating to attain common goals.

- *Assessment procedures focus on identifying children's "zones" and the teaching strategies that best support their progress.* Evaluations of children's progress focus not just on what they have already mastered but on what they can acquire with assistance. In dynamic assessment, the teacher or another trained adult presents the child with challenging tasks and introduces purposeful teaching into the situation. Then the adult assesses the breadth of the child's "zone"—how far the child can progress with assistance—and the teaching style to which the child is most responsive. Teachers use this information to plan activities that promote optimum learning.

- *Experiences for children with deficits and disabilities ensure their participation in challenging, meaningful, collaborative activities.* The same educational principles that spur development in nondisabled children apply to children with deficits and disabilities. When a child's physical or mental problem disrupts opportunities for social participation, education must be directed at restoring that interaction. It must grant the child access to collaboration with adults and peers in meaningful activities. Fostering language and communication is crucial, enabling children with disabilities to join in dialogues with others and to acquire culturally valued ways of thinking and behaving.

- *Teachers and parents build bridges between home and school.* Frequent communication between parents and teachers and many occasions for parents to observe and volunteer in classrooms enhance children's academic achievement. Through strong teacher–parent partnerships, parents learn about effective educational practices and can better support children's learning at home. And teachers gain valuable insights into children's family experiences and cultural backgrounds that they can use to adapt classroom activities to children's learning needs.

A FINAL NOTE

Good parenting and good teaching are challenging, reflective, deliberate endeavors. Depending on the child and the supports in the broader social context, parenting and teaching can be more or less mentally and emotionally taxing, more or less fraught with hurdles to be overcome. In preparing *Awakening Children's Minds*, it has been my goal to create a "zone" for parents and teachers seeking more effective ways to rear and teach young children.

Should the practices described in this book catch hold broadly, their influence promises to be all the more vigorous. Cultures of good parenting and teaching deliver an extra boost to children's well-being. When many parents in a neighborhood are highly involved in children's school life, the impact of parent involvement on children's achievement is magnified.[4] When most or all members of a peer group have parents who combine warmth with reasonable expectations for maturity, young people derive extra benefits in terms of school performance and the ability to resist unfavorable peer pressures.[5] And when excellent early childhood education becomes a team effort of educators, parents, and community members, its effects on learning are stronger and reach many more children.[6]

Parents and teachers who steadfastly engage in dialogues with children can rest assured that their efforts greatly affect the formation of children's minds. Their commitment and involvement are vital for forging a better future for America's children.

NOTES

CHAPTER 1: A NEW VIEW OF CHILD DEVELOPMENT

1. Robinson, J., & Godbey, G., *Time for life.* 1997, College Park: Pennsylvania State University Press.

2. Families and Work Institute Survey, 1995, reported in the *Wall Street Journal,* 1997 March 31, p. 6.

3. U.S. Bureau of the Census, *Statistical abstract of the United States,* 120th ed. 2000, Washington, DC: Government Printing Office.

4. See Ebbeck, J., & Ebbeck, F., Child-care policy in Australia. In L. E. Berk, ed., *Landscapes of development.* 1999, Belmont, CA: Wadsworth, pp. 181–191. For follow-ups of children enrolled in Swedish child-care centers from an early age, see Andersson, B–E., Effects of public day care—A longitudinal study. *Child Development,* 1989. 60: 857–866; Andersson, B–E., Effects of day care on cognitive and socioemotional competence of thirteen-year-old Swedish schoolchildren. *Child Development,* 1992. 63: 20–36; Broberg, A. G., Wessels, H., Lamb, M. E., & Hwang, C. P., Effects of day care on the development of cognitive abilities in 8-year-olds: A longitudinal study. *Developmental Psychology,* 1997. 33: 62–69.

5. Helburn, S. W., ed., *Cost, quality, and child outcomes in child care centers.* 1995, Denver: University of Colorado. Galinsky, E., Howes, C., Kontos, S., & Shinn, M., *The study of children in family child care and relative care: Highlights of findings.* 1994, New York: Families and Work Institute.

6. Cryer, D., & Burchinal, M., Parents as child care consumers. In S. W. Helburn, ed., *Cost, quality, and child outcomes in child care centers,* 1995, Denver: University of Colorado, pp. 203–209.

7. See, for example, Clarke-Stewart, K. A., Interactions between mothers and their young children: Characteristics and consequences. *Monographs of the Society for Research in Child Development,* 1973. 38: No. 6–7, Serial No. 153; Martin, J. A., A longitudinal study of the consequences of early mother–infant interaction: A microanalytic approach. *Monographs of the Society for Research in Child Development,* 1981. 46: No. 3, Serial No. 190. Crain-Thoreson, C., & Dale, P. S., Do early talkers become early readers? Linguistic precocity, preschool language, and emergent literacy. *Developmental Psychology,* 1992. 28: 421–429. Hart, B., & Risley, T. R., *Meaningful differences in the everyday experience of young American children.* 1995, Baltimore: Paul H. Brookes.

8. See, for example, Lewis, M., *Altering fate: Why the past does not predict the future.* 1997, New York: Guilford.

9. See discussions of the long-term developmental consequences of infant–mother attachment that underscore the importance of both quality and consistency of care: Belsky, J., & Cassidy, J., Attachment: Theory and evidence. In M. Rutter & D. Hay, eds., *Development through life.* 1994, Oxford, UK: Blackwell, pp. 373–402; Thompson, R. A., Early sociopersonality development. In W. Damon, series ed., & N. Eisenberg, vol. ed., *Handbook of child psychology: Vol. 3, Social, emotional, and personality development,* 5th ed. 1998, New York: Wiley, pp. 58–65.

10. Hochschild, A. R., *The time bind: When work becomes home and home becomes work.* 1997, New York: Metropolitan Books.

11. Barnett, R. C., & Rivers, C., *She works/he works.* 1996, San Francisco: Harper.

12. See Shapiro, L., The myth of quality time. *Newsweek.* 1997 May 12, p. 65.

13. Ibid.

14. Clark, R., Hyde, J. S., Essex, M. J., & Klein, M. H., Length of maternity leave and quality of mother-infant interaction. *Child Development*, 1997. 68: 364–383; Hyde, J. S., Klein, M. H., Essex, M. J., & Clark, R., Maternity leave and women's mental health. *Psychology of Women Quarterly*, 1995. 19: 257–285.

15. NICHD (National Institute of Child Health and Human Development) Early Child Care Research Network, Child care and mother–child interaction in the first 3 years of life. *Developmental Psychology*, 1999. 35: 1399–1413.

16. Belsky, J., Quantity of nonmaternal care and boys' problem behavior/adjustment at ages 3 and 5: Exploring the mediating role of parenting. *Psychiatry: Interpersonal and Biological Processes*, 1999. 62: 1–20.

17. Hoffman, L. W., Effects of maternal employment in the two-parent family. *American Psychologist*, 1989. 44: 283–292; Williams, E., & Radin, N., Paternal involvement, maternal employment, and adolescents' academic achievement: An 11-year follow-up. *American Journal of Orthopsychiatry*, 1993. 63: 306–312.

18. Greenberger, E., & Goldberg, W. A., Work, parenting, and the socialization of children. *Developmental Psychology*, 1989. 25: 22–35.

19. Moorehouse, M. J., Linking maternal employment patterns to mother–child activities and children's school competence. *Developmental Psychology*, 1991. 27: 295–303.

20. Robinson, J. P., & Godbey, G., Time for life. Also see Parke, R. D., & Buriel, R. Socialization in the family: Ethnic and ecological perspectives. In W. Damon, series ed., & N. Eisenberg, vol. ed., *Handbook of child psychology: Vol. 3, Social, emotional, and personality development*, 5TH ed. 1998, New York: Wiley, pp. 463–552.

21. Coltrane, S., *Family man*. 1996, New York: Oxford University Press; Gottfried, A. E., Maternal employment in the family setting: Developmental and environmental issues. In J. V. Lerner & N. L. Galambos, eds., *Employed mothers and their children*. 1991, New York: Garland, pp. 63–84; Radin, N., Primary caregiving fathers in intact families. In A. E. Gottfried & A. W. Gottfried, eds., *Redefining families: Implications for children's development*. 1994, New York: Plenum, pp. 11–54.

22. Cowan, P. A., Powell, D., & Cowan, C. P., Parenting interventions: A family systems perspective. In W. Damon, series ed., & I. Sigel & K. A. Renninger, vol. eds., *Handbook of child psychology: Vol. 4, Child psychology in practice*, 5TH ed. 1998, New York: Wiley, pp. 3–72.

23. Lerner, J. V., & Abrams, A., Developmental correlates of maternal employment influences on children. In C. B. Fisher & R. M. Lerner, eds., *Applied developmental psychology*. 1994, New York: McGraw-Hill, pp. 174–206; Williams, E., & Radin, N., Paternal involvement, maternal employment, and adolescents' academic achievement: An 11-year follow-up. *American Journal of Orthopsychiatry*, 1993. 63: 306–312.

24. Achenbach, T. M., & Howell, C., Are American children's problems getting worse? A 13-year comparison. *Journal of the American Academy of Child and Adolescent Psychiatry*, 1993. 32: 1145–1154.

25. Farkas, S., & Johnson, J., *Kids these days: What Americans really think about the next generation*. 1997, New York: Public Agenda.

26. Gookin, S. H., & Goodkin, D., *Parenting for dummies*. 1995, Foster City, CA: IDG Books Worldwide; Friel, J. C., & Friel, L. D., *The seven worst things parents do*. 1999, Deerfield Beach, FL: Health Communications.

27. Johnson, D., My blue heaven. *New York Review of Books*. 1998 July 18, p. 15.

28. Burts, D. C., Hart, C. H., Charlesworth, R., Fleege, P. O., Mosley, J., & Thomasson, R. H., Observed activities and stress behavior of children in developmentally appropri-

ate and inappropriate kindergarten classrooms. *Early Childhood Research Quarterly*, 1992. 7: 297–318; Hart, C. H., Burts, D. C., Durland, M. A., Charlesworth, R., DeWolf, M., & Fleege, P. O., Stress behaviors and activity type participation of preschoolers in more and less developmentally appropriate classrooms: SES and sex differences. *Journal of Research in Childhood Education*, 1998. 66: 1346–1359; Stipek, D. J., Feiler, R., Daniels, D., & Milburn, S., Effects of different instructional approaches on young children's achievement and motivation. *Child Development*, 1995. 66: 209–223.

29. See, for example, child psycholoanalyst Selma Fraiberg's widely read book for parents: *The Magic Years*. 1959, New York: Charles Scribner's Sons. The first chapter opens with the story of Frankie, whose parents carefully followed the writings of experts in weaning, toilet training, and preparing him for the arrival of a new baby in hopes of avoiding undue anxieties in their young son. Nevertheless, at age 2, Frankie displayed fears like those of other children his age (e.g., being sucked down the bathroom drain) and, despite thorough sex education, suggested that his parents take his infant sibling back to the dime store.

30. For a more complete description of Piaget's stages, as well as the strengths and limitations of his theory, see Berk, L. E., *Child development*, 5TH ed. 2000, Boston: Allyn & Bacon, Chapters 1 and 6.

31. See Silberman, C. E., *Crisis in the classroom: The remaking of American education*. 1970, New York: Random House.

32. Walberg, H. J., Synthesis of research on teaching. In M. C. Wittrock, ed., *Handbook of research on teaching*, 3RD ed. 1986, New York: Macmillan, pp. 214–229.

33. Berk, L. E., *Child development*, pp. 242–248. (See note 30.)

34. See, for example, Fahrmeier, E. D., The development of concrete operations among the Hausa. *Journal of Cross-Cultural Psychology*, 1979. 9: 23–44.

35. Childs, C. P., & Greenfield, P. M., Informal modes of learning and teaching: The case of Zinacanteco weaving. In N. Warren, ed., *Advances in cross-cultural psychology*, Vol. 2. 1982, London: Academic Press, pp. 269–316.

36. Ceci, S. J., & Roazzi, A., The effects of context on cognition: Postcards from Brazil. In R. J. Sternberg, *Mind in context*. 1994, New York: Cambridge University Press, pp. 119–142.

37. Berk, L. E., *Child development*, pp. 242–248. (See note 30.)

38. Gesell, A., Ilg, F. L., & Ames, L. B., *The infant and child in the culture of today: The guidance of development in home and nursery school,* rev. ed. [1943] 1996, New York: Jason Aronson; Gesell, A., Ilg, F. L., & Ames, L. B., *The first five years of life*. [1946] 1993, New York: Bucaneer Books; Gesell, A., Ilg, F. L., & Ames, L. B., *The child from five to ten*. [1946] 1983, New York: Harper & Row.

39. Spock, B., & Parker, S. J., *Dr. Spock's baby and child care*. 1998, New York: Pocket Books.

40. Ibid., p. 429.

41. Gordon, T., *Parent effectiveness training*, rev. ed. 1990, New York: New American Library.

42. Engelmann, S., & Engelmann, T., *Give your child a superior mind*. 1966, New York: Simon & Schuster, pp. 34, 71.

43. Stipek, D. J., Feiler, R., Daniels, D., & Milburn, S., Effects of different instructional approaches on young children's achievement and motivation. (See note 28.)

44. Elkind, D., *The hurried child: Growing up too fast too soon,* rev. ed. 1988, New York: Addison-Wesley.

45. Ibid., pp. 150–151.

46. Damon, W., *Greater expectations: Overcoming the culture of indulgence in America's homes and schools.* 1995, New York: The Free Press.

47. Ibid., p. xii.

48. Horowitz, F. D., Child development and the PITS: Simple questions, complex answers, and developmental theory. *Child Development,* 2000. 71: 1–10; Lerner, R. M., Theories of human development: Contemporary perspectives. In R. M. Lerner, ed., *Handbook of child psychology: Vol. 1. Theoretical models of human development,* 5th ed. 1998, New York: Wiley, pp. 1–24.

49. Henceforth I refer to nonparental caregivers as teachers, a label more consistent with their role in children's development as clarified by sociocultural theory, which serves as the framework for this book.

50. I am indebted to Pamela Riney-Kehrberg, Department of History, Illinois State University, for suggesting Ise's work.

51. Ise, J., *Sod and stubble.* 1938, New York: Barnes & Noble.

52. Robinson, J. P., & Godbey, G., *Time for life.* (See note 1.)

53. Horowitz, F. D., *Child development and the PITS: Simple questions, complex answers, and developmental theory.* (See note 48.)

54. See, for example, Bronfenbrenner, U., & Morris, P. A., The ecology of developmental processes. In W. Damon, series ed., & R. M. Lerner, vol. ed., *Handbook of child psychology: Vol. 1, Theoretical models of human development,* 5th ed. 1998, New York: Wiley, pp. 535–584; Fischer, K. W., & Bidell, T. R., Dynamic development of psychological structures in action and thought. In W. Damon, series ed., & R. M. Lerner, vol. ed., *Handbook of child psychology: Vol 1, Theoretical models of human development,* 5th ed. 1998, New York: Wiley, pp. 467–561.

55. Fischer, K. W., & Bidell, T. R., Dynamic development of psychological structures in action and thought. (See note 54.)

56. See, for example, Bronfenbrenner, U., & Morris, P. A., The ecology of developmental processes. (See note 54.); Gottlieb, G., Normally occurring environmental and behavioral influences on gene activity: From central dogma to probabilistic epigenesis. *Psychological Review,* 1998. 105: 792–802.

57. Thatcher, R. W., Lyon, G. R., Rumsey, J., & Krasnegor, J., *Developmental neuroimaging.* 1996, San Diego: Academic Press.

58. Greenough, W. T., Wallace, C. S., Alcantara, A. A., Anderson, B. J., Hawrylak, N., Sirevaag, A. M., Weiler, I. J., & Withers, G. S., Development of the brain: Experience affects the structure of neurons, glia, and blood vessels. In N. J. Anastasiow & S. Harel, eds., *At-risk infants: Interventions, families, and research.* 1993, Baltimore: Paul H. Brookes, pp. 173–185.

59. Stiles, J., The effects of early focal brain injury on lateralization of cognitive function. *Current Directions in Psychological Science,* 1998. 7: 21–28.

60. White, B., & Held, R., Plasticity of sensorimotor development in the human infant. In J. F. Rosenblith & W. Allinsmith, eds., *The causes of behavior.* 1966, Boston: Allyn & Bacon, pp. 60–70.

61. See, for example, Roe, K. V., Rose, A., Drivas, A., & Bornstein, R., A curvilinear relationship between maternal vocal stimulation and three-month-olds' cognitive processing: A cross-cultural phenomenon. *Infant Mental Health Journal,* 1990. 11: 175–189; Isabella, R. A., & Belsky, J., Interactional synchrony and the origins of infant–mother attachment: A replication study. *Child Development,* 1991. 62: 373–384.

62. See, for example, Mulrine, A., A preschool with snob appeal. *U.S. News & World Report.* 1999 September 13, pp. 48–49.

63. For further discussion of why intensive early tutoring is at odds with contemporary knowledge of brain development, see Bruer, J., *The myth of the first three years*. 1999, New York: The Free Press.

64. Rothbart, M. K., & Bates, J. E., Temperament. In W. Damon, series ed., & N. Eisenberg, vol. ed., *Handbook of child psychology: Vol. 3. Social, emotional, and personality development*. 1998, New York: Wiley, pp. 105–176.

65. Rothbart, M. K., & Mauro, J. A., Questionnaire approaches to the study of infant temperament. In J. W. Fagen & J. Colombo, eds., *Individual differences in infancy: Reliability, stability and prediction*. 1990, Hillsdale, NJ: Erlbaum, pp. 411–429.

66. Parent ratings of temperament are moderately related to researchers' observations of children's behavior. See Rothbart, M. K., & Bates, J. E., Temperament. (See note 64.)

67. Kagan, J., Biology and the child. In W. Damon, vol. ed., & N. Eisenberg, series ed., *Handbook of child psychology: Vol. 3. Social, emotional, and personality development*, 1998, New York: Wiley, pp. 177–236.

68. Gunnar, M. R., & Nelson, C. A., Event-related potentials in year-old infants: Relations with emotionality and cortisol. *Child Development*, 1994. 65: 80–94; Kagan, J., Biology and the child. (See note 67.); Snidman, N., Kagan, J., Riordan, L., & Shannon, D. C., Cardiac function and behavioral reactivity. *Psychophysiology*, 1995. 32: 199–207.

69. Calkins, S. D., Fox, N. A., & Marshall, T. R., Behavioral and physiological antecedents of inhibited and uninhibited behavior. *Child Development*, 1996. 67: 523–540; Fox, N. A., Bell, M. A., & Jones, N. A., Individual differences in response to stress and cerebral asymmetry. *Developmental Neuropsychology*, 1992. 8: 161–184.

70. Gandour, M. J., Activity level as a dimension of temperament in toddlers: Its relevance for the organismic specificity hypothesis. *Child Development*, 1989. 60: 1092–1098; Miceli, P. J., Whitman, T. L., Borkowski, J. G., Braungart-Riekder, J., & Mitchell, D. W., Individual differences in infant information processing: The role of temperamental and maternal factors. *Infant Behavior and Development*, 1998. 21: 119–136.

71. Chen, X., Rubin, K. H., & Li, Z., Social functioning and adjustment in Chinese children: A longitudinal study. *Developmental Psychology*, 1995. 31: 531–539; Chen, X., Hastings, P. D., Rubin, K. H., Chen, H., Cen, G., & Stewart, S. L., Child-rearing attitudes and behavioral inhibition in Chinese and Canadian toddlers: A cross-cultural study. *Developmental Psychology*, 1998. 34: 677–686.

72. Luthar, S. S., & Zigler, E., Vulnerability and competence: A review of research on resilience in childhood. *American Journal of Orthopsychiatry*, 1991. 6: 6–22; Smith, J., & Prior, M., Temperament and stress resilience in school-age children: A within-families study. *Journal of the American Academy of Child and Adolescent Psychiatry*, 1995. 34: 168–179.

73. Harris, J. R., *The nurture assumption: Why children turn out the way they do*. 1998, New York: The Free Press.

74. Collins, W. A., Maccoby, E. E., Steinberg, L., Hetherington, E. M., & Bornstein, M. H., Contemporary research on parenting: The case for nature and nurture. *American Psychologist*, 2000. 55: 218–232; Gardner, H., Do parents count? *New York Review of Books*. 1998 November 5, pp. 19–22; Kagan, J. A. Parent's influence is peerless. *The Boston Sunday Globe*. 1998 September 13, p. E3; Vandell, D. L., Parents, peer groups, and other socializing influences. *Developmental Psychology*, 2000. 36: 699–710.

75. See, for example, Ceci, S. J., Schooling, intelligence, and income. *American Psychologist*, 1997. 52: 1051–1058; Ceci, S. J., & Hembrooke, H. A., A bioecological model of intellectual development. In P. Moen & G. H. Elder, Jr., *Examining lives in context: Perspectives on the ecology of human development*. 1995, Washington, DC: American Psychological Asso-

ciation; Chase-Landsdale, P. L., Gordon, R., Brooks-Gunn, J., & Klebanov, P. K., Neigh-borhood and family influences on the intellectual and behavioral competence of preschool and early school-age children. In J. Brooks-Gunn, G. Duncan, & J. L. Aber, eds., *Neigh-borhood poverty: Context and consequences for development.* 1997, New York: Russell Sage Foundation.

76. See, for example, Bronfenbrenner, U., *Two worlds of childhood: U.S. and U.S.S.R.* 1970, New York: Russell Sage Foundation; and Fuligni, A. J., & Stevenson, H. W., Time use and mathematics achievement among American, Chinese, and Japanese high school students. *Child Development,* 1995. 66: 830–842, which reports that American teenagers average 18 nonschool hours per week with peers; Japanese teenagers 12 hours; and Tai-wanese teenagers only 9 hours.

77. Gardner, H., Do parents count?, p. 22. (See note 74.)

78. Blanck, G., Vygotsky: The man and his cause. In L. C. Moll, ed., *Vygotsky and edu-cation: Instructional implications and applications of sociohistorical psychology.* 1990, New York: Cambridge University Press, pp. 31–58.

79. Vygotsky was first a teacher, only later a developmental psychologist. This, in part, accounts for the strong emphasis in his theory on social experience—especially dialogues with more experienced cultural members—in children's formation of mind.

80. Vygotsky, L. S., *Thought and language,* A. Kozulin, trans. [1934] 1986, Cambridge, MA: MIT Press.

81. Berk, L. E., *Child development,* see Chapter 9. (See note 30.)

82. Vygotsky, L. S., *Mind in society: The development of higher mental processes,* M. Cole, V. John-Steiner, S. Scribner, & E. Souberman, eds. and trans. [1930–1935] 1978, Cambridge, MA: Harvard University Press.

83. Vygotsky, L. S., The genesis of higher mental functions. In J. V. Wertsch, ed., *The concept of activity in Soviet psychology.* [1960] 1981, Armonk, NY: Sharpe, pp. 144–188.

84. Vygotsky, L. S., The instrumental method in psychology. Ibid, pp. 134–143; Wertsch, J. V., *Vygotsky and the social formation of mind.* 1985, Cambridge, MA: Harvard University Press.

85. Vygotsky, L. S., Thinking and speech. In R. Rieber & A. S. Carton, eds., N. Minick, trans., *The collected works of L. S. Vygotsky: Vol. 1. Problems of general psychology.* [1934] 1987, New York: Plenum, p. 45.

86. Rogoff, B., *Apprenticeship in thinking: Cognitive development in social context.* 1990, New York: Oxford University Press; Rogoff, B., Mistry, J., Göncü, A., Toddlers' guided par-ticipation with their caregivers in cultural activity. In E. A. Forman, N. Minick, & C. A. Stone, eds., *Contexts for learning.* 1993, New York: Oxford University Press, pp. 230–253.

87. Tessler, M., & Nelson, K., Making memories: The influence of joint encoding on later recall. *Consciousness and Cognition,* 1994. 3: 307–326.

88. Greenfield, P. M., You can't take it with you: Why ability assessments don't cross cul-tures. *American Psychologist,* 1997. 52: 1115–1124; Sternberg, R. J. *Successful intelligence.* 1997, New York: Plume.

CHAPTER 2: THE SOCIAL ORIGINS OF MENTAL LIFE

1. Greenfield, P. M., *Notes and references for developmental psychology.* Conference on Making Basic Texts in Psychology More Culture-Inclusive and Culture-Sensitive. 1992 June: Bellingham, WA.

2. Morelli, G., Rogoff, B., Oppenheim, D., & Goldsmith, D., Cultural variation in infants' sleeping arrangements: Questions of independence. *Developmental Psychology,* 1992. 28: 604–613.

3. Ibid.

4. Kawakami, K., *Comparison of mother–infant relationships in Japanese and American families.* Paper presented at annual meeting of the International Society for the Study of Behavioral Development. 1987 July: Tokyo, Japan.

5. Butler, R., & Ruzany, N., Age and socialization effects on the development of social comparison motives and normative ability assessment in kibbutz and urban children. *Child Development,* 1993. 64: 532–543; Nadler, A., Help-seeking as a cultural phenomenon: Differences between city and kibbutz dwellers. *Journal of Personality and Social Psychology,* 1986. 51: 976–982.

6. Wertsch, J. V., A sociocultural approach to socially shared cognition. In L. B. Resnick, J. M. Levine, & S. D. Teasley, eds., *Perspectives on socially shared cognition.* 1991, Washington, DC: American Psychological Association, p. 90.

7. De Wolff, M. S., & van IJzendoorn, M. H., Sensitivity and attachment: A meta-analysis on parental intecedents of infant attachment. *Child Development.* 1997, 68: 571–591.

8. Bell, S. M., & Ainsworth, M. D. S., Infant crying and maternal responsiveness. *Child Development,* 1972. 43: 1171–1190; Hubbard, F. O. A., & van IJzendoorn, M. H., Maternal unresponsiveness and infant crying across the first 9 months: A naturalistic longitudinal study. *Infant Behavior and Development,* 1991. 14: 299–312.

9. Thompson, R. A., Early sociopersonality development. In W. Damon, series ed., & N. Eisenberg, vol. ed., *Handbook of child psychology: Vol. 3, Social, emotional, and personality development,* 5th ed. 1998, New York: Wiley, pp. 25–104.

10. Thompson, R. A., On emotion and self-regulation. In R. A. Thompson, ed., *Nebraska Symposium on Motivation,* Vol. 36. 1990, Lincoln: University of Nebraska Press, pp. 383–483.

11. Elliott, E. S., & Dweck, C. S., Goals: An approach to motivation and achievement. *Journal of Personality and Social Psychology,* 1988. 54: 5–12.

12. Skinner, E. A., Zimmer-Gembeck, M. J., & Connell, J. P. Individual development of perceived control. *Monographs of the Society for Research in Child Development,* 1998. 63: No. 2–3, Serial No. 234.

13. Vygotsky, L. S., *Mind and society: The development of higher mental* processes, M. Cole, V. John-Steiner, S. Scribner, & E. Souberman, eds. And trans. [1930–1935] 1978, Cambridge, MA: Harvard University Press.

14. Ibid., p. 86.

15. Tharp, R. G., & Gallimore, R., *Rousing minds to life: Teaching, learning and schooling in social context.* 1988, New York: Cambridge University Press.

16. Newson, J., & Newson, E., Intersubjectivity and the transmission of culture: On the social origins of symbolic functioning. *Bulletin of the British Psychological Society,* 1975. 28: 437–446.

17. Vygotsky, L. S., *Thought and language,* A. Kozulin, trans. [1934] 1986, Cambridge, MA: Harvard University Press.

18. Ratner, H. H., & Stettner, L. J., Thinking and feeling: Putting Humpty Dumpty together again. *Merrill-Palmer Quarterly,* 1991. 37: 1–26.

19. Adapted from Whitington, V., & Ward, C., Intersubjectivity in caregiver–child communication. In L. E. Berk, ed., *Landscapes of development.* 1999, Belmont, CA: Wadsworth, pp. 109–120.

20. See, for example, Kaye, K., Organism, apprentice, and person. In E. Z. Tronick, ed., *Social interchange in infancy.* 1982, Baltimore: University Park Press, pp. 183–196; Murray, L., & Trevarthen, C., Emotional regulation of interactions between 2-month-olds and their mothers. In T. M. Field & N. Fox, eds., *Social perception in infants.* 1985, Norwood, NJ: ABLEX, pp. 177–197.

21. DeCasper, A. J., & Spence, M. J., Prenatal maternal speech influences newborns' perception of speech sounds. *Infant Behavior and Development,* 1986. 9: 133–150; Morton, J., & Johnson, M. H., CONSPEC and CONLERN: A two-process theory of infant face recognition. *Psychological Review,* 1991. 98: 164–181.

22. Meltzoff, A. N., The human infant as an imitative generalist: A 20-year progress report on infant imitation with implications for comparative psychology. In C. M. Heyes & B. G. Galef, Jr., *Social learning in animals: The roots of culture.* 1996, San Diego: Academic Press, pp. 347–370.

23. Sroufe, L. A., & Waters, E., The ontogenesis of smiling and laughter: A perspective on the organization of development in infancy. *Psychological Review,* 1976. 83: 173–189.

24. Hernandez, F. D., & Carter, A. S., Infant response to mothers and fathers in the still-face paradigm. *Infant Behavior and Development,* 1996. 19: 502; Segal, L. B., Oster, H., Cohen, M., Caspi, B., Myers, M., & Brown, D., Smiling and fussing in seven-month-old preterm and full-term black infants in the still-face situation. *Child Development,* 1995. 66: 1829–1843.

25. Kisilevsky, B. S., Hains, S. M. J., Lee, K., Muir, D. W., Xu, F., Fu, G., Zhao, Z. Y., & Yang, R. L., The still-face effect in Chinese and Canadian 3- to 6-month-old infants. *Developmental Psychology,* 1998. 34: 629–639.

26. Baumwell, L., Tamis-LeMonda, C. S., & Bornstein, M. H., Maternal verbal sensitivity and child language comprehension. *Infant Behavior and Development,* 1997. 20: 247–258; Carpenter, M., Nagell, K., & Tomasello, M., Social cognition, joint attention, and communicative competence. *Monographs of the Society for Research in Child Development,* 1998. 63: No. 4, Serial No. 255.

27. Fenson, L., Dale, P. S., Reznick, J. S., Bates, E., Thal, D. J., & Pethick, S. J., Variability in early communicative development. *Monographs of the Society for Research in Child Development,* 1994. 59: No. 5, Serial No. 242; Carpenter, M., Nagell, K., & Tomasello, M., Social cognition, joint attention, and communicative competence. (See note 26.)

28. Trevarthen, C., & Hubley, P., Secondary intersubjectivity: Confidence, confiding and acts of meaning in the first year. In A. Lock, ed., *Action, gesture, and symbol.* 1978, London: Academic Press, pp. 183–229.

29. Iverson, J. M., Capirci, O., & Caselli, M. C., From communication to language in two modalities. *Cognitive Development,* 1994. 9: 23–43; Namy, L. L., & Waxman, S. R., Words and gestures: Infants' interpretations of different forms of symbolic reference. *Child Development,* 1998. 69: 295–308.

30. Golinkoff, R. M., The preverbal negotiation of failed messages: Insights into the transition period. In R. M. Golinkoff, ed., *The transition from prelinguistic to linguistic communication.* 1983, Hillsdale, NJ: Erlbaum, pp. 58–59.

31. Garvey, C., Requests and responses in children's speech. *Journal of Child Lanugage,* 1974. 2: 41–60; Podrouzek, W., & Furrow, D., Preschoolers' use of eye contact while speaking: The influence of sex, age, and conversational partner. *Journal of Psycholinguistic Research,* 1988. 17: 89–93.

32. Adapted from Whitington, V., & Ward, C., Intersubjectivity in caregiver–child communication, pp. 118–119. (See note 19.)

33. Göncü, A., Development of intersubjectivity in the dyadic play of preschoolers. *Early Childhood Research Quarterly,* 1993. 8: 99–116.

34. Rogoff, B., Cognition as a collaborative process. In W. Damon, series ed., D. Kuhn, & R. S. Siegler, vol. ed., *Handbook of child psychology: Vol. 2. Cognition, perception, and language,* 5th ed. 1998, New York: Wiley, pp. 679–744.

35. Tronick, E. Z., Emotions and emotional communication in infants. *American Psychologist,* 1989. 44: 115–123.

36. Whitington, V., & Ward, C., Intersubjectivity in caregiver–child communication, pp. 109–120. (See note 19.)

37. Trevarthen, C., Communication and cooperation in early infancy: A description of primary intersubjectivity. In M. Bullowa, ed., *Before speech: The beginning of interpersonal communication.* 1979, Cambridge: Cambridge University Press, p. 340.

38. Wood, D. J., Social interaction as tutoring. In M. H. Bornstein & J. S. Bruner, eds., *Interaction in human development.* 1989, Hillsdale, NJ: Erlbaum, pp. 282–303; Wood, D. J., & Middleton, D., A study of assisted problem solving. *British Journal of Psychology,* 1975. 66: 181–191.

39. Berk, L. E., & Winsler, A., *Scaffolding children's learning: Vygotsky and early childhood education.* 1995, Washington, DC: National Assocation for the Education of Young Children.

40. Rogoff, B., Malkin, C., & Gilbride, K., Interaction with babies as guidance in development. In B. Rogoff & J. V. Wertsch, eds., *New directions for child development,* No. 23. 1984, San Francisco: Jossey-Bass, pp. 31–44.

41. Kopp, C. B., The growth of self-regulation: Caregivers and children. In N. Eisenberg, ed., *Contemporary topics in developmental psychology.* 1987, New York: Wiley, pp. 34–55.

42. Berk, L. E., & Winsler, A., *Scaffolding children's learning: Vygotsky and early childhood education.* (See note 39.)

43. Diaz, R. M., Neal, C. J., & Amaya-Williams, M., The social origins of self-regulation. In L. C. Moll, ed., *Vygotsky and education: Instructional implications and applications of sociohistorical psychology.* 1990, New York: Cambridge University Press, pp. 127–154.

44. Sigel, I. E., The relationship between parental distancing strategies and the child's cognitive behavior. In L. Laosa & I. Sigel, eds., *Families as learning environments for children.* 1982, New York: Plenum, pp. 47–86.

45. Kochanska, G., & Aksan, N., Mother–child mutually positive affect, the quality of child compliance to requests and prohibitions, and maternal control as correlates of early internalization. *Child Development,* 1995. 66: 597–615; Kochanska, G., Mutually responsive orientation between mothers and their young children: Implications for early socialization. *Child Development,* 1997. 68: 94–112.

46. Huntsinger, C. S., Jose, P. E., & Larson, S. L., Do parent practices to encourage academic competence influence the social adjustment of young European American and Chinese American children. *Developmental Psychology,* 1998. 34: 747–756.

47. Chao, R. K., Beyond parental control and authoritarian parenting style: Understanding Chinese parenting through the cultural notion of training. *Child Development,* 1994. 65: 1111–1119; Huntsinger, C. S., Jose, P. E., Liaw, F-R., & Ching, W-D., Cultural differences in early mathematics learning: A comparison of Euro-American, Chinese-American, and Taiwan-Chinese families. *International Journal of Behavioral Development,* 1997. 21: 371–388.

48. Rohner, R. P., & Rohner, E. C., Parental acceptance–rejection and parental control: Cross-cultural codes. *Ethnology,* 1981. 20: 245–260.

49. Baumrind, D., & Black, A. E., Socialization practices associated with dimensions of competence in preschool boys and girls. *Child Development,* 1967. 38: 291–327; Denham, S.

A., Renwick, S. M., & Holt, R. W., Working and playing together: Prediction of preschool social-emotional competence from mother–child interaction. *Developmental Psychology,* 1994. 62: 242–249.

50. Eccles, J. S., Early, D., Frasier, K., Belansky, E., & McCarthy, K., The relation of connection, regulation, and support for autonomy to adolescents' functioning. *Journal of Adolescent Research,* 1997. 12: 263–286; Herman, M. R., Dornbusch, S. M., Herron, M. C., & Herting, J. R., The influence of family regulation, connection, and psychological autonomy on six measures of adolescent functioning. *Journal of Adolescent Research,* 1997. 12: 34–67; Luster, T., & McAdoo, H., Family and child influences on educational attainment: A secondary analysis of the High/Scope Perry Preschool data. *Developmental Psychology,* 1996. 32: 26–39; Steinberg, L. D., Darling, N. E., & Fletcher, A. C., Authoritative parenting and adolescent development: An ecological journey. In P. Moen, G. H. Elder, & K. Luscher, eds., *Examining lives in context.* 1995, Washington, DC: American Psychological Association, pp. 423–466.

51. Berk, L. E., & Spuhl, S. T., Maternal interaction, private speech, and task performance in preschool children. *Early Childhood Research Quarterly,* 1995. 10: 145–169; Diaz, R. M., Neal, C. J., & Vachio, A., Maternal teaching in the zone of proximal development: A comparison of low- and high-risk dyads. *Merrill-Palmer Quarterly,* 1991. 37: 83–108; Pratt, M. W., Green, D., MacVicar, J., & Bountrogianni, M., The mathematical parent: Parental scaffolding, parent style, and learning outcomes in long-division mathematics homework. *Journal of Applied Developmental Psychology,* 1992. 13: 17–34; Pratt, M. W., Kerig, P., Cowan, P. A., & Cowan, C. P., Mothers and fathers teaching 3-year-olds: Authoritative parents and adult scaffolding of young children's learning. *Developmental Psychology,* 1988. 24: 832–839; Roberts, R. N., & Barnes, M. L., "Let momma show you how": Maternal–child interactions and their effects on children's cognitive performance. *Journal of Applied Developmental Psychology,* 1977. 13: 363–376.

52. Bruner, J., *Acts of meaning.* 1990, Cambridge, MA: Harvard University Press.

53. Bruner, J., *In search of mind: Essays in autobiography.* 1986, Cambridge, MA: Harvard University Press.

54. Bruner, J., *Acts of meaning.* (See note 52.)

55. Ibid.

56. Bauer, P. J., Development of memory in early childhood. In N. Cowan, ed., *The development of memory in childhood.* 1997. Hove, UK: Psychology Press, pp. 83–111.

57. Brown, R., *A first language: The early stages.* 1973, Cambridge, MA: Harvard University Press.

58. Bloom, L., Language acquisition in its developmental context. In W. Damon, series ed., D. Kuhn & R. S. Siegler, vol. eds., *Handbook of child psychology: Vol. 2, Cognition, perception, and language,* 5th ed. 1998, New York: Wiley, pp. 309–370.

59. Bruner, J., *Acts of meaning,* p. 79. (See note 52.)

60. Observing three mother–toddler pairs in an urban, working-class neighborhood, Miller and Sperry reported an average of 8.5 parent–child narratives per hour. See Miller, P. J., & Sperry, L. L., The socialization of anger and aggression. *Merrill-Palmer Quarterly,* 1987. 33: 1–31.

61. Pillemer, D. B., & White, S. H., Childhood events recalled by children and adults. In H. W. Reese, ed., *Advances in child development and behavior, Vol. 21.* 1989, New York: Academic Press, pp. 297–340.

62. Boyer, K., & Diamond, A., Development of memory for temporal order in infants and young children. In A. Diamond, ed., *Development and neural bases of higher cognitive function.* 1992, New York: New York Academy of Sciences, pp. 267–317.

63. Newcombe, N., & Fox, N. A., Infantile amnesia: Through a glass darkly. *Child Development*, 1994. 65: 31–40; Pillemer, D. B., & White, S. H., Childhood events recalled by children and adults.

64. Bauer, P. J., Development of memory in early childhood. (See note 56.)

65. Howe, M. L., & Courage, M. L., On resolving the enigma of infantile amnesia. *Psychological Bulletin*, 1993. 113: 305–326; Howe, M. L., & Courage, M. L., The emergence and early development of autobiographical memory. *Psychological Review*, 1997. 104: 499–523.

66. Fivush, R., & Hamond, N. R., Autobiographical memory across the preschool years: Toward reconceptualizing childhood amnesia. In R. Fivush & J. A. Hudson, eds., *Knowing and remembering in young children*, 1990. New York: Cambridge University Press, pp. 223–248.

67. McCabe, A., & Peterson, C., Getting the story: A longitudinal study of parental styles in eliciting narratives and developing narrative skill. In A. McCabe & C. Peterson, eds., *Developing narrative structure*. 1991, Hillsdale, NJ: Erlbaum, pp. 217–253; Reese, E., Haden, C. A., & Fivush, R., Mother–child conversations about the past: Relationships of style and memory over time. *Cognitive Development*, 1993. 8: 403–430.

68. Fivush, R., Haden, C., & Adam, S., Structure and coherence of preschoolers' personal narratives over time: Implications for childhood amnesia. *Journal of Experimental Child Psychology*, 1995. 60: 32–56.

69. Haden, C. A., Haine, R. A., & Fivush, R. Developing narrative structure in parent–child reminiscing across the preschool years. *Developmental Psychology*, 1997. 33: 295–307.

70. Miller, P. J., Potts, R., Fung, H., Hoogstra, L., & Mintz, J., Narrative practices and the social construction of self in childhood. *American Ethnologist*, 1990. 17: 292–311.

71. Ibid.

72. Miller, P. J., Fung, H., & Mintz, J., Self-construction through narrative practices: A Chinese and American comparison of early socialization. *Ethos*, 1996. 24: 237–280; Miller, P. J., Wiley, A. R., Fung, H., & Liang, C-H. Personal storytelling as a medium of socialization in Chinese and American families. *Child Development*, 1997. 68: 557–568.

73. Ibid.

74. Miller, P. J., Fung, H., & Mintz, J., Self-construction through narrative practices: A Chinese and American comparison of early socialization, p. 275. (See note 72.)

75. Bruner, J., *Acts of meaning*. (See note 52.)

76. Ibid.

77. Eisenberg, N., Murphy, B. C., & Shepard, S., The development of empathic accuracy. In W. Ickes, *Empathic accuracy*. 1997, New York: Guilford, pp. 73–116.

78. Cassidy, J., Parke, R. D., Butkovsky, L., & Braungart, J. M., Family–peer connections: The roles of emotional expressiveness within the family and children's understanding of emotions. *Child Development*, 1992. 63: 603–618; Dunn, J., Brown, J. R., & Maguire, M., The development of children's moral sensibility: Individual differences and emotional understanding. *Developmental Psychology*, 1995. 31: 649–659; Garner, P. W., Jones, D. C., & Miner, J. L., Social competence among low-income preschoolers: Emotion socialization practices and social cognitive correlates. *Child Development*, 1994. 65: 622–637.

79. Cervantes, C. A., & Callanan, M. A., Labels and explanations in mother–child emotion talk: Age and gender differentiation. *Developmental Psychology*, 1998. 34: 88–98.

80. Dunn, J., Brown, J., Slomkowski, C., Tesla, C., & Youngblade, L. Young children's understanding of other people's feelings and beliefs: Individual differences and their antecedents. *Child Development*, 1991. 62: 1352–1366.

81. Flavell, J. H., & Miller, P. H., Social cognition. In W. Damon, series ed., D. Kuhn & R. S. Siegler, vol. eds., *Handbook of child psychology: Vol. 2. Cognition, perception, and language,* 4th ed. 1998, New York: Wiley, pp. 851–898.

82. Bartsch, K., & Wellman, H. Young children's attribution of action to beliefs and desires. *Child Development,* 1989. 60: 946–964.

83. Chandler, M. J., & Carpendale, J. I. Inching toward a mature theory of mind. In M. Ferrari & R. J. Sternberg, eds., *Self-awareness: Its nature and development.* 1998, New York: Guilford, pp. 148–190. Leekam, S., Children's understanding of mind. In M. Bennett, ed., *The development of social cognition.* 1993, New York: Guilford, pp. 26–61.

84. Marsh, D. T., Serafica, F. C., & Barenboim, C., Interrelationships among perspective taking, interpersonal problem solving, and interpersonal functioning. *Journal of Genetic Psychology,* 1981. 138: 37–48.

85. Vinden, P. G., Junín Quechua children's understanding of mind. *Child Development,* 1996. 67: 1707–1716.

86. Lewis, C., Freeman, N. H., Kyriadidou, C., Maridakikassotaki, K., & Berridge, D. M., Social influences on false belief access—specific sibling influences or general apprenticeship? *Child Development,* 1996. 67: 2930–2947. Ruffman, T., Perner, J., Naito, M., Partin, L., & Clements, W. A., Older (but not younger) siblings facilitate false belief understanding. *Developmental Psychology,* 1998. 34: 161–174.

87. Hughes, C., & Dunn, J., Understanding mind and emotion: Longitudinal associations with mental-state talk between young friends. *Developmental Psychology,* 1998. 34: 1026–1037.

88. Whitehurst, G. J., & Lonigan, C. J., Child development and emergent literacy. *Child Development,* 1998. 69: 849.

89. Butler, S. R., Marsh, H. W., Sheppard, M. J., & Sheppard, J. L., Seven-year longitudinal study of the early prediction of reading achievement. *Journal of Educational Psychology,* 1985. 77: 349–361; Hart, B., & Risley, T. R., *Meaningful differences in the everyday experience of young American children.* 1995, Baltimore: Paul H. Brookes; Share, D. L., Jorm, A. F., MacLean, R., & Matthews, R., Sources of individual differences in reading acquisition. *Journal of Educational Psychology,* 1984. 76: 1309–1324.

90. Hart, B., & Risley, T. R., *Meaningful differences in the everyday experience of young American children;* Helburn, S. W., *Cost, quality and child outcomes in child care centers.* 1995, Denver: University of Colorado.

91. Dickinson, D. K., & Snow, C. E., Interrelationships among prereading and oral language skills in kindergartners from two social classes. *Early Childhood Research Quarterly,* 1987. 2: 1–25.

92. Whitehurst, G. J., & Lonigan, C. J., Child development and emergent literacy. (See note 88.)

93. Bus, A. G., van IJzendoorn, M. H., & Pellegrini, A. D., Joint book reading makes for success in learning to read: A meta-analysis on intergenerational transmission of literacy. *Review of Educational Research,* 1995. 65: 1–21; Scarborough, H. S., & Dobrich, W., On the efficacy of reading to preschoolers. *Developmental Review,* 1994. 14: 245–302.

94. Arnold, D. H., Lonigan, C. J., Whitehurst, G. J., & Epstein, J. N., Accelerating language development through picture book reading: Replication and extension to a videotape training format. *Journal of Educational Psychology,* 1994. 86: 235–243; Whitehurst, G. J., *Long-term effects of an emergent literacy intervention in Head Start.* Paper presented at the biennial meeting of the Society for Research in Child Development. 1997 April: Washington, DC; Whitehurst, G. J., Falco, F., Lonigan, C. J., Fischel, J. E., DeBaryshe, B. D.,

Valdez-Menchaca, M. C., & Caulfield, M., Accelerating language development through picture-book reading. *Developmental Psychology,* 1988. 24: 552–558.

95. Crone, D., *Teachers' reading style and Head Start children's engagement in shared reading.* Paper presented at the Head Start National Research Conference. 1996 June: Washington, DC.

96. Crain-Thoreson, C., & Dale, P. S., Do early talkers become early readers? Linguistic precocity, preschool language, and emergent literacy. *Developmental Psychology,* 1992. 28: 421–429; Purcell-Gates, V., Stories, coupons, and the *TV Guide*: Relationships between home literacy experiences and emergent literacy knowledge. *Reading Research Quarterly,* 1996. 31: 406–428; Whitehurst, G. J., & Lonigan, C. J., Child development and emergent literacy. (See note 88.)

97. Lonigan, C. J., & Whitehurst, G. J., Relative efficacy of parent and teacher involvement in a shared-reading intervention for preschool children from low-income backgrounds. *Early Childhood Research Quarterly,* 1998. 13: 263–290.

98. See, for example, a study comparing caregiver–toddler interaction in four communities—two middle-income urban areas, one in Turkey and one in the United States; a Mayan town in Guatemala; and a tribal village in India. In the middle-income communities, parents often verbally instructed, using techniques that resembled the interaction that takes place in school, where their children will spend years preparing for adult life. In contrast, in the Mayan and Indian communities, adults expected toddlers to take greater responsibility for acquiring skills through keen observation. As the child showed attentive interest, caregivers offered responsive assistance, often nonverbally through demonstration and gesture—communication well suited to conditions in which young children learn by participating in daily activities of adult life. Rogoff, B., Mistry, J., Göncü, A., & Mosier, C., Guided participation in cultural activity by toddlers and caregivers. *Monographs of the Society for Research in Child Development,* 1993. 58: No. 8, Serial No. 236.

99. Kochanska, G., Mutually responsive orientation between mothers and their young children: Implications for early socialization. *Child Development,* 1997. 68: 94–112.

100. Grusec, J. E., & Goodnow, J. J., Impact of parental discipline methods on the child's internalization of values: A reconceptualization of current points of view. *Developmental Psychology,* 1994. 30: 4–19; Turiel, E., The development of morality. In W. Damon, series ed., & N. Eisenberg, vol. ed., *Handbook of child psychology: Vol. 3. Social emotional, and personality development,* 5th ed. 1998, New York: Wiley, pp. 863–932.

101. Fiese, B. H., & Marjinsky, K. A. T., Dinnertime stories: Connecting family practices with relationship beliefs and child adjustment. In B. H. Fiese, A. J. Sameroff, H. D. Grotevant, F. S. Wamboldt, S. Dickstein, & D. L. Fravel, eds., The stories that families tell: Narrative coherence, narrative interaction, and relationship beliefs. *Monographs of the Society for Research in Child Development,* 1999. 64: No. 2, Serial No. 257, pp. 52–68.

102. Blum-Kulka, S., *Dinner talk.* 1997, Mahwah, NJ: Erlbaum.

103. Ibid.

104. Bradley, R. H., & Caldwell, B. M., Home Observation for Measurement of the Environment: A revision of the preschool scale. *American Journal of Mental Deficiency,* 1979. 84: 235–244.

105. See, for example, Bradley, R. H., Caldwell, B. M., Rock, S. L., Ramey, C. T., Barnard, D. E., Gray, C., Hammond, M. A., Mitchell, S., Gottfried, A., Siegel, L., & Johnson, D. L., Home environment and cognitive development in the first 3 years of life: A collaborative study involving six sites and three ethnic groups in North America. *Developmental Psychology,* 1989. 25: 217–235; Klebanov, P. K., Brooks-Gunn, J., McCarton, C., &

McCormick, M. C., The contribution of neighborhood and family income to developmental test scores over the first three years of life. *Child Development,* 1999. 69: 1420–1436.

106. Comstock, G. A., The medium and society: The role of television in American life. In G. L. Berry & J. K. Asamen, eds., *Children and television.* 1993, Newbury Park, CA: Sage, pp. 319–340.

107. Anderson, D. R., Collins, P. A., Schmitt, K. L., & Jacobvitz, R. S., Stressful life events and television viewing. *Communication Research,* 1996. 23: 243–260; Gortmaker, S. L., Must, A., Sobol, A. M., Peterson, K., Colditz, G. A., & Dietz, W. H., Television viewing as a cause of increasing obesity among children in the United States, 1986–1990. *Archives of Pediatric and Adolescent Medicine,* 1996. 150: 356–362.

108. Flavell, J. H., Flavell, E. R., Green, F. L., & Korfmacher, J. E., Do young children think of television images as pictures or real objects? *Journal of Broadcasting and Electronic Media,* 1990. 34: 399–419.

109. Wright, J. C., Huston, A. C., Reitz, A. L., & Piemyat, S., Young children's perceptions of television reality: Determinants and developmental differences. *Developmental Psychology,* 1994. 30: 229–239.

110. Collins, W. A., Children's processing of television content: Implications for prevention of negative effects. *Prevention in Human Services,* 1983. 2: 53–66.

111. Purdie, S. I., Children's processing of motive information in a televised portrayal. *Dissertation Abstracts International,* 1979. 40, Section 2-B: 945–946.

112. Slaby, R. G., Roedell, W. C., Arezzo, D., & Henrix, K., *Early violence prevention.* 1995, Washington, DC: National Association for the Education of Young Children, p. 163.

113. Comstock, G., & Scharrer, E., *Television: What's on, who's watching, and what it means.* 1999, San Diego: Academic Press; Donnerstein, E., Slaby, R. G., & Eron, L. D., The mass media and youth aggression. In L. D. Eron, J. H. Gentry, & P. Schlegel, *Reason to hope: A psychological perspective on violence and youth.* 1994, Washington, DC: American Psychological Association, pp. 219–250; Gerbner, G., & Signorelli, N., *Violence profile, 1967 through 1988–1989. Enduring patterns.* Unpublished manuscript, Annenberg School of Communication. 1990, Philadelphia: University of Pennsylvania.

114. Zillman, D., Bryant, J., & Huston, A. C., *Media, family, and children.* 1994, Hillsdale, NJ: Erlbaum.

115. Levin, S. R., Petros, T. V., & Petrella, F. W., Preschoolers' awareness of television advertising. *Child Development,* 1982. 53: 933–937.

116. Hearold, S., A synthesis of 1,043 effects of television on social behavior. In G. Comstock, ed., *Public communications and behavior,* Vol. 1. 1986, New York: Academic Press, pp. 65–133.

117. Liss, M. B., Reinhardt, L. C., & Fredriksen, S., TV heroes: The impact of rhetoric and deeds. *Journal of Applied Developmental Psychology.* 1983, 4: 175–187.

118. Comstock, G., *Television and the American child.* 1991, Orlando, FL: Academic Press; St. Peters, M., Fitch, M., Huston, A. C., Wright, J. C., & Eakins, D., Television and families: What do young children watch with their parents? *Child Development,* 1991. 62: 1409–1423.

119. Desmond, R. J., Singer, J. L., Singer, D. G., Calam, R., & Colimore, K., Family mediation: Parental communication patterns and the influences of television on children. In J. Bryant, ed., *Television and the American family.* 1990, Hillsdale, NJ: Erlbaum, pp. 253–274.

120. Bronfenbrenner, U., *Two worlds of childhood: U.S. and U.S.S.R.* 1970, New York: Russell Sage Foundation, p. 95.

121. Hetherington, E. M., Bridges, M., & Insabella, G. M., What matters? What does not? Five perspectives on the association between marital transitions and children's adjustment. *American Psychologist*, 1998. 53: 167–184.

122. U.S. Department of Justice., *Crime in the United States*. 1999, Washington, DC: Government Printing Office.

123. Damon, W., *Greater expectations: Overcoming the culture of indulgence in America's homes and schools*. 1995, New York: The Free Press.

124. Hetherington, E. M., Bridges, M., & Insabella, G. M., What matters? What does not? Five perspectives on the association between marital transitions and children's adjustment. (See note 121.)

125. Masten, A. S., & Coatsworth, J. D., The development of competence in favorable and unfavorable environments: Lessons from research on successful children. *American Psychologist*. 1998. 53: 205–220.

126. From Hannah's correspondence to Eva and Charlie, 1999, June 5.

127. Schneider, B., & Stevenson, D., *The ambitious generation: America's teenagers, motivated but directionless*. 1999, New Haven: Yale University Press.

CHAPTER 3: WHY CHILDREN TALK TO THEMSELVES

1. Berk, L. E., Children's private speech: An overview of theory and the status of research. In R. M. Diaz & L. E. Berk, eds., *Private speech: From social interaction to self-regulation*. 1992, Hillsdale, NJ: Erlbaum, pp. 17–53; Berk, L. E., Why children talk to themselves. *Young Children*, 1986. 40 (5): 46–52.

2. Vygotsky, L. S., *Mind in society: The development of higher mental processes*, M. Cole, V. John-Steiner, S. Scribner, & E. Souberman, eds. and trans. [1930–1935] 1978, Cambridge, MA: Harvard University Press; Wertsch, J. V., *Voices of the mind: A sociocultural approach to mental action*. 1993, Cambridge, MA: Harvard University Press.

3. Berk, L. E., Why children talk to themselves. *Scientific American*, 1994. 271 (5): 60–65; Berk, L. E., & Garvin, R. A., Development of private speech among low-income Appalachian children. *Developmental Psychology*, 1984. 20: 271–286.

4. Piaget, J., *The language and thought of the child*, M. Gabain, trans. [1923] 1962, Cleveland, OH: Meridian.

5. Isaacs, S., *Intellectual growth in young children*. 1930, New York: Harcourt Brace.

6. McCarthy, D., The language development of the preschool child. *Monographs of the Institute of Child Welfare*, 1930. Serial No. 4.

7. Vygotsky, L. S., Thinking and speech. In R. Rieber & A. S. Carton, eds., N. Minick, trans., *The collected works of L. S. Vygotsky: Vol. 1, Problems of general psychology*. [1934] 1987, New York: Plenum, p. 45.

8. Ibid.

9. Ibid.

10. Ibid., p. 230.

11. Ibid.

12. Ibid.

13. Berk, L. E., & Garvin, R. A., Development of private speech among low-income Appalachian children. (See note 3.); Kohlberg, L., Yaeger, J., & Hjertholm, E., Private speech: Four studies and a review of theories. *Child Development*, 1968. 39: 691–736; Kirby, K. C., *The development of private speech among two- to five-year-olds in the naturalistic*

preschool setting. Paper presented at the biennial meeting of the Society for Research in Child Development. 1997 April: Washington, DC.

14. Berner, E. S., *Private speech and role-taking abilities in preschool children,* 1971. Unpublished doctoral dissertation, Harvard University, Cambridge, MA; Goudena, P. P., The social nature of private speech of preschoolers during problem solving. *International Journal of Behavioral Development,* 1987. 10: 187–206.

15. Ramirez, J. D., Functional differentiation of social and private speech: A dialogic approach. In R. M. Diaz & L. E. Berk, eds., *Private speech: From social interaction to self-regulation.* 1992, Hillsdale, NJ: Erlbaum, pp. 199–214.

16. Furrow, D., Social and private speech at two years. *Child Development,* 1984. 55: 355–362.

17. Furrow, D., Developmental trends in the differentiation of social and private speech. In R. M. Diaz & L. E. Berk, eds., *Private speech: From social interaction to self-regulation.* 1992, Hillsdale, NJ: Erlbaum, pp. 143–158.

18. Berk, L. E., & Garvin, R. A., Development of private speech among low-income Appalachian children. (See note 3.)

19. Ibid.

20. See, for example, Coles, R., *Children of crisis: Vol. 2. Migrants, sharecroppers, mountaineers.* 1967, Boston: Little, Brown; Hanson, J., & Stevic, R., *Appalachian students and guidance.* 1971, Boston: Houghton Mifflin; Looff, D. H., *Appalachia's children: The challenge of mental health.* 1971, Lexington: University of Kentucky Press; Weller, J., *Yesterday's people: Life in contemporary Appalachia.* 1965, Lexington: University of Kentucky Press.

21. Behrend, D. A., Rosengren, K. S., & Perlmutter, M., The relation between private speech and parental interactive style. In R. M. Diaz & L. E. Berk, eds., *Private speech: From social interaction to self-regulation.* 1992, Hillsdale, NJ: Erlbaum, pp. 85–100.

22. Berk, L. E., & Spuhl, S. T., Maternal interaction, private speech, and task performance in preschool children. *Early Childhood Research Quarterly,* 1995. 20: 271–286.

23. Vygotsky, L. S., *Thought and language,* A. Kozulin, trans. [1934] 1986, Cambridge, MA: MIT Press, p. 30.

24. Ibid.

25. Berk, L. E., Children's private speech: An overview of theory and the status of research. (See note 1.)

26. Nelson, K., ed., *Narratives from the crib.* 1989, Cambridge, MA: Harvard University Press, p. 72.

27. Nelson, K., Monologues in the crib. In K. Nelson, ed., *Narratives from the crib.* 1989, Cambridge, MA: Harvard University Press, pp. 1–23.

28. Levy, E., Monologue as development of the text-forming function of language. In K. Nelson, ed., *Narratives from the crib.* 1989, Cambridge, MA: Harvard University Press, pp. 123–170.

29. Weir, R., *Language in the crib.* 1962, The Hague: Mouton, p. 121.

30. Nelson, K., *Narratives from the crib,* p. 72. (See note 26.)

31. Dore, J., Monologue as a reenvoicement of dialogue. In K. Nelson, ed., *Narratives from the crib.* 1989, Cambridge, MA: Harvard University Press, pp. 231–260.

32. Wertsch, J. V., The regulation of human action and the given–new organization of private speech. In G. Zivin, ed., *The development of self-regulation through private speech.* 1979, New York: Wiley, pp. 79–98; Wertsch, J. V., The significance of dialogue in Vygotsky's account of social, egocentric, and inner speech. *Contemporary Educational Psychology,* 1980. 5: 150–162.

33. Turiel, E., The development of morality. In W. Damon, series ed., & N. Eisenberg, vol. ed., *Handbook of child psychology: Vol. 3. Social, emotional, and personality development,* 4th ed. 1998, New York: Wiley, pp. 307–332.

34. Gralinski, J. H., & Kopp, C. B., Everyday rules for behavior: Mothers' requests to young children. *Developmental Psychology,* 1993. 29: 573–584.

35. Ridderinkhof, K. R., & van der Molen, M. W., Mental resources, processing speed, and inhibitory control: A developmental perspective. *Biological Psychology,* 1997. 45: 241–261.

36. Bronowski, J., Human and animal languages. In J. Bronowski, ed., *A sense of the future.* 1977, Cambridge, MA: MIT Press, pp. 104–131.

37. Vaughn, B. E., Kopp, D. B., & Krakow, J. B., The emergence and consolidation of self-control from eighteen to thirty months of age: Normative trends and individual differences. *Child Development,* 1984. 55: 990–1004.

38. Gralinski, J. H., & Kopp, C. B., Everyday rules for behavior: Mothers' requests to young children. (See note 34.)

39. Kochanska, G., Mutually responsive orientation between mothers and their young children: Implications for early socialization. *Child Development,* 1997. 68: 94–112.

40. Ibid.

41. Bandura, A., Social cognitive theory of moral thought and action. In W. M. Kurtines & J. L. Gewirtz, eds., *Handbook of moral behavior and development: Vol. 1.* 1991, Hillsdale, NJ: Erlbaum, pp. 45–103; Toner, I. J., & Smith, R. A., Age and overt verbalization in delay and maintenance behavior in children. *Journal of Experimental Child Psychology,* 1977. 24: 123–128.

42. Saarni, C., Mumme, D. L., & Campos, J. J., Emotional development: Action, communication, and understanding. In N. Eisenberg, ed., *Handbook of child psychology: Vol. 3. Social, emotional, and personality development,* 5th ed. 1998, New York: Wiley, pp. 237–309.

43. Stipek, D. J., Recchia, S., & McClintic, S., Self-evaluation in young children. *Monographs of the Society for Research in Child Development,* 1992. 57: No. 1, Serial No. 226.

44. Harter, S., & Whitesell, N., Developmental changes in children's understanding of simple, multiple, and blended emotion concepts. In C. Saarni & P. Harris, eds., *Children's understanding of emotion.* 1989, Cambridge: Cambridge University Press, pp. 81–116.

45. Kochanska, G., Socialization and temperament in the development of guilt and conscience. *Child Development,* 1991. 62: 1379–1392.

46. Kochanska, G., Children's temperament, mothers' discipline, and security of attachment: Multiple pathways to emerging internalization. *Child Development,* 1995. 66: 597–615; Kochanska, G., Multiple pathways to conscience for children with different temperaments: From toddlerhood to age 5. *Developmental Psychology,* 1997. 33: 228–240.

47. Thompson, R. A., Emotion regulation: A theme in search of a definition. In N. A. Fox, ed., The development of emotion regulation: Biological and behavioral considerations. *Monographs of the Society for Research in Child Development,* 1994. 59: No. 2–3, Serial No. 240.

48. Thompson, R. A., On emotion and self-regulation. In R. A. Thompson, ed., *Nebraska Symposium on Motivation, Vol 36.* 1990, Lincoln: University of Nebraska Press, pp. 383–483.

49. Kliewer, W., Fearnow, M. D., & Miller, P. A., Coping socialization in middle childhood: Tests of maternal and paternal influences. *Child Development,* 1996. 67: 2339–2357.

50. Aldwin, C., *Stress, coping, and development.* 1994, New York: Guilford; Compas, B., Phares, V., & Ledoux, N., Stress and coping: Preventive interventions for children and adolescents. In L. Bond & B. Compas, eds., *Primary prevention in the schools.* 1989, London: Sage, pp. 319–340.

51. Saarni, C., Emotional competence and self-regulation in childhood. In P. Salovey & D. J. Sluyter, eds., *Emotional development and emotional intelligence.* 1997, New York: Basic Books, pp. 35–66.

52. Eisenberg, M., Fabes, R. A., Shepard, S. A., Murphy, B. C., Guthrie, I. K., Jones, S., Friedman, J., Poulin, R., & Maszk, P., Contemporaneous and longitudinal prediction of children's social functioning from regulation and emotionality. *Child Development,* 1997. 68: 642–664; Eisenberg, N., Guthrie, I. K., Fabes, R. A., Reiser, M., Murphy, B. C., Holgren, R., Maszk, R., & Losoya, S., The relations of regulation and emotionality to resiliency and competent social functioning in elementary school children. *Child Development,* 1997. 68: 295–311.

53. Bates, J. E., Wachs, T. D., & Emde, R. N., Toward practical uses for biological concepts. In J. E. Bates, & T. D. Wachs, eds., *Temperament: Individual differences at the interface of biology and behavior.* 1994, Washington, DC: American Psychological Association, pp. 275–306; Chess, S., & Thomas, A., *Origins and evolution of behavior disorders.* 1984, New York: Brunner/Mazel.

54. Saville-Troike, M., Private speech: Evidence for second language learning strategies during the 'silent' period. *Journal of Child Language,* 1988. 15: 567–590.

55. Ibid., p. 580.

56. Ibid., p. 583.

57. Ibid., p. 585.

58. Olszewski, P., Individual differences in preschool children's production of verbal fantasy play. *Merrill-Palmer Quarterly,* 1987. 33: 69–86; Rubin, K. H. *The private speech of preschoolers who vary with regard to sociability.* Paper presented at the annual meeting of the American Educational Research Association. 1982: New York.

59. Harrist, A. W., Zaia, A. F., Bates, J. E., Dodge, K. A., & Pettit, G. S., Subtypes of social withdrawal in early childhood: Sociometric status and social–cognitive differences across four years. *Child Development,* 1997. 68: 278–294; Wentzel, K. R., & Asher, S. R., The academic lives of neglected, rejected, popular, and controversial children. *Child Development,* 1995. 66: 754–763.

60. Taylor, M., *Imaginary companions and the children who create them.* 1999, New York: Oxford University Press.

61. Ibid., p. 8.

62. Ibid., pp. 14–15.

63. Ibid., p. 22.

64. Mauro, J., *The friend that only I can see: A longitudinal investigation of children's imaginary companions,* 1991. Unpublished doctoral dissertation, University of Oregon; Taylor, M., *Imaginary companions and the children who create them.* (See note 60.)

65. Laursen, B., Hartup, W. W., & Koplas, A. L., Toward understanding peer conflict. *Merrill-Palmer Quarterly,* 1996. 42: 76–102; Rose, A. J., & Asher, S. R., Children's goals and strategies in response to conflicts within a friendship. *Developmental Psychology,* 1999. 35: 69–79.

66. Singer, J. L., Imagination and waiting ability in young children. *Journal of Personality,* 1961. 29: 396–413.

67. Taylor, M., & Carlson, S. M., The relation between individual differences in fantasy and theory of mind. *Child Development,* 1997. 68: 436–455.

68. Taylor, M., Cartwright, B. S., & Carlson, S. M., A developmental investigation of children's imaginary companions. *Developmental Psychology,* 1993. 29: 276–285.

69. Bach, L. M., Chang, A. S., & Berk, L. E., *The role of imaginary companions in the development of social skills and play maturity.* Paper presented at the biennial meeting of the Society for Research in Child Development. 1999: Albuquerque, NM.

70. Krafft, K. C., & Berk, L. E., Private speech in two preschools: Significance of open-ended activities and make-believe play for verbal self-regulation. *Early Childhood Research Quarterly,* 1998. 13: 637–658.

71. Saville-Troike, M., Private speech: Evidence for second language learning strategies during the 'silent' period. (See note 54.)

72. Berk, L. E., Children's private speech: An overview of theory and the status of research. (See note 1.)

73. Berk, L. E., & Spuhl, S. T., Maternal interaction, private speech, and task performance in preschool children. (See note 22.)

74. Behrend, D. A., Rosengren, K. S., & Perlmutter, M., A new look at children's private speech: The effects of age, task difficulty, and parent presence. *International Journal of Behavioral Development,* 1989. 12: 305–320.

75. Behrend, D. A., Rosengren, K. S., & Perlmutter, M., The relation between private speech and parental interactive style. (See note 21.); Goudena, P. P., The social nature of private speech of preschoolers during problem solving. (See note 14.)

76. In a recent study, Katrina Gillingham and I sought to determine whether 2- to 6-year-olds would continue to engage in play in a laboratory, with an adult present, after we asked them not to talk during the play period because a class next door needed things "perfectly quiet." Although the children reduced their self-talk to whispers, no child in the study was able to continue playing without talking to himself or herself. See Gillingham, K., & Berk, L. E. *The role of private speech in the early development of sustained attention.* Paper presented at the biennial meeting of the Society for Research in Child Development. 1995: Indianapolis.

77. Berk, L. E., & Garvin, R. A., Development of private speech among low-income Appalachian children. (See note 2.); Berk, L. E., Relationship of elementary school children's private speech to behavioral accompaniment to task, attention, and task performance. *Developmental Psychology,* 1986. 22: 671–680; Bivens, J. A., & Berk, L. E., A longitudinal study of the development of elementary school children's private speech. *Merrill-Palmer Quarterly,* 1990. 36: 443–463.

78. Beaudichon, J., Nature and instrumental function of private speech in problem solving situations. *Merrill-Palmer Quarterly,* 1973. 19: 117–135; Fuson, K. C., The development of self-regulating aspects of speech: A review. In G. Zivin, ed., *The development of self-regulation through private speech.* 1979, New York: Wiley, pp. 135–217.

79. Azmitia, M., Expertise, private speech, and the development of self-regulation. In R. M. Diaz & L. E. Berk, eds., *Private speech: From social interaction to self-regulation.* 1992, Hillsdale, NJ: Erlbaum, pp. 101–122; Behrend, D. A., Rosengren, K. S., & Perlmutter, M., A new look at children's private speech: The effects of age, task difficulty, and parent presence. (See note 74.); Bivens, J. A., & Berk, L. E., A longitudinal study of the development of elementary school children's private speech. (See note 77.); Gaskill, M. N., & Diaz, R. M., The relation between private speech and cognitive performance. *Infancia y Aprendizaje,* 1991. 53: 45–58.

80. Bivens, J. A., & Berk, L. E., A longitudinal study of the development of elementary school children's private speech. (See note 77.); Berk, L. E., Relationship of elementary school children's private speech to behavioral accompaniment to task, attention, and task performance. (See note 77.)

81. Berk, L. E., & Spuhl, S. T., Maternal interaction, private speech, and task performance in preschool children. (See note 22.); Duncan, R. M., & Pratt, M. W., Microgenetic change in the quantity and quality of preschoolers' private speech. *International Journal of Behavioral Development,* 1997. 20: 367–383.

82. Krafft, K. C., & Berk, L. E., Private speech in two preschools: Significance of open-ended activities and make-believe play for verbal self-regulation. (See note 70.)

83. See, for example, Berk, L. E., & Spuhl, S. T., Maternal interaction, private speech, and task performance in preschool children. (See note 22.); Frauenglass, M. H., & Diaz, R. M., Self-regulatory functions of children's private speech: A critical analysis of recent challenges to Vygotsky's theory. *Developmental Psychology,* 1985. 21: 357–364.

84. Comparisons across studies that have used identical observational procedures yield this estimate of the extent to which private speech rises with the onset of formal schooling. See Berk, L. E., Relationship of elementary school children's private speech to behavioral accompaniment to task, attention, and task performance. (See note 77.); Bivens, J. A., & Berk, L. E., A longitudinal study of the development of elementary school children's private speech. (See note 77.); and Krafft, K. C., & Berk, L. E., Private speech in two preschools: Significance of open-ended activities and make-believe play for verbal self-regulation. (See note 70.)

85. See Chapter 1, page 11–12, and Chapter 2, page 40.

86. Deutsch, F., & Stein, A. H., The effects of personal responsibility and task interruption on the private speech of preschoolers. *Human Development,* 1972. 15: 310–324; Diaz, R. M., Padilla, K. A., & Weathersby, E. K., The effects of bilingualism on preschoolers' private speech. *Early Childhood Research Quarterly,* 1991. 6: 377–393; Frauenglass, M. H., & Diaz, R. M., Self-regulatory functions of children's private speech: A critical analysis of recent challenges to Vygotsky's theory. (See note 83.)

87. Berk, L. E., Relationship of elementary school children's private speech to behavioral accompaniment to task, attention, and task performance. (See note 77); Kohlberg, L., Yaeger, J., & Hjertholm, E., Private speech: Four studies and a review of theories. (See note 13.)

88. Berk, L. E., & Landau, S., Private speech of learning disabled and normally achieving children in classroom academic and laboratory contexts. *Child Development,* 1993. 64: 556–571. Berk, L. E., & Landau, S., *Private speech in the face of academic challenge: The failure of impulsive children to "get their act together."* Paper presented at the biennial meeting of the Society for Research in Child Development. 1997 April: Washington, DC; Berk, L. E., & Potts, M. K., Development and functional significance of private speech among attention-deficit hyperactivity disordered and normal boys. *Journal of Abnormal Child Psychology,* 1991. 19: 357–377.

89. Berk, L. E., & Garvin, R. A., Development of private speech among low-income Appalachian children. (See note 3.); Berk, L. E., & Landau, S., Private speech of learning disabled and normally achieving children in classroom academic and laboratory contexts. (See note 88.); Kohlberg, L., Yaeger, J., & Hjertholm, E., Private speech: Four studies and a review of theories. (See note 13.)

90. Goudena, P. P., The problem of abbreviation and internalization of private speech. In R. M. Diaz & L. E. Berk, eds., *Private speech: From social interaction to self-regulation.* 1992, Hillsdale, NJ: Erlbaum, pp. 215–224; Wertsch, J. V., The regulation of human action and the given–new organization of private speech. In G. Zivin, ed., *The development of self-regulation through private speech.* 1979, New York: Wiley, pp. 79–98.

91. Diaz, R. M., & Berk, L. E., A Vygotskian critique of self-instructional training. *Development and Psychopathology,* 1995. 7: 369–392.

92. Piper, W., *The little engine that could.* 1930, New York: Platt, pp. 18–19.

93. Willoughby, E. M., *Boris and the monsters.* 1980, Boston: Houghton Mifflin, p. 24.

94. Ibid., p. 29.

95. Ramirez, J. D., The functional differentiation of social and private speech: A dialogic approach. In R. M. Diaz & L. E. Berk, eds., *Private speech: From social interaction to self-regulation.* (See note 15.)

CHAPTER 4: LEARNING THROUGH MAKE-BELIEVE PLAY

1. Erikson, E., *Childhood and society.* 1950, New York: Norton.

2. Garvey, C., *Play.* 1990, Cambridge, MA: Harvard University Press.

3. Piaget, J., *Play, dreams, and imitation in childhood.* 1932, New York: Norton.

4. Piaget, J., Response to Brian Sutton-Smith. *Psychological Review,* 1966. 73: 111–112.

5. Vygotsky, L. S., *Mind in society: The development of higher mental processes,* M. Cole, V. John-Steiner, S. Scribner, & E. Souberman, eds. and trans. [1930–1935] 1978, Cambridge, MA: Harvard University Press, p. 101.

6. Ibid., p. 102.

7. Mischel, W., & Baker, N., Cognitive appraisals and transformations in delay behavior. *Journal of Personality and Social Psychology,* 1975. 31: 254–261.

8. Vygotsky, L. S., *Mind in society: The development of higher mental processes,* p. 97. (See note 5.)

9. Corrigan, R., A developmental sequence of actor–object pretend play in young children. *Merrill-Palmer Quarterly,* 1987. 33: 87–106; O'Reilly, A. W., Using representations: Comprehension and production of actions with imagined objects. *Child Development,* 1995. 66: 999–1010.

10. Vygotsky, L. S., *Mind in society: The development of higher mental processes,* p. 98. (See note 5.)

11. Vygotsky, L. S., Imagination and creativity in childhood. *Soviet Psychology,* [1930] 1990. 28: 64–96.

12. Sternberg, R. J., & Lubart, T. I., Investing in creativity. *American Psychologist,* 1996. 51: 677–688.

13. Vygotsky, L. S., *Mind in society: The development of higher mental processes.* (See note 5.)

14. Ibid., p. 99.

15. Ibid., p. 100.

16. Seliger, M. & Kahn, L., eds., *When they came to take my father: Voices of the Holocaust.* 1996, New York: Arcade, p. 34.

17. Vygotsky, L. S., *Mind in society: The development of higher mental processes.* (See note 5.)

18. Ibid., pp. 102–103.

19. Connolly, J. A., & Doyle, A. B., 1984. Relations of social fantasy play to social competence in preschoolers. *Developmental Psychology,* 1984. 20: 797–806; Elias, C. L., & Berk, L. E., *Self-regulation in young children: Is there a role for sociodramatic play?* Paper presented at the biennial meeting of the Society for Research in Child Development. 1999 April: Albuquerque, NM; Singer, D. G., & Singer, J. L., *The house of make-believe.* 1990, Cambridge, MA: Harvard University Press.

20. Ruff, H. A., & Lawson, K. R., Development of sustained, focused attention in young children during free play. *Developmental Psychology,* 1990. 26: 85–93; Ruff, H. A., Lawson, K. R., Parinello, R., & Weissberg, R., Long-term stability of individual differences in sustained attention in the early years. *Child Development,* 1990. 61: 60–75.

21. Lawson, K. R., Parinello, R., & Weissberg, R., Long-term stability of individual differences in sustained attention in the early years. (See note 20.)

22. Kirby, K. C., *Development of private speech among 2- to 5-year-olds in the naturalistic preschool setting.* Poster presented at the biennial meeting of the Society for Research in Child Development. 1997 April: Washington, DC.

23. Newman, L. S., Intentional and unintentional memory in young children: Remembering versus playing. *Journal of Experimental Child Psychology,* 1990. 50: 243–258.

24. Roskos, K., & Neuman, S. B., Play as an opportunity for literacy. In O. N. Saracho & B. Spodek, eds., *Multiple perspectives on play in early childhood education.* 1998, Albany: State University of New York Press, pp. 101–102.

25. See, for example, Pellegrini, A. D., & Galda, L., The effects of thematic-fantasy play training on the development of children's story comprehension. *American Educational Research Journal,* 1982. 19: 443–452; Silvern, S. B., Taylor, J. B., Williamson, P. A., Surbeck, E., & Kelley, M. F., Young children's story recall as a product of play, story familiarity, and adult intervention. *Merrill-Palmer Quarterly,* 1986. 32: 73–86.

26. Pellegrini, A. D., The construction of cohesive text by preschoolers in two play contexts. *Discourse Processes,* 1982. 5: 101–108; Pellegrini, A. D., The narrative organization of children's fantasy play. *Educational Psychology,* 1985. 5: 17–25.

27. Dickinson, D., & Moreton, J., *Predicting specific kindergarten literacy skills from three-year-olds' preschool experiences.* Paper presented at the biennial meeting of the Society for Research in Child Development. 1991 April: Seattle, WA.

28. Ervin-Tripp, S., Play in language development. In B. Scales, M. Almy, A. Nicolopoulou, & S. Ervin-Tripp, eds., *Play and the social context of development in early care and education.* 1991, New York: Teachers College Press, p. 90.

29. Bergen, D., & Mauer, D., Symbolic play, phonological awareness, and literacy skills at three age levels. In K. A. Roskos & J. F. Christie, eds., *Play and literacy in early childhood: Research from multiple perspectives.* 2000, Mahwah, NJ: Erlbaum, pp. 45–62.

30. Galda, L., Pellegrini, A., & Cox, S., Preschoolers' emergent literacy: A short-term longitudinal study. *Research in the Teaching of English,* 1989. 23: 292–310; Pelegrini, A. D., & Galda, L., Longitudinal relations among preschoolers' symbolic play, metalinguistic verbs, and emergent literacy. In J. Christie, ed., *Play and early literacy development.* 1991, Albany: State University of New York Press, pp. 11–33.

31. Ibid.

32. Dyson, A. H., Emerging alphabetic literacy in school contexts: Toward defining the gap between school curriculum and child mind. *Written Communication,* 1984. 1: 5–55.

33. Moshman, D., & Franks, B. A., Development of the concept of inferential validity. *Child Development,* 1986. 57: 153–165.

34. Dias, M. G., & Harris, P. L., The influence of the imagination on reasoning by young children. *British Journal of Developmental Psychology,* 1990. 8: 305–318.

35. Flavell, J. H., Green, F. L., & Flavell, E. R., Development of knowledge about the appearance–reality distinction. *Monographs of the Society for Research in Child Development,* 1987. 51: No. 1, Serial No. 212.

36. Custer, W. L., A comparison of young children's understanding of contradictory representations in pretense, memory, and belief. *Child Development,* 1996. 67: 678–688.

37. Schwebel, D. C., Rosen, C. S., & Singer, J. L., Preschoolers' pretend play and theory of mind: The role of jointly constructed pretense. *British Journal of Developmental Psychology,* 1999. 17: 333–348.

38. Hughes, C., & Dunn, J., Understanding mind and emotion: Longitudinal associations with mental-state talk between young friends. *Developmental Psychology,* 1998. 34: 1027–1037.

39. Youngblade, L. M., & Dunn, J., Individual differences in young children's pretend play with mother and sibling: Links to relationships and understanding of other people's feelings and beliefs. *Child Development*, 1995. 66: 1472–1492.

40. Ibid.

41. See, for example, Fodor, J. A., A theory of the child's theory of mind. *Cognition*, 1992. 44: 283–296; Trawick-Smith, J., A qualitative analysis of metaplay in the preschool years. *Early Childhood Research Quarterly*, 1998. 13: 433–452.

42. Some researchers take an intermediate position, viewing pretend play as a vital basis for the preschool child's beginning grasp of mental representation. See, for example, Leslie, A. M., Some implications for mechanisms underlying the child's theory of mind. In J. W. Astington, P. L., Harris, & E. R. Olson, eds., *Developing theories of mind.* 1988, New York: Cambridge University Press, pp. 19–46. Others believe that preschoolers do not regard pretend play as involving the mind at all but rather think of it as a type of action. They argue that an appreciation of pretend as representation is not present until 6 to 8 years of age. See, for example, Lillard, A. S., Playing with a theory of mind. In O. N. Saracho & B. Spodek, eds., *Multiple perspectives on play in early childhood education.* 1998, Albany: State University of New York Press, pp. 11–33.

43. Lillard, A. S., Young children's conceptualization of pretend: Action or mental representational state? *Child Development*, 1993. 64: 372–386.

44. Lillard, A. S., Body or mind: Young children's categorization of pretense. *Child Development*, 1996. 67: 1717–1734.

45. Carpendale, J. I., & Chandler, M. J., On the distinction between false belief understanding and subscribing to an interpretive theory of mind. *Child Development*, 1996. 67: 1686–1706; Flavell, J. H., Green, F. L., Flavell, E. R., & Grossman, J. B., The development of children's knowledge about inner speech. *Child Development*, 1997. 68: 39–47; Taylor, M., Cartwright, B. S., & Bowden, T., Perspective taking and theory of mind: Do children predict interpretive diversity as a function of differences in observers' knowledge? *Child Development*, 1991. 62: 1334–1351.

46. Chandler, M. J., & Carpendale, J. I., Inching toward a mature theory of mind. In M. Ferrari & R. J. Sternberg, eds., *Self-awareness: Its nature and development.* 1996, New York: Guilford, pp. 148–190.

47. Krafft, K. C., & Berk, L. E., Private speech in two preschools: Significance of open-ended activities and make-believe play for verbal self-regulation.

48. Gillingham, K., & Berk, L. E. *The role of private speech in the early development of sustained attention.* Paper presented at the biennial meeting of the Society for Research in Child Development. 1995: Indianapolis.

49. Elias, C. L., & Berk, L. E., *Self-regulation in young children: Is there a role for sociodramatic play?* (See note 19.)

50. Singer, D. G., & Singer, J. L., *The house of make-believe.* (See note 19.)

51. Ibid.

52. Curie, E., *Madame Curie.* 1938, New York: Doubleday, Doran; Quinn, S., *Marie Curie, a life.* 1995, New York: Simon & Schuster.

53. Quinn, S., *Marie Curie, a life,* p. 27. (See note 19.)

54. Wagner-Martin, L., *Sylvia Plath: A literary life.* 1999, New York: St. Martin's Press.

55. McCabe, J., *Charlie Chaplin.* 1978, New York: Doubleday.

56. Singer, D. G., & Singer, J. L., *The house of make-believe,* p. 288. (See note 19.)

57. See, for example, El'konin, D., *Psikhologia igri* (The psychology of play). 1978, Moscow: Izdatel'stvo Pedagogika; Garvey, C., *Play,* 1990, Cambridge, MA: Harvard University Press;

Haight, W. L., & Miller, P. J., *Pretending at home: Early development in a sociocultural context.* 1993, Albany: State University of New York Press.

58. Haight, W. L., & Miller, P. J., *Pretending at home: Early development in a sociocultural context.* (See note 57.)

59. See also, Miller, P., & Garvey, C., Mother–baby role play: Its origins in social support. In I. Bretherton, ed., *Symbolic play.* 1984, New York: Academic Press, pp. 101–130; Smolucha, L., & Smolucha, F., Post-Piagetian perspectives on pretend play. In O. N. Saracho & B. Spodek, eds., *Multiple perspectives on play in early childhood education.* 1998, Albany: State University of New York Press, pp. 34–58.

60. Kavanaugh, R. D., Whitington, S., & Cerbone, M. J., Mothers' use of fantasy in speech to young children. *Journal of Child Language,* 1983. 10: 45–55.

61. Haight, W. L., & Miller, P. J., *Pretending at home: Early development in a sociocultural context.* (See note 57.)

62. Ibid.

63. Ibid.

64. Ibid.

65. See, for example, McGhee, P. E., *Humor: Its origin and development.* 1979, San Francisco, CA: Freeman; Shultz, T. R., A cognitive-developmental analysis of humour. In A. J. Chapman & H. C. Fox, eds., *Humour and laughter: Theory, research, and applications.* 1976, New Brunswick, NJ: Transaction, pp. 11–36.

66. Johnson, K. E., & Mervis, C. B., First steps in the emergence of verbal humor: A case study. *Infant Behavior and Development,* 1997. 20: 187–196.

67. Dunn, J., & Woodking, C., Play in the home and its implications for learning. In B. Tizard & R. Dienstbier, eds., *Nebraska Symposia on Motivation,* Vol. 36. 1977. London: Heinemann, pp. 45–58; Fiese, B., Playful relationships: A contextual analysis of mother–toddler interaction and symbolic play. *Child Development,* 1990. 61: 1648–1656; Haight, W. L., & Miller, P. J., *Pretending at home: Early development in a sociocultural context.* (See note 57); O'Connell, B., & Bretherton, I., Toddlers' play alone and with mother: The role of maternal guidance. In I. Bretherton, ed., *Symbolic play.* 1984, New York: Academic Press, pp. 337–368; Slade, A., A longitudinal study of maternal involvement and symbolic play during the toddler period. *Child Development,* 1986. 58: 367–375; O'Reilly, A. W., & Bornstein, M. H., Caregiver–child interaction in play. In M. H. Bornstein & A. W. O'Reilly, *New directions for child development,* No. 59. 1993, San Francisco: Jossey-Bass, pp. 55–66; Tamis-LeMonda, C. S., & Bornstein, M. H., Habituation and maternal encouragement of attention in infancy as predictors of toddler language, play and representational competence. *Child Development,* 1989. 60: 738–751; Zukow, P. G., The relationship between interaction with the caregiver and the emergence of play activities during the one-word period. *British Journal of Developmental Psychology,* 1986. 4: 223–234.

68. Fiese, B., Playful relationships: A contextual analysis of mother–toddler interaction and symbolic play. (See note 67.)

69. Stilson, S. R., & Harding, C. G., Early social context as it relates to symbolic play: A longitudinal investigation. *Merrill-Palmer Quarterly,* 1997. 43: 682–693.

70. Feldman, R., & Greenbaum, C. W., Affect regulation and synchrony in mother–infant play as precursors to the development of symbolic competence. *Infant Mental Health Journal,* 1997. 18: 4–23.

71. Rubin, K. H., Fein, G. G., & Vandenberg, B., Play. In P. Mussen, series ed., & E. M. Hetherington, vol. ed., *Handbook of child psychology: Vol. 4. Socialization, personality, and social development,* 4th ed. 1983, New York: Wiley, pp. 693–744.

72. Elicker, J., Englund, M., & Sroufe, L. A., Predicting peer competence and peer relationships in childhood from early parent–child relationships. In R. D. Parke & G. W. Ladd, eds., *Family–peer relationships: Modes of linkage.* 1992, Hillsdale, NJ: Erlbaum, pp. 77–102.

73. Piaget, J., *The language and thought of the child*, M. Gaban, trans. [1923] 1962, Cleveland, OH: Meridian.

74. Forman, E. A., & McPhail, J., A Vygotskian perspective on children's collaborative problem-solving activities. In E. A. Forman, N. Minick, & C. A. Stone, eds., *Contexts for learning.* 1993, New York: Cambridge University Press, pp. 323–347; Kobayashi, Y., Conceptual acquisition and change through social interaction. *Human Development,* 1994. 37: 233–241.

75. Göncü, A., Development of intersubjectivity in the dyadic play of preschoolers. *Early Childhood Research Quarterly,* 1993. 8: 99–116.

76. Howes, C., & Clemente, D., Adult socialization of children's play in child care. In H. Goelman, ed., *Children's play in day care settings.* 1994, Albany: State University of New York Press, pp. 20–36.

77. File, N., The teacher as guide of children's competence with peers. *Child & Youth Care Quarterly,* 1993. 22: 351–360.

78. Ibid.

79. Tudge, J. R. H., & Rogoff, B., Peer influences on cognitive development: Piagetian and Vygotskian perspectives. In M. H. Bornstein & J. S. Bruner, eds., *Interaction in human development.* 1987, Hillsdale, NJ: Erlbaum, pp. 17–40.

80. Bronson, M. B., *The right stuff for children birth to 8: Selecting play materials to support development.* 1995, Washington, DC: National Association for the Education of Young Children. To order this book, contact NAEYC, 1509 16TH Street, N.W., Washington, DC 20036-1426, phone (800) 424-2460.

81. Huston-Stein, A. C., Fox, S., Greer, D., Watkins, B. A., & Whitaker, J., The effects of action and violence on children's social behavior. *Journal of Genetic Psychology,* 1981. 138: 183–191; Singer, J. L., & Singer, D. G., "Barney and Friends" as entertainment and education: Evaluating the quality and effectiveness of a television series for preschool children. In J. K. Asamen & G. L. Berry, eds., *Research paradigms, television, and social behavior.* 1998, Thousand Oaks, CA: Sage, pp. 305–367; Tower, R. B., Singer, D. G., Singer, J. L., & Biggs, A., Differential effects of television programming on preschoolers' cognition, imagination, and social play. *American Journal of Orthopsychiatry,* 1979. 49: 265–281.

82. Bronson, M. B., *The right stuff for children birth to 8: Selecting play materials to support development.* (See note 80.)

83. McLoyd, V. C., Warren, D., & Thomas, E. A. C., Anticipatory and fantastic role enactment in preschool triads. *Developmental Psychology,* 1984. 20: 807–814.

84. Neuman, S. B., & Roskos, K., Literacy objects as cultural tools: Effects on children's literacy behaviors in play. *Reading Research Quarterly,* 1992. 27: 203–225.

85. Smith, P. K., & Connolly, K. J., *The ecology of preschool behaviour.* 1980, Cambridge, England: Cambridge University Press.

86. Caldera, Y. M., Huston, A. C., & O'Brien, M., Social interactions and play patterns of parents and toddlers with feminine, masculine, and neutral toys. *Child Development,* 1989. 60: 70–76; Ruble, D. N., & Martin, C. L., Gender development. In W. Damon, series ed., & N. Eisenberg, vol. ed., *Handbook of child psychology: Vol. 3. Social, emotional, and personality development,* 5th ed. 1998, New York: Wiley, pp. 933–1016.

87. Repetti, R. L., Determinants of children's sex stereotyping: Parental sex-role traits and television viewing. *Personality and Social Psychology Bulletin,* 1984: 10: 457–468.

88. Kinsman, C. A., & Berk, L. E., Joining the block and housekeeping areas: Changes in play and social behavior. *Young Children,* 1979. 35(1): 66–75.

89. Roopnarine, J. L., Hossain, Z., Gill, P., & Brophy, H., Play in the East Indian context. In J. L. Roopnarine, J. E. Johnson, & F. H. Hooper, eds., *Children's play in diverse cultures.* 1994, Albany: State University of New York Press, pp. 9–30.

90. Goldstein, J., Aggressive toy play. In A. D. Pellegrini, ed., *The future of play theory.* 1995, Albany: State University of New York Press, pp. 127–147.

91. See, for example, Goldstein, J. H., Sex differences in toy play and use of video games. In J. H. Goldstein, ed., *Toys, play, and child development.* 1994, New York: Cambridge University Press, pp. 110–129; Irwin, A. R., & Gross, A. M., Cognitive tempo, violent video games, and aggressive behavior in young boys. *Journal of Family Violence,* 1995. 10: 337–350.

92. Kinder, M., Contextualizing video game violence: From Teenage Mutant Ninja Turtles to Mortal Kombat 2. In P. M. Greenfield & R. R. Cocking, eds., *Interacting with video.* 1996, Norwood, NJ: Ablex, pp. 25–37.

93. Phillips, C. A., Rolls, S., Rouse, A. & Griffiths, M. D., Home video game playing in schoolchildren—A study of incidence and patterns of play. *Journal of Adolescence,* 1995. 18: 687–691.

94. Wright, J. C., & Huston, A. C., *Effects of educational TV viewing of lower income preschoolers on academic skills, school readiness, and school adjustment one to three years later. Report to Children's Television Workshop.* 1994, Center for Research on the Influences of Television on Children, University of Kansas, Lawrence.

95. Kohut, A., *The role of technology in American life.* 1994, Los Angeles: Times Mirror Center for the People and the Press; Kraut, R., Patterson, M., Lundmark, V., Kiesler, S., Mukopadhyay, T., & Scherlis, W., Internet paradox: A social technology that reduces social involvement and psychological wellbeing? *American Psychologist,* 1998. 53: 1017–1031.

96. Bailey, D. A., & Rasmussen, R. L., Sport and the child: Physiological and skeletal issues. In F. L. Smoll & R. E. Smith, eds., *Children and youth in sport: A biopsychological perspective.* 1996, Dubuque, IA: Brown & Benchmark, pp. 187–199.

97. Smith, R. E., & Smoll, F. L., The coach as a focus of research and intervention in youth sports. In F. L. Smoll & R. E. Smith, eds., *Children and youth in sport: A biopsychological perspective.* 1996, Dubuque, IA: Brown & Benchmark.

98. Smith, R. E., & Smoll, F. L., Coaching the coaches: Youth sports as a scientific and applied behavior setting. *Current Directions in Psychological Science,* 1997. 6: 16–21.

CHAPTER 5: HELPING CHILDREN WITH DEFICITS AND DISABILITIES

1. Vygotsky, L. S., *The collected works of L. S. Vygotsky: Vol. 2. The fundamentals of defectology,* R. W. Rieber & A. S. Carton, eds., J. E. Knox & C. B. Stevens, trans. 1993, New York: Plenum.

2. Ibid.

3. Ibid.

4. Goldin-Meadow, S., Mylander, C., & Butcher, C., The resilience of combinatorial structure at the word level: Morphology in self-styled gesture systems. *Cognition,* 1995. 56: 88–96; Goldin-Meadow, S., Butcher, C., Mylander, C., & Dodge, M., Nouns and verbs in a self-styled gesture system: What's in a name? *Cognitive Psychology,* 1994. 27: 259–319.

5. Morford, J. P., & Goldin-Meadow, S., From here and now to there and then: The development of displaced reference in homesign and English. *Child Development*, 1997. 68, 420–435.

6. Kegl, J., Senghas, A., & Coppola, M., Creation through contact: Sign language emergence and sign language change in Nicaragua. In M. DeGraff, ed., *Language creation and language change: Creolization, diachrony, and development.* 1999: Cambridge, MA: MIT Press, pp. 179–237.

7. Keller, H. A., *Story of my life.* 1968, New York: Lancer.

8. Ibid., p. 35.

9. Keller, H. A., *My religion.* 1927, Garden City, NY: Doubleday, p. 153; Lash, J. P., *Helen and teacher.* 1980, New York: Delacorte.

10. Keller, H. A., *Teacher.* 1955, New York: Doubleday.

11. Keller, H. A., *The world I live in.* 1920, New York: Century, pp. 113–114.

12. Lash, J. P., *Helen and teacher.* (See note 9.)

13. Einhorn, L. J., *Helen Keller, public speaker.* 1998: Westport, CT: Greenwood Press, p. xxiii.

14. Vygotsky, L. S., *The collected works of L. S. Vygotsky: Vol. 2. The fundamentals of defectology.* (See note 1.)

15. Hatton, D. D., Bailey, D. B., Jr., Burchinal, M. R., & Ferrell, K. A., Developmental growth curves of preschool children with vision impairments. *Child Development*, 1997. 68: 788–806.

16. Fraiberg, S., *Insights from the blind: Comparative studies of blind and sighted infants.* 1977, New York: Basic Books; Tröster, H., & Brambring, M., Early motor development in blind infants. *Journal of Applied Developmental Psychology*, 1993. 14: 83–106.

17. Clifton, R. K., Perris, E., & Bullinger, A., Infants' perception of auditory space. *Developmental Psychology*, 1991. 27: 161–171; Litovsky, R. Y., & Ashmead, D. H., Development of binaural and spatial hearing in infants and children. In R. H. Gilkey & T. R. Anderson, eds., *Binaural and spatial hearing in real and virtual environments.* 1997, Mahwah, NJ: Erlbaum, pp. 571–592.

18. Fraiberg, S., *Insights from the blind: Comparative studies of blind and sighted infants.* (See note 16.); Tröster, H., & Brambring, M., Early motor development in blind infants. (See note 16.)

19. Bai, D. L., & Bertenthal, B. I., Locomotor status and the development of spatial search skills. *Child Development*, 1992. 63: 215–266; Campos, J. J., & Bertenthal, B. I., Locomotion and psychological development. In F. Morrison, K. Lord, & D. Keating, eds., *Applied developmental psychology, Vol. 3.* 1989, New York: Academic Press, pp. 229–258.

20. Campos, J. J., Kermoian, R., & Zumbahlen, M. R., Socioemotional transformations in the family system following infant crawling onset. In N. Eisenberg & R. A. Fabes, eds., *New directions for child development*, No. 55. 1992, San Francisco: Jossey-Bass, pp. 25–40.

21. Mayes, L. C., & Zigler, E., An observational study of the affective concomitants of mastery in infants. *Journal of Child Psychology and Psychiatry*, 1992. 33: 659–667.

22. Hatton, D. D., Bailey, D. B., Jr., Burchinal, M. R., & Ferrell, K. A., Developmental growth curves of preschool children with vision impairments. (See note 15.)

23. Tröster, H., & Brambring, M., Early social-emotional development in blind infants. *Child: Care, Health and Development*, 1992. 18: 207–227.

24. Erin, J. N., Language samples from visually impaired four- and five-year-olds. *Journal of Childhood Communication Disorders*, 1990. 13: 181–191; Fraiberg, S., *Insights from the blind: Comparative studies of blind and sighted infants.* (See note 16.)

25. Finn, D. M., & Fewell, R. R., The use of play assessment to examine the development of communication skills in children who are deaf–blind. *Journal of Visual Impairment*

and Blindness, 1994. 88: 349–356; Rettig, M., The play of young children with visual impairments: Characteristics and interventions. *Journal of Visual Impairment and Blindness,* 1994. 88: 410–420; Rogers, S. J., Cognitive characteristics of handicapped children's play: A review. *Journal of the Division for Early Childhood,* 1988. 12: 161–168.

26. Ibid.

27. Tröester, H., & Brambring, M., The play behavior and play materials of blind and sighted infants and preschoolers. *Journal of Visual Impairment and Blindness,* 1994. 88: 421–432.

28. Preisler, G. M., 1993. A descriptive study of blind children in nurseries with sighted children. *Child: Care, Health and Development,* 1993. 19: 295–315.

29. Keller, H. A., *The world I live in,* pp. 104–105. (See note 11.)

30. Vygotsky, L. S., *The collected works of L. S. Vygotsky: Vol. 2. The fundamentals of defectology,* pp. 105, 108. (See note 1.)

31. Ibid., p. 100. See also, Newman, J. R., *The world of mathematics,* Vol. 4. 1956, New York: Simon & Schuster, p. 2372.

32. Fraiberg, S., *Insights from the blind: Comparative studies of blind and sighted infants.* (See note 16); Rogow, S., *Helping the visually impaired child with developmental problems: Effective practice in home, school, and community.* 1988, New York: Teachers College Press.

33. Moore, V., & McConachie, H., Communication between blind and severely visually impaired children and their parents. *British Journal of Developmental Psychology,* 1994. 12: 491–502.

34. Tröester, H., & Brambring, M., The play behavior and play materials of blind and sighted infants and preschoolers. (See note 27.)

35. Vygotsky, L. S., *The collected works of L. S. Vygotsky: Vol. 2. The fundamentals of defectology,* p. 100. (See note 1.)

36. Mayberry, R. I., The importance of childhood to language acquisition: Evidence from American Sign Language. In J. C. Goodman & H. C. Nusbaum, eds., *The development of speech perception: The transition from speech sounds to spoken words.* 1994, Cambridge, MA: MIT Press, pp. 57–90.

37. Jamieson, J. R., Visible thought: Deaf children's use of signed and spoken private speech. *Sign Language Studies,* 1995. 86: 63–80.

38. Spencer, P. E., & Lederberg, A., Different modes, different models: Communication and language of young deaf children and their mothers. In L. B. Adamson & M. A. Romski, eds., *Communication and language acquisition: Discoveries from atypical development.* 1997, Baltimore: Paul Brookes, pp. 203–230.

39. Brinich, P. M., Childhood deafness and maternal control. *Journal of Communication Disorders,* 1980. 13: 75–81; Lederberg, A. R., & Mobley, C. E., The effect of hearing impairment on the quality of attachment and mother–toddler interaction. *Child Development,* 1990. 61: 1596–1604; Meadow, K. P., Greenberg, M. T., Erting, C., & Carmichael, H., Interactions of deaf mothers and deaf preschool children: Comparisons with three other groups of deaf and hearing dyads. *American Annals of the Deaf,* 1981. 126: 454–468; Meadow-Orlans, K. P., & Steinberg, A. G., Effects of infant hearing loss and maternal support on mother–infant interactions at 18 months. *Journal of Applied Developmental Psychology,* 1993. 14: 407–426; Spencer, P. E., & Meadow-Orlans, K. P., Play, language, and maternal responsiveness: A longitudinal study of deaf and hearing infants. *Child Development,* 1996. 67: 3176–3191; Wedell-Monning, J., & Lumley, J., Child deafness and mother–child interaction. *Child Development,* 1980. 51: 766–774.

40. Spencer, P. E., & Lederberg, A., Different modes, different models: Communication and language of young deaf children and their mothers. (See note 38.)

41. Jamieson, J. R., Teaching as transaction: Vygotskian perspectives on deafness and mother–child interaction. *Exceptional Children*, 1994. 60: 434–449; Jamieson, J. R., Instructional discourse strategies: Differences between hearing and deaf mothers of deaf children. *First Language*, 1994. 14: 153–171.

42. Jamieson, J. R., Visible thought: Deaf children's use of signed and spoken private speech. *Sign Language Studies*, 1995. 86: 63–80.

43. Folven, R. J., & Bonvillian, J., The transition from nonreferential to referential language in children acquiring American Sign Language. *Developmental Psychology*, 1991. 27: 806–816.

44. Brown, P. M., Prescott, S. J., Rickards, F. W., & Paterson, M. M., Communicating about pretend play: A comparison of the utterances of 4-year-old normally hearing and deaf or hard-of-hearing children in an integrated kindergarten. *Volta Review*, 1997. 99: 5–17; Darbyshire, J., Play patterns in young children with impaired hearing. *Volta Review*, 1977. 79: 19–26; Higginbotham, D., & Baker, B., Social participation and cognitive play differences in hearing-impaired and normally hearing preschoolers. *Volta Review*, 1981. 83: 135–149; Spencer, P. E., & Meadow-Orlans, K. P., Play, language, and maternal responsiveness: A longitudinal study of deaf and hearing infants. (See note 39.)

45. Casby, M. W., & McCormack, S. M., Symbolic play and early communication development in hearing-impaired children. *Journal of Communication Disorders*, 1985. 18: 67–78. Spencer, P. E., & Meadow-Orlans, K. P., Play, language, and maternal responsiveness: A longitudinal study of deaf and hearing infants. (See note 39); Spencer, P. E., The association between language and symbolic play at two years: Evidence from deaf toddlers. *Child Development*. 67: 867–876.

46. Marschark, M., *Psychological development of deaf children*. 1993, New York: Oxford University Press.

47. Spencer, P. E., Bodner-Johnson, B. A., & Guttfreund, M. K., Interacting with infants with a hearing loss: What can we learn from mothers who are deaf? *Journal of Early Intervention*, 1992. 16: 64–78.

48. Lederberg, A. R., & Everhart, V. S., Communication between deaf children and their hearing mothers: The role of language, gesture, and vocalizations. *Journal of Speech, Language, and Hearing Research*, 1998. 41: 887–899.

49. Coryell, J., & Holcomb, T. K., The use of sign language and sign systems in facilitating the language acquisition and communication of deaf students. *Language, Speech, and Hearing Services in Schools*, 1997. 28: 384–394; Gallaway, C., & Woll, B., Interaction and childhood deafness. In C. Gallaway & B. J. Richards, ed., *Input and interaction in language acquisition*. 1994, Cambridge, UK: Cambridge University Press, pp. 197–218.

50. Moores, D. F., *Educating the deaf, 5th ed.* 2000, Boston: Houghton Mifflin.

51. Musselman, C. R., Lindsay, P. H., & Wilson, A. K., The effect of mothers' communication mode on language development in preschool deaf children. *Applied Psycholinguistics*, 1988. 9: 185–204.

52. Swisher, M. V., Conversational interaction between deaf children and their hearing mothers: The role of visual attention. In P. Siple & S. D. Fischer, ed., *Theoretical issues in sign language research: Vol. 2. Psychology*. 1991, Chicago: University of Chicago Press, pp. 111–134; Swisher, M. V., Learning to converse: How deaf mothers support the development of attention and conversational skills in their young children. In P. E. Spencer & C. J. Erting, eds., *The deaf child in the family and at school*. 2000, Mahwah, NJ: Erlbaum, pp. 21–39.

53. Marschark, M., *Psychological development of deaf children*, p. vii. (See note 46.)

54. Prinz, P. M., & Strong, M., ASL proficiency and English literacy within a bilingual deaf education model of instruction. *Topics in Language Disorders,* 1998. 18: 47–60.

55. For example, deaf children have been taught visual symbols to stand for various handshapes and handsigns that resemble English sounds. In each of these systems, they acquire an intermediate set of symbols aimed at facilitating decoding of written language. See, for example, Sutton, V., *Sign Writing.* 1996, Deaf Action Committee: www.signwriting.org; Smith-Stubblefield, S., Roseberry-McKibbin, C., & Hanyak, R., *See the sound with visual phonics: A new approach to articulation/phonological training.* Paper presented at the annual meeting of the American Speech and Hearing Association. 1994: New Orleans.

56. Hakuta, K., Ferdman, B. M., & Diaz, R. M., Bilingualism and cognitive development: Three perspectives. In S. Rosenberg, ed., *Advances in applied psycholinguistics: Vol. 2. Reading, writing, and language learning.* 1987, New York: Cambridge University Press, pp. 284–319.

57. Bialystok, E., Effects of bilingualism and biliteracy on children's emerging concepts of print. *Developmental Psychology,* 1997. 33: 429–440; Ricciardelli, L. A., Bilingualism and cognitive development: Relation to threshold theory. *Journal of Psycholinguistic Research,* 1992. 21: 301–316.

58. Vygotsky, L. S., *The collected works of L. S. Vygotsky: Vol. 2. The fundamentals of defectology,* p. 118. (See note 1.)

59. American Psychiatric Association, *Diagnostic and statistical manual of mental disorders,* 4th ed. 1994, Washington, DC: Author.

60. Barkley, R. A., *Taking charge of ADHD.* 1995, New York: Guilford.

61. Weiss, G., & Hechtman, L. T., *Hyperactive children grown up.* 1993, New York: Guilford.

62. In a study comparing attention to television in 6- to 12-year-old boys with and without ADHD, the ADHD boys, who were extremely inattentive in their classrooms, attended to TV programming to a high degree. Their attention was equivalent to that of non-ADHD agemates as long as distracting toys were not in the room. Also, recall of information from TV programs was similar for both groups of boys. See Landau, S., Lorch, E. P., & Milich, R., Visual attention to and comprehension of television in attention-deficit hyperactivity disordered and normal boys. *Child Development,* 1992. 63: 928–937.

63. Barkley, R. A., *Attention-deficit hyperactivity disorder: A handbook for diagnosis and treatment.* 1990, New York: Guilford.

64. American Psychiatric Association, *Diagnostic and statistical manual of mental disorders,* 4th ed. (See note 59.)

65. Gaub, M., & Carlson, C. L., Gender differences in ADHD: A meta-analysis and critical review. *Journal of the American Academy of Child and Adolescent Psychiatry,* 1997. 36: 1036–1045.

66. Sherman, D. K., Iacono, W. G., & McGue, M. K., Attention-deficit hyperactivity disorder dimensions: A twin study of inattention and impulsivity–hyperactivity. *Journal of the American Academy of Child and Adolescent Psychiatry,* 1997. 36: 745–753; Zametkin, A. J., Attention-deficit disorder: Born to be hyperactive? *Journal of the American Medical Association,* 1995. 273: 1871–1874.

67. Biederman, J., & Spencer, T. J., Genetics of childhood disorders: XIX, ADHD, part 3: Is ADHD a noradregenergic disorder? *Journal of the American Academy of Child & Adolescent Psychiatry,* 2000. 39: 1330–1333; Cook, E. H., Stein, M. A., Ellison, T., & Unis, A. S., Attention-deficit hyperactivity disorder and whole-blood serotonin levels: Effects of comorbidity. *Psychiatry Research,* 1995. 57: 13–20; Faraone, S. V., & Biederman, J., Neurobiology of attention-deficit hyperactivity disorder. *Biological Psychiatry,* 1998. 44: 951–958; Faraone,

S. V., Biederman, J., Weiffenbach, B., Keith T., Chu, M. P., Weaver, A., et al., Dopamine D-sub-4 gene 7-repeat allele and attention deficit hyperactivity disorder. *American Journal of Psychiatry*, 1999. 156: 768–770.

68. Novak, G. P., Solanto, M., & Abikoff, H., Spatial orienting and focused attention in attention-deficit hyperactivity disorder. *Journal of Psychophysiology*, 1995. 32: 546–559; Riccio, C. A., Hynd, G. W., Cohen, M. J., & Gonzalez, J. J., Neurological basis of attention deficit hyperactivity disorder. *Exceptional Children*, 1993. 60: 118–124.

69. Lyoo, K., Noam, G. G., Lee, C. K., Lee, H. K., Kennedy, B. P., & Renshaw, P. F., The corpus callosum and lateral ventricles in children with attention-deficit hyperactivity disorder: A brain magnetic resonance imagining study. *Biological Psychiatry*, 1996. 40: 1060–1063.

70. Berquin, P. C., Gidd, J. N., Jacobsen, L. K., Burger, S. D., Krain, A. L., Rapoport, J. L., & Castellanos, F. X., Cerebellum in attention-deficit hyperactivity disorder: A morphometric MRI study. *Neurology*, 1998. 50: 1087–1093; Castellanos, F. X., Giedd, J. N., Marsh, W. L., Hamburger, S. D., Vaituzis, A. C., Dickstein, D. P., et al., Quantitative brain magnetic resonance imaging in attention-deficit/hyperactivity disorder. *Archives of General Psychiatry*, 1996. 53: 607–616; Mostofsky, S.H., Reiss, A. L., Lockhart, P., & Denckla, M. B., Evaluation of cerebellar size in attention-deficit hyperactivity disorder. *Journal of Child Neurology*, 1998. 13: 434–439.

71. Barkley, R. A., *ADHD and the nature of self-control.* 1997, New York: Guilford.; Bernier, J. C., & Siegel, D. H., Attention-deficit hyperactivity disorder: A family ecological systems perspective. *Families in Society*, 1994. 75: 142–150; Landau, S., Children with attention deficits and disinhibited behavior. In L. E. Berk, ed., *Landscapes of development.* 1999, Belmont, CA: Wadsworth, pp. 373–390.

72. Barkley, R. A., *Taking charge of ADHD.* (See note 60.)

73. Lahey, B. B., & Loeber, R., Attention-deficit/hyperactivity disorder, oppositional defiant disorder, conduct disorder, and adult antisocial behavior: A life span perspective. In D. M. Stoff, J. Breiling, & J. D. Maser, eds., *Handbook of antisocial behavior.* 1997, New York: Wiley, pp. 51–59.

74. Milberger, S., Biederman, J., Faraone, S. V., Guite, J., & Tsuang, M. T., Pregnancy, delivery and infancy complications and attention-deficit hyperactivity disorder: Issues of gene–environment interaction. *Biological Psychiatry*, 1997. 41: 65–75.

75. Danforth, J. S., Barkley, R. A., & Stokes, T. F., Observations of parent–child interactions with hyperactive children: Research and clinical implications. *Clinical Psychology Review*, 1991. 11: 703–721.

76. Patterson, G. R., Performance models for parenting: A social interactional perspective. In J. E. Grusec & L. Kuczynski, eds., *Parenting and children's internalization of values.* 1997, New York: Wiley, pp. 193–226.

77. Whalen, C. K., & Henker, B., The social worlds of hyperactive children. *Clinical Psychology Review*, 1985. 5: 1–32.

78. Atkins, M. S., Pelham, W. E., & Licht, M., A comparison of objective classroom measures and teacher ratings of attention deficit disorder. *Journal of Abnormal Child Psychology*, 1985. 13: 155–167.

79. Campbell, S. B., Endman, M. W., & Bernfeld, G., Three-year follow-up of hyperactive preschoolers into elementary school. *Journal of Child Psychology and Psychiatry*, 1977. 18: 239–249.

80. Landau, S., & Milich, R., Assessment of children's social status and peer relations. In A. M. LaGreca, ed., *Through the eyes of the child.* 1990, Boston: Allyn & Bacon, pp. 259–291.

81. Hartup, W. W., The company they keep: Friendships and their developmental significance. *Child Development,* 1996. 67: 1–13; Vandell, D. L., & Hembree, S. E., Peer social status and friendship: Independent contributors to children's social and academic adjustment. *Merrill-Palmer Quarterly,* 1994. 40: 461–477.

82. Pelham, W. E., Jr., & Bender, M. E., Peer relationships in hyperactive children: Description and treatment. In D. D. Gadow & I. Bialer, eds., *Advances in learning and behavioral disabilities,* Vol. 1. 1982, Greenwich, CT: JAI Press, pp. 365–436.

83. Whalen, C. K., Henker, B., & Granger, D. A., Social judgment process in hyperactive boys: Effects of methylphenidate and comparisons with normal peers. *Journal of Abnormal Child Psychology,* 1990. 18: 297–316.

84. Erhardt, D., & Hinshaw, S. P., Initial sociometric impressions of attention-deficit hyperactivity disorder and comparison boys: Predictors from social behaviors and nonbehavioral variables. *Journal of Consulting and Clinical Psychology,* 1994. 14: 340–344.

85. George, T. P., & Hartmann, D. P., Friendship networks of unpopular, average, and popular children. *Child Development,* 1996. 67: 2301–2316; Parker, J. G., & Asher, S. R., Friendship and friendship quality in middle childhood: Links with peer group acceptance and feelings of loneliness and social dissatisfaction. *Developmental Psychology,* 1993. 29: 611–621.

86. Bagwell, C. L., Newcomb, A. F., & Bukowski, W. M., Preadolescent friendship and peer rejection as predictors of adult adjustment. *Child Development,* 1998. 69: 140–153; Parker, J. G., & Asher, S. R., Peer relations and later personal adjustment: Are low-accepted children at risk? *Psychological Bulletin,* 1987. 102: 357–389.

87. Black, B., & Logan, A., Links between communication patterns in mother–child, father–child, and child–peer interactions and children's social status. *Child Development,* 1995. 66: 255–271; Pettit, G. S., Clawson, M. A., Dodge, K. A., & Bates, J. E., Stability and change in peer-rejected status: The role of child behavior, parenting, and family ecology. *Merrill-Palmer Quarterly,* 1996. 42: 267–294.

88. Barkley, R. A., Behavioral inhibition, sustained attention, and executive functions: Constructing a unifying theory of ADHD. *Psychological Bulletin,* 1997. 121: 65–94.

89. Ibid.

90. Barkley, R. A., *Taking charge of ADHD.* (See note 60.)

91. Berk, L. E., & Landau, S., Private speech of learning disabled and normally achieving children in classroom academic and laboratory contexts. *Child Development,* 1993. 64: 556–571; Berk, L. E., & Landau, S., *Private speech in the face of academic challenge: The failure of impulsive children to "get their act together."* Paper presented at the biennial meeting of the Society for Research in Child Development. 1997 April: Washington, DC; Berk, L. E., & Potts, M. K., Development and functional significance of private speech among attention-deficit hyperactivity disordered and normal boys. *Journal of Abnormal Child Psychology,* 1991. 19: 357–377.

92. Ibid.

93. Alessandri, S. M., Attention, play, and social behavior in ADHD preschoolers. *Journal of Abnormal Child Psychology,* 1992. 20: 289–302.

94. Barkley, R. A., *ADHD and the nature of self-control.* (See note 71.) Greenhill, L. L., Halperin, J. M., & Abikoff, H., Stimulant medications. *American Academy of Child and Adolescent Psychiatry,* 1999. 38: 503–512.

95. Ibid.

96. Barkley, R. A., *Taking charge of ADHD*. (See note 60.); Brown, R. T., Carlson, C. L., & Bunner, M. R., Effects of methylphenidate on the academic performance of children with attention-deficit hyperactivity disorder and learning disabilities. *School Psychology Review,* 1993. 22: 184–198; Brown, R. T., Dingle, A., & Landau, S., Overview of psychopharmacology in children and adolescents. *School Psychology Quarterly,* 1994. 9: 4–25; Greenhill, L. L., Halperin, J. M., & Abikoff, H., Stimulant medications. (See note 94.)

97. Milich, R., The response of children with ADHD to failure: If at first you don't succeed, do you try, try again? *School Psychology Review,* 1993. 23: 11–28.

98. Berk, L. E., & Potts, M. K., Development and functional significance of private speech among attention-deficit hyperactivity disordered and normal boys. (See note 91.)

99. Barkley, R. A., *Taking charge of ADHD*. (See note 60.); Campbell, S. B., Hyperactivity in preschoolers: Correlates and prognostic implications. *Clinical Psychology Review,* 1985. 5: 405–428.

100. Brown, R. T., Carlson, C. L., & Bunner, M. R., Effects of methylphenidate on the academic performance of children with attention-deficit hyperactivity disorder and learning disabilities. (See note 96); Erhardt, D., & Hinshaw, S. P., Initial sociometric impressions of attention-deficit hyperactivity disorder and comparison boys: Predictors from social behaviors and nonbehavioral variables. (See note 84.)

101. Barkley, R. A., *Taking charge of ADHD*. (See note 60); Greenhill, L. L., Halperin, J. M., & Abikoff, H., Stimulant medications. (See note 94.); Landau, S., Children with attention deficits and disinhibited behavior. (See note 71.)

102. Safer, D., Zito, J., & Fine, E., Increased methylphenidate usage for attention deficit hyperactivity disorder in the 1990s. *Pediatrics,* 1996. 98: 1084–1088.

103. Angold, A., & Costello, E., Stimulant treatment for children: A community perspective. *Pediatrics,* in press.

104. Jensen, P. S., Kettle, L., Roper, M. T., Sloan, M. T., & Dulcan, M. K. Are stimulants overprescribed? Treatment of ADHD in four U.S. communities. *Journal of the American Academy of Child and Adolescent Psychiatry,* 1999. 38: 797–804.

105. Zito, J. M., Safer, D. J., dos Reis, S., Gardner, J. F., Boles, M., & Lynch, F., Trends in prescribing of psychotropic medications to preschoolers. *Journal of the American Medical Association,* 2000. 283: 1025–1030.

106. Campbell, S. B., Hyperactivity in preschoolers: Correlates and prognostic implications. (See note 99.)

107. Ibid.

108. Barkley, R. A., *Taking charge of ADHD*. (See note 60.)

109. Pelham, W. E., Pharmacotherapy for children with attention-deficit hyperactivity disorder. *School Psychology Review,* 1993. 22: 199–227.

110. Barkley, R. A., *Taking charge of ADHD*. (See note 60.)

111. Landau. S., Children with attention deficits and disinhibited behavior. (See note 71.)

112. Shure, M. B., Interpersonal cognitive problem solving: Primary prevention of early high-risk behaviors in the preschool and primary years. In G. W. Albee & T. P. Gullotta, eds., *Primary prevention works.* 1997, Thousand Oaks, CA: Sage.

113. Erhardt, D., & Hinshaw, S. P., Initial sociometric impressions of attention-deficit hyperactivity disorder and comparison boys: predictors from social behaviors and nonbehavioral variables. (See note 84.)

114. Barkley, R. A., *Taking charge of ADHD*. (See note 60.)

115. Landau, S., Children with attention deficits and disinhibited behavior. (See note 71.)

116. Jacob, R. B., O'Leary, K. D., & Rosenblad, C., Formal and informal classroom settings: Effects on hyperactivity. *Journal of Abnormal Child Psychology*, 1978. 6: 47–59.

117. Mosteller, R., The Tennessee study of class size in the early school grades. *Future of Children*, 1995. 5: 113–127.

118. Vygotsky, L. S., *The collected works of L. S. Vygotsky: Vol. 2. The fundamentals of defectology.* (See note 1.)

119. Gindis, B., The social/cultural implication of disability: Vygotsky's paradigm for special education. *Educational Psychologist*, 1995. 30: 77–81.

CHAPTER 6: LEARNING IN CLASSROOMS

1. I am grateful to Carol Owles for inspiration for the story of Tamara. Much of the description of Tamara and her classroom — and all the comments of parents — are derived from Carol's extensive case study of an award-winning teacher. For purposes of illustrating Vygotsky-based classroom practices, I have also drawn on observations of several outstanding teachers I have known over the years, integrating their unique qualities and classroom practices into Tamara's characterization. Because Tamara is a composite, I refer to her by a different name from the one used by Carol in her case study. See Owles, C. S., *Living, learning, and literacy in an early childhood classroom: The successes and struggles of one good teacher*, 2000. Unpublished doctoral dissertation, Champaign-Urbana: University of Illinois.

2. Moll, L. C., & Whitmore, K. F., Vygotsky in classroom practice: Moving from individual transmission to social transaction. In E. A. Forman, N. Minick, & C. A. Stone, eds., *Contexts for learning.* 1993, New York: Oxford University Press, pp. 19–42.

3. Vygotsky, L. S., *Thought and language*, A. Kozulin, trans. [1934] 1986, Cambridge, MA: MIT Press, pp. 188–189.

4. Ibid.

5. Vygotsky, L. S., *Selected psychological investigations.* Moscow: Izdstel'sto Akademii Pedagog-icheskikh Nauk SSSR, p. 278.

6. Vygotsky, L. S., *Thought and language.* (See note 3.)

7. Adapted from Owles, C. S., *Living, learning, and literacy in an early childhood classroom: The successes and struggles of one good teacher,* pp. 45–46. (See note 1.)

8. Ibid.

9. Vygotsky, L. S., *Mind in society: The development of higher mental processes*, M. Cole, V. John-Steiner, S. Scribner, & E. Souberman, eds. and trans. [1903—1935] 1978, Cambridge, MA: Harvard University Press.

10. Ibid., pp. 117–118.

11. Goodman, K. S., *What's whole in whole language?* 1986, Portsmouth, NH: Heinemann; Watson, D. J., Defining and describing whole language. *Elementary School Journal,* 1989. 90: 129–141.

12. Sacks, C. H., & Mergendoller, J. R., The relationship between teachers' theoretical orientation toward reading and student outcomes in kindergarten children with different initial reading abilities. *American Educational Research Journal,* 1997. 34: 721–739.

13. Hatcher, P. J., Hulme, C., & Ellis, A. W., Ameliorating early reading failure by integrating the teaching of reading and phonological skills: The phonological linkage hypothesis. *Child Development*, 1994. 65: 41–57.

14. Adams, M. J., Treiman, R., & Pressley, M., Reading, writing, and literacy. In W. Damon, series ed., & D. Kuhn & R. S. Siegler, vol. eds., *Handbook of child psychology: Vol. 2. Cognition, perception, and language*, 5th ed. 1998, New York: Wiley, pp. 275–355.

15. Tulviste, P., *The cultural-historical development of verbal thinking*. 1991, Commack, NY: Nova Science Publishers.

16. Campbell, J. R., Voelkl, K. E., & Donahue, P. L., *NAEP 1996 trends in academic progress*. 1997, Washington, DC: Government Printing Office.

17. Goodlad, J., *A place called school*. 1984, New York: McGraw-Hill.

18. Tharp, R. G., & Gallimore, R., *Rousing minds to life*. 1988, New York: Cambridge University Press.

19. Jones, E., & Nimmo, J., *Emergent curriculum*. 1994, Washington, DC: National Association for the Education of Young Children.

20. Katz, L. G., & Chard, S. C., The project approach. *Scholastic Early Childhood Today*. 1998 March 12, pp. 43–44.

21. This project is described in Katz, L., & Chard, S. C., *Engaging children's minds: The project approach*, 2nd ed. 2000, New York: Ablex.

22. Two excellent, practical guides to carrying out projects in early childhood classrooms are Chard, S. C., *The project approach: Making curriculum come alive*. Books 1 and 2. 1998, New York: Scholastic; and Helm, J. H., & Katz, L., *Young investigators: The project approach in the early years*. 2001, New York: Teachers College Press.

23. Inagaki, K., Piagetian and post-Piagetian conceptions of development and their implications for science education in early childhood. *Early Childhood Research Quarterly*, 1992. 7: 115–133.

24. Palincsar, A. S., *Beyond reciprocal teaching: A retrospective and prospective view*. Raymond B. Cattell Early Career Award Address at the annual meeting of the American Educational Research Association. 1992 April: San Francisco; Palincsar, A. S., & Brown, A. L., Reciprocal teaching of comprehension-fostering and monitoring activities. *Cognition and Instruction*, 1984. 1: 117–125.

25. Palincsar, A. S., & Klenk, L., Fostering literacy learning in supportive contexts. *Journal of Learning Disabilities*, 1992. 25: 211–225.

26. Palincsar, A. S., Brown, A. L., & Campione, J. C., First-grade dialogues for knowledge acquisition and use. In E. A. Forman, N. Minick, & C. A. Stone, *Contexts for learning*. 1993, New York: Oxford University Press, pp. 47–48.

27. Ibid., p. 49.

28. Rosenshine, B., & Meister, C., Reciprocal teaching: A review of nineteen experimental studies. *Review of Educational Research*, 1994. 64: 479–530.

29. Palincsar, A. S., Brown, A. L., & Campione, J. C., First-grade dialogues for knowledge acquisition and use. (See note 26.)

30. Yackel, E., Cobb, P., Wood, T., Wheatley, G., & Merkel, G., The importance of social interaction in children's construction of mathematical knowledge. National Council of Teachers of Mathematics, ed., *Yearbook of the National Council of Teachers of Mathematics*. 1990, Reston, VA: Author, p. 14.

31. McClain, K., Cobb, P., & Bowers, J., A contextual investigation of three-digit addition and subtraction. National Council of Teachers of Mathematics, ed., *Yearbook of the National Council of Teachers of Mathematics*, 1998. Reston, VA: Author, pp. 141–150.

32. McClain, K., Cobb, P., & Bowers, J., A contextual investigation of three-digit addition and subtraction. (See note 31); Yackel, E., Cobb, P., Wood, T., Wheatley, G., & Merkel, G., The importance of social interaction in children's construction of mathematical knowledge. (See note 30.)

33. McClain, K., Cobb, P., & Bowers, J., A contextual investigation of three-digit addition and subtraction. (See note 31.)

34. Cobb, P., Wood, T., & Yackel, Discourse, mathematical thinking, and classroom practice. In E. A. Forman, N. Minick, & C. A. Stone, eds., *Contexts for learning.* 1993, New York: Oxford University Press, pp. 91–119.

35. Yackel, E., Cobb, P., Wood, T., Wheatley, G., & Merkel, G., The importance of social interaction in children's construction of mathematical knowledge. (See note 30.)

36. Cobb, P., Wood, T., Yackel, E., Nicholls, J., Wheatley, G., Trigatti, B., & Perlwitz, M., Assessment of a problem-centered second-grade mathematics project. *Journal for Research in Mathematics and Education,* 1991, 22: 3–29.

37. Cobb, P., Wood, T., Yackel, E., & Perlwitz, M., A follow-up assessment of a second-grade problem-centered mathematics project. *Educational Studies in Mathematics,* 1992. 23: 483–504.

38. Ibid.

39. Forman, E. A., & McPhail, J., Vygotskian perspective on children's collaborative problem-solving activities. In E. A. Forman, N. Minick, & C. A. Stone, eds., *Contexts for learning,* 1993, New York: Cambridge University Press, pp. 323–347; Kobayashi, Y., Conceptual acquisition and change through social interaction. *Human Development,* 1994. 37: 233–241; Tudge, J. R. H., Processes and consequences of peer collaboration: A Vygotskian analysis. *Child Development,* 1992. 63: 1364–1379.

40. Ellis, S., Klahr, D., & Siegler, R. S., *The birth, life, and sometimes death of good ideas in collaborative problem solving.* Paper presented at the meeting of the American Educational Research Association. 1994, April: New Orleans.

41. Ellis, S., & Gauvain, M., Social and cultural influences on children's collaborative interactions. In L. T. Winegar & J. Valsiner, eds., *Children's development within social context,* Vol 2. 1992, Hillsdale, NJ: Erlbaum, pp. 155–180.

42. Holloway, S., *Beyond the "average native": Cultural models of early childhood education in Japan.* Paper presented as part of the Workshop on Global Perspectives on Early Childhood Education. 1999, April: Washington, DC: National Academy of Sciences.

43. Bempechat, J., & Drago-Severson, E., Cross-national differences in academic achievement: Beyond etic conceptions of children's understandings. *Review of Educational Research,* 1999. 69: 287–314; Hatano, G., Introduction: Conceptual change—Japanese perspectives. *Human Development,* 1994. 37: 189–197.

44. LaPointe, A. E., Askew, J. M., & Mead, N. A., *Learning mathematics.* 1992, Princeton, NJ: Educational Testing Service; LaPointe, A. E., Mead, N. A., & Askew, J. M., *Learning science.* 1992, Princeton, NJ: Educational Testing Service; U.S. Department of Education, *Pursuing excellence: A study of U.S. fourth-grade, eighth-grade, and twelfth-grade mathematics and science achievement in international context.* 1997–1998, Washington, DC: Government Printing Office.

45. Berk, L. E., Vygotsky's theory: The importance of make-believe play. *Young Children,* 1994. 50(1): 30–39; Katz, L. G., Evangelou, D., & Hartman, J. A., *The case for mixed-age grouping in early education.* 1990, Washington, DC: National Association for the Education of Young Children; Roopnarine, J. L., Aheduzzaman, M., Donnely, S., Gill, P., Mennis, A., Arky, L., Dingler, K., McLaughlin, M., & Talukder, E., Social-cognitive play behaviors and playmate preferences in same-age and mixed-age classrooms over a 6-month period. *American Educational Research Journal,* 1992. 29: 757–776.

46. Azmitia, M., Peer interaction and problem solving: When are two heads better than one? *Child Development*, 1988. 59: 87–96; Radziszewska, B., & Rogoff, B., Influence of adult and peer collaboration on the development of children's planning skills. *Developmental Psychology*, 1988. 24: 840–848.

47. Brody, G. H., Graziano, W. G., & Musser, L. M., Familiarity and children's behavior in same-age and mixed-age peer groups. *Developmental Psychology*, 1983. 19: 568–576; Howes, C., & Farver, J., Social pretend play in 2-year-olds: Effects of age of partner. *Early Childhood Research Quarterly*, 1987. 2: 305–314.

48. Ibid.; Gelman, R., & Shatz, M., Appropriate speech adjustments: The operation of conversational constraints on talk to two-year-olds. In M. Lewis & L. A. Rosenblum, eds., *Interaction, conversation, and the development of language*. 1978, New York: Wiley, pp. 27–61.

49. Jensen, M. K., & Green, V. P., The effects of multi-age grouping on young children and teacher preparation. *Early Child Development and Care*, 1993. 91: 25–31; Pratt, D., On the merits of multiage classrooms: Their work life. *Research in Rural Education*, 1986. 3: 111–116.

50. Winsler, A., & Diaz, R. M., Private speech in the classroom: The effects of activity type, presence of others, classroom context, and mixed-age grouping. *International Journal of Behavioral Development*, 1995. 18: 463–487.

51. Renninger, K. A., Developmental psychology and instruction: Issues from and for practice. In W. Damon, series ed., & I. Sigel & K. A. Renninger, vol. eds., *Handbook of child psychology: Vol 4. Child psychology and practice*. 1998, New York: Wiley, pp. 211–274.

52. Burns, R. B., & Mason, D. A., Class formation and composition in elementary schools. *American Educational Research Journal*, 1998. 35: 739–772.

53. Webb, N. M., Nemer, K. M., & Chezhik, A. W., Equity issues in collaborative group assessment: Group composition and performance. *American Educational Research Journal*, 1998. 35: 607–651.

54. Owles, C. S., *Living, learning, and literacy in an early childhood classroom: The successes and struggles of one good teacher*, p. 99. (See note 1.)

55. Bodrova, E., & Leong, D. J., Scaffolding emergent writing in the zone of proximal development. *Literacy Teaching and Learning*, 1998. 3(2): 1–18.

56. Ibid.

57. Vygotsky, L. S., *Mind in society: The development of higher mental processes*. (See note 9.)

58. Lidz, C. S., *Practitioner's guide to dynamic assessment*. 1991, New York: Guilford; Lidz, C. S., Dynamic assessment: Psychoeducational assessment with cultural sensitivity. *Journal of Social Distress and the Homeless*, 1997. 6: 95–111.

59. See, for example, Budoff, M., Measures for assessing learning potential. In C. S. Lidz, ed., *Dynamic assessment: An interactional approach to evaluating learning potential*. 1987, New York: Guilford, pp. 173–195; Feuerstein, R., *Dynamic assessment of retarded performers: The Learning Potential Assessment Device*. 1979, Baltimore: University Park Press.

60. Campione, J. C., & Brown, A. L., Linking dynamic assessment with school achievement. In C. S. Lidz, ed., *Dynamic assessment: An interactional approach to evaluation of learning potential*. 1987, New York: Guilford, pp. 173–195.

61. See McRel Early Literacy Advisor Web Site at www.mcrel.org/resources/literacy/road.

62. Brown, A. L., & Ferrara, R. A., Diagnosing zones of proximal development. In J. Wertsch, ed., *Culture, communication, and cognition*. 1985, New York: Cambridge University Press, pp. 273–305; Tzuriel, D., & Feuerstein, R., Dynamic group testing for prescriptive teaching: Differential effects of treatment. In H. C. Haywood & D. Tzuriel, eds., *Interactive testing*. 1992, New York: Springer-Verlag, pp. 187–206.

63. Grigorenko, E. L., & Sternberg, R. J., Dynamic testing. *Psychological Bulletin,* 1998. 124: 75–111.

64. Lidz, C. S., *Practitioner's guide to dynamic assessment.* (See note 58.)

65. Brown, A. L., Transforming schools into communities of thinking and learning about serious matters. *American Psychologist,* 1997. 52: 399–413.

66. Connors, L. J., & Epstein, J. L., Parent and school partnerships. In M. H. Bornstein, ed., *Handbook of parenting: Vol. 4. Applied and practical parenting.* 1996, Mahwah, NJ: Erlbaum, pp. 437–458; Grolnick, W. S., & Slowiaczek, M. L., Parents' involvement in children's schooling: A multidimensional conceptualization and motivational model. *Child Development,* 1994. 65: 237–252; Stevenson, D. L., & Baker, D. P., The family–school relation and the child's school performance. *Child Development,* 1987. 58: 1348–1357.

67. Peshkin, A., *Growing up American: Schooling and the survival of community.* Prospect Heights, IL: Waveland Press.

68. Greenfield, P. M., & Suzuki, L., Culture and human development: Implications for parenting education, pediatrics, and mental health. In I. E. Sigel & K. A. Renninger, eds., *Handbook of child psychology: Vol. 4. Child psychology in practice,* 5th ed. 1998, New York: Wiley, pp. 1059–1109.

69. Owles, C. S., *Living, learning, and literacy in an early childhood classroom: The successes and struggles of one good teacher,* pp. 135–136. (See note 1.)

70. Ibid., pp. 16, 153.

71. In addition to Vygotsky, Malaguzzi mentions Urie Bronfenbrenner, John Dewey, Frederick Froebel, Howard Gardner, Johann Pestalozzi, Jean Piaget, and others. See Malaguzzi, L., History, ideas, and basic philosophy. In C. Edwards, L. Gandini, & G. Forman, eds., *The hundred languages of children: The Reggio Emilia approach—advanced reflections.* 1997, Norwood, NJ: Ablex, pp. 49–97.

72. Gandini, L., Fundamentals of the Reggio Emilia approach to early childhood education. *Young Children,* 1993. 49: 4–8; Malaguzzi, L., History, ideas, and basic philosophy. (See note 71.)

73. Filippini, T., The role of the pedagogista: An interview with Lella Gandini. In C. Edwards, L. Gandini, & G. Forman, eds., *The hundred languages of children: The Reggio Emilia approach—advanced reflections.* 1997, Norwood, NJ: Ablex, pp. 127–137.

74. Edwards, C., Partner, nurturer, and guide: The roles of the Reggio teacher in action. In C. Edwards, L. Gandini, & G. Forman, eds., *The hundred languages of children: The Reggio Emilia approach—advanced reflections.* 1997, Norwood, NJ: Ablex, pp. 179–198.

75. Malaguzzi, L., For an education based on relationships. Trans L. Gandini. *Young Children,* 1993. 49(1): 9–12.

76. Gandini, L., Educational and caring spaces. In C. Edwards, L. Gandini, & G. Forman, eds., *The hundred languages of children: The Reggio Emilia approach—advanced reflections.* 1997, Norwood, NJ: Ablex, pp. 161–178.

77. Vecchi, V., The role of the atelierista: An interview with Lella Gandini. In C. Edwards, L. Gandini, & G. Forman, eds., *The hundred languages of children: The Reggio Emilia approach—advanced reflections.* 1997, Norwood, NJ: Ablex, p. 140.

78. Forman, G., Multiple symbolization in the long jump project. In C. Edwards, L. Gandini, & G. Forman, eds., *The hundred languages of children: The Reggio Emilia approach to early childhood education.* 1993, Norwood, NJ: Ablex, pp. 171–188.

79. Malaguzzi, I., History, ideas, and basic philosophy. (See note 71.)

80. Katz, L. G., & Chard, S. C., Documentation: The Reggio Emilia approach. *Principal,* 1997. 76(May): 16–17; Vecchi, V., The role of the atelierista: An interview with Lella Gandini. (See note 77.)

81. Tharp, R. G., & Gallimore, R., *Rousing minds to life.* (See note 18.)

82. Au, K. H., A sociocultural model of reading instruction: The Kamehameha Elementary Education Program. In S. A. Stahl & D. A. Hayes, eds., *Instructional models in reading.* 1997, Mahwah, NJ: Erlbaum, pp. 181–202; Tharp, R. G., Institutional and social context of educational practice and reform. In E. A. Forman, N. Minick, & C. A. Stone, eds., *Contexts for learning.* 1993, New York: Oxford University Press, pp. 269–282; Tharp, R. G., Intergroup differences among Native Americans in socialization and child cognition: An ethnogenetic analysis. In P. M. Greenfield & R. Cocking, eds., *Cross-cultural roots of minority child development.* 1994, Hillsdale, NJ: Erlbaum, pp. 87–105.

83. Tharp, R. G., & Gallimore, R., *Rousing minds to life.* (See note 18.)

84. Children's Defense Fund, *The state of America's children: Yearbook 2000.* 2000, Washington, DC: Author.

85. Cost, Quality, and Outcomes Study Team, Cost, quality, and child outcomes in child care centers: Key findings and recommendations. *Young Children,* 1995. 50(4): 40–44.

86. Galinsky, E., Howes, C., Kontos, S., & Shinn, M., *The study of children in family child care and relative care: Highlights of findings.* 1994, New York: Families and Work Institute.

87. Hausfather, A., Toharia, A., LaRoche, C., & Engelsmann, F., Effects of age of entry, day-care quality, and family characteristics on preschool behavior. *Journal of Child Psychology and Psychiatry,* 1997. 38: 441–448; Howes, C., Relations between early child care and schooling. *Developmental Psychology,* 1988. 24: 53–57; Howes, C., Can the age of entry into child care and the quality of child care predict adjustment to kindergarten? *Developmental Psychology,* 1990. 26: 292–303; Lamb, M. E., Nonparental child care: Context, quality, correlates, and consequences. In W. Damon, series ed., & I. E. Sigel & K. A. Renninger, vol. eds., *Handbook of child psychology: Vol. 4. Child psychology in practice,* 5th ed. 1998, New York: Wiley, pp. 73–133; Phillips, D. A., Voran, M., Kisker, E., Howes, C., & Whitebook, M., Child care for children in poverty: Opportunity or inequity? *Child Development,* 1994. 65: 472–492.

88. Bredekamp, S., & Copple, C., eds*., Developmentally appropriate practice in early childhood programs,* rev. ed. 1997, Washington, DC: National Association for the Education of Young Children.

89. Galinsky, E., Howes, C., Kontos, S., & Shinn, M., *The study of children in family child care and relative care: Highlights of findings.* (See note 86.); Helburn, S. W., ed*., Cost, quality and child outcomes in child care centers.* 1995, Denver: University of Colorado; Howes, C., Phillips, D. A., & Whitebook, M., Thresholds of quality: Implications for the social development of children in center-based child care. *Child Development,* 1992. 63: 449–460.

90. Adapted from Bredekamp, S., & Copple, C., eds., *Developmentally appropriate practice in early childhood programs.* (See note 88.)

91. U.S. Department of Education*, Pursuing excellence: A study of U.S. fourth-grade, eighth-grade, and twelfth-grade mathematics and science achievement in international context.* (See note 44.)

92. Stevenson, H. W., & Lee, S.-Y., Contexts of achievement: A study of American, Chinese, and Japanese children. *Monographs of the Society for Research in Child Development,* 1990. 55: No. 1-2, Serial No. 221; Stevenson, H. W., Learning from Asian schools. *Scientific American,* 1992. 267(6): 32–38.

93. Campbell, J. R., Voelkl, K. E., & Donahue, P. L., *NAEP 1996 trends in academic progress.* 1997, Washington, DC: Government Printing Office; Campbell, J. R., Hombo, C.M., & Mazzeo, J. *NAEP 1999 trends in academic progress.* 2000, Washington, DC: Government Printing Office.

94. Carnegie Task Force on Learning in the Primary Grades, *Years of promise: A comprehensive learning strategy for America's children: Executive summary.* 1996, New York: Carnegie Corporation.

95. Bredekamp, S., & Copple, C., eds., *Developmentally appropriate practice in early childhood programs,* p. 141. (See note 88.).

96. Ibid.

CHAPTER 7: THE CHILD IN CONTEMPORARY CULTURE

1. Harter, S., The perceived competence scale for children. *Child Development,* 1982. 53: 87–97; Marsh, H. W., Smith, I. D., & Barnes, J., Multidimensional self-concepts: Relations with sex and academic achievement. *Journal of Educational Psychology,* 1985. 77: 581–596.

2. See Damon, W., *Greater expectations: Overcoming the culture of indulgence in America's homes and schools.* 1995, New York: The Free Press.

3. Feiring, C., & Taska, L. S., Family self-concept: Ideas on its meaning. In B. Bracken, ed., *Handbook of self-concept.* 1996, New York: Wiley, pp. 317-373.

4. Hughes, J. N., Cavell, T. A., & Grossman, P. B., A positive view of self: Risk or protection for aggressive children? *Development and Psychopathology,* 1997. 9: 75–94.

5. Harter, S., The development of self-representations. In W. Damon, series ed., & N. Eisenberg, vol. ed., *Handbook of child psychology: Vol. 3. Social, emotional, and personality development,* 5TH ed. 1998, New York: Wiley, pp. 553–618.

6. U.S. Bureau of the Census, *Statistical abstract of the United States,* 120th ed. 2000, Washington, DC: Government Printing Office.

7. Greenfield, P. M., *Mind and media: The effects of television, video games, and computers.* 1984, Cambridge, MA: Cambridge University Press.

8. U.S. Bureau of the Census, *Statistical abstract of the United States,* 120th ed. (See note 6.)

9. Clements, D. H., Teaching creativity with computers. *Educational Psychology Review,* 1995. 7: 141–161.

10. Cunningham, A. E., & Stanovich, K. E., Early spelling acquisition: Writing beats the computer. *Journal of Educational Psychology,* 1990. 82: 159–162.

11. Clements, D. H., Teaching creativity with computers; Clements, D. H., & Nastasi, B. K., Computers and early childhood education. In M. Gettinger, S. N. Elliott, & T. R. Kratochwill, eds., *Advances in school psychology: Preschool and early childhood treatment directions.* 1992, Hillsdale, NJ: Erlbaum, pp. 187–246.

12. Clements, D. H., Metacomponential development in a LOGO programming environment. *Journal of Educational Psychology,* 1990. 82: 141–149.

13. Bronson, M., *The right stuff for children birth to 8.* 1995, Washington, DC: National Association for the Education of Young Children.

14. Audrey, A., & Schep, S., *How babies are made.* 1984, Boston: Little, Brown.

15. Mayle, P., *Where did I come from?* 1986, New York: Lyle Stuart.

16. Cole, J., *How I was adopted.* 1995, New York: Morrow Junior Books.

17. Straus, M. A., *Beating the devil out of them: Corporal punishment in American families.* 1994, San Francisco: Jossey-Bass.

18. Straus, M. A., Sugarman, D. B., & Giles-Sims, J., Spanking by parents and subsequent antisocial behavior of children. *Archives of Pediatric and Adolescent Medicine,* 1997. 151: 761–767.

19. Holden, G. W., Coleman, S. M., & Schmidt, K. L., Why 3-year-old children get spanked: Determinants as reported by college-educated mothers. *Merrill-Palmer Quarterly,* 1995. 41: 431–452.

20. Goodnow, J. J., Analyzing agreement between generations: Do parents' ideas have consequences for children's ideas? In I. E. Sigel, A. McGillicuddy-DeLisi, & J. J. Goodnow, eds., *Parental belief systems.* 1992, Hillsdale, NJ: Erlbaum, pp. 293–317.

21. Larzelere, R. E., Schneider, W. N., Larson, D. B., & Pike, P. L., The effects of discipline responses in delaying toddler misbehavior recurrences. *Child & Family Behavior Therapy,* 1996. 18: 35–57.

22. Hoffman, M. L., Affective and cognitive processes in moral internalization. In E. T. Higgins, D. N. Ruble, & W. W. Hartup, eds., *Social cognition and social development: A sociocultural perspective.* 1983, Cambridge, UK: Cambridge University Press, p. 246.

23. Krevans, J., & Gibbs, J. C., Parents' use of inductive discipline: Relations to children's empathy and prosocial behavior. *Child Development,* 1996. 67: 3263–3277.

24. Mussen, P., & Eisenberg-Berg, N., *Roots of caring, sharing, and helping.* 1977, San Francisco: Freeman; Turiel, E., The development of morality. In W. Damon, series ed., & N. Eisenberg, vol. ed., *Handbook of child psychology: Vol. 3. Social, emotional, and personality development,* 5th ed. 1998, New York: Wiley, pp. 863–932.

25. Kochanska, G., Mutually responsive orientation between mothers and their young children: Implications for early socialization. *Child Development,* 1997. 68: 597–615.

26. Kochanska, G., Aksan, N., & Koenig, A. L., A longitudinal study of the roots of preschoolers' conscience: Committed compliance and emerging internalization. *Child Development,* 1995. 66: 1752–1769.

27. Kochanska, G., Socialization and temperament in the development of guilt and conscience. *Child Development,* 1991. 62: 1379–1392; Kochanska, G., Mutually responsive orientation between mothers and their young children: Implications for early socialization. (See note 25.)

28. Thomas, A., & Chess, S., *Temperament and development.* 1977, New York: Brunner/ Mazel.

29. Coplan, R. J., Rubin, K. H., Fox, N. A., Calkins, S. D., & Stewart, S. L., Being alone, playing alone, and acting alone: Distinguishing among reticence and passive and active solitude in young children. *Child Development,* 1994. 65: 129–137; Rubin, K. H., & Coplan, R. J., Social and nonsocial play in childhood: An individual differences perpsective. In O. N. Saracho & B. Spodek, eds., *Multiple perspectives on play in early childhood education.* 1998, Albany: State University of New York Press, pp. 144–170.

30. Chen, X., Rubin, K. H., & Li, D., Social functioning and adjustment in Chinese children: A longitudinal study. *Developmental Psychology,* 1995. 31: 531–539.

31. Weisz, J. R., Chaiyasit, W., Weiss, B., Eastman, K. L., & Jackson, E. W., A multimethod study of problem behavior among Thai and American children in school: Teacher reports versus direct observations. *Child Development,* 1995. 66: 402–415.

32. Crick, N. R., & Ladd, G. W., Children's perceptions of their peer experiences: Attributions, loneliness, social anxiety, and social avoidance. *Developmental Psychology,* 1993. 29: 244–254; Harrist, A. W., Zaia, A. F., Bates, J. E., Dodge, K. A., & Pettit, G. S., Subtypes of social withdrawal in early childhood: Sociometric status and social–cognitive differences across four years. *Child Development,* 1997. 68: 278–294; Rubin, K. H., Bukowski, W., & Parker, J. G., Peer interactions, relationships, and groups. In N. Eisenberg, ed., *Handbook of child psychology: Vol. 3. Social, emotional, and personality development,* 5th ed. 1998, New York: Wiley, pp. 619–700.

33. Davies, P. T., & Cummings, M. T., Marital conflict and child adjustment: An emotional security hypothesis. *Psychological Bulletin*, 1994. 116: 387–411.

34. Emery, R. E., & Laumann-Billings, L., An overview of the nature, causes, and consequences of abusive family relationships: Toward differentiating maltreatment and violence. *American Psychologist*, 1998. 53: 213–220.

35. Ibid.

36. Coie, J. D., & Dodge, K. A., Aggression and antisocial behavior. In N. Eisenberg, ed., *Handbook of child psychology: Vol. 3. Social, emotional, and personality development*, 5th ed. 1998, New York: Wiley, pp. 779–862.

37. Falbo, T., Social norms and the one-child family: Clinical and policy implications. In F. Boer & J. Dunn, eds., *Children's sibling relationships.* 1992, Hillsdale, NJ: Erlbaum, pp. 71–82.

38. Falbo, T., & Polit, D., A quantitative review of the only-child literature: Research evidence and theory development. *Psychological Bulletin*, 1986. 100: 176–189.

39. Brody, G. H., Stoneman, Z., & McCoy, J. K., Forecasting sibling relationships in early adolescence from child temperaments and family processes in middle childhood. *Child Development*, 1994. 65: 771–784; Dunn, J., Temperament, siblings, and the development of relationships. In W. B. Carey & S. C. McDevitt, eds., *Prevention and early intervention.* 1994, New York: Brunner/Mazel, pp. 50–58.

40. Dunn, J., & Kendrick, C., *Siblings: Love, envy and understanding.* 1982, Cambridge, MA: Harvard University Press; Volling, B. L., & Elins, J. L., Family relationships and children's emotional adjustment as correlates of maternal and paternal differential treatment: A replication with toddler and preschool siblings. *Child Development*, 1998. 69: 1640–1656.

41. MacKinnon-Lewis, C., Starnes, R., Volling, B., & Johnson, S., Perspectives of parenting as predictors of boys' sibling and peer relations. *Developmental Psychology*, 1997. 33: 1024–1031; Stocker, C. M., & McHale, S. M., The nature and family correlates of preadolescents' perceptions of their sibling relationships. *Journal of Social and Personal Relationships*, 1992. 9: 179–195.

42. Nelson, K., Structure and strategy in learning to talk. *Monographs of the Society for Research in Child Development, 1972.* 38: No. 1–2, Serial No. 149; Reznick, J. S., & Goldfield, B. A., Rapid change in lexical development in comprehension and production. *Developmental Psychology*, 1992. 28: 406–413.

43. Teele, D. W., Klein, J. O., Chase, C., Menyuk, P., Rosner, B. A., & The Greater Boston Otitis Media Study Group. Otitis media in infancy and intellectual ability, school achievement, speech, and language at 7 years. *Journal of Infectious Diseases*, 1990. 162: 685–694; Vernon-Feagans, L., Manlove, E. E., & Volling, B. L., Otitis media and the social behavior of day-care-attending children. *Child Development*, 1996. 67: 1528–1539.

44. Feagans, L. V., Kipp, E., & Blood, I., The effects of otitis media on the attention skills of day-care-attending toddlers. *Developmental Psychology*, 1994. 30: 701–708; Roberts, J. E., Burchinal, M. R., & Campbell, F., Otitis media in early childhood and patterns of intellectual development and later academic performance. *Journal of Pediatric Psychology*, 1994. 19: 347–367.

45. Cameron, M. B., & Wilson, B. J., The effects of chronological age, gender, and delay of entry on academic achievement and retention: Implications for academic redshirting. *Psychology in the Schools*, 1990. 27: 260–263; Jones, M. M., & Mandeville, G. K., The effect of age at school entry on reading achievement scores among South Carolina students. *Remedial and Special Education*, 1990. 11: 56–62; Morrison, F. J., Griffith, E. M., & Alberts,

D. M., Nature–nurture in the classroom: Entrance age, school readiness, and learning in children. *Developmental Psychology,* 1997. 33: 254–262.

46. Carlton, M. P., & Winsler, A., School readiness: The need for a paradigm shift. *School Psychology Review,* 1999. 28: 338–352.

47. Dennebaum, J. M., & Kulberg, J. M., Kindergarten retention and transitional classrooms: Their relationship to achievement. *Psychology in the Schools,* 1994. 31: 5–12.

48. Dornbusch, S. M., Glasgow, K. L., & Lin, I.-C., The social structure of schooling. *Annual Review of Psychology,* 1996. 47: 401–427.

49. Bredekamp, S., & Copple, S., *Developmentally appropriate practice in early childhood programs,* rev. ed. 1997, Washington, DC: National Association for the Education of Young Children.

50. Carlton, M. P., & Winsler, A., School readiness: The need for a paradigm shift. (See note 46.)

51. Crystal, D. S., Chen, C., Fuligni, A. J., Stevenson, H. W., Hsu, C.-C., Ko, H.J., Kitamura, S., & Kimura, S., Psychological maladjustment and academic achievement: A cross-cultural study of Japanese, Chinese, and American high school students. *Child Development,* 1994. 65: 738–753.

52. See, for example, National Center for Education Statistics, *National Assessment of Educational Progress 1996 Mathematics Report Card for the Nation and the States.* 1997, Washington, DC: Government Printing Office. In this nationally representative sample of American children and adolescents who took achievement tests in a range of subjects, fourth-grade boys outperformed fourth-grade girls in mathematics.

53. Bielinski, J., & Davison, M. L., Gender differences by item difficulty interactions in multiple-choice mathematics items. *American Educational Research Journal,* 1998. 35: 455–476; Hyde, J. S., Fenema, E., & Lamon, S. J., Gender differences in mathematics performance: A meta-analysis. *Psychological Bulletin,* 1990. 107: 139–155.

54. Kerns, K. A., & Berenbaum, S. A., Sex differences in spatial ability in children. *Behavior Genetics,* 1991. 21: 383–396.

55. Casey, M. B., Muttall, R., Pezaris, E., & Benbow, C. P., The influence of spatial ability on gender differences in mathematics college entrance test scores across diverse samples. *Developmental Psychology,* 1995. 31: 697–705.

56. See, for example, Collaer, M. L., & Hines, M., Human behavioral sex differences: A role for gonadal hormones during early development? *Psychological Bulletin,* 1995. 118: 55–107; Finegan, J. K., Niccols, G. A., & Sitarenios, G., Relations between prenatal testosterone levels and cognitive abilities at 4 years. Developmental Psychology, 1992. 28: 1075–1089.

57. Baenninger, M., & Newcombe, N., Environmental input to the development of sex-related differences in spatial and mathematical ability. *Learning and Individual Differences,* 1996. 7: 363–379; Subrahmanyam, K., & Greenfield, P. M., Effect of video game practice on spatial skills in girls and boys. In P. M. Greenfield & R. R. Cocking, eds., *Interacting with video.* 1996, Norwood, NJ: Ablex, pp. 95–114.

58. Eccles, J., Wigfield, A., Harold, R. D., & Blumfeld, P., Age and gender differences in children's self- and task perceptions during elementary school. *Child Development,* 1993. 64: 830–847.

59. Eccles, J. S., Jacobs, J. E., & Harold, R. D., Gender-role stereotypes, expectancy effects, and parents' role in the socialization of gender differences in self-perceptions and skill acquisition. *Journal of Social Issues,* 1990. 46: 183–201; Lummis, M., & Stevenson, H. W., Gender differences in beliefs about achievement: A cross-cultural study. *Developmental Psychology,* 1990. 26: 254–263.

60. Catsambis, S., The path to math: Gender and racial-ethnic differences in mathematics participation from middle school to high school. *Sociology of Education,* 1994. 67: 199–215; Ruble, D. N., & Martin, C. L., Gender development. In W. Damon, series ed., & N. Eisenberg, vol. ed., *Handbook of child psychology: Vol. 3. Social, emotional, and personality development,* 5th ed. 1998, New York: Wiley, pp. 933–1016.

61. Elliott, E. S., & Dweck, C. S., Goals: An approach to motivation and achievement. *Journal of Personality and Social Psychology,* 1988. 54: 5–12.

62. Butler, R., Information seeking and achievement motivation in middle childhood and adolescence: The role of conceptions of ability. *Developmental Psychology,* 1999. 35: 146–163.

63. National Center for Education Statistics, *National assessment of educational progress 1999: Trends in academic progress.* 2000, Washington, DC: Government Printing Office; U.S. Bureau of the Census, *Statistical abstract of the United States,* 120th ed. (See note 6.)

64. Updegraff, K. A., McHale, S. M., & Crouter, A. C., Gender roles in marriage: What do they mean for girls' and boys' school achievement? *Journal of Youth and Adolescence,* 1996. 25: 73–88.

65. Halpern, D. F., *Sex differences in cognitive abilities,* 3rd ed. 2000, Mahwah, NJ: Erlbaum; Campbell, J. R., Hombo, C. M., & Mazzeo, J., *NAEP 1999 trends in academic progress.* 2000, Washington, DC: Government Printing Office.

66. Diamond, M., Johnson, R., Young, D., & Singh, S., Age-related morphologic differences in the rat cerebral cortex and hippocampus: Male–female; right–left. *Experimental Neurology,* 1983. 81: 1–13.

67. Halpern, D. F., *Sex differences in cognitive abilities,* 3rd ed. (See note 65.)

68. Hyde, J. S., & Linn, M. C., Gender differences in verbal ability: A meta-analysis. *Psychological Bulletin,* 1998. 104: 53–69.

69. Eccles, J. S., Jacobs, J. E., & Harold, R. D., Gender-role stereotypes, expectancy effects, and parents' role in the socialization of gender differences in self-perceptions and skill acquisition. (See note 59.)

70. Good, T. L., & Brophy, J. E., *Looking in classrooms,* 8th ed. 1999, New York: Addison-Wesley.

71. Briggs, F., *Children's views of the world.* Invited lecture. 2000 April 12: Illinois State University, Normal, IL.

72. Preston, R. C., Reading achievement of German and American children. *School and Society,* 1962. 90: 350–354.

73. Hetherington, E. M., Bridges, M., & Insabella, G. M., What matters? What does not? Five perspectives on the association between marital transitions and children's adjustment. *American Psychologist,* 1998. 53: 167–184.

74. Wallerstein, J. S., Corbin, S. B., & Lewis, J. M., Children of divorce: A ten-year study. In E. M. Hetherington & J. Arasteh, eds., *Impact of divorce, single parenting, and stepparenting on children.* 1988, Hillsdale, NJ: Erlbaum, pp. 198–214.

75. Hetherington, E. M., Bridges, M., & Insabella, G. M., What matters? What does not? Five perspectives on the association between marital transitions and children's adjustment. (See note 73.)

76. Cherlin, A. J., Furstenberg, F. F., Jr., Chase-Lansdale, P. L., Kiernan, K. E., Robins, P. K., Morrison, D. R., & Teitler, J. O., Longitudinal studies of effects of divorce on children in Great Britain and the United States. *Science,* 1991. 252: 1386–1389.

77. Guidubaldi, J., & Cleminshaw, H. K., Divorce, family health and child adjustment. *Family Relations,* 1985. 34: 35–41.

78. Amato, P. R., & Keith, B., Parental divorce and adult well-being: A meta-analysis. *Journal of Marriage and the Family,* 1991. 53: 43–58.

79. Simons, R. L., & Johnson, C., Mothers' parenting. In R. L. Simons & Associates, eds., *Understanding differences between divorced and intact families.* 1996, Thousand Oaks, CA: Sage, pp. 45–63.

80. Camara, K. A., & Resnick, G., Interparental conflict and cooperation: Factors moderating children's post-divorce adjustment. In E. M. Hetherington & J. D. Arasteh, ed., *Impact of divorce, single parenting, and stepparenting on children.* 1988, Hillsdale, NJ: Erlbaum, pp. 169–195; Clarke-Stewart, K. A., & Hayward, C., Advantages of father custody and contact for the psychological well-being of school-age children. *Journal of Applied Developmental Psychology,* 1996. 17: 239–270.

81. Vygotsky, L. S., *Sobraniye sochinenii* [Collected works], Vol. 5. 1983, Moscow: Pedagogika, p. 212.

CONCLUSION: A VISION FOR PARENTING
AND EDUCATIONAL PRACTICE

1. Bronfenbrenner, U., & Ceci, S. J., Nature–nurture reconceptualized in developmental perspective: A bioecological model. *Psychological Review,* 1994. 101: 568–586; *American Psychologist,* 2000. 55: 218–232. Collins, W. A., Maccoby, E. E., Steinberg, L., Hetherington, E. M., & Bornstein, M. H., Contemporary research on parenting: The case for nature and nurture. *American Psychologist,* 2000. 55: 218–232.

2. See, for example, Chen, X., Liu, M., Li, B., Cew, G., Chen, H., & Wang, L., Maternal authoritative and authoritarian attitudes and mother–child interactions and relationships in urban China. *International Journal of Behavioral Development,* 2000. 24: 119–126. Collins, W. A., Harris, M. L., & Susman, A., Parenting during middle childhood. In M. H. Bornstein, ed., *Handbook of parenting, Vol. 1. Children and parenting.* 1996, Mahwah, NJ: Erlbaum, pp. 65–90; Eccles, J. S., Early, D., Frasier, K., Belansky, E., & McCarthy, K., The relation of connection, regulation, and support for autonomy to adolescents' functioning. *Journal of Adolescent Research,* 1997. 12: 263–286; Luster, T., & McAdoo, H., Family and child influences on educational attainment: A secondary analysis of the High/Scope Perry Preschool data. *Developmental Psychology,* 1996. 32: 26–39; Petit, G. S., Bates, J. E., & Dodge, K. A., Supportive parenting, ecological context, and children's adjustment: A seven-year longitudinal study. *Child Development,* 1997. 68: 908–923; Steinberg, L. D. Darling, N. E., & Fletcher, A. C., Authoritative parenting and adolescent development: An ecological journey. In P. Moen, G. H. Elder, & K. Luscher, eds., *Examining lives in context.* 1995, Washington, DC: American Psychological Association, pp. 423–466; Werner, E., & Smith, R., *Overcoming the odds: High risk children from birth to adulthood.* Ithaca, NY: Cornell University Press.

3. Rothbart, M., & Bates, J., Temperament. In W. Damon, series ed., & N. Eisenberg, vol. ed., *Handbook of child psychology: Vol. 3. Social, emotional, and personality development.* 1998, New York: Wiley, pp. 105–176.

4. Darling, N., & Steinberg, L., Community influences on adolescent achievement and deviance. In J. Brooks-Gunn, G. Duncan, & L. Aber, eds., *Neighborhood poverty: Context and consequences for children: Conceptual, ethodological, and policy approaches to studying neighborhoods,* Vol. 2. New York: Russell Sage Foundation, pp. 120–131.

5. Fletcher, A., Darling, N., Steinberg, L., & Dornbusch, S., The company they keep: Relation of adolescents' adjustment and behavior to their friends' perceptions of authoritative parenting in the social network. *Developmental Psychology,* 1995. 31: 300–310.

6. Brown, A. L., Transforming schools into communities of thinking and learning about serious matters. *American Psychologist,* 1997. 52: 399–413; Tharp, R. G., & Gallimore, R., *Rousing minds to life: Teaching, learning, and schooling in social context.* New York: Cambridge University Press.

Teachers (*continued*)
  partnerships with parents, 206–7, 215, 219, 250; partnerships with schools, 207–8; peer-coaching of, 211; private speech of children, listening to, 105–6; qualifications, 215, 219; ratio of teacher to child, 214–15, 218; reciprocal teaching, 194–97; shared understanding with child, 42–46. *See also* Classrooms; Kindergartens; Preschools
Team sports, children's participation in, 20–21
Television viewing: ADHD children's viewing, 162–63; adults' viewing, 20–21; children's viewing, 66–69, 139, 143, 223
Temperament of children, 25–27, 29, 233; ADHD children on medication, 173
Testing. *See* Dynamic assessment; IQ
Time issues for children: schedule of activities, 144; television viewing, 223
Time issues for parents, 19–22, 220; free time, amount of, 20–21; job vs. family time, 5, 6–10; monitoring of children's experiences and, 7; quality time, 4, 6–7, 22; quantity of time involved, 7, 20, 246; questions for parents, 21
Time out, 177, 227–29
Toddlers: crib speech, 84–87, 104; make-believe play, 113–14; shared understanding with adult, 43–44; speech of, 53; toys for, 139
Toys, 138–42, 225–26
Traditional education: flexibly organized classrooms vs., 102; independence emphasized, 37; negative effects of, 248; open education vs., 13–14; whole-class lessons, 189–90, 242
Transition classes between kindergarten and first grade, 237–39
Turn taking, 135
TV. *See* Television viewing
Twins and ADHD, 164

Vaughn, B., 89
Video games, 143–44, 224–25, 240
Violence, 220; juvenile offenders, 70; television and, 68, 223; toys and, 143–44, 224, 226

Visually impaired children. *See* Blind children
Vocabulary development. *See* Language skills of children
Vygotsky, L. S., theories of: adult role in child development, 137, 220; classroom learning, 184, 185, 187–88, 190, 194, 196, 198, 200, 201, 204, 208, 210, 248; game play, 118, 119; imaginative play, 110–11, 112, 113, 115–16, 119, 124, 127–28, 129, 135, 145; private speech, 77, 78–79, 80–81, 83–84, 99, 100, 102, 127–28; sociocultural theory, 32–34, 38, 245; special-needs children, 147–49, 155, 157, 159, 161, 180, 244; zone of proximal development, 40–41, 60

Warmth of adult-child relationship, 50–51, 73, 221, 224, 246, 248. *See also* Authoritative parenting
Watson, J., 11
Where Did I Come From? (P. Mayle), 227
White, B., 24
Whitehurst, G., 62, 63, 64
Whole-class lessons, 189–90, 242
Whole-language movement, 188
Willoughby, E. M., 105
Winsler, A., 202
Wish fulfillment aspect of make-believe play, 111–12
Wood, T., 197
Writing. *See* Literacy development

Yackel, E., 197

Zinacanteco Indian children, 15, 23
Zone of proximal development, 40–69; building a support system for knowledge and skills, 46–64, 72; creating the zone, 42–69, 72, 245; dynamic assessment and, 204–5, 249; game play and, 118, 249; importance of, 73; make-believe play and, 110–11; private speech used by children in, 100; shared understanding, 42–46, 72; teaching in the zone, 185. *See also* Scaffolding